T0354377

PROVOCATIVE
COLUMNS

PROVOCATIVE COLUMNS

✦

*A Liberal Rabbi Reflects on Beliefs,
Israel & American Politics*

Bruce Warshal

iUniverse, Inc.
New York   Bloomington

PROVOCATIVE COLUMNS
A Liberal Rabbi Reflects on Beliefs, Israel & American Politics

iUniverse books may be ordered through booksellers or by contacting:

iUniverse
1663 Liberty Drive
Bloomington, IN 47403
www.iuniverse.com
1-800-Authors (1-800-288-4677)

Because of the dynamic nature of the Internet, any Web addresses or links contained in this book may have changed since publication and may no longer be valid. The views expressed in this work are solely those of the author and do not necessarily reflect the views of the publisher, and the publisher hereby disclaims any responsibility for them.

ISBN: 978-1-4401-3381-7 (pbk)
ISBN: 978-1-4401-3382-4 (ebk)

Printed in the United States of America

iUniverse rev. date: 5/11/2009

For Lynne, my wife of 49 years, my harshest critic and demanding editor, yet done with compassion and love. She has saved me from many embarrassments.

Acknowledgements

I want to thank my three children, Eric, Michael and Sue for their encouragement to compile this collection of columns; Justo Rey, the CEO of the Forum Publishing Group, the publishers of the *Jewish Journal*. The more people I aggravated the more he stood up for the freedom of the press; Alan Goch, the editor of the *Journal*, who made it easy for me to write these columns, especially when I was after deadline; and Andrew Polin, the long-time editor of the paper, who has become as a family member. I learned much about journalism from him.

Introduction

This book is a selection of columns that I wrote for the *Jewish Journal* of South Florida beginning in May, 2003. I had the privilege of publishing this paper from 1991. I was part of a management team that purchased the paper in 1995. In 1998 we sold it to the Tribune Company (publishers of the *Chicago Tribune*, the *Los Angeles Times* and many other papers). When I retired as the publisher and assumed the title of publisher emeritus, a state of being that requires little exertion, I began writing weekly columns, possibly out of boredom, but, more importantly, out of a belief that the Jewish community needed a frank discussion of issues that too often are not confronted.

Many of these columns upset individual Jews and portions of the Jewish institutional community. Some of these views could not be expressed in most other Jewish newspapers because the majority of those papers in America are controlled by Jewish Federations or Jewish community boards that parrot the talking points of the establishment. When I published the *Jewish Journal* I established the policy that the paper itself would not print a weekly editorial but would instead present six opinion pieces that reflect the broad spectrum of Jewish opinions on both religion and politics. The Tribune Company has continued this approach and I can safely say that the *Journal* has one of the most exciting op-ed sections in any American Jewish publication.

This book includes a selection of those columns. It is not intended to be read linearly from page one onward. One can read columns at random or focus in on particular topics. I caution that there is a sequence in the order of columns within some of these categories and that it may be more rewarding to read those columns in the order in which they appear.

Looking at the Table of Contents you see that the book is divided into three parts. Part One is entitled Judaism: Part Two, Israel; and Part Three, United States. But I write from the viewpoint of a rabbi and my sense of Jewishness suffuses this entire book, not merely Part One. Also, these parts are not thematically hermetically sealed. There is much overlap. This is most evident in Part Three. My discussion of issues that affect this country such as death with dignity, gay rights, capital punishment or creationism could have been included in the Judaism, Part One section when I write of the religious basis for my opinions.

I have included the publication date of each column because it often presents the context of the discussion. Since many of these columns were written years apart I have had to restate certain basic assumptions in the later columns; thus there is a minimal amount of redundancy throughout the book. I have not attempted to rectify this since it would destroy the basic structure of an individual column.

I have attempted to choose "evergreen" columns that shed some light on issues that are important at the present time, but many of these columns focus on hot issues or events of former years. I have included them because what we learned from them still affects our lives. This is especially true of the columns on Guantanamo, civil rights abuses under President George W. Bush and the Bush Doctrine of the legitimacy of preventive war. As of this writing I expect that President Obama will rectify many of these excesses, but it is important to review these topics so that we will never have to live through them again.

I have included three columns on Bush's attempt to privatize Social Security, even though President Obama will not pursue this course. I have done so because Senator McCain promised privatization if he were elected. I believe that whenever the White House reverts to Republican occupancy we can expect this issue to re-emerge. Unfortunately some issues seem never to be resolved. In July, 2005 I wrote the column on genocide in Darfur included in this book and now, almost five years later, it is still relevant.

As a columnist I have been limited to approximately 800 words a week, and at times 1200 words. I have often yearned for the ability to write a three or four thousand word essay on some of these topics. Space limitation is both a curse and a blessing. It has forced me to be succinct and to discipline my thoughts. But it has also left me with issues that I wish I could have explored but ended up "on the cutting table," so to speak. I have overcome this at times by writing a series of columns on one issue, some of which are included here.

A newspaper column presents the writer with the challenge to present complex issues in every-day language. It forces one to use the vernacular rather than academic lingo. I believe that this is a plus rather than a negative. This is especially true when discussing Jewish belief systems. I purposely use that phrase rather than Jewish philosophy or theology. We should be able to speak about sophisticated beliefs in simple language. As I mention in one of the columns, I am frustrated with philosophers or theologians who leave you mystified after reading them. If an idea is worth something it should be able to be communicated simply.

I mentioned above that some of these columns may disturb the reader. Possibly subconsciously that is intentional in that I believe that the role of a columnist and a rabbi is to challenge conventional wisdom. In fact that should be the role of religion as well. As I discuss in Part One, religion should challenge us as much as soothe us. The greatest danger for any religion is to put us to sleep. The same can be said for a columnist. Hopefully I will not do that to you. I am accessible. My email address is brucewarshal@comcast.net and I am open to any comments of praise or condemnation. Happy reading.

Bruce Warshal
March, 2009

Table of Contents

PEACE PROCESS

General Considerations

Terrorism

PART ONE—JUDAISM BELIEF SYSTEMS

One Man's Opinions – Jewish Beliefs, Part I
1/25/05

Looking over my past columns I realize that I've written a lot about politics and government, albeit from a Jewish viewpoint, but I am a working rabbi and should stick to the religious business a little more often. So this will be the first of a two part series on Jewish belief systems, not to use the fancy words of theology or philosophy. What occasioned these columns is that I was rifling through some old files and chanced upon the *Commentary* symposium, "The State of Jewish Beliefs." That magazine asked the original questions in 1966 and updated those 30 years later in 1996. Now almost 40 years later they are still relevant. Remember that there are no correct answers to these questions, only personal opinions. So here go the questions and my answers.

Do you believe in God?

It depends on your definition of God. Rabbi Mordechai Kaplan, the founder of the Reconstructionist movement, defined God in pantheistic terms, God being the cosmos that emerged from the chaos of the Big Bang. God becomes the ideal harmony that we all seek. More traditionalists define God as a supernatural presence not of this world. Which one do I believe? I don't know. Who says that we have to have all the answers? I am continually challenging my own beliefs and changing them as I schlep through life.

Do you believe the Torah to be divine revelation?

Absolutely not, not one word, including the Ten Commandments. I believe that the Torah was written by man seeking God. This will be the subject for next week's column.

Do you accept the binding nature of any, some, or all of the commandments?

Many of the 613 commandments are binding upon us because we know them to be true, i.e. do not murder or steal. But they are not binding upon us because they come from God. All morality is shaped by mankind. This is a scary thought, yet it is also an exciting opportunity for us. Each generation must review all of the commandments and test them against our continuing growth of knowledge. As one example: The Torah railed against homosexuals. Today we understand the biological underpinnings and redefine what is right or wrong.

In what sense do you believe the Jews are the chosen people of God?

In no sense. Since I do not believe in revelation (God does not break into the natural order), again to be discussed in detail next week, I cannot believe that God chooses any one people over another. I also find this concept to be counter productive in dealing with other faith communities. It is a conceit that they do not quite understand.

What is the distinctive role of the Jewish people in the world today?

We do not have a distinctive role. As with other faith communities we must strive to find the meaning of existence, the meaning of God. We must ask ourselves, how God would want us to act. But that process is shared by all faiths. Our one advantage is that we do it in a liberal and intelligent context (or at least my brand of Judaism does it that way). But there are other faith communities that do likewise.

What is the distinctive role of Jewish messianism in the world today?

There is none. Waiting for the messiah, whether it is for the return of Jesus or Menachem Shneerson, is a useless exercise. Messianism entered Judaism during a period of oppression as a last resort concept. We have outgrown the idea.

How have the Holocaust and the existence of the state of Israel influenced your faith, your religious identity, your observance?

This is a tough question, not easily answered in the context of a relatively short newspaper column. The short of it is that there is not a Jew alive who has not been influenced by the Holocaust and the existence of the state of Israel. But our Master Story is still meeting God at Sinai (whether you believe it literally or symbolically, as I do), seeking eternal truths through our relationship with God, and not dwelling on the Holocaust. The Holocaust should be remembered for the universal message that it teaches – the ever-present potential for mankind to lapse into barbarianism, but it cannot be the foundation for a healthy, vibrant Judaism. Only the process of seeking God can do that.

As for Israel, it enriches our peoplehood when it exhibits compassion and it embarrasses us when it reverts to the status of just another powerful nation-state. There is no doubt that Zionism has been the dominant feature of Judaism in the last half century, but I believe that its role in sustaining Jewish identity will wane in the next half century. Finally, it would be obscene to believe that God had a plan for the rising of the state out of the ashes of the Holocaust. No just God would sacrifice 6 million innocents for the sake of a state.

Which aspects of American life offer the greatest stimulus to Jewish belief, and which offer the greatest challenge?

The open and free American society that beckons each of us to participate as equals is both a stimulus and challenge to Judaism. Contrary to the Jewish defense agencies, which will remain nameless to protect the guilty, anti-Semitism is no longer a serious problem in America. On the contrary, assimilation is our major problem, and this assimilation is a response to the fact that Jews are both welcomed and hated to the same extent as any other ethnic or religious group in this country. We can either bemoan this fact and long for the ghettos where we had no assimilation problems, or we can affirmatively embrace those men and women whom our children are marrying and welcome them into Judaism. How we respond will determine our future Judaism in America.

What is your assessment of the current denominational and ideological divisions within American Judaism? Are you worried about Jewish religious unity?

I'm not worried. Judaism was never monolithic. There has never been a period in our history when there was only one kind of Judaism. We have been arguing with one another for 3,000 years. Why should we stop now? Actually our divisions make us strong. We are a challenging people and we should continue to challenge one another concerning Jewish belief systems. I am sure that I am aggravating some Jews in this column, and that is good. All of us should be a little aggravated to keep the brain working.

Do you see any prospect of a large-scale revival of Judaism in America?

I don't see a large-scale revival, but neither do I believe that we will wither -- if we are serious about outreach. We must become more proactive in our presentation of Judaism. We have a great religion. It's time that we welcome others to share it. Proselytizing was the initial Jewish position before it was reversed in the Talmudic period. Now it's time to get back to our roots.

One Man's Opinion – Jewish Beliefs, Part II
2/1/05

Last week I answered a series of questions on Jewish beliefs posed by *Commentary* magazine in a symposium called "The State of Jewish Beliefs." For all of the people whom I did not annoy or offend then, I will continue the dialogue. I do not try to be contentious (my wife says that I really do), but I think that it is time that Jews speak in a more modern idiom with belief systems that appeal to people living in the 21st century. All of the peripheral questions aside, I believe that there is one core question that has to be answered by every Jew.

That question is whether you believe in revelation or not. Put starkly, did God say to Moses on that barren mountain called Sinai, "Moishe, take a ballpoint and I will dictate to you what mankind is supposed to believe"? Or is the Torah the product of man reaching toward God? Note that I love the Sinai story. It is my paradigm for man searching for God. It is the Master Story for Judaism. I just don't take it literally.

When I was a kid growing up in a small coal town in Pennsylvania I was told that there were three kinds of Judaism: Orthodox (the really religious), Conservative (sensible committed Jews like my family) and the *goyim* (Reform Jews who weren't sure they were Jewish). Well, they lied to me. There are only two kinds of Jews – those who believe in revelation and those who don't.

Here's why I can't believe that God took his time to speak to us. First, if we believe that Torah is revealed to us by God, then the product had better be perfect. God would not be a second rate law giver. If God went to law school it would be Yale, not Podunk From God we expect perfection, not a C-plus paper. Let's look at the Torah and see how perfect it is.

There are nonsense prescriptions in the sense of making no-sense. God tells Jews we are not allowed to wear clothing with a mixture of linen and wool (Shatnez). No explanation. I can't see the utility of this advice. Even in the Ten Commandments God warns the Jews that if they don't follow them he will afflict the sins of the fathers onto the 3rd and 4th generations. Not a noble thought. It took the prophet Ezekiel to refute this at a later date. God delivers the ten plagues on the Egyptians even though it is God himself that hardens Pharaohs' heart so that he denied Moses' request to let his people go. How can he punish someone (including killing all the first-born of the Egyptians) for an act that God himself preordained? We can go on ad infinitum, but I think that we can see that Torah is less than a perfect product, a state of being that we would expect from God.

Second, if God took his time out to meet with Jews on Mount Sinai some 3,250 years ago, why hasn't he returned since? Has he forgotten the way? This is a serious philosophical problem -- why is there not continuing revelation? Jews believed in the Oral Law coming from God as written in the Talmud, but after that we deny continuing revelation. Why? It makes sense that God would want to update us. Catholicism solves this problem by positing the concept that God gives continuing revelation through the Pope, thus the concept of the infallibility of the Pope. Protestants solve this problem by hearkening back to the prophets. Thus when Oral Roberts proclaims that God speaks to him, he is merely fulfilling God's intention to keep in touch.

Third, if you believe in the original revelation, it makes perfect sense that you can believe in later revelations, be it through Jesus, Muhammad or Joseph Smith at Palmyra, New York (the Mormon scriptures). Actually, Palmyra is a much more civilized location than Sinai. For one the weather is better and there are much better hotels for the receivers of the revelation. Of all religions, Bahai is the most consistent. It believes in the original revelation to Jews and all succeeding revelations. In technical terms, it is the most syncretistic religion on earth. I solve this problem quickly. I don't believe in the original or succeeding revelations.

All of the above does not mean that I disrespect Torah. On the contrary, Torah is an inspiration to me. It reflects my people's quest to find God. Even when my ancestors struck out (as in Abraham's intention to sacrifice Isaac —what was he thinking?) I find lessons to live by today. But I don't find God's word. I find man's words and man's evolution toward a more civilized humanity.

Being a non-revelationary Jew solves some philosophical problems for me and probably creates others. To begin, the problem of evil is lessened. I don't have to ask where God was during the Holocaust or any other genocide. He just doesn't break into the natural order. You have a problem with evil – direct that problem to your fellow man (or woman). Obviously the concept of the Chosen People is forsaken. I discussed that last week. I don't think it's such a great loss. I'm content to seek God on an equal footing with other faith communities. I don't have to be chosen.

The concept of prayer does change. I can't pray to God for good marks on my examination, a new bike for Hanukah or the eradication of the cancer in my body. A God who does not reveal truth, who does not break into the natural order, does not answer prayer. But I do a lot of praying. To me prayer is introspection and I enjoy communing with God, even though intellectually I know that there is no answer. Actually there is an answer, if my prayers have an effect upon me so that I begin to face my problems, even if I can't fully solve them.

As for ethics, as we discussed last week, all ethics are man-made. There are no absolutes, to the great consternation of fundamentalists everywhere. In truth, even if you believe that God said, "Thou shall not murder", it is still up to us to determine what exactly is murder? Self defense, killing in war, abortion – are these murders or are they justified? So we are left with mankind trying to figure this thing out. Thus there are no absolutes, just relative moral principles. This fits my non-revelationary stance very well.

So what happened to all those Orthodox, Conservative, Reform, Reconstructionist, Humanistic and Hasidic Jews that exist today? If there are only two kinds of Jews, why do we have all those organizations? The answer is that we will continue to define our Judaism through these streams, primarily based on aesthetics. Do we want more or less Hebrew in the service? Do we want a three hour or a one hour service? To me, all of those decisions are secondary as to what kind of a Jew I think I am. As long as I have defined my relationship to God (either through revelation or not) then where I *daven* is secondary and can change with the seasons. If you know your core, all else is commentary.

Jewish Beliefs, Part III
3/8/05

This is a column that I had no intention to write. I have always shied away from writing too much about "religion," making this column into another Dvar Torah. Rabbi Weiss does an excellent job each week in this newspaper writing the Dvar Torah. He doesn't need my help. Rather I have attacked social, political and ethical topics, using my religious outlook as applied to those issues. Judaism is the unstated underpinning to most of my columns.

That is basically the definition of what we once called the social action rabbi, sometimes labeled prophetic Judaism. That was my entry into the rabbinate and is still basically my orientation 35 years later. I respect the modern trend of seeking spirituality in Reform Judaism, but as an ever-evolving rationalist I tell people that if they really want spirituality they should find a good cause and march on a picket line. There they will find real spirituality. It's pretty obvious that my wife, Lynne, and I are graduates of the civil rights movement of the sixties. We participated in our share of sit-ins and picket lines. As a civil rights, activist lawyer I may have made my greatest contribution to this world.

Having said all of the above, it does not mean that I do not strive for religious insights, for beliefs that will help me make sense of a sometimes senseless world, for personal beliefs that will help me make sense of a sometimes confused inner self. So, the last week of January and the first week of February I wrote two columns sharing Jewish beliefs through my eyes. To my surprise, I have received more feedback through email and personal contact on those columns than I have on any others in the last almost two years since I have been writing in the *Journal*.

Encouraged by all of this, I will now attempt to further explain my relationship with God. I don't have to decide what or who God is. I certainly do not believe that he breaks into the natural order to reveal eternal truths or to direct world affairs, as I discussed at length in my column of early February. I leave that to my president who believes that God is directing his actions. (God help us all, if his God is really doing that.) There I go again, getting political rather than "religious."

But who is God and what role can he play in my life? I can't answer that directly, but I can say that I am constantly questing to define my relationship to him. Essentially God is a process for me, rather than a defined outcome. The quest is what really counts, the conclusions are secondary. There can be many answers, each person finding his or her personal conclusions. In my book there are only personal truths that each one of us carves out of our lifelong quests. As an example, when a born-again says to me that "Jesus Saves," I always answer in the affirmative, since he obviously saves that person. I don't believe that there is any one truth, certainly not in the realm of theology.

Here's the core of my quest: Torah says that man is made in the image of God. What could this mean? It certainly doesn't mean that God has human features. (If that were the case I would argue that God has a very large nose, since God is a Jewish God.) What it does mean to me is that each generation has to sit down and make a list of the attributes that we would assign to God and then try to emulate them. A simple beginning: God is certainly honest, not crooked; compassionate, not distant; loving, not hating and so on. If we really worked on this, our list could fill volumes. After the exercise of what God is, then we have a template to follow. We have our own revelation, our own God that we find after our personal quests. And the list will vary with individuals and certainly varies over generations. As an example, one generation may brand homosexuality as evil while a succeeding generation may describe it as just another variation of nature. One thing is for sure, God is there for us to find and define. He is not there to dictate to us.

All of the above is possible for Jews simply because the traditional Jewish salvation system did not include beliefs. Jews made it into the afterlife in rabbinic Judaism based on mitzvot. If you were a decent human being, you were not denied salvation. This is in contrast to Christianity that posited the idea that you had to believe that Jesus died for your sins to be accepted in the great beyond. Being just a decent human being wasn't enough. Beliefs were superimposed on actions. (This was the byproduct of the concept of original sin. It's actually a sophisticated system if you accept the original premises. I don't knock it; I just don't believe it.) Getting back to Judaism, since my salvation (whether we now define that as an afterlife or just the feeling of spiritual fulfillment in life) depends on deeds alone, I am free to enter into my personal quest and my own personal relationship to God, knowing that even if my conclusions were wrong on some absolute cosmic grading scale, my errors in belief do not put my salvation in jeopardy. Our liberal salvation system is the basis of our liberal religion.

But if each of us comes to different conclusions in our questing, what holds Judaism together? The answer: Community. We come together to pray. We share the same synagogue and even the same prayers, but each of us has slightly different religions. But our community, our sense that we are all Jews, no matter what we think, is the glue that binds us together. Let me clearly define our community by, once again, referring to Christianity. Christians have a wonderful sense of community, but it comes after belief. If you believe a certain way, you are enveloped by a warm and embracing Baptist community. If you change your beliefs a little, you lose that community and embrace, possibly a Presbyterian community. Change again, and you may become an Episcopalian. In Christianity you can think your way out of your community and into another.

In contrast, in Judaism you can't think yourself out of your synagogue, the only boundary being that if you accept Christ you are no longer a Jew (which is what makes the Jews for Jesus movement bogus). Community, whether it is expressed through the synagogue, the JCC, the Federation or the local kosher delicatessen, is always there and is always accepting. How else can we explain our embrace of so many Jewish atheists? They are no less Jewish than we who *daven* in the synagogue. Actually they are often found *davening* in the synagogue. Isn't Judaism wonderful?

Jewish Beliefs, Ethics, Part IV
3/15/05

My gosh, we have gotten to part four in a series. I had no intention of dwelling on belief systems, but I think that this column is a natural extension of last week's.

In my previous columns I indicated that I believe that Torah (in its broadest sense, including Talmud) is the work of mankind striving toward God. Thus all of the commandments are man-made. Put in its starkest form, there are no absolute laws. All morals and ethics are relative, the product of each generation's strivings. This is most disturbing to the literally billions of people who want to be told in absolute terms what to believe and how to act. As I have discussed before, the belief in absolutes is actually an illusion. The Torah tells us to honor our fathers and mothers. But it is left to us to determine what "honor" means. Do we honor by paying for the finest nursing home care or are we abandoning them? Do we honor by visiting them once a week or once a month? We are told not to murder, and as I asked in a previous column, is abortion murder, is self defense murder, and is assisted suicide to end a life of pain murder? Absolutes may exist on paper, but in real life we are all left to determine our own morality, not a rabbi or priest or any other religious authority.

But just because something feels right, does that make it moral? There must be some structure that gives us guidance, short of dictating to us. Let me share with you the system that I find most helpful in my personal quest. I rely on the philosopher Martin Buber. He was a German Jewish theologian who made aliyah to Israel in 1938. He taught at Hebrew University until his death in 1965.

Buber wrote a small book entitled "I-Thou." It's not an easy book to read. I've read it twice and I tell you that there are parts of it that still mystify me. (Why can't philosophers write in plain English, or in his case, plain German?) But while standing on one foot (in the great tradition of Rabbi Hillel) let me summarize its message.

Buber believed that there are two essential relationships in life: I-Thou and I-It. An I-Thou relationship is where one tries to understand the essence of the Other, to truly understand his or her fears, aspirations, dreams, the things that make us real human beings, not just human machines that eat, drink, defecate and reproduce. The true humanity of the Other is the Thou that we seek to identify. In contrast, an I-It relationship is where we are not interested in the Other as a Thou, but only in using the Other, the way we would use a machine, as an It.

If I need a hammer, I pick it up and slam it against a nail. It is an it. It has no feelings. It is there to be used. I have a perfect I-It relationship to it. The problem is that people use other people in I-It relationships. As relates to people, Buber maintains that the closer we come to I-Thou relationships, the more moral we become. The closer that we come to I-It relationships in our dealings with other people, the more immoral we become.

Let's get down to some real examples. Obviously, murder is immoral under the I-Thou, I-It paradigm. You can't understand the true essence of another human being if you just killed him. (Killing him sort of ceases the dialogue). Cheating, stealing and other forms of deceit detract from the wholeness of the Other whom we are obliged to respect and know fully. Thus under the I-Thou system adultery is always wrong because it involves cheating on another person (the husband or wife).

Let us assume that a worker hates his boss but invites him to his Shabbat dinner for obvious business advantage. On the surface this looks like a real mitzvah, in the tradition of Abraham who welcomed strangers into his tent. Based on the revelation theory of absolute truths decreed to us by God, we have no transgression here. But based on Buber's I-Thou system, we have an immoral act. (Immoral may be a strong word, but it has a great element of I-It, of using the other person.) Actually, using the I-Thou, I-It system creates a higher level of morality than the old Ten Commandments route.

Let's talk about sex. It always grabs our attention. Under the I-Thou system, if two unmarried people love each other and treat other with tenderness and understanding within an I-Thou relationship, then their sex is moral. Now let us assume that a married man is no longer in love with his wife, but she does not know it. He continues to sleep with her exclusively either because he is too busy to find another, is afraid of AIDS, or is just plain lazy. When he has sexual relations with his wife, he is merely using her to satisfy his carnal desire. To the outside world he is a moral man in a marital relationship. Under the I-Thou system he is using her, making her an It, the same way one uses a machine. He is less than moral.

How about two young people who meet at an upscale bar on the Upper West Side of New York and decide to have a one night stand, no strings attached, no promises made? To begin, they are both using one another, but with each other's knowledge, no deception involved. It is certainly not an I-Thou relationship. They are not trying to find the true humanity in each other. But it is not an I-It relationship in that one is using the other without his or her knowledge, the kind of I-It games that people use to manipulate others.

So we have here a perfect example of what we have in most human relationships – the grey world in which we live between the pure white of I-Thou and the utter blackness of I-It. Understanding that we are human and thereby destined to live in this grey area on the ethics continuum, it is our challenge to assess each of our actions and honestly ask ourselves, are our relationships closer to I-Thou than to I-It? If something feels right to us, it may be an indication that we are closer to I-Thou, but there is no guarantee. We have to ponder whether we are using another person, somehow turning him or her into an It.

I have been asked what the Jewish definition of sin is. The Hebrew word for sin is *chet,* which means an arrow. Sin is missing the mark. It is not an absolute. The closer we get to I-Thou the less we sin; the closer to I-It, the more we sin. It is an arrow with a moving target. Defining sin is a process that purifies our actions.

Speaking of Black, White & Greys
5/17/05

My wife tells me that I'm writing too much about politics, sounding too much like a lawyer and not enough like a rabbi. So here is my take on what we get out of religion. (Like E.F. Hutton of old, when the wife speaks, I listen; so this is the first in a two-part series.)

We turn to religion for many things: for standards (that's why the Ten Commandments are such a big hit); for succor to get us through this life (that's why the yizkor service speaks to me); and for a construct to answer the big question – what's it all about, what's the meaning of life? After all is done, and we look at our children, grandchildren and great grandchildren, when we contemplate the end for ourselves, what was the meaning of the whole experience?

I think that's why as we get older we get more interested in religion, not just to cram for the finals, but to make sense out of the whole journey that we can now put into perspective over decades of time. Standards are important. So is receiving comfort and support through life cycles, but putting the whole picture together, answering the big question – why have I experienced this journey? – is the real payoff of religion.

The problem is that it is not an easy question and there is no ready answer. It is a question to which ultimately there may be no answer, but the question must still be pondered. This is not a modern query. Our rabbis in the Talmud asked the very same question, but in a much more dramatic form. Our rabbis, almost two thousand years ago, contemplated whether the whole experience of life was worth anything -- maybe we should never have been born. Talk about angst! You think we developed it in the twenty-first century? It's surprising that the rabbis asked this question, but the Talmud's answer is even more surprising: It would have been better if we had never been born, but (and this is a very big but) God ordained life, and now it is our challenge to make sense of that life.

Many of us try to make sense of this life by turning to religion. Some of us find good answers, some find bad answers (remember that the KKK burned a cross in the name of Jesus, Yigal Amir assassinated Yitzhak Rabin in the name of Adonai and the Ayatollah Khomeini distorted a whole nation in the name of Allah), and some find partial answers, ambiguous answers, and just no answers. It is this process that I want to share with you.

First, the process is a difficult endeavor. Most people don't like difficult tasks. They prefer life neatly wrapped in a half-hour sitcom in 22 minutes of narrative, leaving eight minutes for advertising consumer products, which are dearer to their hearts than philosophy. People want answers, but they want quick answers. You can't explain the meaning of life in a sound byte. Remember the Graduate: Plastics, Benjamin. That's what people want – good advice in one word. God, Bruce. Actually, plastics wasn't bad advice for the past 40 years. But God may not be as accurate an answer, at least not a one word explanation of God. However, ironically, as we gain more knowledge about the universe, as technologically we become more sophisticated, almost as a reaction to the complexity of life, we seem to be turning to simple answers about its ultimate meaning. We see astronauts turning to born-again religion, doctors and lawyers turning to fundamentalist Judaism – looking for easy, sure answers.

I don't have those easy, sure answers. My liberal Judaism is much more complex. I am reminded of my first year class at Yale Law School. In the

Socratic method of teaching, of asking question upon question, we discussed this particular problem and ended with six or seven possible answers. In my naiveté (I was young) I asked the professor, "But, sir, what is the correct legal answer?" He replied (with a certain tinge of contempt), "We don't teach answers here. If you want simple answers, go to Podunck Law School. At Yale we can only teach you sophisticated questions, some of which will have no answers, others partial answers, and some will have answers at a given time, which will then change for the next generation. Answers are not important in life. The right questions are crucial to a vital legal system."

That was a powerful response that has stayed with me throughout my life. The right questions are vital to a philosophical or religious quest. I may never get the answers, or, if found, answers can change over a lifetime. I have come to savor a good question, to see complex beauty in all the shades of grey between those sure answers of black and white. Unanswered questions are a source of mystery to me, intellectual and emotional challenges that enrich my life, rather than frustrate me. Liberal Judaism allows me to contemplate the greys. Sometimes I get clear answers, other times not.

A discussion at our Shabbat dinner table highlighted this whole issue for me. We had a guest whose young mother had just died, and this occasioned a discussion concerning the afterlife. One person thought that God had a reason for this death and that her mother was needed in some kind of an afterlife. Another Jew at the table said that she believed that there was no afterlife. I sat there non-committal. I really don't know if there is an afterlife. I certainly want to believe in it for both emotional and intellectual reasons. Remember that the great rational philosopher Immanuel Kant posited an afterlife as a necessary ingredient to his Ethical Imperative. Yet as much as I want to believe, there is a voice inside me that says you cannot be sure; that eternal existence is a concept beyond my human ken.

So the answer is that I do and I don't believe on alternate days (like alternate-side street parking in New York City) and worse yet, I do and I don't believe at the same time. You talk about greys – I'm part of the rainbow coalition. I have every shade of color in the universe, every shade of grey plastered over this issue. I have more questions than Carter has liver pills (to use an old trite phrase) and fewer answers than a Yale law professor has to a first year class.

But this is Jewishly acceptable. All three opinions on the afterlife (yes, no and maybe) expressed at our Shabbat dinner table were derived from Jewish tradition. The Sadducees (the ancient priests) denied afterlife. The Pharisees (the rabbis of the Talmud) invented the concept. Later, Spinoza (17th century) denied it. Orthodoxy restates it. Early Reform denied it. Present day Reform finds it once again. Mordecai Kaplan and the Reconstructionists denied it. I certainly find support in our tradition for not being able to make a decision. Judaism always understood the doubter. The Talmud was meticulous in reporting all minority positions, even as it declared the majority decisions of the rabbis as the word of God.

Ultimately all answers are personal – the correct answer for me, but not necessarily truth for all human beings. The important point is that my Judaism has allowed me to ask many questions without putting a straight-jacket on my beliefs. And even more important, Judaism has not demanded of me a surety of commitment beyond my capability. Judaism is truly a thinking person's religion because it respects the questions more than the answers.

Next week: A comparison of Jewish fundamentalism with Liberal Judaism.

Liberal Judaism in Perspective
5/24/05

Last week I discussed the greys (rather than the black and white) of religious questing –the idea that questions are more important than answers, and that my religion wasn't meant to be dogma, but rather a quest to put life together. This is Judaism as a way of life, rather than a set catechism.

I am aware that is not the definition of Judaism for all people. That is understandable since we know that there is no such thing as a single Judaism. Orthodoxy itself has a multiplicity of gradations, and Chabad-Lubavich is as different from my liberal Judaism as Jehovah Witnesses are from Unitarians – essentially different religions. Be it Chabad, be it the transplanted Williamsburg fanatic on the West Bank, be it the Orthodox establishment legally recognized as the only legitimate Judaism in Israel, be it an ultra Orthodox congregation here in South Florida, there are Jews out there who will tell you that answers are more important than questions, and that their specific answers constitute the whole of Judaism.

The problem is that these people deride the liberal quest and, in plain English, say that I'm really a *goy* (or is that plain Yiddish?). My response to them is the same as my response to born-again Christians – they practice a different religion than I do and they do not impact upon my quest. No, that is not true. My response to fundamentalist Christians is much more benign, simply because they do not challenge my Jewish authenticity. I am angered at my Jewish fundamentalist brethren for trying to highjack a religion that continued to evolve over almost four millennia. Now they want to stop time and say that they have the one final answer. In other words, I believe that liberal Judaism is the inheritor of traditional rabbinic Judaism, rather than these judgmental fundamentalists, who would never report a minority opinion, as our forefathers did in the Talmud, if their lives depended on it.

Note my reaction. I am angered. Anger is a healthy emotion. I am not cowed. I am not apologetic. I am not feeling guilty for practicing a religion different from my grandparents or parents. I know that I am an authentic Jew, not a watered-down Jew, as Jewish fundamentalists would describe me. Yet too many liberal Jews think that they are faded Xerox copies of the original, because they do not practice as many rituals or say as many *brachas* as their more Orthodox-fundamentalist brethren. Ironically, they give more money to these Orthodox charities out of guilt – some "real" Jews should remain alive – than they do to the Conservative or Reform movements. They give money to people who deny their very legitimacy as Jews, and they feel good and more Jewish as they do this.

Let me speak for liberal Jews: We must not think of ourselves as ersatz Jews. We do not pray as much as fundamentalists do, certainly not three times a day. We do not study as much as they do, certainly we do not sit in *yeshivot* all day studying Talmud, supported by the Israeli government. We do not obsess about religion and think about it day and night as they do. And to all of the above I am going to give you a surprising response from a committed rabbi: It is healthy that we do not do all of this.

Seeking God and the meaning of life is a healthy and rewarding endeavor, but if that's all that we do, then we will all end up like the Christian monk who lived in a cave overlooking Saint George's monastery on the road to Jericho. He prayed to God all day, lived a solitary life there without human contact. His food was hoisted to him on a dolly three times a day. I am sure that he considered all other Christians less committed than he, less authentic than he. In Jewish terms, he out-*frummed* the *frum*. In my terminology, he was a fanatic who added nothing to the Christian continuum. Liberal Jews can always be out-Jewed by any Jewish fundamentalist, simply because liberal Jews are not fanatics.

To say that I am a good Jew does not mean that religion must totally dominate me. My life should be filled with good things, but not dominated by them. Good food, but not gluttony. Good sex, but not sexual obsession. Good times, but not constant partying. Good reading, but not constant intellectualism (otherwise I become an intellectual bore, even to myself). Good nationalism (I love this nation), but not jingoism.

Balance – the Greek golden mean. We can learn from the Greek and western tradition, as well as from Judaism. That is the genius of liberal Judaism. It has taken world knowledge, Greek philosophy, Buddhist contemplation etc., and filtered them through our intellects and emotions into an ever-evolving Judaism.

Balance. Judaism is a central and important part of my life. But it is not the only part. Fundamentalist Jews would have us feel guilty over this. To the contrary, they should feel guilty for rejecting all the wonderful aspects of life that to them are meaningless, from classical music to Marlins baseball.

Balance. The Talmud (tractate Gittin, 70a) understood this concept. It stated: "There are eight things that are harmful in large quantities, but good in small quantities. They are: traveling, sexual intercourse, wealth, work, wine, sleep, hot baths and blood-letting." I would **not** add liberal religion to this list because I think that this is healthy in portions greater than small. But the Talmud understood balance. We cannot let our religion consume us. We cannot let anything consume us.

Balance means that there is always someone out there who can out-Jew you. Speaking to liberal Jews: We must always remember that we are authentic Jews. We are not in a race with our fundamentalist co-religionists for the Super-Jew trophy, although in our way we are super-Jews. We are the ones who keep the wonderful Talmudic intellectual tradition of questing in life. With less ritual, with no *payesin*, with no guaranteed answers, often with more questions than answers, we are mainstream, authentic Jews.

Make no apologies. Feel no guilt. Continue to ask questions, knowing that there are no definitive answers. Use tradition. Relate to our enriching history. But everything in balance. This is the glorious, intellectually and emotionally satisfying religion of liberal Judaism. It's not perfect, but it's pretty darn good.

Liberal Judaism Doesn't Need a *Hechsher*
1/8/08

I enjoy reading the columns of Rabbi Avi Shafran in the *Jewish Journal* since he is an accomplished writer, albeit a fundamentalist believer. Last month he favorably critiqued the new Reform prayer book, since, from his point of view, it represents a return to tradition. Here's the rub: he assumes that his brand of ultra-Orthodoxy is true Judaism and liberal forms of Judaism are inauthentic. This column is dedicated to the refutation of that premise. In fact, the opposite is true: ultra-Orthodoxy is the deviation while liberal forms of Judaism (Reform, Conservative, Reconstructionist, Humanistic etc.) reflect "authentic" Judaism, if there is such a concept of authenticity in religious discourse.

Let me explain. Judaism, like all religions, has been constantly changing since its inception some four thousand years ago. Before 621 BCE (before the Common or Christian era) there were many temples spread throughout Israel. At that time the priests consolidated power in the Temple in Jerusalem. Their control of Judaism was relatively short-lived because a few hundred years later a new class of scholars, called rabbis, arose to challenge their religious leadership.

The priests believed that Judaism was to be based solely on the Torah, while the rabbis thought that the religion had to progress with new concepts and new rituals. They wrote the Mishnah and Gemara (the Talmud) based on the belief that the Oral Law was given to Moses on Mount Sinai as well as the Torah. The Oral Law was the foundation of the Talmud.

It is this rabbinic interpretation that is the basis of all forms of modern expressions of Judaism. In other words, the priests could not hold the religion static, especially after they were put out of business by the Romans who destroyed the Second Temple in 70 CE. Under rabbinic Judaism, through *halachic* interpretation, Judaism evolved for the next thousand years.

The problem was that Jews increasingly lived under adverse conditions imposed by the Catholic Church and national movements infused with anti-Semitism. We think of the Inquisition as an occurrence in 1492 when Jews were expelled from Spain. Actually, it began under Pope Innocent III who died in 1216 and as early as 1242 an inquisitorial committee condemned the Talmud in Paris. The first burning of Jews at the stake took place in France in 1288. The Inquisition lasted until 1834 and thrived in many countries that were under the influence of the Church. In Spain alone, 28,540 Jews were burned at the stake and over 300,000 Jews were forcibly converted.

But that wasn't the only *tzouris* we had. Bogdan Khmelnitski (sometimes spelled Chmielnicki) led a Ukrainian uprising against Polish rule in 1648. Coupled with his hatred of Poland, he was a rabid anti-Semite. In 1648-49 Khmelnitski destroyed 300 Jewish communities and killed 100,000 Jews. This was truly a holocaust since he massacred Jews simply because they were Jews. In that sense he is the closest historical anti-Semite to Hitler.

But there's more *tzouris*. Shabbetai Zevi was born in 1626 and was only 22 years old at the time of the Khmelnitski massacres. He was a charismatic manic-depressive who would go into sullen hibernation only to emerge with great energy. He eventually declared himself the Messiah (*Moshiach*). The Jewish population of Europe that was beleaguered under the stresses of the Inquisition and the Khmelnitski massacres turned to Shabbetai Zevi with a sense of excitement. It is estimated that 50 percent of European Jews came under his spell. It all ended in humiliating disaster when Zevi was arrested by the Sultan in Constantinople and given the choice of converting to Islam or being put to death. He converted in 1666, leaving the Jews bereft of hope.

Entering the eighteenth century Judaism was in a shambles. The rabbis circled the wagons and stressed strict adherence to old-time religion. Consolidation and separation from the gentile community was needed to protect the remnants of Jews. Religious evolution and innovation, especially in the wake of Shabbetai Zevi, was the last thing that they wanted or needed. Thus began a period of religious sterility. Judaism stopped evolving.

It was not until the Enlightenment that new ideas began to enter Judaism and that the religion began to naturally evolve once again. Modern liberal forms of Judaism began to flourish. What we call ultra-Orthodox Judaism, as espoused by very articulate spokespeople like Rabbi Shafran, is the direct descendant of the ossified Judaism of Eastern Europe that developed in the wake of the Inquisition, Khmelnitski and Zevi. It is a stagnant form of Judaism because it fights natural evolution.

If there is such a thing as "authentic" Judaism, it is found in the various forms of liberal Judaism that are practiced in the United States today. So, thank you Rabbi Shafran for your comments on the new Reform prayer book, but liberal Judaism doesn't need your *hechsher* (approval).

The Mind of a Fundamentalist – God Controls History
9/9/08

The minds of fundamentalist religious thinkers never cease to amaze me. Take Rabbi Avi Shafran as an example. He is a brilliant writer and is director of public affairs for Agudath Israel of America. A month ago the *Jewish Journal* published his opinion piece in which he opined that, although Jewish tradition tells us that Divine intervention ended in biblical times, he sees the hand of God protecting Israel today.

Rabbi Shafran writes "sensitive Jews saw Divine fingerprints" on Israel's amazing victory in the Six Day War in 1967 as well as the 1976 Entebbe rescue. These "miracles" emanate directly from God controlling history, a biblical concept called Providence.

Rabbi Shafran sees God's hand in the "frustrated plots against Jews... the miracles that consist not of something happening but of something not happening." He continues: "Every time a Palestinian terrorist is intercepted, or has a 'work accident' – his explosives detonating in his lap rather than in the Jewish crowd he had targeted – that, too, is a miracle."

But the concept of Providence, God controlling history, has negative as well as positive aspects. God, in the process of controlling history, punishes as well as protects. We see this concept playing itself out in the Christian community as well. After September 11, 2001, both Jerry Falwell and Pat

Robertson agreed on the TV show "The 700 Club" that God caused the death of almost 3,000 innocents in New York City since he was punishing America because of "pagans, and the abortionists, and the feminists, and the gays and the lesbians." Falwell also attributed Katrina's devastation of New Orleans to the fact that the lesbian talk host, Ellen DeGeneres, hailed from that city.

The Rev John Hagee believes that God controls history. He recently received a standing ovation at the AIPAC conference by Jewish conservatives at the mere mention of his name (he was absent since he was disavowed by John McCain). He has sermonized that God created the Holocaust because Jews immigrated to America instead of Israel. There are two blasphemies here. One is against God – the very idea that God would cause the death of six million Jews because they didn't follow his desires distorts religious sensibilities beyond recognition. The second blasphemy is against my own family. Hagee is saying that my *bubie* and *zayde* who reached these shores in 1898 are part of the reason that Hitler destroyed European Jewry.

Lest you snicker too loudly at these Christian Neanderthals, let us look at their Jewish counterparts. Last year the former Sephardic Chief Rabbi of Israel, Mordecai Eliyahu, declared that the victims of the Holocaust were made to suffer because of the sins of the Reform Movement. On the pirate Israeli haredi radio station *Kol Ha'emet* (The Voice of Truth) Eliyahu was asked for which sin the Holocaust victims were punished. He chose the Reform Movement because "those redactors of the Jewish faith began in Germany." He continued, "We learn from this that it is forbidden to attempt to change Judaism."

Rabbi Eliyahu has not progressed beyond the Book of Deuteronomy, written in either the 13th century BCE (if you are Orthodox) or the 7th century BCE (if you believe modern scholarship). In any case he is not living in the 21st century. Deuteronomy states that the good are rewarded and the sinners punished by God here on earth. This means that if you have a disease or other *tzouris* you must have done something wrong and you are receiving your just rewards from God. The Book of Job was written precisely to refute this kind of thinking. Judaism does progress.

This brings us to Rabbi Eliyahu's second point: "We learn that it is forbidden to attempt to change Judaism." It is precisely this mindset that produces the far right in Christianity and the Taliban and bin Ladens in Islam. All religions evolve and to deny this reality stops evolution and freezes our quest for truth and for a meaningful relationship to God into a time warp. I refuse to live in either the 13th or 7th centuries BCE.

But where are our more liberal Jewish voices? Steve Bayme, American Jewish Committee's Director of Contemporary Jewish Life, after reviewing Rabbi Eliyahu's diatribe writes: "Particularly absent are the voices of moderate

Orthodox rabbis and leaders who are willing to repudiate the odious divisiveness of these statements...Modern Orthodox institutions seem incapable of acting as brake and corrective to the extremism of the Orthodox Right. The collapse of Modern Orthodoxy – historically a bridge between Orthodox and non-Orthodox Jews – constitutes a grave setback not only to its own noble principles and beliefs but to the unity of the Jewish people globally."

We Jews can rightly complain that liberal Muslims have not been vigorous enough in repudiating their fundamentalist wing which threatens to engulf their religion. But we also have our own religious fanatics on the West Bank causing harm and havoc to the Palestinians living there, and we neither speak out against their actions nor against their fundamentalist mindset that produce their atrocities.

If God controls history, Then He/She has a weird sense of justice.

Serious Thoughts Coming From a So-So Movie
11/11/08

My Father My Lord is an Israeli movie that is currently playing throughout South Florida. It received praise from the *New York Times* reviewer and 3 ½ stars from *Newsday*, and it won the Best Film Award at the Tribeca Film Festival. I found it to be exceedingly slow of pace, and I love slow movies. Its world was so constricted that I felt claustrophobic, but it was, for all of its faults, an important study of the ultra-Orthodox community in Israel. (My wife gave it one star and she was being kind, which is her nature.) If you are planning to see this movie maybe you should stop reading this column because I will tell you too much about its plot.

OK, you're still with me. The movie tells the story of an ultra-Orthodox rabbi who is so concerned with his relationship to God and His commandments that he ignores his wife and child. When his young child, approximately ten years old, enters his study he is too busy to talk to him. He is so obsessed in saying prayers for every human function that he has no time for his conjugal obligations to his passive wife. As the Orthodox know there are blessings to be recited for every occasion including the acts of eating, drinking, awakening, going to sleep and even defecation.

Into the rabbi's small but safe environment enters tragedy when the adorable child drowns in the Dead Sea. By the end of the movie the rabbi can no longer preach to his congregation, although he still forces himself to pray with intensity to a God that allowed his son to die. The mother of the child sits in the balcony of the shul and slowly and contemplatively drops prayer books over the balcony into the men's section in a symbolic rejection of God.

The philosophical core of the movie is when the rabbi, before the tragic loss of his son, is lecturing to his congregation about providence. The concept of providence is that God controls all of history. The rabbi explains that there is general providence for all the species on earth. Any one dog will die solely by chance, but God protects the continued existence of the species. In his narrow view of the world the rabbi explains that God has a special relationship to Torah-True Jews but that God does not protect non-practicing Jews or gentiles. For them no personal providence exits. Then his child dies.

This opens us to the question that any person who has lost a husband, wife, or child asks: How can God have let this happen? My simple answer is there is no providence for the world. God does not intervene in history. People live and die by fate at random. God has nothing to do with the human travail. This does not mean that I reject God. I believe in the ultimate meaning of existence, in a force of nature, in a human ideal that we label God. I believe that the concept of an afterlife is a sophisticated idea, although I have no personal position, either for or against.

What I am left with is a faith that is not carved in stone as it was for the central character in My Father My Lord. There is great room in my system for doubt. Rather than diminishing it, this enriches my religious life. The following prayer from the new Reform prayer book eloquently expresses this: "Doubting is but the forefront of faith, a faith in the infinite growth of an unbounded creation. A doubting age is one of restlessness and discontent with what is current; a doubt is an idea that is still alive. To doubt that the past has uncovered all things is to express faith that many things are still to be uncovered. To doubt that we have grown to our full stature and knowledge is to express faith that we may develop into beings of such power and dignity that we cannot as yet imagine what shall be."

Prayer then becomes introspection and communion with our personal God, but not a pipeline to His or Her personal ear. I do not anthropomorphize God. My prayer is merely my attempt to attune myself with the awesome nature of divinity. When I say a *mishebarach* for the ill in my synagogue I know that I am not curing the ill, but I am doing something more important – I am attaching my soul to the soul of someone in need. I am making myself more human and better equipped to help that person to the best of my human capabilities.

Unlike the rabbi in My Father My Lord, who views religion as the obligation to serve God through a series of rituals, I view religion as a tool of mankind that we use to become better human beings. Unlike the rabbi of the movie, for me religion affords a process of continual growth, not exclusion.

As I grow I understand that providence is in our own hands and is not limited to the few ultra-Orthodox Jews, as in the movie; or, for that matter, the few ultra-Orthodox Muslims or the born agains who believe that only the very few "real" Christians will be swept up to God in the Rapture.

Of course, I consider myself a movie maven, and I don't recommend My Father My Lord for its cinematic excellence, but I do believe that it can inspire just the kind of dialogue that I share with you today. So it wasn't a complete waste of time, yours or mine.

Finding God in an Ambiguous World
5/30/06

Contemporary life is confusing, especially in this country after September 11, 2001. Simple instinctive beliefs are challenged. There are many different ways to look at the world, and there are many different interpretations of truth and ethical conduct. For many of us this is a new degree of autonomy that does not necessarily provide tranquility; rather, it confuses and complicates life. It denies us the surety that we expected from religion. It throws us into a sea of turmoil when we were expecting a safe harbor. It's not what we wanted from religion.

Many may view this situation and see chaos. I see vitality and intellectual excitement. I revel in the many choices open to a liberal Jew as he or she seriously confronts religion in an attempt to find belief

I admit that this is not everyone's predisposition. A certain percentage of the population, both Christian and Jew, is looking for clear and certain answers to clearer and more certain questions. These people are looking for unambiguous solutions in the face of an ever-increasingly ambiguous world. In Christianity we call them fundamentalists. In Judaism, we call them Orthodox or Hasidic. My description is not meant to be pejorative. I do not fault their quest, nor do I impugn their intellect. I just don't see the world in their light. What I find exceedingly difficult, they find self-explanatory. This does not prove that they are overly simplistic; on the contrary, it may prove that I am overly skeptical. I cannot argue what is the correct way. I can merely tell you what my way is.

There is one certain fact, with which everyone, Jew and Christian, fundamentalist and liberal, agrees, and that fact is that we live in a very indeterminate, complex world where statesmanship disintegrates into terrorism, where priests shed their collars, where women shed other apparel, where "morality" sheds its pretense, where the shortest distance between two points is not necessarily a straight line, where God is and isn't, where mankind feels that he or she cannot pray, and prays to God for the ability to pray.

We live in the turmoil of change that is faster than our ability to understand these changes. And even after the end of the cold war, we find ourselves in an unsafe environment, both physically and emotionally. Emotionally we long to return to simpler times, but intellectually we know that is impossible. We are in constant future time warp from which we cannot escape. Such is our existence.

In the face of the above, mankind is burdened by two decisions. The first is the agony of whether there is a religious answer. The second, to which I alluded above, is how sure, how all-inclusive, how definitely rewarding he or she wants that answer to be.

In answer to the chaotic world that I perceive, I consciously find my God, posit his existence, which is not to say that I create him. It is to say that I find him in his pre-existent state, much as a scientific person discovers the reality of existence, but in no way creates such reality. Of course, the difference is that the scientific person can verify his or her truth, at least until a new theory of relativity proves him/her wrong, while the philosophical or theological person can only verify truth by the affect such truth has upon his or her own personal life. This is certainly a less tangible truth than many seek; but then the mistake is not in the answer, but in the seeker.

Whoever asks for universal truths asks too much. Each person must face and define the world in its chaos, and yes, also in its beauty, in his or her own terms. It cannot be denied that reality out there differs for each person, even though we may agree on the general shape of the beast. All theological answers are by necessity personal, for they are merely reflections of personal questions and personal reality. But that reality and those personal questions and answers are real, as real as pre-existent logarithms, and certainly as real to the seeker as life itself.

If all answers are real, also they are all true. If I can face the beast of life, if in the chaos I can discern beauty and meaning, if I can do this by finding what for me is the pre-existing God, then I have as large a portion of truth as I personally will ever need.

I have made the religious choice. Now I must go on to my second decision: How sure, how all-inclusive, can that decision be, given the post-modern state of my psychology?

I fault not those who find the one and perfect answer. I cannot, and I suspect that many other liberal religionists cannot. If I could believe that God revealed his law (at Sinai or any other place) to me, then by definition I would be Orthodox. I would have a surety that dispels doubt, which obliterates ambiguity, which clearly defines my orders and my obligations to the Almighty. Alas, I cannot make this commitment. I do not find his revelation.

I find merely God, the Nameless, and with my human pretensions I proceed to define and circumscribe he who cannot be defined or circumscribed. But I do find him. I freely choose the religious answer, because for me this is the only possible response to the chaotic world that I perceive. This choice is a choice of faith, irrational in the sense that it cannot be proved by sensory perception, but not irrational if by that word we connote a mode of thought less worthy or less intellectual than rational constructs.

But the question still remains: faith in what, or how much faith? I have often heard the bromide that Orthodoxy is the hardest kind of Judaism, Conservative less hard, and of course, Reform the easy way out. On the scale of difficulty, all the disciplines, including kashrut and Shabbat, weigh but as a feather compared to the onus of choice that is incumbent upon every liberal Jew. The difficulty of it all is enough to drive one into fundamentalism, into Orthodoxy.

This point cannot be overstated. (Be prepared for a paragraph-long sentence!) If we merely find God, if God did not reveal his answers to us, if we are all seekers rather than order-takers, if we have to personally decide first whether to believe and then what to believe, if we have to fashion our own rituals and redefine them in each generation, if we have to live in a world where there are many rights and that what is wrong may well be wrong for you but right for me; in short, if we have to find our own God and define our own relationship to him, then this burden, this quest is by far the most difficult of all religious endeavors. It is all consuming and makes the surety of Orthodoxy appear to be an easy path to God, lacking the turmoil inherent in our choices.

But all is not bleak. (Be prepared for another paragraph-long sentence!) For those who grow by questing, for those who see the potential of changing relationships, for those whose basic belief in God is not destroyed by the fact that such belief does not chart faith as a well-defined road map, for those who find commitment enriched by the adventure of the possibility of change and variation, for those who are not satisfied with the one answer for now and for all times -- for those people the Nameless shall be named and renamed. His presence shall be felt not as a monolith, but in the sweet music of orchestration upon a familiar theme. Such are the vibrations of liberal Judaism.

Science versus Religion?
3/13/07

A close relative, an atheist who keeps kosher, insisted that I read two books that recently have been on the best sellers list: "The God Delusion" by Richard Dawkins and "The End of Faith" by Sam Harris. My ophthalmologist, Howard Goldman, has been feeding me stories on the relationship between religion and science from the Science Tuesday section of the *New York Times* because he knows that I tend to overlook that section. I recently attended *shul* in New York to pray a little and relax but was confronted with a notice that the synagogue was sponsoring a lecture entitled "Science and Religion: Concord or Discord."

OK, I get the message. This is something I should write about. Not only is the synagogue sponsoring lectures on this subject, but the John Templeton Foundation has been holding symposia across this land in its attempt to reconcile religion with science. It even awards $1.5 million each year to the winner of the Templeton Prize, a scientist or writer who contributes most to this field. (Maybe I should sharpen my pencil.) Recently there was sort of an anti-Templeton conclave of scientists at the Falk Institute in La Jolla, California. At that conference Nobel laureate physicist Steven Weinberg warned that "the world needs to wake up from its long nightmare of religious belief." That was the tenor of the symposium.

So I bought the Dawkins and Harris books and was extremely underwhelmed. These scientists are objecting to fundamentalist religion that I find philosophically simplistic and politically dangerous. But the problem is that they insist upon including me in their company. Harris comments: "The religious moderate is nothing more than a failed fundamentalist," and "Religious moderates are, in large part, responsible for the religious conflict in our world, because their beliefs provide the context in which scriptural literalism and religious violence can never be adequately opposed." I find this reasoning as simplistic as the logic of the fundamentalists against whom he rails.

Dawkins is more judicious in his language but still fails to distinguish between liberal and fundamentalist religion. There are basically three definitions of God. The first is labeled theistic. It is a belief in a God that breaks into the natural order, reveals his or her desires in a holy book and answers prayer. Deism defines God as an amorphous spirit that exists but does not intervene in worldy affairs. There is no revelation nor is there a direct answer to prayer. (This was certainly the God of Jefferson, Hamilton, Franklin and many more of our founding fathers.) The third position is pantheism which does not define God as a personality but that all laws, forces and manifestations of the self-existing universe are God. (This was the God of Spinoza, Einstein and Rabbi Mordecai Kaplan, who founded the Reconstructionist Movement, as well as the God of many Reform and Conservative rabbis.)

The problem is that Dawkins does not recognize belief in a pantheistic God as religion. He writes that many Jews believe this but are "confused and confusing" because of their "willingness to label as 'religion' the pantheistic reverence which many of us share with its most distinguished exponent, Albert Einstein." But what academic degree gives Dawkins the right to define what religion is or to what the word God applies? I do not define science for him and he does not have the right to define me or anyone else out of the religious stream.

The problem is further exacerbated by the fact that these writers define religion from a Christian perspective. If a Christian asks you, "What is your religion?" he or she is really asking, "What do you believe?" You are a Methodist, Catholic, Jehovah Witness, etc. We Jews can believe many things but still belong to the same synagogue. Judaism is a religious culture that encompasses many different belief systems. It is an inherently liberal religion, albeit capable of being distorted by our own fundamentalists. But it is a religion in which most scientists can feel comfortable.

Harris stresses that religion has been the reason for slaughter and wars throughout history. This is undeniably true. But so has nationalism, and no one is calling for One World government. I for one do not want to do away with the differences between Italian, Chinese, French and other cultures that come with nationalism. Hitler wanted to conquer the world in the name of nationalism, not religion. Pol Pot and Mao killed millions in the name of communism and Stalin was an avowed atheist. Religion is not the only impetus for mass slaughter.

Harris uses a bit of legerdemain and fancy wordplay to answer this. In relation to Stalin and Mao he writes, "Although these tyrants paid lip service to rationality, communism was little more than a political religion." Does this mean that all intensely held beliefs are automatically religious? In that case, religion is truly the scourge of mankind. As for Hitler, he writes, "Knowingly or not, the Nazis were the agents of religion." Tell that to the Christian clerics whom Hitler murdered. Is Harris qualified to psychoanalyze Hitler?

Both writers have an intense dislike of the bible. They quote the most heinous portions that every liberal religionist would eschew. This is relevant to the fundamentalists, who are the cause of their ire. But it is not relevant to the modern Jew who looks upon the bible and the Talmud as the history of our people reaching toward God, not the word of God delivered from On High. Sure, the bible has some very difficult passages. What rational person would think that God directed him to sacrifice his child? If one marries and finds that his bride is not a virgin, she can be stoned to death. Slavery is acceptable in the bible. So what. I learn as much from my ancestors who struck out in their quest to find meaning as I do from the prophets who hit home runs and who teach me how to love mankind.

The problem with these scientists who attack religion is that they define it as a set of beliefs that God gives to mankind. I define religion as a journey, a continuing quest to find meaning and morality, a process, not an end – and the beliefs change over time. But these beliefs grow organically from earlier beliefs and there is no need to scuttle the earlier documents that have much to teach us, even if they are not perfect.

Yes, fundamentalism is dangerous. The Muslim kind can produce a 9/11. The Christian and Jewish kind can stifle stem cell research, introduce "intelligent design" instead of evolution and destroy separation of church and state. For me, Christian fundamentalism is much more dangerous than Muslim fanaticism. The latter can sadly kill a few thousand people, but Christian fundamentalism is attempting to change the very nature of our society and kill the soul of our multi-cultured country.

The bottom line is that bashing all forms of religion (liberal and fundamentalism) discredits the scientific community and is self defeating. The *New York Times* reported that on the third day of the La Jolla conference a scientist critiqued the discussion: "With a few notable exceptions the viewpoints have run the gamut from A to B. Should we bash religion with a crowbar or only with a baseball bat?" He then turned to Sam Harris and said, "I think that you and Richard (Dawkins) are remarkably apt mirror images of the extremists on the other side and that you generate more fear and hatred of science." That's my conclusion about both of their books. Religion bashing is no way to convince Americans to support science.

Value of Religion
6/13/06

Several years ago I read a blurb in a newspaper that some academic did a study that showed that religious people enjoyed life more than non-religious people. I found that to be a little preposterous, so, at the time, I never gave it a second thought. I threw the newspaper into the recycling bin, being a good citizen, and I forever lost the footnote as to who came to this startling conclusion. However, the thought stayed in my mind. Are religious people really happier than non-religious people? Then I thought, maybe he or she was really correct. But why? Why does religion allow us to enjoy life more than our secular brethren?

Upon further contemplation, I have concluded that religion, especially Judaism, enriches our lives in six different ways. To be honest, I wanted to arrive at seven ways, since it is a mystical number in Judaism; but alas, I can only provide six explanations. So here are the six contributions that religion gives to the individual.

First, religion gives us community, something everyone seeks. The world is not community. We need sub-groups, with our own histories and myths and *buba maises*. We need the warmth of knowing that we share some commonality with a smaller portion of the six billion people on this globe. Judaism specializes in community.

Second point: Religion provides for us a sensitivity to time and its meaning. It provides cycles by which we can count the seasons and delineate the passage of time. My favorite Henny Youngman joke: He said he was an atheist, but he gave it up – no holidays. Counting time is important to the human psyche.

When I was in law school in the late nineteen fifties I waited on tables in one of those coffee shops/bars/small bohemian playhouses that were so fashionable at the time. I served beverages while four intense young actors on a slightly raised stage performed Jean-Paul Sartre's famous play "No Exit". I can never forget the experience because each and every night, for over fifty nights, while I served drinks, they acted. "No Exit" will never have an exit in my mind. The play is a definition of hell. Four dead people sit on stools and talk, and talk and talk and talk. You see the definition of hell to Sartre is undifferentiated time. There is no end to just sitting and talking. He understood the human need for segmentation, for beginnings and ends. We in Judaism have a special holiday to celebrate a cycle. It's called Simhat Torah, where we celebrate nothing more than the end of the Torah cycle and the beginning of another. We punctuate and consecrate time through the Sabbath and our many other holidays

The third contribution of religion is more ephemeral, more philosophical, more difficult to define, yet is just as real and equally as important. Religion provides for us a vehicle to ask the question, what is the meaning of life? Or to put it in a more popular form, what's it all about, Alfie? We may never know, really, what it's all about. We may just have to live and hope and quest; but religion, and I am speaking here of Judaism in particular, can at least give us a lift, helping us along the way, in our journey and search for meaning. It's not a vehicle that's guaranteed to bring us to the end of the quest, but it can help us to move toward our destination. Nationalism can't do it. Consumerism can't do it. Hedonism can't do it. Judaism at least helps us to do it.

The fourth contribution of religion to our lives is that it gives us the rituals of consolation. This cannot be underestimated. During times of stress or mourning we have tradition and structure to turn to. Ritual solemnifies, dignifies and validates our existence. We don't just merely lose a loved one. Religion allows us to contemplate the meaning of, and add dignity to, a life that we mourn. It provides structure during the *shiva* period. It provides remembrance through the *yizkor* service. It provides community, once again, through the need for a *minyan*. Religion is an institutionalized friend that musters all our living friends into action. Can non-religious people do without all of this? Of course they can, and they do. But I maintain that they do it less well, that they are left with voids that could have been partially filled by the warmth of religious tradition and ritual.

Fifth value of religion: It provides for us an ethical system. For some that means a God-given set of commandments (ten sounds like a good number) or 613 *mitzvot*. For others, religion provides a structure in which we search for the image of God and we find our ethics in the striving of mankind toward God, not from pronouncements on high. But it is religious structure through which we quest. Personally, I trace my ethical system to both the biblical prophets and the philosophy of Martin Buber. I am inspired by Amos, Micah and other early Jews who sought to make this world better in the name of God. It is all religion no matter what your basis. Can people be ethical and upright without religion? Of course, but they are forsaking a valuable tool. It is like constructing a house with only one hammer, while religion can make it easier by providing you a whole toolbox.

Sixth and final point: Religion provides us with a set of beliefs, a definition of God. This point is related to, but distinct from, point number three, where we talked about the meaning of life. Even a Jewish atheist knows what God he rejects and what *shul* he won't step into. For many the existence of God gives hope that there is something beyond this life. For others God provides the basis of ethics, consolation and meaning in life. God is the bedrock of western religion. He is not needed in Buddhism, a religion I deeply respect, but cannot reconcile with my own sense of self and worth (but that is another story). But he is needed in Judaism, Christianity and Islam.

But who is he? Or more precisely, what is he? My religious bent is that I don't believe in a personal God that breaks into the natural order and reveals his truth. To me, God is the mystery of existence, the unknowable that makes life something more than merely being, and the indefinable urge to grope for meaning. I find hope and joy out of the mystery, such joy that I call it God. Others may find despair, and they may show no interest in God or religion. I do not fault them. Neither do I pity them. I just feel sad for them, because they deny themselves the richness of the religious journey. This brings us back to our original newspaper story. As human beings the non-religious may be no better nor worse than we who practice religion, but it seems they are a tad bit sadder.

My Ethical Will
12/12/06

My daughter suggested that I do not write enough about Judaism, separate from Israel and politics. Literally ten minutes after that conversation I was thumbing through some documents and came upon my ethical will that I wrote 13 years ago when I was merely 57. Rereading that, I have come to the conclusion that I still stand behind it.

Ethical wills are an old Jewish tradition. For centuries Jews, both obscure and prominent, have been writing these missives to their progeny. The ethical will that follows reflects my own religious synthesis. I share it with you and I invite you to eavesdrop into a personal communication.

Dear Eric, Michael and Sue: I have no idea how much wealth I shall leave you upon my death. This depends on two important variables – how long I can remain gainfully employed and how long I live. Actually, I hope to live to Zayde's age of 97, in the process consuming much of my savings, thus leaving you little tangible wealth. But in this ethical will that I give you today, I hope that I am leaving you great wealth.

If, God forbid, mom pre-deceases me, then you will be responsible for my remains. Therefore, I want to speak to you of burial and mourning issues. Keep a closed casket. Remember me not in death, but as I lived. That is the Jewish way. And let me die as I have lived – cheaply. Do not purchase a fancy casket. Save the money and enjoy it or give it as *tzedakah*. Remember me with joy as well as tears. Celebrate my sense of humor with a joke during the eulogy. Remember some ludicrous situation in which I have been involved and recount it as ballast against the tendency to induct into sainthood all recently deceased.

The traditional Jewish mourning practice is to recite kaddish two times a day for eleven months. It has the value of bringing people back to the synagogue, but it will have no value for me once I am gone. Remember that all mourning practices are for the bereaved, not for the dead. Recite kaddish to connect yourselves to your parents and grandparents. Recite it when you wish and how often you wish. There is a discipline in mourning as well as in other aspects of life, and you may wish to recite kaddish every day or at Shabbat services for some period of time in my memory. But feel no guilt. If you wish to celebrate my memory by viewing one significant movie once a week for eleven months, then I applaud you from my resting place. As I have grown older I have personally found the yizkor services for Yom Kippur, Sukkot, Pesach and Shavuot to be spiritually uplifting. They ground me to the memories and the loves that I have lost and so they help me lead a more reflective and fuller life today. Since you are in your early and mid-twenties I bring them to your attention now for future utilization, hoping that these yizkor services can be as meaningful to you as they have been to me.

Speaking of Jewish ritual, I am aware that today all Jews are Jews by choice, whether you are natural born or not. We live in a society that does not require religious practice and in many ways discourages it. That is not all bad, for inherent in such a society are great personal liberties. Yet within that context I believe that there are many rewards to be found in a religious commitment. My children, I cannot tell you what kind of Judaism to practice. In fact, if your practice is identical to mine then you haven't lived a reflective life. Religion is the reflections of each generation's quest for meaning and God, and I don't expect your quest to be identical to mine. I cannot even ask you to believe in God, since I cannot define what that term means to me. It is all part of the quest.

I can ask that you don't succumb to a fundamentalism. I fear people who know the one sure path to God and eternity, whether that path is packaged as part of Islam, Christianity or Judaism. During times of stress in your lives it may appear tempting to turn to the security and solace that these systems provide, yet they are as fool's gold – they glitter and give immediate satisfaction, but they cannot provide a framework for a lifetime of spiritual growth. In the liberal tradition, always understand that your religious beliefs are absolutely true for you but not necessarily for anyone else; but that does not negate their truth for you.

I am aware that at your age prayer is not an important part of your existence. But I remind you that a good *chazzan* can transport you into a world of reflection and a familiar prayer can ground you in a memory that will give you new insight and enhance your life's journey. A full life should be a mixture of planning and impulse, of carefree behavior and of discipline. To err in one direction you become a fool, in the other direction you become a compulsive bore. Within this balance that I advise you to seek, you can utilize prayer. Earlier I spoke of the yizkor services. I would also recommend Simchat Torah, the High Holy Days and, of course, Shabbat. Don't nudge God too often. Every Sabbath is not necessary (as I have shown you in practice!). If you have a choice between a family Shabbat dinner, with the rituals including *zemirot* (singing) and the *birkat*, choose that over the shul. I believe that it will be more important to you and your children.

As you know, when you grew up we defined Shabbat as a family day. We went to the movies, the zoo, and the beach – all things that an Orthodox Jew would not consider to be holy. What the outside world did not see was the consecration of time by shared family experiences each and every Shabbat. You were not even allowed to attend birthday parties for friends on Shabbat because that would take you away from the family unit. I recommend this discipline of joy and suggest that you practice it with your own children. Of course, Shabbat dinner. We may not see one another throughout the week, but we must share Shabbat dinner. That is another joyful law of our household that has been operable even in your adulthood. Continue it when both mom and I are gone. I think that it will serve you well.

In many ethical wills that I have read, parents have admonished their children to remain Jewish. I cannot do that. Of course I want you to continue the traditions, but more than that I want your lives to be fulfilled. I want you to be Jews for yourselves, not for me, because I believe the religion, or at least the liberal stream of the religion that we practice, is a wonderful vehicle to use in your search for meaning, solace and warmth in life. Within this context I want you to marry Jews. Of course, a convert is a full-fledged Jew. You have me at a disability because you know that I will not say kaddish over you if you intermarry. But you also know that many of the enrichments of our shared lives (such as Shabbat dinner) cannot be appreciated by a non-Jew. Ultimately the humanity of your spouse is more important than religion; but the combination of humanity, decency and a shared religious heritage is the ideal that you should pursue.

Remember the Holocaust, but don't dwell on it. Take your spouses and children to the Holocaust Museum in Washington and to Yad V'Shem in Jerusalem. Let them understand that fate has chosen us Jews as witnesses to the world for the human potential towards evil. Learn the correct lesson from the Holocaust. It is not that gentiles naturally hate Jews and that we should distrust them and hold ourselves apart. Rather, it is the most hateful of many holocausts that people have wreaked upon others. The Shoah (the Holocaust) speaks to all humanity through Jews. Judaism believes that we are born neither with original sin nor original purity. We humans have within us the capability to do amazing acts of kindness as well as atrocious acts of evil. This is the universal message of the Shoah. As Jews, remember the Holocaust, but let it not dominate your Judaism, for a vital religion has to be built on more affirmative foundations. Remembrance and sadness are part of religion but cannot be its dominant themes if we are to continue using religion as a life enhancing tool.

Speaking of the Holocaust is a good segue to the ultimate goal of Judaism, which is its universal message. Judaism preaches redemption for all people, whether they are Jews or not. This is the reason that Pesach is my favorite holiday. We do not celebrate the journey of Jews from slavery to freedom; rather we recite the paradigm for the redemption of all peoples from slavery to freedom. This, our most Jewish and particularistic holiday, is also our most universalistic holiday. To me, my children, Pesach encapsulates Judaism's basic message – all people, not just Jews, are important to God. You are aware that I do not believe that we are the chosen people. All of our literature reflects mankind groping towards God. I do not believe God breaks into the natural order. God has not chosen us or any other people. We have chosen God. I believe that Jews are an interesting and unique people because of the religious traditions that we have created; but remember, my children, that that religious tradition requires us to cherish and to recognize the humanity of people of all beliefs and all races. I would be greatly disappointed if you were to become Jews who care only for other Jews to the exclusion of the rest of humanity.

A word about *tzedakah*: You have grown up in a family where you have been taught the need to give back to society. Choose your own charities, but be committed to something. Ideally I believe that your charities should encompass both Jewish and non-Jewish interests. Remember that none of us is self-made. I have had the advantage of a middle class upbringing that stressed education. With my identical biological makeup, if I were born into a dysfunctional family in an American slum, I cannot guarantee that I would have risen above my environment. Be not full of yourselves and remember the adage, there but for the grace of God go I. With this sense of humility commit yourselves to a life *of tzedakah*. I am not asking you to deprive yourselves of basics, but before you feast on every innovative status symbol, put some money aside for *tzedakah*. You will find your own humanity in this endeavor.

A word about Israel: Although Eric and Michael have spent meaningful time in Israel as adults, I regret that Sue, by her own choice, has only been there as a child. We will try to rectify that in the near future. (This has been done.) It is difficult to tell you to love Israel, since that will come only through your own experiences. I know that Israel is an imperfect country, and there is much about Israeli society that is a source of great annoyance. Yet it is the only country on this planet that is uniquely Jewish, and what happens there will inevitably affect your own personal equilibrium.

Therefore, I charge you to become active Zionists, to work for the benefit of Israel, to support liberal causes within that country that will reflect the best within Judaism. Support those causes that will make Israel a light unto the nations, rather than a stronghold for religious fundamentalism and xenophobia. Israel is not just another country. In many ways it is your country, spiritually if not physically. It is odd because it is not quite nationalism (for we are Americans, not Israelis) and it is not religious (in that Judaism is much greater than the land of Israel), but Israel does play a role within our Jewish psyche as the physical embodiment of our four thousand year religious journey. Go there often, and form your own attachments and resentments. But go there.

As my final "legacy of intangibles" I want to leave you with some thoughts on values, relationships and temperament having nothing to do with religion. I know that you are honest, and I believe that your sense of ethics is family and society based and only secondarily from religious thought. Whatever its source, stay honest. There will be many temptations in your lives, but remember my admonition. Remain religious in the sense of the definition of religion as what you do when you know that no one will ever know. Remain ethical and religious for yourselves.

As equally important as honesty, stay compassionate. The greatest legacy my father gave to me was a passion for the underdog. In your desire to succeed, don't identify too closely with the establishment. Understand the wisdom and humanity found in the workshop as well as in the boardroom. Care about people whom society generally doesn't care about. Do not let material success desensitize your spirit.

I know that you have been reared in Boca Raton and in many respects this is a disability. Houses, autos, clothes and jewelry are not the real things of value in life. I have not taken a vow of poverty and neither do I expect you to. But learn from what Michael calls the "yuppie scum." Life should not be a frenetic quest for the latest status symbols. Learn from the empty people you see trying to look successful in life.

Which brings us to relationships: Your mother and father are not unique. Relationships need not break up every other year and you can spend a lifetime with a mate in marital harmony. Contrary to what your friends from unhappy and broken homes tell you, you need not bicker or constantly fight. Find a spouse to share a deep and tranquil love. This is your ultimate salvation in life.

My children, I wish you lives as rewarding as mine has been to this point. I hope that this, my ethical will, in some small way helps you to achieve that. I need not tell you to care for your mother and to love and care for each other. May you have long and happy lives.

Love, Abba.

JEWISH COMMUNITY
Thinking Out Of The Box

Part One
8/5/03

Thinking out of the box is not easy, nor is the product of that thought easily accepted. Creative artists have faced resistance to new ideas throughout history. In modern times, new forms in music and literature have been panned. George Gershwin's *Porgy and Bess* was savaged by the critics and his *American in Paris* was called "pedestrian," which is ironic because it is a piece of music about walking through Paris. Critics rejected both *The Sleeping Beauty* and *Swan Lake* by Tchaikovsky because they created a new paradigm for ballet music. And the list can go on. New ideas, new paradigms that do not fit into our accepted, inherited intellectual boxes, are considered either heresy or discarded as worthless.

There is no field of endeavor that is more resistant to new ideas, to thinking out of the box, than religion. In this, the first of a series of three columns, I intend to present ideas that rabbis may think heretical or, if not, are afraid to discuss for fear of congregational retribution. In other words, some of these ideas may startle you, anger you, bother you, maybe even challenge you. Any of the above would validate my role as a columnist and as a rabbi who wants to foster meaningful Jewish dialogue.

Here we go: Let us openly admit that many inherited rituals no longer speak to us and should be discarded or at least de-emphasized (meaning merely tolerated). A prime example of this is *kashrut* (keeping kosher).

Orthodox Jewish scholars will tell you that kosher means cleanliness only in a ritual sense. It has nothing to do with physical cleanliness. The old "pig is bad because of trichinosis" routine was an apologetic, a lame explanation

35

to non-Jews to justify our odd eating habits that were so different from the majority culture.

Kashrut has always been merely a discipline, a ritual, to daily remind one that he or she is a Jew, and also to bind the Jewish community together. As long as the majority of Jews adhered to it, it was a good discipline. But it was not an edict from God, unless you believe that both the Torah and Talmud are revelations from the Almighty, in which case you are part of the 6 percent of American Jews who are Orthodox, and are not part of this discussion. But if you are a part of the other 94 percent who call themselves Reform, Conservative, Reconstructionist, Renewal, Humanistic, gastronomic, or any other variety of Judaism, then you have to agree with the premise that *Kashrut* was a man-made ritual to meet the needs of the generation that established it.

It's a new generation and the discipline no longer works. When the same realization faced the Catholic Church, it dropped its existing discipline. No longer do Catholics have to refrain from eating meat on Friday, as the remembrance of the day of crucifixion. When a ritual ceases to work, a non-orthodox intelligent establishment drops it and directs its energies to other more creative ways of showing religiosity.

But the liberal Jewish establishment, which should include the Conservative movement, has not done this. The vast majority of Jews have voted on this issue – they have ignored *kashrut*. Well over 99 percent of Reform Jews and approximately 97 percent of Conservative Jews do not keep kosher. Well, some do keep kosher only in their homes. I guess they feel at least their dishes will go to heaven. By their eating habits, the vast majority of Jews have affirmed that any God who would create lobster tail and then tell mankind that he cannot eat it, is a sadistic and cruel deity who should be avoided at all cost.

The problem is that the hierarchy is not listening. The Conservative movement has turned its rabbinate into a priesthood over this issue. A congregational board comprised entirely of *hazar* eating Jews would fire a Conservative rabbi who openly ate a Big Mac at MacDonald's. They have turned their rabbis into priests who should remain celibate while the rest of us enjoy carnal pleasure.

The Reform movement is not much better. An ever increasing number of young Reform rabbis are keeping kosher in their quest to "feel Jewish." The problem is that their congregants aren't feeling Jewish in the same way, and the gap between spiritual leader and the congregation is widening. Actually, if someone feels good keeping kosher, I have no quarrel with him/her. For a small group of liberal Jews it is still a meaningful ritual. My quarrel is with a small group of Reform rabbis and the whole Conservative rabbinate that continue to hock their congregants over *kashrut*, an essentially dead ritual

Be creative. Find new rituals. It is time for rabbis to stop making their congregants feel guilty over what is for them an empty ritual. Guilt does not create community; it destroys it. Guilt does not enhance religious devotion; it diminishes it. Let us move on. For those few who still find meaning in keeping kosher, I encourage them to continue to enhance their own satisfaction. However, beyond *kashrut*, let us all move on to serious religious questions.

Thinking Out Of The Box, Part Two
8/12/03

Human beings are taught to think in terms of paradigms and metaphors. We are taught to organize data and items in certain patterns to make sense of otherwise chaotic phenomena. In other words, we are taught to create little boxes into which we can compartmentalize our data and our thought processes. On the whole, these little boxes are not harmful, for they provide structure human beings so desperately need.

But I am reminded of the Chinese blessing, which is, "May you live during interesting times," and the Chinese curse, which is, "May you live during interesting times." There is no free lunch. With the blessing comes the curse. So it is with thinking in boxes. The blessing is that we have structure in which we can solidly build a storehouse of knowledge. The curse is that this structure inhibits original thinking – what we call today, thinking out of the box.

Out of the box, here is my second installment, in a three part series, on a new Jewish perspective.

Legal rules do not make you a Jew. Rather, in my opinion, sharing of community makes you Jewish. Thus all of the controversy over matrilineal and/or patrilineal descent is actually irrelevant. Let me explain by way of an example. When I was a rabbi in Ann Arbor, Michigan, I had a congregant who was married to a Jew, but was Christian-born. He had been practicing Judaism with his wife for twenty years but had never "converted." Both his knowledge and his practice of Judaism far exceeded that of most of my other congregants.

One day he asked me to convert him. My natural reaction was: Since you have been practicing Judaism all these years, why didn't you do this sooner? His answer was simple. His father was a Protestant minister, and while his father was alive he would not hurt him by formally rejecting Christianity, yet he always felt himself Jewish.

And he was right. He was a Jew all those years. In my conversion classes

I required six months of study. I required none for him. I was really not converting him. I was merely telling the world by conventional standards – a formal ceremony – what was an existential reality: He was Jewish because he was part of our community.

When I taught conversion classes, at the end of the six-month period a *Bet Din* (a panel of rabbis) would perform a ceremony that would "convert" the person. In truth, that was not when that person became a Jew. He or she really became Jewish when somewhere along the way he began saying "we Jews" rather than "you Jews." The reality of acceptance of our community made him Jewish, not some ceremony conducted by rabbis. During the Holocaust there were "non-Jewish" spouses who chose to go to the death camps with their Jewish mates and who died because of their acceptance of the fate of the Jewish community. Is there a reader who could tell me that they did not die as Jews? The conversion ceremony was not needed. Community, not legalisms, determined their fate and religion.

What does this mean? It means that the acceptance of patrilineal descent by the Reform movement is helpful in defining who is a Jew, in that as long as the majority of Jews remain in a thought process contained in a little legal box, it is a hook to legally define someone as being part of a community. But being part of the Jewish community -- any community – isn't really defined by legal strictures. It is defined by every-day occurrences, by living as a Jew. A piece of paper, a rabbi's *hekshur* does not make one a Jew. A lifetime of Jewish communal living does.

What does this mean? It means that the definition of being a Jew is fuzzy. We lose set boundaries – and people love set boundaries. They make definitions in life so simple. Boundaries are good when you're buying property, but they're lousy when you are trying to define complex relationships. Life is not lived in sharply defined black and white. Most of it is lived in that fuzzy gray area between good and bad, right and wrong, success and failure, and love and hate. Fuzzy boundaries are what life is made of. And fuzzy boundaries are what define Judaism. We should learn to live with them.

And finally, this leads to one very practical suggestion. All of us have daughters-in-law, friends, acquaintances or others whom we know who are not "converted" Jews, but who are raising Jewish children, who are attending Jewish functions, who are tied to our community by a series of complex bindings. Don't be quick to label them as Christians or in any other way as outsiders. Without a formal conversion, they may be more Jewish than some of "us." Inclusion should be our first instinct, not exclusion, for inclusion creates community, which is the ultimate definition of Judaism.

Thinking Out Of The Box, Part Three
8/19/03

This is the last of a three part series on thinking out of the box on religious issues. If I haven't offended you in the last two weeks, beware, I may today

Zionism is dead. Thank God Israel is alive, but the Zionist ideal that has been the preoccupation of American Jewry from the founding of the state to the turn of the millennium will no longer sustain our Jewish identity. Yes, it will for most of us, because we are senior citizens with long memories; but Zionism will not be a reason for being Jewish to our grandchildren.

If we are honest with ourselves, we should have realized that commingling of nationalism and religion has been a recipe for repression and disaster throughout history. Why should we have thought that we Jews could do it any better than the literally thousands of others who have failed? When religion is the bedrock of a national state, you end up with intolerance of your minority at best, or an inquisition at worst.

It is true that less than perfect neighbors surround Israel, but they are human and have some valid historical and moral claims on the land. We deny their humanity when a West Bank settler was convicted a few years back of kicking to death an eleven-year-old Palestinian child and given six months community service as punishment by an Israeli court. Such conduct becomes an embarrassment to Jewish ethics. We expect more from a Jewish state and a Jewish court.

Internally, Israel has disappointed us as well. We are old enough to remember restrictive covenants in land deeds in the United States. We Jews were forbidden to live among those who felt our presence would disturb their perfect world of white Anglo-Saxon dominance. We were too boisterous, too foreign, and too un-Christian. The United States Supreme Court ruled in 1948 that restrictive covenants were illegal, and now we can live where we choose, as it should be in any decent, humane and liberal democracy.

Back to Israel. Approximately 85 percent of Israeli land is under restrictive covenants against Israeli Arab citizens. A few years ago this was challenged by an Israeli Arab couple that wanted to purchase a home in a new development, but were denied because they were not Jewish. The Supreme Court of Israel ruled in their favor, declaring restrictive covenants inimical to true democracy. However, Israel is a democracy without a constitution, and the Supreme Court is not the final authority. The Knesset quickly overturned the Supreme Court and overwhelmingly reinstated restrictive covenants as the law of the land.

How can American Jews, who have been victims of such gruesome discrimination, continue to condone, if in no other way than by our silence,

Israeli discrimination against its own citizens? Is this the state that is supposed to sustain Jewish identity for our grandchildren? I doubt it. It is a sad statement and will anguish many of us to verbalize it, but the Zionist ideal is dead.

* * * * *

Contrary to what my *Bubbe* and *Zayde* told me, the most important single group in this world is not Jews, but is humanity. Humanity is the bottom line. We are merely a sub-group adding to the richness of God's mosaic, called humanity. And we should start thinking in those terms.

This really is not new to Judaism. Of the major religions, Judaism may be the most universalistic in its scope. The prophets Isaiah and Micah and Amos spoke of all humanity, not merely Jews. But centuries of persecution have narrowed our focus. A Jewish life has become more important than a non-Jewish life. As a defense mechanism to discrimination against us, we developed a sense of superiority over our neighbors who were not quite as bright as we since they had *goyishe kups*.

This narrow, parochial distinction of Judaism thrives today in right-wing Orthodoxy, which eschews a broader world-view. Please note I am not talking about Modern Orthodoxy, but of a rigid Orthodoxy that is trying to make the phrase "modern Orthodoxy" an oxymoron.

Given the choice of my children or grandchildren marrying a right-wing Satmar Hasidic Jew or a sophisticated Episcopalian, Unitarian or Presbyterian, hands down I welcome the Christian into my family, because his or her world-view coincides with mine, although it is expressed through another religious tradition. The Satmar-Hasidic world-view, although very "Jewish" down to the *titzies* and *payesin*, negates my world-view.

It is time for liberal Jews to understand that we are the natural inheritors of rabbinic Judaism as it continues to evolve and that ultra-Orthodox Judaism does not represent "authentic" Judaism, but rather is a reflection of a retrogressive and ossified Judaism, a fundamentalism that faltered by the side of the highway while the rest of the religion traveled down the road of evolutionary change.

In other words, we are not a pale reflection of the real Judaism of our grandfathers: rather we are the authentic Judaism of our generation, with a healthy world-view that recognizes the humanity of all mankind. The bottom line is not Jews, but humanity.

For better or worse, my thoughts are out of the box.

Intermarriage and Outreach

Facing the Reality of Intermarriage
10/23/07

Somewhere between 40 and 50 percent of Jewish weddings today are intermarriages. For Jews between ages 18 to 25, fully 52% live in households where one parent is not Jewish. Currently there are over one million intermarried households, comprising 33% of all married households containing a Jew.

Even when we don't sit shiva (and, thank God, that is an increasingly rare phenomenon) how does the Jewish community react to an intermarriage? The answer is – poorly. The Orthodox are in denial concerning their increasing rate of intermarriage. Except for the far, far right wing who live totally isolated lives from the American mainstream, Orthodoxy faces the same forces of assimilation as do liberal Jews. But what of the Conservative and Reform responses?

The Conservative Movement talks in terms of sensitivity, but in reality does not welcome an intermarried Jew or his or her spouse. The intermarried couple is looked upon as somewhat subversive to Jewish survival. Most important, a Conservative rabbi is *forbidden* to perform an intermarriage ceremony.

But in this column I want to focus on the Reform Movement. Yes, we are doing a lot better than the Orthodox or Conservative Movements, but we are far from perfect. Reform synagogues are reaching out to some extent, but not enough. My biggest gripe with my movement is that the Central Conference of American Rabbis (the Reform rabbinical association) still disapproves of a rabbi officiating at an intermarriage ceremony. Here the key word is *disapproves*, rather than forbids. Fortunately, a sizable percentage of Reform rabbis do intermarriages. When I performed life-cycle events, I performed mixed-marriage ceremonies under certain circumstances. If the couple decided that the children would be reared as Jews, I jumped at the chance to welcome the non-Jew into the family, even if he or she was not converting.

41

Let me share with you a real case from Ann Arbor, Michigan, where I was a rabbi during the early 1970's. The girl's name was Sarah. She was from Detroit and was a graduate of the Solomon Schechter Day School. His name was John. He was the son of a nominally Christian University of Michigan professor who was an atheist. Consequently John had never entered a church in his life. John grew up with Jews and felt totally at home with bagels, lox, chicken soup and even Jewish guilt.

Both Sarah and John decided that their children would attend the same day school as she did and that they would join a synagogue together. Obviously, no Christianity would be in their home. I asked John why he would not convert. He answered, "Maybe someday I will. My father and mother's atheism was their journey, not necessarily mine. But I'm only 23 years old and I am not ready to label myself anything at this time. If I were to acknowledge any religious identity, it would certainly be Jewish. But I am very happy that Sarah is Jewish and that my children will be Jewish. But, rabbi, one thing is for sure, I am not going to convert to satisfy in-laws or you. If and when I convert, it will be to satisfy my own spiritual journey on my own time schedule."

Wow, how do you answer that? He was perfectly logical. And what service to Judaism or to the couple would I perform if I refused to do that marriage? In fact, I performed the ceremony with joy and with the conviction that I was serving Judaism in the best way possible. It is time for the official body that represents Reform rabbis to change its stance. We live in a new world and we have to change to meet the challenges that it brings to us.

Beyond just having the rabbi officiate at an intermarriage ceremony, the Reform movement needs a new and revitalized outreach program to intermarried Jews and their spouses and to non-Jews who could become converts to Judaism. It is not merely a need for increased numbers; we need new blood, new excitement, and new genes in our gene pool – in short, a massive Outreach program.

We must face up to the realization that in our open American society which most of us affirmatively embrace (certainly not wanting to return to the shtetl) being Jewish is an option, not a state of being. The bottom line is that in America all Jews are Jews-by-Choice, not just converts. This implies that we must continually outreach to unaffiliated and marginal natural-born Jews, intermarried couples and even to non-Jews who are "Jew curious," to use a nice phrase that I borrow from Paul Golin of the Jewish Outreach Institute.

It's a new world and Judaism never was, and shouldn't be, a closed social club to outsiders. It's time to openly embrace intermarried couples and to proselytize those millions of Americans who have no religion despite the origin of their birth. Next week I will further amplify on this topic of Outreach.

Outreach to Intermarrieds and Non-Jews
10/30/07-

Last week I discussed intermarriage and our need to reach out to intermarried couples. Today I want to continue that conversation as well as talking about a general Outreach program to non-Jews who are potential converts.

Outreach is not a new idea. Almost 40 years ago when I was a pulpit rabbi in Ann Arbor, Michigan I spoke of Outreach. I proposed that we Jews should open reading rooms in upscale shopping malls with people trained to talk to prospective converts and that we should advertise in newspapers welcoming non-Jews into our Introduction to Judaism classes. Well, the reading rooms never happened, but rabbis are beginning to reach out through newspaper advertisements.

Today I would go further. I would propose that Federations hire a cadre of young rabbis from all the movements to especially work with intermarried couples and to proselytize to the general community, just as we support rabbis as community chaplains to reach out to unaffiliated hospitalized Jews. These outreach rabbis should be specially trained at their respective seminaries and should receive the same salaries that a typical congregational rabbi earns. In South Florida, if the Federations allocated just one percent of their campaigns to outreach, as does Boston, we would have approximately $700,000 annually to spend on enriching Judaism through conversion and through a greater percentage of kids being raised as Jews by intermarried couples.

The call for a conversionary movement goes back to the survivor of the Holocaust and great Rabbi Leo Baeck, who as early as 1949 challenged the Jewish community on this issue. Rabbi Alexander Schindler (who installed me as Rabbi of Touro Synagogue in New Orleans in 1975), then the head of the Reform Movement, "shocked" the Jewish establishment by calling for proselytizing among non-Jews in 1979: "We live in America today. No repressive laws restrain us. The fear of persecution no longer inhibits us. There is no earthly reason now why we cannot reassume our ancient vocation and open our arms wide to all newcomers." The Conservative leader Rabbi Harold Schulweis has called for proactive conversion. In a 1997 *Moment Magazine* article he wrote: "Why not open our arms to those who seek a spiritual way of life?...The logic is clear and so is the theology. Judaism is not an exclusive club of born Jews."

There is much to do if we are to become a more welcoming community to non-Jews. First, we should train those whom the prospective converts first meet – the receptionists at synagogues and Jewish community centers and the ushers at Shabbat services. Next, we should better train our prospective rabbis at our seminaries as to the importance of outreach to both intermarried couples and to potential converts. Also, we should send our existing corps of rabbis back for re-training and reprogramming. Finally, every Jew should wake up to our new environment and realize that we no longer live in the *shtetl* and that we must adapt to our new surroundings. It's time we think differently and think big.

One wonderful example of thinking big was presented by my friend and colleague Charles Sherman, who is the rabbi of the Reform congregation in Tulsa, Oklahoma. Rather than excluding the non-Jewish spouse from the bima (as prescribed by the Conservative Movement) he announced that non-Jewish spouses who raise their children in Judaism are "heroes in our midst." I love that phrase, "heroes in our midst."

Rabbi Sherman wrote: "They are providing their children a religious identity different from their own. An interfaith couple's commitment to raise Jewish children is difficult for some non-Jewish grandparents. (Think of it in the reverse situation.) Non-Jewish parents in interfaith marriages make this sacrificial decision for a variety of reasons – because they understand that they need to teach their child one faith and give their children a single religious identity. Because they realize that their Jewish spouse, however loosely connected to Judaism, will be unable to support a Christian upbringing for their child. Because they love their spouses and children enough and respect Judaism enough to make a very real sacrifice. These sacrifices are made for the welfare of the family." Thus he labels them "heroes in our midst."

Rabbi Sherman further comments, "And aside from the family itself, the key beneficiary is the Jewish people. Therefore, I believe that we must assure that our Temple is a place where these non-Jewish parents are comfortable to worship, learn and socialize." But beyond making these statements, he did something significant and wonderful. On a Shabbat evening he invited all the non-Jewish spouses in the congregation to join him on the bima as he expressed on his own behalf and on behalf of the congregation their deepest gratitude to those who are raising their children as Jews. Rabbi Sherman asked God's blessing upon them, as they bless us by their sacrificial acts, and he asked the entire congregation to join in the blessing for these non-Jewish spouses.

Now that's what I call Outreach! And that is what I call an act of great personal humanity. Rather than rejection, it was a statement of universalism, mixed with our particularistic needs.

It's a new world and Judaism had better understand the need for Outreach if it wants to survive.

It's Time for Jewish Outreach
12/27/04

I just received the latest newsletter of the Jewish Outreach Institute (JOI) which is located in New York City. It is a fine organization that is beginning to make inroads into traditional Jewish thought patterns concerning outreach to unaffiliated and intermarried couples. (For more information email info@joi.org.)

A serious outreach program by the organized Jewish community is long overdue. Just looking at statistics proves this. The recent National Jewish Population Study showed that although almost all Jews celebrate Passover and Hanukkah, less than 40% affiliate with any Jewish organization (and that included synagogues, JCCs, Hadassah, etc.).

Looking at intermarriage, the statistics are even more startling. The same study reports that of all Jews age 18 to 25, 52% live in a household where one parent is not Jewish. Currently there are over one million intermarried households, comprising 33% of all married households containing a Jew. Obviously outreach to non-Jews is essential to Jewish survival.

Outreach is not a new 20th or 21st century concept. During the rabbinic period the rabbis read Torah in the open marketplace on Mondays and Thursdays. This was the genesis of our current practice to read Torah in the synagogues on Monday and Thursday mornings, (not just on Shabbat). The marketplace is where we should be. Thirty-five years ago as a young rabbi I maintained that organized religion should be like a floating crap game – where the action is.

JOI delineates three different kinds of outreach. First, public space Judaism. This includes lighting Hanukkah menorahs in shopping malls (not public property) or sukkah building at Home Depot. Think about it. More Jews go to Home Depot each week than attend religious services. When my son was married six years ago he was registered at Bloomingdales and Home Depot! Think about Jewish programming in the Passover food aisle of Publix. The idea is that Jews will unintentionally stroll into a Jewish experience.

The second category is destination events that require prior knowledge of the time and place of the programs, such as street fairs, Jewish film festivals, author readings in Barnes and Noble. They should be placed in public areas (excluding synagogues or JCCs) where the marginal Jews or prospective Jew can have a low pressure experience that hopefully will open the door to a deeper involvement in our community.

The third JOI component is an open door, welcoming stance by our Jewish institutions, especially the synagogues. I believe that we have done a poor job in this area. We live in South Florida with the highest percentage of elderly in the nation. Anyone attending services quickly realizes that they are peopled by senior citizens. Yet how many of our synagogues reach out to those among us who cannot drive to *shul*? How many provide van service to those who would love to share a Shabbat experience? If we don't reach out to those who are already Jewish, it is not surprising that we don't adequately welcome potential converts and those married to Jews.

We know that synagogues advertise in the *Jewish Journal* and the secular press to sell High Holy Day tickets. How many of them advertise throughout the year just to welcome people to a Shabbat service? No money is involved -- just come for free. Is this not important to us? And, most surprisingly, many do not realize that services are free. Rabbi Joy Levitt of the new JCC on the Upper West Side of Manhattan taught a section of a class for expectant mothers. She urged them to check out one of the 17 synagogues on the Upper West Side. She reports: "One woman in the class raised her hand and remarked that she hadn't known that you could walk into a synagogue if you weren't a member. She was an investment banker. She was Jewish. She lived in Manhattan and she didn't know this. Even more surprising were the nods around the room, indicating that most of the people sitting there didn't know this either." This gives us an idea about how much outreach we need.

We need to reach the children of the intermarried as soon as possible. Preschool education is where we should start. However, the price of admission is often steep. Pre-schools are money-making machines for most synagogues. Since the profits on the pre-school float adult programming as well as the rabbi's salary, it would be difficult to convince them to lower the price. But we need a new paradigm. Jewish pre-schools should be free for any Jew, and especially the children of intermarried Jews. Presently Birthright Israel provides a free trip to Israel for any Jewish college student without showing need. This program is funded by Jewish philanthropists. They are interacting with the child 15 years too late. Get him/her into a Jewish pre-school and you can start him on the road to a Jewish identity so that you won't have to send him to Israel to find one.

Smart businessmen know that every problem also presents an opportunity. We can bewail the non-affiliated or we can outreach. We can deplore intermarriage or we can embrace the couple and enrich Judaism. Intermarriage can surely enrich us. The Jew-by-Choice brings a new gene pool, a new perspective that makes us look at our own religion that we often practice by rote, and very often a new enthusiasm that many of us lose upon being a bar or bat mitzvah. Many a Jew has come back to his or her religion simply because he or she intermarried.

Just looking at population numbers; if every Jew married another Jew, our tribe would still decrease in size due to our low birth rates. Yet if 50% of Jews intermarry and only 65% of the children of those intermarried couples choose Judaism, the Jewish community grows by 15% each generation. As Rabbi Kerry Olitzky of the JOI puts it, "If we really want to ensure the Jewish future in America, the road to growth runs through intermarried households."

It's time to take outreach seriously.

Reaching Out is Good for Judaism
1/2/07

Everyone is *geshrying* about intermarriage and how it will diminish our American Jewish community. Some alarmists have predicted that our numbers will fall to only one million in 50 years from our current six million. Well, sit back and chill – intermarriage may actually be increasing our numbers.

According to a demographic study released in November by the Jewish Federation of Boston and reported in the *Boston Globe*, the Jewish community there has unexpectedly grown due primarily to the fact that with an intermarriage rate somewhere around 50 percent fully 60 percent of the children in those marriages are being reared as Jews. Without boring you with the mathematical calculation, this means that we pick up an extra 10 percent over what we would have had if Jews married only Jews.

Boston community leaders said that this growth is a direct result of a decision by the Boston Jewish community to welcome interfaith families starting in the 1970's. The Combined Jewish Philanthropies in Boston spends about one percent of its annual budget on programs aimed at interfaith families. This is ten times greater than the national average.

Spurred by this report I went back and read Gary Tobin's book, "Opening the Gates – How Proactive Conversion Can Revitalize the Jewish Community," which I should have read seven years ago when it was first published. Tobin was at Brandeis and is now at the University of Judaism in Los Angeles. He is one of the more creative thinkers in the Jewish community. It's very nice that we get 60 percent of the kids in an intermarriage, but it would be even nicer if more people converted into Judaism.

Tobin reviews some of the usual arguments against an active conversionary movement. Jews don't proselytize – it's against our religion. This is a half truth. The biblical Book of Ruth was written especially to buttress a proselytizing movement in Judaism. The Macabbeans actually force-converted the Idumean empire into Judaism approximately 100 BCE. It was only after the Roman Empire embraced Christianity and it became a capital offense for a

Jew to convert a Christian that we Jews quickly got out of the conversionary business. That is when the rule that a Jew must turn away a prospective convert three times was instigated. Today we live in a free country and we have a great religion that we should want to share with others.

The most shocking part of his book describes how unprepared we are to welcome prospective Jews into our fold. The first step for any convert is usually approaching a synagogue. As part the research for his book Tobin surveyed 45 synagogues across the United States. The survey presented a simple request to the first person who answered the phone: "I am interested in becoming Jewish, and I would like to have some information on the process of conversion." The survey noted the respondent's tone of voice, the outcome of the request, and information received.

Tobin reports: "For the most part, the person answering the phone at the synagogues was cold or neutral. Many of them seemed surprised or flustered ... Only seven of the forty-five people who answered the phone offered information, whether in the form of brochures on Introduction to Judaism classes or dates and times of classes...The overall impression, however, was that a request for information on conversion was either surprising ("Conversion? Oh my!"), an inconvenience ("Call back when we're not so busy") or simply unwelcome ("Ugh").

Reaction to My Outreach Column
1/16/07

My recent column on outreach and conversion brought me a few very interesting, intelligent and extensive emails. Let me share them with you.

One person stressed the non-acceptance by natural born Jews toward converts. He wrote: "Convert or not, a Christian who enters or tries to enter into Jewish community life all too often encounters what is best described as Jewish tribal culture which can be exclusionary in the extreme. Too many Jews, perhaps because of our centuries old (until recently) history of religious discrimination at the hands of Christians, tend to have a race memory suspicion or resentment of the Goyim....This leads to the one glaring omission in your column. What good is having the rabbinate way out front when a substantial portion of their congregations lags far behind and subverts the rabbinic effort?"

Suspicion and non-acceptance were certainly the rule in past generations, but I question whether that is the case today. In our open society where approximately 50% of young Jews intermarry, there is a new understanding in the Jewish community. One merely has to look at the many rabbis who are converts and the leaders of congregations and Federations who are also converts. Personally I know of Reform and Conservative rabbis who are married to converts. I question whether this writer who is a senior citizen is not reflecting the sensibilities of a previous generation. Also, I believe that the rabbis lag behind the lay people these days. The vast majorities in Conservative and Reform congregations want their rabbis to perform intermarriages, but the entire Conservative rabbinate and a majority of Reform rabbis will not officiate at a mixed marriage.

Another writer commented on the obstacles to a conversionary outreach. He writes: "Ritual vs. Belief. Even Reform temples are swinging towards Ritual in a big way. In my view, the only way to attract a significant number of converts is to clearly enunciate Beliefs along with Ritual. Ritual can attract a few wandering souls, but only a cogent statement of Beliefs can broaden the appeal to the general public (before Ritual entraps them!)."

I don't look upon ritual as an entrapment. I agree that beliefs are important, but the lure of Judaism for me is that beliefs are not a straightjacket. Christianity is founded upon the one core belief that Jesus died for humankind's sins. If one cannot make the commitment to vicarious atonement he or she cannot find salvation in bedrock Christianity. In contrast bedrock Judaism teaches that salvation depends solely on human conduct (mitzvot) and that all people, not only Jews, are saved if they are righteous.

This means that there can be many different Jewish belief systems, and that's what makes it exciting for me. The quest to find meaning in life, morality amidst this unfinished world, and ultimately some definition of God (if not God himself or herself), is what makes Judaism exciting. It is an intellectually fulfilling religion. But if all this questing can arrive at many different answers, what then holds us together? Ritual. Not entrapping ritual but rituals that can take these intellectual commitments and transform them into our daily lives.

The Passover seder is a prime example. It is one thing to profess freedom, but it is another to ritualize its importance by remembering that we were once slaves ourselves. Eighteen hundred years ago the Talmud (not some Reform rabbi) commented that Pesach celebrates the concept that all peoples must travel from slavery to freedom, not merely Jews going from Egyptian bondage to self-determination in Israel. Passover is the most ritually particularistic Jewish holiday at the same time being the most universalistic in its outreach to all humanity. Ritual is the basis of Jewish community, but it is not exclusionary. Any non-Jewish spouse or convert can quickly attach himself or herself to Jewish ritual.

Another writer comments that intermarriage is a good thing: "Any system that maximizes human happiness is a good thing, and allowing people to love across religious lines increases overall happiness." He gets no argument from me. As much as I am committed to Judaism, both as a Jew and a rabbi, I fully recognize that Judaism is a tool of mankind to enhance life, and people are not tools of religion. But I point out that I can say this because of our liberal salvation system. The same cannot be said for bedrock Christianity.

He further argues: "Intermarriage contributes to the process of religious evolution, which I generally think is a good thing. Whenever two individuals or peoples mix – Canaanites with Hebrews, Inca with other tribes – their cultures and belief systems usually intermingle, adapting and producing a culture superior to its predecessors." Again I cannot deny that there is core validity to his argument. Historically bumping up against Hellenistic culture and Western civilization has enriched Judaism. We did this without intermarrying, but intermarriage is one way of assimilating different cultures into our own. As a rabbi and father I can say that since Judaism risks losing adherents through intermarriage, it is safer to counsel in-marriage to our young, but that is not a damnation of intermarriage. Certainly intermarriage brings a new gene pool into our tribe which no doubt enriches us. For me the key is not to exclude outside cultures and beliefs, but to Judaicize them. Our job is to creatively accept these new influences for the enrichment of Jewish tradition.

Finally this writer complains, "I think that one big weakness of reform Jewish worship is the 'absence' of God…Atheistic Jews are probably far more common – and readily accepted within the reform community – than Jews who believe that there is in fact a God who sets everything in motion or who, God forbid, intervenes in human events…My point? Judaism will only really expand significantly if and when it appeals to more people on an emotional level. Not everyone is receptive to sterile, human-oriented intellectualism."

Well, I believe in God, but not a God who intervenes in human affairs. Obviously the writer does, in which case he has to explain to me where God was during the Holocaust and where is he now when we need him in Darfur. But he has a point – Judaism cannot be merely a collection of intellectualisms (no religion can). But to have emotion we need rituals, not entrapping rituals (whatever that means), but liturgical and communal rituals that define and explicate the universal message of Judaism in an authentic Jewish manner.

These rituals are easily assimilated into one's personality. They need not exclude the non-Jewish spouse or the potential convert. On the contrary, they will induce others to join us. The days of Classical Reform are gone. It's now time to rejoice with song and emotional commitment to a liberal religion that can be expressed in emotive terms. It's also time to invite other seekers of meaning to join us.

Anti-Semitism and Victim Mentality

Hysteria Over Anti-Semitism In America
2/17/04

Last month the American Jewish Committee (AJC) released its 2003 Annual Survey of American Jewish Opinion. It reflected that 97% of American Jews believe that anti-Semitism is either a very serious problem (37%) or somewhat of a problem (60%), and 49% believe that it is increasing.

These perceptions are incredulous to me. How did we get there? It is obvious that American Jews believe the scare tactics and false alarms that are being fed to them by Jewish organizations looking to extract money from their pockets.

I have received solicitation letters from these organizations with large pictures of skinheads on the envelopes. They truly frightened me, which of course was the intent. Fear raises money. The mantra goes on. American Jewish Congress, the Wiesenthal Center, the Anti Defamation League (ADL) and many other Jewish organizations repeat it. It is a disservice to our community.

The same AJC opinion poll indicated that 82% of American Jews believe that anti-Semitism is either a serious problem on college campuses (28%) or somewhat of a problem (54%). This is equally incredulous to me. An out-of-town Hillel director recently privately confirmed to me that it is just not true. Yes, there is Arab propaganda against Israel, just as there is Jewish agitation against the Palestinians, as has been the case for the last thirty or forty years. But, no, there is absolutely no increase in anti-Semitism on his campus.

Then why doesn't he speak out? Why fight the establishment? If they want to believe that, and it brings very needed money into Hillel coffers, why complain? His was an honest, cynical evaluation. He didn't foster the hysteria, but let them enjoy their paranoia, especially if it financially helps a good program (and Hillel is a great program, and I am proud to serve on its Broward/Palm Beach Board).

Let me share with you a very personal evaluation of the "proof" of anti-Semitism in this country. My personal story: About eleven years ago, when I was publishing the *Jewish Journal*, a rock band was booked into the Florida Atlantic University auditorium. Its name was Elvis Hitler. The Palm Beach Chapter of the ADL protested this as an anti-Semitic outrage. We sent a *Jewish Journal* reporter to interview the leader of the band. We asked this young punk rocker if he knew who Hitler was. Well, he knew that he was sort of a bad guy. He had no knowledge of the Holocaust. We asked him why he chose the name of Elvis Hitler. He answered that he thought it would bring some attention to the group, but that he was having second thoughts, since it was turning out to be too negative. This ignorant young rocker had no idea what Jews were, let alone whether he had a negative opinion of them. Yet this was officially reported as an anti-Semitic incident by the ADL.

That same year a young skinhead in West Palm Beach distributed crudely written anti-Semitic flyers. He stuffed them in the free newspaper racks throughout the city, maybe 25 or 30 locations. This was a definite anti-Semitic act. But since he stuffed them in 25 boxes throughout the city, the ADL listed it as 25 different anti-Semitic acts. Needless to say that at the end of that year they were able to report a large rise in anti-Semitism in Palm Beach County. People believe these statistics. Statistics don't lie, we are told. Well, maybe they do. I am reminded of Benjamin Disraeli's famous statement: "There are three kinds of lies – lies, damn lies and statistics."

For the record, I question all ADL, AJ Congress and Wiesenthal Center statistics. Although I disagree with many positions of the American Jewish Committee (AJC), and they are not above grandstanding on Israel to raise money, I do believe in the integrity of their research. But please note, the AJC is not, repeat *not* claiming an increase in anti-Semitism in this country.

Common sense tells each and every one of us that life is good for Jews here. When is the last time that you personally were accosted or even slighted for being Jewish? Excluding criticism of Israel, which you may consider anti-Semitic, but which I don't (we will discuss this in the third segment of this series), when is the last time that you picked up a newspaper and read anything that is even faintly anti-Semitic? It is practically unheard of in the United States.

Even after an American Jew, Jonathan Pollard, was found to have spied for a Jewish state against this country, there was no outcry of dual loyalty against our community. Certainly, at that point, if the anti-Semites were lurking just below the veneer of civility, they would have emerged. Nothing happened.

We all have lived through a period of history when Jews were either denied entrance or held to a quota at our elite universities. When I earned my graduate degrees at Yale in the late fifties and early sixties, there was a strict 6% quota for Jews in the undergraduate program. Thankfully, this kind of anti-Semitism is part of our country's history, along with segregation and slavery. How anti-Semitic can this country be, when a Shapiro can become president of Princeton, a Levin president of Yale and a Rudenstine, and now a Larry Summers, president of Harvard? Our job is to wake up and smell the roses, to live in the present and not the past.

About six years ago the American Jewish Committee did research on the level of anti-Semitism in America. Roughly they found that 85% of Americans welcomed a Jewish son-in-law or daughter-in-law. It was true that about 15% did not, and that portions of those people were anti-Semitic. But the study showed that over 15% of Americans disliked Puerto Ricans, Catholics, Blacks, Asians, even Wasps. We are an equal-opportunity hating country.

The point is that Jews are disliked or even hated to no greater extent that any other group in our society. We are not singled out. Anti-Semitism is not a problem. There is no society in this world where each group is totally accepted by all other groups. Even in Israel, we have Ashkenazic Jews who look down on Sephardic Jews and others who look down on black Ethiopian Jews, and many who resent the Russian immigrant Jews. No society, including Israel or this country, is without prejudice.

In August of 2003 the Pew Research Center for the People and the Press reported that 10% of Americans would not vote for an otherwise qualified Jewish presidential candidate. But the survey also showed that 8% would not vote for an otherwise qualified Catholic. And the margin of error for the survey was 2% -- which means that Jews are no worse off than the seventy-some million Catholics in this country. Sad to say fully 38% would not vote for an otherwise qualified Muslim. That's a figure this country should be ashamed of. If you take respected research seriously, the bottom line is that Jews in the United States are no more discriminated against than any other group. What else can we ask for?

Our problem is not anti-Semitism, but assimilation. With an intermarriage rate of somewhere between 40 to 50 percent we run the risk of annihilation, not through rejection but from acceptance. The danger is not being hated, but being loved to death. I am amused when the same rabbi gives his anti-Semitism warning in the Friday night sermon and his intermarriage warning in his *Shabbat* morning sermon. Did it ever occur to him that we couldn't be hated and loved to death at the same time?

We are as illogical as the real anti-Semite who accuses us of being communists and powerful capitalists who control the world, at the same time. We are either capitalists or communists, but we can't be both simultaneously. We are either hated or loved, but not both at the same time.

I have been an executive director of a Federation, and I believe that there are many good, affirmative aspects of Judaism upon which to raise money. Unfortunately, many Jewish organizations take the easy road and use scare tactics, emphasizing an anti-Semitic problem that does not really exist.

The ADL, Lies & Victim Mentality
6/7/05

The front page of the *Jewish Journal* the week of April 19th reported that the Anti-Defamation League declared in its annual report that anti-Semitic incidents in Florida had risen a whopping 69 percent in the previous year. Rather than accepting these statistics staff writer Shani McManus did an admirable job of investigative reporting.

The ADL claimed 36 anti-Semitic incidents in Palm Beach County, including a West Palm Beach synagogue defaced with a swastika. The *Jewish Journal* called every known synagogue in West Palm Beach and could not verify this incident. Palm Beach County Sheriff Rick Bradshaw reports only four hate crimes and he further stated, "We have not seen an increase in the volume of hate crimes." The ADL reported 64 anti-Semitic acts in Broward County, yet Captain Richard Moss of the BSO, who is Jewish, stated, "I don't think that we've seen anything in the past year that could be classified a hate-crime. We have not had (any reports) of anyone being called a slur in public, and no reports of graffiti." The ADL claimed 33 anti-Semitic acts in Miami-Dade County, yet McManus reports that a spokesperson for the Miami-Dade Police Department said that the only incident of a hate-crime that she could recall was a report of someone painting a swastika on a mosque!

Let me tell you the aftermath of that article. I decided to do some investigative journalism myself. I questioned the *Jewish Journal* reporter (certainly not demanding to know her sources, either open or anonymous), but she did admit that a very prominent professional leader of another Jewish organization in South Florida confided to her that he does not believe any statistic issued by the ADL, but that he could not say this on the record. As a rabbi and former Jewish Federation director I can tell you that over the years many Jewish professionals have also told me the same thing, always "off the record," that judicious protection against being controversial.

Therein lies the problem. We are so civilized that we cannot tell the truth. It reminds me of a column that I wrote in mid 2003 discussing criticism of President Bush. Then *New York Times* columnist Bill Keller (now Executive Editor) wrote that Bush's information on Weapons of Mass Destruction was "dissembling." That's a fancy word, which Webster's New World Dictionary defines as "to conceal the truth." In contrast, in Britain, where they are less delicate in public discourse, Max Hastings, a veteran British war correspondent, wrote that Blair's actions were based on "deceit," and he added "and it stinks." It's all about calling a thing by its common name. My name for ADL statistics is lies, in the tradition of Benjamin Disraeli's famous statement that there are three kinds of lies—lies, damn lies and statistics. And for the record, it stinks.

How does the ADL get away with this mass deception? The simple answer is that it builds upon a victim mentality that pervades our community. Our leaders, for reasons of money raising and other factors, have constantly told us that we live in world of "us against them." In this great tradition, recently Ariel Sharon told a group of teenagers on the March of the Living, "Always remain vigilant and trust no one but ourselves. Jews can only rely on themselves." Our *Jewish Journal* columnist Leonard Fein astutely wrote, "To trust no one means to suspect everyone. To suspect everyone is to ensure that no one will offer a hand; it is a self-fulfilling prophecy. What a shabby self-portrait we paint when we present ourselves as the eternal victim, utterly alone in a hostile world."

How one reads history is crucial. The *Raleigh News & Observer* recently reported that students at one of North Carolina's larger Christian schools are reading "Southern Slavery, as it Was," a booklet that explains a biblical justification for slavery and asserts, "that slaves weren't treated as badly as people think." The booklet also calls slavery "a relationship based upon mutual affection and confidence."

As horrifying as this story is, the realization that history is anything that the current generation wishes to inculcate in its youth is even more terrifying. Is there no absolute truth to be found in history? Yes and no. One would expect that some simple dates are incontrovertible. It would be hard to teach that the invasion of Pearl Harbor occurred on July 4, 1942 instead of December 7, 1941. But even the most basic premises are challenged. You can read "scholarly" articles on the Internet that prove that the Holocaust is a Jewish propaganda lie. It's not unreasonable that some people would think this, given the fact that some people believe that slavery was "a relationship based upon mutual affection and confidence."

How one views history has an important effect on our Judaism. History is not cut and dried. There is always controversy concerning what actually happened, and even when the basic facts are agreed upon, there is inevitably disagreement as to the significance and the conclusions drawn from these facts. In plain words, one can read Jewish history in many different ways.

Yes, we have been defeated twice by the Romans and then oppressed by the Holy Roman Empire. But we have had long stretches of history where we were the dominant power and religion and, sad to say, we oppressed our neighbors. We have been up, and we have been down. Unfortunately, many of us have been brought up thinking that Jews were always helpless and the world constantly oppressed us. This has led to a ghetto mentality that it is us against the world, and the logical conclusion is, "Only Jews help other Jews in the end." Having been a Jewish Federation director I can attest that this was a most potent sentence in raising money.

But it's not true. We have to stop looking at the world and reading history with a victim mentality. Everyone is not anti-Semitic. The world is not out to get us. The news media in general is neither anti-Israel nor anti-Jewish. Looking at the world through eyes that are distorted by a victim mentality produces a surrealistic landscape that only we Jews seem to recognize. When others object to our perceptions we take this as further proof that they are anti-Semitic.

It is important that we correct this state of affairs before we lose total contact with reality. If we don't catch ourselves we will be writing booklets that declare that the slaves really had wonderful lives. Talking about reality, we had better come to our senses and begin to publicly challenge the lies of the ADL. Someone has to tell the king that he's not wearing clothes.

Fear–Mongering and the Anti-Defamation League
12/16/08

This past month I attended a lecture by the Deputy National Director of the Anti-Defamation League at a local synagogue. Before I begin my critique let me put the current level of anti-Semitism in this country in perspective.

About ten years ago the American Jewish Committee reported that 85 percent of Americans would welcome a Jew as a son or daughter in law. Doesn't sound like an avalanche of anti-Semitism to me. The Pew Research group recently found that ten percent of Americans would not vote for a Jew as president even if he or she were qualified. Pew also reported that eight percent would not vote for a Catholic. It appears that we are not special. We are in the same boat as the over 70 million American Catholics.

In fact, about ten percent of Americans hate everyone else. Ten percent hate Puerto Ricans, white Anglos, Italians, etc. Thus there is no Jewish problem here. If anything we are loved and respected far more than any other ethnic or religious group in this country. We are a mere two percent of the population, yet we comprise 14 percent of the Senate, seven percent of the House of Representatives and 22 percent of the Supreme Court.

The recent financial crisis started on Monday, September 29th on the eve of Rosh Hashanah. It wasn't until Wednesday after sunset that the Senate voted on the bail-out package. The House didn't vote on it until Thursday because it was in recess for the two days of Rosh Hashanah. Joseph Aaron of the *Chicago Jewish News* commented: "The greatest financial crisis since the Great Depression, a crisis some feared would lead to a second Great Depression and everyone took in stride that things would just have to wait while the Jews spent two days blowing the shofar. The Jews, all five or so million in a country of more than 300 million...Talk about G-d bless America."

It's true that about ten percent of Americans are prejudiced against Jews, African-Americans and other religious and ethnic minorities. That means that there are about 30 million prejudiced people, some of whom will use the N-Word or burn an African-American Church or deface a synagogue with a swastika. We're a big country and it is easy to gather these isolated incidents and present a power-point presentation that would frighten the average person who will not put it within the context of the greater acceptance of society.

This brings us to the recent speech by Ken Jacobson of the ADL entitled, "Anti-Semitism and the Financial Crisis." He highlighted statements from Internet hate sites: The financial crisis was caused by Jews; the collapse of Lehman Brothers was caused by the transfer of $400 billion to Israeli banks; and it was caused by Jewish bankers to get rich. ADL representatives handed out a slick 24-page booklet quoting a series of these statements. Of course it included a solicitation card for the ADL, an organization that has perfected the use of scare tactics to elicit money from fearful and insecure Jews.

Let me make a comment on the supposed rise of anti-black hatred in the country since the election of Barack Obama. The *New York Times* reported on the destruction of a black church in Massachusetts by arsonists on the night of the election. The AP reports that chatter among white supremacists on the Internet has increased since Election Day and that anti-black graffiti has risen since then.

Does this mean that the country is becoming more prejudiced? Of course not. The election of an African-American president shows how far this country has come. It has pushed many people to confront their own unconscious bigotry and to overcome it. It has brought whites and blacks together. Yes, it has also brought agitation from the ten percent who will never change, but that agitation is a sideshow to the miraculously changing American experience.

Thus it is with the American Jewish experience. We will always have the bigots on the Internet, but they are not a threat to our existence and are not part of the American mainstream. Their presence should not be used by the ADL to scare money out of us.

Of course we should continue to monitor their activity, but do we need a national organization like ADL with 29 offices in this country and three abroad, budgeted at $50 million per year, to do this? It could be accomplished at a small fraction of this money by the community relations councils of local Jewish Federations.

With $50 million we could send thousands of children to a Jewish summer camp or enroll them in a Jewish Day School or send them to visit Israel. We could subsidize synagogues so they can service families who cannot afford dues. The list could go on. The point is that organizations like the ADL play upon Jewish paranoia and look to the past, not to the future. We should not let the fears of a past generation distort the use of our limited resources to the detriment of a future generation.

Putting the Holocaust in Perspective
5/6/08

This past Thursday (the 26th of Nisan) we commemorated Yom Hashoah, Holocaust Memorial Day, which is an official holiday on the calendars of all branches of Judaism. More than 60 years after the end of the Shoah the unanswered question remains as to where this historical event fits into the philosophical structure of Judaism.

The new Yad Vashem memorial in Jerusalem is truly outstanding and no one can experience it without being shaken to the core. But I have an important criticism. There is no mention of the other victims that shared our same fate under the Nazis – the Romani (Gypsies), gays, Jehovah Witnesses and the defectives. The last gallery at Yad Vashem presents the founding of the State of Israel and then one emerges from a subterranean tunnel onto a dramatic balcony that oversees the hills of Jerusalem.

The symbolism and the message are very clear: out of the Holocaust the State of Israel rises. Certainly world compassion for the plight of Jews had some effect on the United Nation's partition vote in November of 1947, but there can be no philosophical connection between the founding of Israel and the Holocaust. Surely the Holocaust was not the price that God required for the existence of Israel. It would be blasphemy to think that six million Jews were slaughtered as a result of some Divine plan. Then the question must be asked as to why Yad Vashem focuses solely on Israel to the total exclusion of the universal message of the Shoah. The answer is that it, like many other Jewish institutions, is caught up in a victim mentality.

The true message of the Holocaust is a universal warning: look what evil mankind is capable of inflicting on one another. Talmudic Judaism taught that within each of us are two inclinations, the evil (*yetzer ha ra*) and the good (*yetzer tov*). The message is that every generation and every individual human being has to struggle to determine which inclination will predominate. Judaism does not believe in original sin or original purity. The Holocaust, and all subsequent and previous (as in the Armenian) genocides teach us that we must always work toward peace and universal understanding.

Contrast this to the particularistic reading of history – look what the *goyim* did to us; you can't rely on anyone but another Jew; never again, so that we can legitimize our dehumanization of our enemies, justified by our remembrance of the Shoah; an obsession with Jewish pain rather than Jewish joy: a drowning in victim mentality.

This is not to say that we should not remember and teach the Holocaust, but it is to say that the Holocaust cannot become the basis for Jewish continuity. Our Master Story should remain our meeting God at Sinai, whether we interpret that literally or symbolically (i.e. a myth). The Sinai experience reflects our seeking affirmative answers to the meaning of life and morality. This dramatically contrasts with a Judaism that is based on the remembrance of the Shoah.

Sixteen years ago Rabbi Ephraim Buchwald, director of education at the famous Orthodox Lincoln Square Synagogue in New York City, wrote a searing opinion piece in the *Miami Herald*, entitled "The Holocaust is killing American Jews." It has stayed with me these many years. He wrote: "Obsessing over the Holocaust is exacting a great price. It is killing American Jews…(t)he priority seems to be the building of Holocaust memorials – such as the dramatic 'reaching hand' sculpture and museum in Miami Beach. Over half a billion dollars has already been pledged or spent to build 19 Holocaust memorials and 36 research centers or libraries in America. Some cities, such as Los Angeles, have two or three Holocaust memorials competing with each other…

"It is quite likely that a young Jew today knows who Hitler and Eichmann were, but has no idea of Rabbi Akiva and Maimonides. We've reached the absurd point where the only feature of Judaism with which our young Jews identify is that of the Jew as victim – murdered, cremated, or turned into a lampshade. Is there no joy in Jewish life?… No wonder our young Jews are turned off and walking away from their heritage."

The real danger of an unhealthy emphasis on the Shoah is that it distorts the use of our limited community funds. Every dollar invested in Holocaust memorials takes away from investment in Jewish education, Jewish camping, Israel programming, senior services and a host of other needs of a vibrant and living American Jewish community.

Caveat: I am not negating the remembrance of the Holocaust. I take pride that I chaired the Florida Commissioner of Education's Holocaust Task Force where we implemented Holocaust education in our public schools under a mandate from the legislature. Never should we forget, but never should we obsess. The Shoah should be a part of our Jewish history but not the dominant part of our Jewish psyches. We can learn from Aristotle, even if he wasn't Jewish. We should follow his golden mean -- everything should be in moderation and in perspective.

MUSINGS

Is the Lubavitcher Rebbe the Messiah?
3/20/07

A few months ago I was walking in Times Square (New York City) and there were two Chabadnicks handing out literature proclaiming that the Rebbe, Menachem Schneerson, was the Messiah (Moshiach). They were in competition with a guy up the street with a sign proclaiming the end of the world and that Jesus will save us if we believe in him.

Being a curious person, or maybe just a contentious one, I approached the Chabad-Lubavitchers and asked how the Rebbe could be the Messiah since he died in 1994 and was buried in Queens? They responded that he really wasn't dead and that the person buried in the grave in Queens was his father-in-law. I walked away amused and a little irritated that these jokers were there in the name of Judaism.

Last month my wife, Lynne, and I were in the subterranean 42nd Street subway station and another Chabad Chasid was distributing literature. Not to offend him, heaven forbid, I took what he was offering. It is this handout that I want to discuss. Hold on to your seats, because this stuff is amazing (that's a polite adjective for ludicrous).

"America's efforts to safeguard peace around the world are critical elements in actualizing the redemption, as proclaimed by the prophet of our generation, the Lubavitcher Rebbe king Messiah (Moshiach) shlita (who lives forever)... America can be proud...in meriting the blessing of exceeding success with which the Rebbe king Messiah shlita blessed the U.S. armed forces in their holy mission in Iraq." Never mind that Schneerson has been dead 13 years but is able to bless this latest war, making it a holy mission. No one told these people that it has not been a success. The rest of the country seems to understand that, but it hasn't gotten to Chabad headquarters in Brooklyn yet.

There's more: On January 31, 1992 the United States and the Soviet Union signed a bilateral nuclear disarmament treaty. The next day the Rebbe declared this the fulfillment of Isaiah's prophecy of peace. Most important, "the Rebbe king Messiah shlita (who lives forever) stated that the decision of the superpowers to abolish nuclear armament production and establish a new world order based on justice was a direct result of the rabbinic ruling" (by the Rebbe).

It gets even better: The treaty was signed at the United Nations building in New York City "which is the world capital and headquarters of the Rebbe king Messiah shlita." And the construction of the building was completed in 1951 (5711), "the same year that Rebbe king Messiah shlita officially assumed leadership." Here's the punch line: "The reason the U.N. is situated in New York is that the leader of our generation resides in that city."

The pamphlet further tells me that the 1991 Gulf War was part of God's redemption and that it was foretold in Jewish Midrash. Also, the Rebbe prophesied the death of Saddam Hussein in 2007 as well as North Korea's agreement to limit its nuclear plans in the six-nation talks in Beijing on February 12, 2007. You may not realize that date corresponds to 24 Shevat on the Hebrew calendar, "the day on which President Bush announced the reduction and nullification of nuclear weapons, fifteen years ago. An event mentioned by the Rebbe king Messiah shlita (who lives forever) and referred to as his direct impact on the nations. In summary, there is no doubt that we are standing in the time of the actual redemption, as the Rebbe king Messiah shlita's prophecies are fulfilled completely, one after the other. Be ready for the rest of the prophecies! They're coming any second!"

The handout also said that Judaism is against free choice and gay rights. It wasn't included in the pamphlet, but the Rebbe also denied evolution. If he were alive (I'm sorry, I forgot he still lives) he would be a major proponent of "intelligent design."

One thing I learned: a woman's place is in the home. "A home needs to be tidy and organized, but also pleasant looking. The paint should match and the curtains and furniture should look nice…Indeed, this task is the responsibility of the women and girls, who have a better taste for beauty and luxury."

I was invited to the Messiah's house at 770 Eastern Parkway, Brooklyn for a blessing. If I couldn't do that I was directed to a web site where I could ask for a blessing from the Rebbe (who really did die in 1994). There was space on the web site to explain my personal needs to the Rebbe and I was promised an answer within seconds. It then stated: "If you don't understand the Hebrew, please write down the volume and page numbers and ask someone from your local Chabad house to translate it for you."

The pamphlet comes directly from 770 Eastern Parkway, so I assume that it is official Chabad doctrine. I am told that there are sophisticated local Chabad rabbis that do not believe the above, but I don't hear their voices. Until I hear them say that they do not believe that the Rebbe is the Messiah, I assume that they do. I also assume that they believe that the United Nations sits in New York because of the Rebbe, etc..

No responsible Jewish authority would accept the Messianic Jews (Jews for Jesus) as authentic Jews. Is there a difference between Jesus and Menachem Schneerson as the Messiah? Why do we feel comfortable *davening* with Chabad and not with the Jews for Jesus? Why do we invite Chabad emissaries into our Day Schools and into our Reform and Conservative religious schools to bake matzah? Would we invite Jews for Jesus to bake matzah for our children? And why do liberal Jews build Chabad houses? I think I know that answer – these Lubavitchers remind them of their grandfathers and in some sad way they look upon them as more authentic Jews.

This brings us to the crux of the matter. The pamphlet described above states: "The Rebbe of every generation provides spiritual life force for the whole generation. We, on our part, must do all we can to be 'connected' to him, only then can we receive all our physical and spiritual needs from him." That's not Judaism. We don't need Jesus, Menachem Schneerson or any other Chasidic guru to find God. The essence of mainstream Judaism (Orthodox through Humanism) is that we can have a direct relationship with God. The word rabbi means merely teacher. No one stands between a Jew and his or her God. That's the distortion that Chasidism introduced into Judaism, whether a particular Chasidic rabbi believes that the Rebbe is the Messiah or not.

Upon leaving the subway station the Chabadnick gave me a nice business-sized laminated card with the Rebbe's picture on it with the words emblazoned "Moshiach (Messiah)." He also gave me a beautiful 9 x 11 colored picture of the Rebbe, with the same message in Hebrew. Needless to say, I'm not going to put it on my wall.

A *Shaitel* Crisis in Brooklyn
6/22/04

I'm not making this up. It's a real story some of you may have missed from the *New York Times* on May 14th. It seems that there was panic in Borough Park (Brooklyn, for the one reader who doesn't know Borough Park). In Israel "one of the most respected Jewish authorities in the ultra-Orthodox world" Rabbi Yosef Shalom Elyashiv issued a ban on wigs (*shaitels*) from India.

It seems that Indian women shed their locks in Hindu temples and the cutting may have played some part in a Hindu pantheistic religious ceremony. Since such a ceremony is considered idolatrous, according to Rabbi Elyashiv, the *shaitels* made from this hair would be *traif.*

Panic set in. One woman in Brooklyn exclaimed: "You have to hope whatever you have is good, otherwise you put a thousand dollars in the garbage." It was reported that in Israel ultra-Orthodox Jews were burning Indian wigs in bonfires. Until they could verify whether their *shaitels* came from India or not, observant women were turning to snoods to cover their hair. A snood is a baglike cloth hair covering.

The *Times* reported that when the Uptown Girl Snood Factory Outlet in Borough Park opened at 11 a.m. the day after the ban a line was already at the door. Michelle Aaron, the manager, said, "Thank God, today's been great." Noting that it was the second anniversary of her father's death, she continued, "He sent me a blessing." Which at least proves that a catastrophe for one person can be a blessing for another. "God works in mysterious ways." Oops, that's a New Testament quote.

Besides snickering in our liberal armchairs, let's contemplate what this says about Judaism. First, there is a long tradition of modesty for women in Judaism and women's hair has been considered a sexual turn-on. Red hair was especially considered simultaneously passionate and traitorous, which may explain why red hair was attributed to Judas in early Christian art. The wearing of hair loose and exposed in the street by married women was considered immoral during rabbinic times. Such conduct would establish a legal cause for divorce and the wife would forfeit her dowry.

During the Middle Ages Jewish married women cut or shaved their hair and covered their heads with kerchiefs, the forerunners of snoods. It was during the sixteenth century that the great Rabbi Judah Katzenellenbogen and other rabbinic authorities began to allow women to wear a wig in place of the kerchief. In the last few centuries most women have forsaken the wig or kerchief, exposing their natural hair.

So we see that Borough Park is not out of the mainstream of rabbinic or Middle Age Judaism. The rest of the Jewish religious community moved on to a new sense of propriety, and these women remained, for better or worse, four or five centuries behind. All of this highlights the fact that there is no right or wrong, just a difference of opinion based on a chasm of four or five centuries. It's a matter of aesthetics, not philosophy.

But there is an important point in all of this. Notice that prohibition is centered on the woman. It is her licentiousness that is the focus of attention, not the males. This confirms that most of our rabbinic sages were male chauvinist pigs (kosher pigs of course). We have a sexist tradition that must be squarely confronted. If a married woman produces a child out of wedlock she is an adulteress and that infant is a *mamzer* (a bastard) who according to Torah is to be excluded from the Jewish community for ten generations. If a married male produces a child out of wedlock with an unmarried woman he is not an adulterer and the child is not a *mamzer*. He is just exercising his right to take a second wife. The panic in Borough Park reflects a society that is male dominated. There is no comparable focus on male propriety and modesty.

The *Times* reported that at least one ultra-Orthodox woman was not too perturbed by this whole affair. Chaya Lewis, an administrative assistant at a school in Crown Heights commented: "We do everything everybody else does, yet we have guidelines. If this is a problem, we're going to find a way." It is this "finding a way" that bewilders me as a modern reform Jew. Modesty by not showing sensuous hair upon your head is the objective. So you purchase a thousand, yes and even a two thousand, dollar *shaitel* and parade out in public. Excuse me. Show me a woman whose hair can be as perfect and appealing and downright sexy as a two thousand dollar wig and I'll show you a beauty contest winner, and there are not many of them around. The use of flattering wigs totally negates the original intent of the prohibition. Either there's something wrong with this system or I'm totally confused.

There's something else that eludes me. Even if the hair from India were cut as part of a Hindu pantheistic ceremony, how does this make the wig *traif*? Does the Hindu ceremony rub off on the strands of hair? Does it send subliminal messages through the warp of the wig into the cranium that can turn an observant Jewish woman into an atheist? That's the danger, since pantheism is the concept that the universe conceived as a whole is God. There is no external God other than the laws of nature that are manifested in the existing universe. To some that's atheism, to others that's God. Rabbi Mordecai Kaplan, the founder of the Reconstructionist Movement, believed in the pantheistic definition of God. Good thing he wasn't in the wig business. He would have starved, or worse, they would have burned his wigs in a bonfire.

One last little quibble. It refers to the manager of the Uptown Girl Snood Factory Outlet. Since it was the second anniversary of her father's death, she believed that he sent her a blessing in the form of a great day's business. Since when is this normative Judaism? The next time I go to a Yizkor service should I bring a tally of my family's financial standing and see if I can negotiate some help from the beyond?

The sum of this exercise is that Judaism is not monolithic. From the outside we Jews may all look alike, just as some Jews believe that all Christians are the same. But that is manifestly not true. I am still looking for something that I have in common with these denizens of Borough Park. When I find it, I'll let you know.

Jews for Jesus – They're After Me Again
7/25/06

This month 200 Jews for Jesus missionaries converged on New York City in their annual drive to obliterate Judaism by converting us to Christianity. There is nothing new here except that this year they have a generous budget of $1.4 million. They are using an extensive media campaign as well as their usual street evangelizing. Needless to say, the Jewish community is not too happy about this. The *New York Times* reported that Jewish groups (from Orthodox to Reform) are "barely able to contain their loathing" for Jews for Jesus. In fact "loathing" may be too mild a word. Personally, I share in this response.

Let me explain why. I have no problem with Christian proselytizing. When someone knocks on my door I politely reply that I am not interested. I respect their First Amendment right of free speech and I even respect their commitment to their religion. I admit that I do not understand their belief that God would consign five billion non-Christians to hell because they do not accept that Jesus died for their sins. Personally I will run that risk and argue with God when my time comes.

Let's understand that Jews for Jesus is not just a group of ex-Jews who believe in Jesus and want to spread the word. It is an organization that is funded by the mainstream evangelical Christian movement (those right-wing fundamentalists who scare the heck out of me). While it uses ex-Jews on the street, its administrative staff is Christian. It is part of a long Christian tradition to either force us or lure us into Christianity. Given the history of that campaign, a history that contains a few little problems such as the Inquisition, my Jewish ire begins to rise.

As long as I am just a part of the amorphous other five billion people on earth who do not accept Jesus as my Savior, I don't mind being targeted. But when they specifically zero in on Jews, I'm upset. (And they are quite determined in their approach to us. They have literature in Hebrew, Yiddish and Russian.) When they single me out they are saying that Judaism is inauthentic and our bible is only a preliminary statement that must be completed by the teachings of the New Testament. I don't expect others to believe as I do, but I don't like them standing in my face and telling me that I'm incomplete.

I have no difficulty with individuals who want to leave Judaism and enter Christianity. As I welcome converts into Judaism I have to respect those who go in the other direction. I believe in the right of each person to find the religion that meets his or her needs. My complaint is not with seekers of meaning, no matter where that quest leads them. Unlike some of my fellow religionists, I respect ex-Jews who find Jesus – as long as they identify themselves as authentic Christians, not as fulfilled Jews.

You just can't remain a Jew and believe in Christian dogma. Here's the reason why: the structures of the two religions are antithetical. Christianity is built around a theological statement that Jesus died for our sins (vicarious atonement). Christian holidays reflect this essential element --Christmas as the birth of Christ and Easter as his death and resurrection.

In contrast, the essential element of Judaism is non-theological. Look at our holiday cycle. Jews celebrate Hanukah, the saving of the *people* from the Seleucid Greek Empire; Purim, the saving of the *people* by Queen Esther from destruction by the wicked Haman: Passover, the retelling of the *people* Israel going from slavery to freedom; Shavuot, the giving of the Torah to the *people* Israel. Need I go on? It becomes obvious that the essential element in Judaism is the people, or put in another way, peoplehood or community.

Every Jew instinctively understands this. He or she may not believe as his/her fellow Jew does, but they both recognize that they are part of the same peoplehood. First we find our peoplehood, and then we seek our theology. Abraham founded a people, not a theology except for the broad concept of monotheism. Christianity reverses the process. If you are a Baptist, you have a wonderful peoplehood in that community. If you modify your Christian beliefs and decide to become an Episcopalian, you lose your Baptist community and have to start all over again with essentially a new community. In Judaism you can believe what you want (short of proclaiming Jesus your Savior). You have the option of leaving Reform for Orthodoxy or vice-versa, or leaving both to become a gastronomic atheistic Jew – but you never lose your peoplehood (community).

The other main difference between the two religions is that the salvation system in traditional Christianity (especially the evangelical variety into which Jews for Jesus fits) is based on belief. If Jesus died for your sins and you believe this, then you're saved. For Judaism, you make it into the great beyond by doing mitzvot, good deeds. Your beliefs are irrelevant. You just can't square these two opposite approaches to salvation, which means you can't remain a Jew while proclaiming your belief in Jesus. You're either *milchik* or *fleyshik* (milk or meat), or as one New York Jewish leader put it, "We don't believe you can be a carnivorous vegetarian."

This is not a question of Jew versus Christian. Mainstream Christian movements, including Catholicism, are adamantly against any conversionary movement that targets Jews separate from the general population. The Christian Scholars Group on Christian-Jewish Relations (an organization consisting of 22 Christian scholars, theologians, historians and clergy from six Protestant denominations and the Roman Catholic Church) issued this statement in 2002: "Christians should not target Jews for conversion. Christian worship that teaches contempt for Judaism dishonors God."

To which I say, "Amen." And when I'm in New York (the week after I write this) I intend to say that to the Jews-for-Jesus guy who stops me on the street. I'm going to say that and probably a few other choice words.

Who killed Jesus – Jews or Romans?
8/26/03

Mel Gibson is a pretty good actor. I loved his Lethal Weapon series. But he is a lousy historian and theologian. The problem is that he invested $25 million of his own money to produce and direct "The Passion," a movie about Jesus' final 12 hours that puts the blame for his crucifixion on the Jews.

In 1965 the Second Vatican Council cleared the Jews of deicide, but Gibson, who is part of a breakaway Catholic group that calls itself Traditionalist Catholic, rejects this. In a *New York Times Magazine* article in March Gibson's father was quoted as saying that the Vatican Council was "a Masonic plot backed by the Jews" and that the Holocaust was a charade. More troubling, Gibson is relying on Anne Catherine Emmerich, an early 19th century German nun, for source material. Emmerich also wrote that Jews killed Christian children to procure their blood.

The question is: who is right – Mel Gibson or the Vatican Council? Who killed Jesus, the Romans or the Jews? Even though there are no Romans around to defend themselves and we Jews are here to argue our case, historical honesty points to the Romans.

No Jewish Motive

Although killing for power is replete in Jewish history, as unfortunately it is in the history of all peoples, there is no Jewish tradition for killing for theological reasons. Sadly, burning at the stake for the sake of beliefs is a legacy of our daughter religion Christianity.

Jesus, whom most Christian scholars would characterize as an ethical teacher, would not have been a threat to the Jewish religious establishment of the First Century even if his teachings radically differed from the Jewish norm (although many scholars seem to indicate that this was not the case).

Indeed there were many strains of Jewish thought at the time of Jesus. The Pharisees, Sadducees, Essenes and Hasidim (not related to modern day Hasidim) were all part of a cauldron of emerging Jewish religious thought. Historically, they did not crucify one another.

Roman Motivation

Continuing our search for motivation, the gospels indicate that Jesus was crucified and that Pilate wrote upon the cross, "Jesus of Nazareth, The King of the Jews." When Pilate asked the Jews, "Shall I crucify your King?" the chief priest protested, "We have no king but Caesar." This questioning reflects Roman concern for the possibility of Jews having a king (i.e. political leader) other then Caesar.

Jesus lived in tumultuous times. The Romans were vigilant against incipient Jewish insurrection. This vigilance was not without good cause. The Jews of the First Century had aspirations to reestablish an independent Jewish state. Merely 36 years after the death of Jesus, the Jews staged a bloody four-year war against Rome that ended in the destruction of Jerusalem and the Second Temple. The last stand of the zealots at Massada is a well-known part of this history. Again in the years 132-135 the Jews staged a second unsuccessful major offensive against Rome.

The Romans were not paranoid. They had every reason to fear the least bit of evidence concerning a challenge to their rule over Judea. The Jews were not a docile subject people. They were a difficult and stiff-necked adversary. It is historically consonant with what scholars know of First Century Judea to believe that Jesus was crucified by the Romans for political reasons, justified or unjustified.

At this point I must say that I believe that individual Jews were involved in the crucifixion of Jesus, Jews who were functionaries of Roman power, but not the Jewish establishment that was busy preparing insurrection against Rome.

In all occupations there are quislings and corroborators. The term quisling for traitor refers to the Norwegian Vidkun Quisling who facilitated Nazi rule of Norway. Even a covey of quislings would not lead us to the conclusion that Norway or the Norwegian people as a whole had complicity with the loathed Nazis.

So it was in ancient Judea. I do not doubt that the Romans used Jewish agents in the network of rule and those agents were a part of most Roman crucifixions. Having said this, there is no doubt that the crucifixion of Jesus was a Roman act to further the ends of Roman rule.

Wrong Court – Wrong Timing

It is related that Jesus was brought before a religious Sanhedrin (Bet Din). A Sanhedrin composed of 23 members did try capital cases. Most important cities in Judea had a Jewish court of this nature. But the gospels tell us that this Jewish court sentenced Jesus on the eve of Passover or on the day itself. (The gospels differ as to the exact timing.) Jewish sources clearly indicate that no authentic Jewish court would be in session at those times (Mishnah Sanhedrin 4:1). This would be analogous to saying that a Florida court convicted a defendant and sentenced him to death on December 25th. We are aware that no American court is in session on this day.

Any court operating in the middle of the night or at daybreak during the religious season referred to in the gospels could not have been an authentic Jewish court, but would have to have been an illegitimate creature of Roman domination.

Wrong Method

Every nation has its favorite method of capital punishment. Historically England had its gallows, France its guillotine, New York its electric chair, California its gas chamber, etcetera. Name the method of capital punishment and you can almost isolate the geography and the nationality of the executioner.

Crucifixion was as alien to Judaism as it was common to Roman rule. The fact is that the traditional biblical method of execution was stoning and that a religious Sanhedrin had the right to inflict only four modes of capital punishment: stoning, burning, decapitation and strangling. Jewish law did not permit crucifixion. The fact that Jesus was crucified and not put to death in another fashion indicates that the Romans, not the Jews, killed him. It is as simple as that.

I really do wish that Mel Gibson would do a fifth Lethal Weapon movie. I would cough up my six bucks to see it. But I also wish that he would not foist his antediluvian religious convictions upon the world and thereby libel Jews for the crime of deicide. Don't forget to look for his movie "The Passion" in your local theater in the not too distant future, and just sit at home. Put the six bucks in the *pushke* instead.

PART TWO - ISRAEL
CRITICISM OF ISRAEL

Ground Rules for Relating to Israel
11/16/04

I have been accused of being overly critical of Israel at times, so I believe that it is time to discuss "where I am coming from." Let me share with you three tenets that form the basis of my emotional attachment to that land.

First point: We American Jews have to become more sophisticated concerning Israel. The chauvinists and simpletons among us tell us that we cannot hold Israel to a higher standard than we would hold any other nation-state, and to do so is a form of anti-Semitism. I say, "baloney." I will always hold Jews as individuals and Israel as a nation to a higher standard. If we don't, why be Jews and why have a Jewish state?

Of course I will criticize Israel more harshly for allowing torture or discriminatory practices toward its minorities than I would for, let us say, Norway or Cambodia. Israel is my relative, and if a relative goes astray we judge. If a stranger errs, we may utter a word of disapproval but move on to other things. With a relative, you don't move on, you stay there and you try to fix the situation.

I have been accused of having two standards, one for Israel and one for the Palestinians. I plead guilty. Although I respect Palestinian culture, I don't expect perfection. With Israel, I know that there cannot be perfection, but I expect an above-average showing. Why? Because they are Jews. If we can't expect the best from Jews, then once again, why bother being Jews? When I read that the Israeli mafia has invaded America and that there is a street war going on in Prague, of all places, between factions of the Israeli mafia, it makes me wonder what a Jewish state has wrought. I do hold them to higher standards, just as I hold America to higher standards.

Second Point: As much as I love Israel, I love Judaism more. The two are not synonymous. Israel, the land and its history and the modern state, are only a part of my Judaism. We are a religion first, not merely a nationality. By nationality I am American. By peoplehood and religion, I am Jewish. This is an important truth that cannot be overemphasized, even though it has been the basis in history for anti-Zionist beliefs. Not only is Israel merely a part of Judaism, but also we must recognize the danger that the State of Israel and Zionism could destroy the religion. This process takes different forms in America and Israel.

In this country, for the last half of the twentieth century we have allowed our love of Israel to eclipse our religious commitments. It was more important to give to the UJA than to join a synagogue. The definition of a good Jew was not someone who followed the mitzvot, but someone who pledged the most money to Federation, no matter how that money was obtained. This was certainly the case with many a Wall Street manipulator. Our major leaders for over half a century were religiously ignorant, but were experts in Middle East politics.

Our Jewish day camps, day schools and synagogues played second fiddle to missions to Israel, where we basked in the image of the super Jew after the Six Day War in 1967. We reveled in seeing an Israeli F-16 fly the skies, but ignored prayer and community at home. The result has been a gradual reduction in synagogue membership and Jewish identification among the young. This Zionism of the super Jew began to wither as the world began to realize that Israel was taking on the trappings of just another successful country entering the ranks of world powers, with all the defects inherent therein.

In Israel, the Jewish state has done much to destroy Judaism, or at least the kind of Judaism that I, as a liberal Jew, practice. I am telling you nothing that you do not know when I remind you that Israel is a working theocracy. It is a country that is ruled by a religious establishment that does not recognize any form of Judaism other than a right wing Orthodoxy. Reform or Conservative rabbis are not recognized by the state and cannot perform either burials or marriages. All rabbis in synagogues in Israel are paid by the state, except Reform or Conservative.

There is no open religious dialogue that would challenge the stranglehold of Orthodoxy. The result of this arrangement is that about 80% of the Israelis are secular and a large portion of them are even antagonistic to religion. They are Jews by nationality, but not by religion. This causes them great problems when they migrate to America or other Diaspora countries. They have great difficulty in redefining their identities as religious Jews. Many remain just Israelis, who proclaim that some day they will return to that land, although very few actually do. Their children's ties to Judaism become even more problematic.

So… let us acknowledge that there is a danger in Zionism in that while it can enrich our Judaism, it has the potential to destroy it as well. Saying this is not an anti-Zionist act. It is merely an acknowledgement that we must put our Zionism and love of the State of Israel in the broader context of our commitment and love of Judaism, an ancient religion that has at various times survived and even thrived when there was no State of Israel, when the Zionist dream was not actively pursued.

It is not the intent of this column to attack specific issues concerning Israel, be they West Bank settlements, terrorism, the isolation of Arafat, the progress or should I say non-progress of peace talks, the discrimination against its Arab minority or the myriad of other problems that confront that country. I am merely trying to define the posture from which I approach these questions, the mental set that dictates how I look at the world, Judaism and Israel.

Finally, there is a third point I would like to make. This will complete the third leg of a stable stool upon which I perch. The point is: Although I am a Jew committed to the existence and prosperity of Israel, I must acknowledge that there is equity and truth to be found on both sides of the struggle between Palestine and Israel.

Too often we American Jews denigrate Arabs as if they were foreign interlopers who act only out of anti-Semitic animus. The truth is that they have as legitimate a claim to the land as we have. That is the tragic fact of history. As the colonial power withdrew, there were two equally valid claims upon the land, both with historical precedent and both with sizable indigenous populations there. In fact, we know that there were more Arabs than Jews.

They, too, deserved self-determination, as we sought it for ourselves. The tragedy of history is that in 1948 Arab leadership would not settle for half a loaf. The tragedy continues. In 2004, when a new Palestinian leadership is willing to settle for merely a portion, a sizable percentage of Israelis, who happen to be part of the government coalition, are as insistent on having the whole loaf as was Arab leadership 57 years ago.

The realization that we do not possess all of the truth and honor in this world should precede any analysis of Middle East politics. We American Jews must not automatically assume that Arabs are wrong and Jews are right. We are a good people, but we are not angels, superhuman beings who never err. Jews and a Jewish state are struggling with complex issues, just as is the rest of this world. Thus, unlike the stance of AIPAC, which proclaims the discredited motto, "my country right or wrong", it is permissible, even preferable, to recognize nuance and subtlety. It is permissible to criticize because very often criticism is the best medicine. Without criticism none of us would grow.

But that criticism must come from love, sometimes tough love, but love nonetheless. With this mindset in hand, I look forward to discussing Israel with you in future columns.

Criticizing Israel from a Distance
11/27/07

If there is one thing that sends the American Jewish community into spasms of vitriolic attacks it is criticism of Israel. Rarely does it take the time to analyze the criticism; rather it circles the wagons and waits for the Indians to attack. In reality, it shuts down all criticism that does not conform to the community's party line, except for a few dissident voices in opinion pieces in the *Jewish Journal*, one of the few Jewish newspapers that are not owned by a Jewish Federation or other Jewish communal entities. In other words, it's a real paper, not a house organ.

One of the big arguments against American Jews criticizing Israel is that these critics are not living there and do not understand the real issues involved. This, of course, applies to the American Jewish establishment itself because its spokespersons are also not there. What makes their view from these shores any wiser than the critic's view? In truth, both the Right and the Left should continue to comment on Israeli policy.

The argument that we are not there and we do not feel their pain is fallacious. It is precisely because we are not there that we can have a clearer perception of reality. It is analogous to seeing a French impressionist painting. Up very close all you can perceive is a series of little painted stripes. The picture does not come into focus. Only when you place some distance between the viewer and the canvas can you see the whole picture clearly.

Sometimes political and geographic distance can actually be an advantage. I can think of two instances in American history when this was true. In the mid 1840's Alexis de Tocqueville visited this country and described American life in his famous book. He was a foreigner with a foreign perception, yet historians agree that if you really want to know what American life was like during this period, you have to read de Tocqueville, not our domestic commentators. His distance allowed him to see things in which we were too involved. He saw the whole forest, not merely the trees.

The second instance that I make reference to is when Gunnar Myrdal, a Swedish economist and politician (and future Nobel Prize winner) wrote a book in 1944 entitled "An American Dilemma: The Negro Problem and Modern Democracy." He so clearly painted the complete picture that his book was widely read by Washington policy makers, including President John Kennedy. It was referenced by the Court in the 1954 Brown v. Board of Education decision. It can be argued that Gunnar Myrdal's book, written by a foreigner with insights that only distance could provide, was a major catalyst for our political resolve to deal with our segregation policies in this country

There is a large minority of Israelis who criticize their own government's mishandling of the peace process, but they need to hear liberal voices from American Jews and gentile friends if they are to succeed. The fact is that the average man-in-the-street Israeli, whether out of cultural conditioning from a century-old disposition to look down on Arab society, or from shell shock emanating from a continuous conflict that seems never to end, does not have the ability to put himself into the shoes of his adversary. He cannot empathize with the Palestinian aspirations for statehood. He seems incapable of understanding the humanity of the "enemy."

Without this, it becomes a zero-sum game, namely one side must win and the other must lose. This leaves little room for compromise and a win-win conclusion. Unfortunately it opens the door to a modern Greek tragedy, a lose-lose situation where two peoples destroy life for each other – two stubborn Semitic cousins who cannot find their way out of the forest for they can only see the proximate trees before them.

With love and compassion I fret that Israel will not find peace in my lifetime, unless something dramatic occurs with the help of our American government, and I am not optimistic about the upcoming Annapolis, Maryland conference (but we will have to wait and see what happens). I do not say that Israel will be the sole fault of this tragic end, but it will be an equal partner with the Palestinians in steering this disastrous course.

This brings us back to the need for criticism of Israeli policy. As an American I love this country enough to vigorously criticize the Bush administration. As a Jew I love Israel enough to criticize the Olmert administration, which, if American Jews knew enough about Israeli politics, they would equate with the Bush fiasco. And I do this from a geographical and emotional distance that allows me to see some things that the average Israeli cannot.

In Praise of President Jimmy Carter
1/23/07

Jimmy Carter's book "Palestine, Peace Not Apartheid" is rising on the best seller list. As of Sunday, January 14, it was number five. If the Jewish establishment continues its attack on the book, it could rise to number one in the near future.

The use of the word apartheid as applied to Israel seems to be the lightning rod that evokes cries of anguish and anger from Jews. But Carter makes it very plain in the book and in the series of interviews following its publication that he is referring to Israeli occupation of the West Bank and Gaza and not to Israel itself. But this matters little to the American Jewish establishment that cannot abide any criticism of Israel.

To begin, let me say that there are many parts of the Carter book of which I can be critical, but taking a gestalt view he is correct. His three main points are that pro-Israel lobbyists stifle debate in this country, Israelis are guilty of human rights offenses in the occupied territories and that American newspapers are not critical of Israel. He writes as a friend who appears to be exasperated with Israel. This does not help him in his argumentation, but neither does it detract from its truths. For this he is vilified.

Abe Foxman of the Anti-Defamation League shouted, "I believe that he is engaging in anti-Semitism." Simon Wiesenthal Center: "Carter abandons all objectivity." David Harris of the American Jewish Committee: ""Outlandishly titled book... compromises any pretense to objectivity and fairness." The right-wing ZOA that maintains that "Judea and Samaria are historically, legally and religiously Jewish land ...Jews have more right to live in Judea and Samaria than many other people" declares that Carter's book is "inaccurate, shallow and vicious."

The establishment trotted out the ubiquitous Alan Dershowitz who called President Carter a "hypocrite" and a "bully." Look who's calling him a bully. Dershowitz is peeved because the president will not debate him. But who is he to demand an equal podium with Jimmy Carter? For me the most interesting critic is Emory University professor Kenneth Stein who had previously written a book with Carter. He resigned from his affiliation with the Carter Center. I have known Ken since we were both graduate students at Yale and he is an honest and decent person, but he is also a cautious and establishment personality. I wonder how much pressure from the Jewish community, both overt and psychological, played into his decision, even unconsciously. He attacks Carter's book beginning with, "a title too inflammatory to even print."

But is it? Its very truth may inflame such reaction. The respected

Israeli human rights organization B'Tselem reports: "Israel has created in the Occupied Territories a regime of separation based on discrimination, applying two separate systems of law in the same area and basing the rights of individuals on their nationality. This regime is the only one of its kind in the world, and is reminiscent of distasteful regimes from the past, such as the apartheid regime in South Africa." In another report B'Tselem maintains that the West Bank "bears striking similarities to the racist Apartheid regime," and even "entails a greater degree of arbitrariness than was the case with the regime that existed in South Africa."

Shmuel Rosner, a conservative columnist for *Haaretz* (the *New York Times* of Israel), writes: "Arguing about apartheid is pointless. There is enough material evidence to prove that apartheid exists in the occupied territories in one form or another. If you argue about the use of this word, you lose. If you argue that Israel is blameless you lose also. The only argument you can make against Carter is about context and the bigger picture." I agree that very often Carter loses the context battle, but I believe that he is correct on the bigger picture.

In September of 2003 I wrote a column in which I quoted Avraham Burg from an article he wrote for *Yediot Aharonot* (Israel's largest newspaper). Burg is an Orthodox Jew who has served as the Speaker of the Knesset as well as the Chairman of the Jewish Agency (the group that spends all the UJA money raised in the United States). He speaks about the grand highways on the West Bank that are built exclusively for Israelis: "Traveling on the fast highway that takes you from Ramot on Jerusalem's northern edge to Gilo on the southern edge, a 12-minute trip that skirts barely a half-mile west of the Palestinian roadblocks, it's hard to comprehend the humiliating experience of the despised Arab who must creep for hours along the pocked, blockaded roads assigned to him. One road for occupier, one road for the occupied."

This past summer I traveled on another of these for-Jews-only roads coming back from a visit to illegal outposts on the West Bank. I was overcome with a feeling of shame and remorse. What have we come to? Apartheid was the precise word that came to my lips, but more importantly, struck at my heart. My Jewish soul ached. On that same trip I visited Hebron. Immediately adjacent to that city is a memorial for Baruch Goldstein who in 1994 murdered 29 Muslims as they prayed in the mosque in Hebron. His headstone is consciously the same size as Rabin's and devout Jewish West Bank settlers pray at his grave and adorn it with flowers.

As I walked through the central marketplace of Hebron which is now desolate, I saw signs in Hebrew that read Revenge and Death to the Arabs. According to a 1997 agreement between Netanyahu and Arafat this neighborhood, which is part of an area designated as H-2, was supposed to be used by both Arabs and Jews. Precisely because of this fact, the American government spent $2 million to build sidewalks and streetlamps to refurbish it. But alas, no Palestinians are allowed to enter the area and the 500 Jewish settlers have excluded the over 100,000 Palestinians who live in Hebron from entering.

The problem is that the Israeli Army has no jurisdiction over the settlers in the territories who are under Israeli law. The Palestinians are under military control. When settlers have an attack against Arabs, the Army can watch but cannot intervene. Only the Israeli police who are not present can intervene. The bottom line is that the soldiers are in Hebron to protect the settlers from the Palestinians. But there is no one to protect the Palestinians from the settlers.

Riding back on a Jews-only road a prominent Los Angeles Jew who has raised millions for Israel said to our Jewish Israeli guide who toured us through the West Bank settlements and Hebron, "My God, you are making me an anti-Semite." Experiencing the reality of a cruel occupation, not American Jewish talking points in support of Israel, makes you realize the legitimacy of President Carter's use of the word apartheid.

He can be forgiven for his mistakes in the book because his message is good for Israel --Palestinians and Israelis must compromise and come to peace; otherwise there will continue to be apartheid. President Carter is not to be denigrated; rather, he is to be applauded because his message is what will ultimately save the soul of Israel.

West Bank Checkpoints and Apartheid
1/30/07

This is an extension of last week's column entitled "In Praise of President Jimmy Carter."   As discussed last week, there has erupted in the Jewish community an avalanche of calumny against Carter for using the word apartheid in describing Israel's relationship to the Palestinians in the West Bank.

One email I received (along with an article from *The Jewish Press*, a right-wing Orthodox publication out of Brooklyn) proclaimed: "It was no secret that Jimmy Carter was a Jew/Israel-hater since the late 70's." An ordinarily liberal rabbi in Boca Raton wrote a letter to his congregation describing Carter's book "Palestine, Peace Not Apartheid" as having "an obscene misleading title."

This ignores the fact that the word is in common use in Israeli publications in their own domestic dialogue. They recognize a reality that American Jews cannot bring themselves to confront. One American Jew who used the word in an opinion piece in the *New York Times* in August of 2003 was the late Rabbi Arthur Hertzberg, ex-president of the American Jewish Congress and NYU professor. Certainly Hertzberg was not a Jew-hater, but he was a person who recognized reality.

President Carter's definition of apartheid is the "forced separation of two peoples in the same territory with one of the groups dominating or controlling the other." It is an exceedingly accurate description of the West Bank. The motivation of apartheid in South Africa was racial while the Israelis use this domination for the purpose of expansion of Jewish settlements. To the person being controlled this is an irrelevancy – life is still unbearable.

I have personally witnessed the degradation that ordinary Palestinians experience at West Bank roadblocks. A checkpoint on the border of Israel proper is justifiable, but most of the 522 roadblocks are within the West Bank cutting off village from village and countryside from urban areas. The ex-Deputy Mayor of Jerusalem Meron Benvenisti writes: "(The roadblocks) are all designed for one purpose: to show who has the power to control the lives of Palestinians. Small groups of young, inexperienced and frightened soldiers serve as the agents of the power that forces millions of people to behave according to arbitrary rules that interrupt the most basic routines of their lives. This domination is implemented for the most part without any need for force, by exploiting the fear of the Palestinians."

Benvenisti continues: "The disdain for the Palestinians and the arrogant use of a mentality of submissiveness is reflected not only by the roadblocks themselves but by the checking procedures, which are conducted without any sensitivity to the dignity and needs of the Palestinians, who are expected to wait in line in silence or else be 'punished.' Colonial regimes have always been based on the arrogance of a small number of soldiers who controlled the lives of millions of natives with minimal force, and a dependence on deterrence, which guaranteed the inferior status of those subject to their authority."

An editorial this past month in *Haaretz* (the *New York Times* of Israel) lamented that the number of roadblocks increased by 27 percent under the current Olmert coalition since its inception this past summer. It commented: "The world of the West Bank checkpoints…looks like a laboratory experiment designed to test the limits of the human capacity to adapt to impossible conditions… workers who are unable to leave their villages and towns in order to support their families, students who cannot get to their exams and parents who cannot reach the doctor to get antibiotics for their children…In addition, there are about 150 flying checkpoints every week, which make it impossible for the Palestinians to plan a daily schedule." (A flying checkpoint is a portable barrier that is quickly moved from one location to another.)

If this critique were offered by an American Jew, our community would brand him or her a traitor (you should read my hate mail). If it came from a gentile, we would declare him an anti-Semite. If from an elected politician, we would work for his defeat. If from an ex-President, we would lose all perspective and become apoplectic. But it is reality. As Benvenisti writes: "Those who believe that 'the ideology of Greater Israel has been shelved" should understand that the roadblocks symbolize the expropriation of the West Bank territories without annexation, albeit with the addition of the creation of Palestinian 'reservations.'" That's another way of describing apartheid.

This past summer I traveled to the West Bank city of Ramallah and met with Zahira Kamal, the Minister of Women's Affairs in the Fatah government before its defeat by Hamas. She lives in Jerusalem and teaches in Ramallah, a twenty minute drive. Due to the roadblocks it takes her two hours each way to commute and many times she is unable to return to her home in Jerusalem. Kamal looks at the checkpoints through the eyes of a women's advocate. Seventy-eight percent of Palestinians are under 40-years-old and 51 percent are women. With a high fertility rate, one-third of these women is pregnant and must walk through checkpoints to get to hospitals.

Kamal talks about women who need chemotherapy who are detained at checkpoints and the plight of rural women when checkpoints close as evening approaches. Rural women in labor at night cannot get to a hospital. She knows of at least six women who were forced to give birth over the telephone. The doctor does not hang up until he or she hears the cry of the newborn.

Not many American Jews, or for that matter, not many Israelis, travel to the West Bank and see for themselves the degradation heaped upon the Palestinians. Doctors, lawyers and academics along with laborers and housewives are treated like children by wet-behind-the-ears 18-year-old soldiers brandishing guns. It is the rawest form of "forced separation of two peoples in the same territory with one of the groups dominating or controlling the other," Carter's definition of apartheid. Carter calls it apartheid. I call it Un-Jewish.

If you really love Israel, visit there. My wife Lynne and I will be returning this coming summer. Israel is a wonderful country in many respects and you owe it to yourself to experience it. But, if you really love Israel, don't be swept away in the American Jewish hysteria of defending an indefensible policy toward the Palestinians. The *Palm Beach Post* editorialized concerning the ADL's critique of Carter: "Mr. Foxman sounds like those Republicans who contend that any criticism of President Bush's policies during wartime is unpatriotic."

If you want to be a patriotic Jew, stand up for Israel when she deserves it, but criticize when she needs it. I know that I love America enough to protest when she is going in the wrong direction, as I have done during the Vietnam era and presently during our folly in Iraq. As a Jew I love Israel enough to criticize with the same vigor, disregarding the pathetic and sick response of the Jewish establishment over President Carter's flawed but essentially correct book. Israel needs your love and your criticism.

More Reaction on President Carter
2/6/07

The uproar over President Carter's book ""Palestine, Peace Not Apartheid" has not abated in the Jewish community, so I shall add one more column to the dialogue (and then, hopefully, we shall go on to another topic).

In response to last week's column on West Bank checkpoints I received a heartfelt email from a dear friend. She is European born, reared in Israel and now an American. She embodies the perspective of Eastern Europe, Israel and South Florida with a keen sensibility.

Commenting on both Zel Lurie's column and mine she wrote: "Both of you may be right, but it hurts my heart to see what is happening nowadays. There is enough anti-Semitism in the world and Carter's book is going to inflame it even more. This is what we need right now? In my youth and even later any time a Jew was found guilty of something the first thought was, 'what are the goyim going to think?' I still have the same mentality. I am reading now (quite belatedly) Chiam Herzog's Living History and I cry reading about the heroism and the sacrifices of our yideleh during the War for Independence. Were those sacrifices and the ones in the wars that followed in vain?" She signed her email, "Your sad friend."

It's interesting that my friend is not denying the reality of what is happening on the West Bank and neither is she spewing simplistic rebuttal points that are being distributed within the Jewish community. What she is doing is baring a broken Jewish heart and in this I share her pain. Indeed, were those sacrifices in vain? My answer must be that they were in vain only if Israel loses its way among the righteous. David Ben Gurion was often quoted as saying that he wanted the Jewish state to be as normal as all other countries.

Well, it can't be. If Israel is no better than the rest of this messed up world, we as Jews have failed. The more than 500 checkpoints on the West Bank that I discussed last week that are part of a Greater Israel strategy and reek pain and suffering upon the "enemy" are an affront to Jewish ethics. If they are the real face of Israel (and I believe that they are not – that the majority in

Israel really wants peace, not more land) then in truth those young men who sacrificed with their lives died in vain.

This is the reason that it is incumbent on every Jew, in Israel and in the Diaspora, to praise when appropriate and to criticize when needed. I don't like criticizing Israel. I get no joy from writing these columns, but I am compelled by my sense of Jewish ethics. In fact I am a captive of my Jewish ethics. Recently I read "Disgace," a novel by the South African Nobel Prize winning writer J.M. Coetzee, that comments on that society. But I was surprised to find that Coetzee is no longer from South Africa since he recently immigrated to Australia.

And this is my dilemma: While Coetzee can give up the fight, can move from one country to the next, leaving his anguish behind as he finds a new identity – I can do none of that. If I move to Sydney or Timbuktu, I still carry my Jewish identity, my sense of Jewish history and ethics. My friends Amos, Micah, Isaiah and their fellow travelers follow me wherever I go. And Israel, the only Jewish state in this world, is part of that Jewish identity, for better or worse. I'm stuck with it, and it's stuck with me.

That is the mystic tie between the Diaspora and Israel. With this tie comes not only the right but the obligation to comment, not just to praise, but seriously to comment. A few minutes before I began this column I received another email from a reader who wrote: "I am a survivor from France and my love and dedication to Israel is absolute and this includes my right to question." This is a right that many American Jews would deny him.

Going back to my friend's original email and her feeling that the Carter book may spur increased anti-Semitism. I, too, was reared in an environment that asked the key question: "What are the goyim going to think?" Except that I was not in Europe or Israel, but in a small coal town in Pennsylvania with 60 other Jewish families. Unlike my friend, I have "outgrown" this mentality. I am no longer a defenseless Jew wandering the earth. Let them think what they want. Especially as I get older, I am more concerned with what I think about myself.

I also realize that we Jews are not perfect (If we were, what would I write about?) and that criticism of Jews in the United States or the State of Israel is not automatically anti-Semitic. ADL's Abe Foxman can claim, "I believe that he (Carter) is engaging in anti-Semitism," but that does not make it so. In any case, criticism from any quarter is so vital to a healthy Israel and Judaism that an increase in anti-Semitism is a danger that we will have to face. But I sincerely doubt that it is a great danger.

Meanwhile the uproar continues. The *Forward* reported that President Carter received a standing ovation from students and faculty after his speech in defense of his book at Brandeis University. After Carter left the gymnasium to catch a commercial flight back to Georgia, Harvard Professor Alan Dershowitz assumed the podium and took one of the cheapest shots that I have heard in many a year. The *New York Times* reported Dershowitz's response: "There are two different Jimmy Carters. You have heard the Brandeis Jimmy Carter today, and he was terrific. I support almost everything he said. But if you listen to the Al Jazeera Jimmy Carter, you'll hear a very different perspective."

I ask: Where is there one iota of evidence to show that Carter speaks one way to Jews and another way to others, including Arabs? One thing you can say for President Carter, whether you like him or not, he has been pretty consistent in his speeches. He's not running for office, so he can be honest to his own beliefs. I believe that Dershowitz's "swift-boating" Carter will not play well in the Jewish community. We are too sophisticated to swallow that trick out of the playbook of Karl Rove. Hopefully we can keep the dialogue on a higher level.

Final comment: Yossi Beilin, Knesset member, former Justice Minister in Israel, formulator of the Oslo Peace Accords and the leader of the Meretz Party, wrote a column this past week for the *Forward* under the heading, "Carter Is No More Critical of Israel Than Israelis Themselves." He personally hesitated to use the word apartheid to describe the present situation on the West Bank, but he concluded: "Somewhere down the line...the destructive nature of occupation will turn Israel into a pariah state, not unlike South Africa under apartheid." That's why President Carter's book is so important.

A Footnote on Carter and Dershowitz
3/6/07

Alan Dershowitz has been the most outspoken critic of Carter. His recent column has been emailed to practically everyone who has an email address. In it he attacks Carter's personal integrity because the Carter Center has received money from Arab sources and Carter once borrowed money from BCCI, a now defunct Arab-owned bank that was "virulently anti-Israel." He writes: "The entire premise of (Carter's) criticism of Jewish influence on American foreign policy is that money talks. It is Carter, not me, who has made the point that if politicians receive money from Jewish sources, then they are not free to decide issues regarding the Middle East for themselves. It is Carter, not me, who has argued that distinguished reporters cannot honestly report on the Middle East because they are being paid by Jewish money. So, by Carter's own standards, it would be almost economically 'suicidal' for Carter 'to espouse a balanced position between Israel and Palestine.' By Carter's own standards, therefore, his views on the Middle East must be discounted."

I agree with Dershowitz's premise that money buys political support. Our lobbyists in Washington have proved that point. We have the best Congress that money can buy. But this does not apply to Carter. At his Brandeis speech he specifically answered a student's question concerning financial support for the Carter Center from Arab sources. He responded that he instructed his staff to go through every donation and they found that only two percent of their donations came from Arab sources, and nearly all of that money has gone to development projects in Africa. Furthermore, there has always been transparency. All of their donations have been made public.

This has not stopped Dershowitz from writing that, "It pains me to say this, but I now believe that there is no person in American public life today who has a lower ratio of real to apparent integrity than Jimmy Carter ... He is no better than so many former American politicians who, after leaving public life, sell themselves to the highest bidder and become lobbyists for despicable causes. That is Jimmy Carter's sad legacy."

It is apparent that Dershowitz has taken on the hatchet-man mantle for the Jewish establishment. He is to the more sedate Jewish leaders what Nixon was to Eisenhower. What would induce him to take such a stance? Well, I called a Jewish Federation director and asked a simple question – what is Dershowitz's current speaking fee? He replied that it was between $55,000 to $60,000 per speech. "Who pays that kind of money?" I asked. He replied that it is Jewish Federations and other national Jewish organizations. I would assume that, since Dershowitz speaks frequently throughout the country, he makes much more off the national Jewish establishment than he does from his professorship at Harvard. But, of course, his politics would not be affected by this since he is not an ex-politician.

I am afraid that Dershowitz is in the same position as Newt Gingrich, who was pushing for the impeachment of Clinton at the same time that he was having an affair with his intern, while cheating on his third wife (or was it his second?). The analogy is correct except that Clinton was actually diddling Monica while President Carter is not guilty of Dershowitz's slander. But this does not get Dershowitz off the hook, or the Jewish establishment that has apparently bought him.

President Carter is Leading the Way Toward Peace
4/29/08

President Jimmy Carter has once again upset the Bush administration, the Olmert government and American Jewry by traveling to Damascus to meet with the Hamas leader Khaled Meshal. Here at home the Jewish establishment continues its demonization of Carter as an enemy of Israel, and in Israel proper Olmert follows his American managers by refusing to meet with Carter when he was there. This is in spite of the fact that 64 percent of Israelis are in favor of direct talks with Hamas.

As I noted in my column of March 18-20, an impressive array of military experts in Israel also agree that there is no alternative to talking with Hamas. These include former Shin Bet head Yaacov Peri, former National Security Advisor Giora Eiland, former IDF Chief of Staff Shaul Mofaz and former chief of the Mossad Efriam Halevy. On this point the liberal peace movement agrees with the military men. Former Knesset Member Uri Avneri wrote an open letter to President Carter on behalf of Gush Shalom, the Israeli Peace Block, "to congratulate you on your wise and courageous decision to meet in Damascus with Hamas leaders."

Former Israeli Foreign Minister Shlomo Ben Ami recently met with senior Bush administration officials in Washington and urged that the administration change its Gaza policy of toppling the Hamas government to promoting a reconciliation of Hamas with Fatah as prelude to direct peace talks with Hamas as part of a unity Palestinian government.

Earlier this month Fatah and Hamas attempted reconciliation under the aegis of the Yemeni government and signed a joint commitment to that end. It would have been the first step toward meaningful peace negotiations. Unfortunately Vice President Dick Cheney was in Ramalah the very next day and convinced the Palestinian Authority president, Mahmud Abbas, to fudge on the agreement

This adamant refusal to include Hamas and Israel's continued expansion of West Bank settlements bring us to the question whether Israel wants peace or just more land. Since the Annapolis peace conference in late November of last year Defense Minister Ehud Barak has approved construction of nearly 1,000 new settlement housing units. A new Peace Now report indicated that from August to February construction took place at 101 settlements. The report showed a dramatic rise in Israeli construction in Arab East Jerusalem. Since Annapolis tenders have been issued for 750 units there. There are also plans for an additional 3,648 units to be built in East Jerusalem. Just last week the *New York Times* reported that an additional 100 units have been authorized for the West Bank.

Haaretz, the paper of record in Israel, editorialized: "Had Peace Now not published reports from time to time, it is doubtful anyone would have been aware of the continuing construction in the settlements." The editorial commented that one would never know this listening to the proclamations of Ehud Olmert. It further stated: "The dynamic of deception is continuing. Deception of the Americans, deception of the voters for parties that etched peace on their standard, deception of the Palestinians and above all self deception."

Israeli duplicity has moved a long-time supporter of Israel, Rabbi Henry Siegman, past director of the American Jewish Congress and the Synagogue Council of America and a professor at the University of London, to literally cry out that "Israel's various governments, from 1967 until today, have never had the intention of allowing (a Palestinian state) to come into being."

He continues, in a recent *The Nation* article, that "It would be one thing if Israeli governments had insisted on delaying a Palestinian state until certain security concerns have been dealt with. But no government serious about a two-state solution to the conflict would have pursued, without letup, the theft and fragmentation of Palestinian lands, which even a child understands makes Palestinian statehood impossible." Indeed, Siegman calls this "a colonial enterprise that disgraces what began as a noble Jewish national liberation struggle," and he concludes that "further peace conferences, no matter how well intentioned, make their participants accessories to one of the longest and cruelest deceptions in the annals of international diplomacy."

The Palestinians are not stupid. They see their country being gobbled up by Israel. We may call them terrorists but they see themselves as freedom fighters protecting their own national aspirations. The only way to avoid a military confrontation with Hamas (and Hezbollah thrown in) is to stop the West Bank settlements and East Jerusalem expansion and to get down to serious negotiations with all Palestinians, including Hamas.

It's time that we stop demonizing President Carter and heed his leadership. He is leading us toward our own salvation.

Reassessing Kissinger, Carter and Baker
7/1/08

I have just completed Aaron David Miller's book "The Much Too Promised Land – America's Elusive Search for Arab-Israeli Peace." Miller is now with the Woodrow Wilson International Center for Scholars, but for the last two decades he served as an advisor to six secretaries of state where he helped formulate policy on the Middle East and the Arab-Israeli peace process. Most important for the following discussion, he is from a prominent Jewish family (his father was a good friend of Yitzhak Rabin) and is certifiably a friend of Israel.

Now for the surprise – Miller argues that the three most important contributions to Middle East peace were made by Henry Kissinger, Jimmy Carter and James Baker. This may discomfort many Jews who have made an industry of demonizing both Carter and Baker.

Miller credits Kissinger with two important decisions. First, during the Yom Kippur War in 1973 when Israel's armaments dwindled dangerously, Kissinger convinced Nixon to airlift new supplies in the face of Soviet objections. When Brezhnev threatened to intervene, with Nixon's approval Kissinger actually raised the nuclear threat level to force the Soviet leader to back down.

Kissinger's second decision was to pressure both Golda Meir and Moshe Dayan not to destroy the Egyptian Third Army which was surrounded by Israel in the Sinai. He astutely reasoned that it would have precluded any future peace negotiations with Egypt and would have toppled Anwar Sadat and in Kissinger's words, "(Israel) would have had a Saddam in Cairo."

This was not done without a certain amount of bloodletting. Kissinger called Israel's Ambassador to the United States, Simcha Dinitz, and informed him, "You will not be permitted to destroy this army." Nixon backed Kissinger, saying, "I'm prepared to pressure the Israelis to the extent required, regardless of the domestic political consequences." (As a certified Nixon-hater, I begrudgingly admit to his foreign policy astuteness and fortitude in this case.) The subsequent Israeli-Egyptian peace treaty proved Kissinger correct.

This leads us to Jimmy Carter. It was his personal persistence that made the Camp David peace accords between Israel and Egypt possible. Miller comments that, "Camp David was Jimmy Carter's show." It was not an easy two weeks. For the last 11 days Begin and Sadat never met face to face. Carter had to shuffle back and forth between them. At one point Sadat had packed his bags and was preparing to leave. Carter had to threaten Sadat with the end of their personal friendship and the disruption of the United States-Egyptian relationship. Carter wrote, "And he went over in a corner by himself and he came back and said, 'I'll stay.'" In his memoirs former Israeli president Ezer Weizman wrote that no American president had helped Israel as much as Jimmy Carter.

Concerning Carter's calling for a Palestinian homeland and the pressure that it brought upon him by AIPAC and the Jewish community, he told Miller, "I just finally said to hell with it. I did what I think was best, and I think that if that gets a permanent peace for Israel, they will forgive. I lost support for the first time in history, certainly since 1948, from the Jewish community in 1980." That's how we repay our friends. We're still demonizing him for telling the truth about conditions on the West Bank.

Secretary of State James Baker engineered the Madrid peace conference in 1991. He had to drag Premier Yitzhak Shamir to the table as well as many of the Arab participants. It took him nine months, nine Middle East trips and sixty thousand-plus miles to put the conference together. Its importance was not in any substantive agreements, but in breaking taboos and opening channels of dialogue. Miller contends that without Madrid there could never have been an Oslo Accord in 1993 or a subsequent Jordanian-Israeli peace agreement.

Unfortunately Jews only remember Baker as the person who told Shamir that Israel would not receive $10 billion in loan guarantees unless he froze West Bank settlements. AIPAC went berserk. Baker was demonized, along with Carter. History has proven Baker correct. The major obstacle to peace is those settlements.

Miller writes: "Those who argue that Bush (Senior) and Baker lacked the kind of gut pro-Israel affinity of a Reagan, Shultz, or Clinton are absolutely right; those who argue that Bush and Baker were anti-Semites or unreasonably harsh on Israel are wrong." The fact is that three of the four state department advisors on Baker's team were Jews: Dennis Ross, whom Aaron Miller characterizes as having a "strong Jewish identity," Dan Kurtzer, an Orthodox Jew who was previously a dean at Yeshiva University, and Miller. Anti-Semites do not assemble a team the likes of them.

Yet in 2004 when John Kerry suggested that he would utilize both Carter and Baker as emissaries to the Middle East if he were elected president, the Jewish community went apoplectic and Kerry had to apologize for his faux pas.

I suggest that Jews read Miller's book. For a bright people, we often make bad assumptions.

PEACE PROCESS
General Considerations

Lessons from the Six Day War
6/5/07

Where were you on June 5, 1967? It's one of those dates that very few Jews will forget. It is seared into my memory along with VJ Day (the end of World War II for our younger readers), the day Franklin D. Roosevelt died and the day that John F. Kennedy was shot.

My wife, Lynne, and I had just returned in March from nine months in Israel where I was studying for the rabbinate at Hebrew Union College in Jerusalem. Back in Cincinnati on June 5th we were jolted into fear and anxiety by the start of the Six Day War until it became evident what the outcome would be. This week we celebrate the 40th anniversary of that momentous war.

When in Jerusalem the previous year, we would peer into the Old City from a high point near the base of Jaffa Road where we could overlook the no-man's land that separated the Jewish new city of Jerusalem from the historic walled city that included the Western Wall and other important Jewish sites. After June 5th Jerusalem became whole, not only physically but emotionally, for every Jew. Who can forget General Motte Gur and the Israeli soldiers taking the Kotel (Western Wall)?

But it didn't end there. In the last 40 years Israel has annexed vast areas of land around the historic city into the municipal borders. And with the annexation of the E-1 corridor that connects the West Bank city of Maale Adumim with Jerusalem the combined land mass will cut the West Bank in half and preclude a viable peace treaty with the Palestinians in the future.

It's all very well for us to proclaim that Jerusalem is the spiritual core of

Judaism, but what is Jerusalem? Its current southern border now approaches the immediate outskirts of Bethlehem. This is not the city of our forefathers. The bottom line is that we Jews have to realize that Jerusalem is also a spiritual core for Islam and that we must find a way to accommodate their needs as well as ours if we want peace. Jerusalem must remain a whole city that in some way is shared with our Palestinian cousins.

Another legacy of the Six Day War is the occupation of the West Bank and Gaza and what that means for the soul of Israel. I and others have written about the morality of ruling over another people for 40 years and the inevitable cruelty it places upon them. For the first 20 years of the occupation it was fashionable among Jews to characterize it as a "benevolent occupation." There is no such thing as benevolence when you are controlling the lives of others. Occupation brings out the worst in the occupier as well as the occupied.

As much as I care for the Palestinians, since all people are God's children, I care more for the Israelis because they are my people. I make no excuses for this. It is a natural response. And it is precisely because of this that I want to see the occupation ended. Forty years is more than enough. The occupation is killing the spiritual soul of Israel. Its 18-year-old children are conscripted into the IDF and taught to rule over women and children at checkpoints in the West Bank and to raid Arab houses in the middle of the night. These are lessons in desensitization. Brutality has entered into the Israeli psyche. Wife-beating and other violent crimes are now as common in Israel as in our American society. Jews are not immune to immoral behavior. Whether we like it or not, Israeli social scientists have seen the causal connection between a deterioration of civil society in Israel with the 40-year occupation.

Another legacy of the Six Day War was a sense of Jewish supremacy that can only be characterized as Chutzpah. The swift destruction of the Arab armies created the caricature of the Super Jew, and we American Jews basked in its reflected glory. It was a good antidote to the stereotype of the passive Jew who walked silently into the gas chambers and to the timidity of the middle class American Jewish suburbanite. But it carried with it a hubris that inhibited diplomacy and compromise.

We Jews have always quoted Abba Eban's bon mot that the Arabs have never missed a chance to miss a chance at peace. But historical facts have come to light, with the declassification of the minutes of the Israeli Cabinet meetings, which show that from 1970 to 1973 the Egyptians made fully seven private proposals for peace that were rejected by Israel. Eban wanted to talk, but Golda Meir as prime minister convinced the Cabinet to reject them. This was a direct result of the hubris generated by the Six Day War. The Yom Kippur War could have been avoided and 2,838 slain Israeli soldiers would have lived had there been the understanding that compromise and diplomacy are better than relying on military superiority. In the end Israel did compromise, thanks to President Carter and the Camp David accords.

Today we have a chance to rectify that error in regard to the Palestinians. The current Arab world is as different from their grandparents as Olmert is from Ben Gurion or as the city-dwelling Israeli technology guru is from the kibbutznick-farmer of the 1950's. It's a new world, and the Saudis are presenting a reasonable peace plan for a comprehensive solution. Yet Israel will not talk to them or directly to the Palestinians. It is reminiscent of Golda Meir's response to the Egyptians. It is also as dumb as Bush's insistence that the United States will not talk to Iran or North Korea. It is a fact that peace will never come unless a country talks to its enemies. Talking to friends is pleasant, but talking to enemies is productive. The category of enemy includes those you despise, including Hamas and anyone else the Palestinians democratically elect.

In 1967 we Jews divided the world into good guys and bad guys and the swift Israeli victory validated this morality play. It was a simple scenario that fed our communal emotional needs. Life is no longer simple. Today we understand that there is an element of truth in both the Israeli and Palestinian narratives. To avoid a modern-day Greek tragedy in which we have to live through another round of death and destruction, some movement in the peace process must be initiated.

Someone should tell AIPAC, the ZOA and other strident American Jewish supporters of Israel that they do no service to Israel by reinforcing Olmert's refusal to negotiate. Not to promote a peace process is to ignore the mistakes that were made in the aftermath of the Six Day War and to ignore the lessons that we should have learned from those mistakes.

What We Can Learn From the Yom Kippur War
9/28/04

I am writing this between Rosh Hashanah and Yom Kippur. Each year as the Day of Atonement approaches, I think about that time 31 years ago when Israel's existence hung in the balance during the Yom Kippur War. These many years later it is now our obligation to learn as much as we can from that history.

I suggest a dense and scholarly book written about four years ago entitled 'The Iron Wall" by Avi Shlaim. He is an Israeli who teaches international relations at Oxford. His book is important because it relies upon newly declassified minutes of the Israeli Cabinet meetings during that period. We get an illuminating view of all the major players.

Contrary to the almost mythic reverence in which Golda Meir is held by American Jews, Shlaim paints a negative portrait: "She had an exceptionally strong and decisive personality, being imperious, overbearing, and intolerant of opposition. Subtlety and ambiguity were alien to her character, and she had a remarkable capacity for simplifying complex problems. She saw the world in black and white, without intermediate shades of gray. Her confidence that in any debate her party, her country, and she were in the right was without limits. And it was this burning conviction of always being in the right that made it so difficult to reason with her." The sophisticated Cambridge-educated Abba Eban shared this assessment. He quipped that Meir chose to use only 200 words, although her vocabulary extended to 500.

Using these declassified Israeli sources, Shlaim argues that the arrogance that followed the decisive 1967 victory produced intransigence on the part of Israel that rebuffed repeated attempts by Egypt and the United States to find a peace formula. He quotes Abba Eban concerning this hubris: "The rhetoric of 1973 is almost inconceivable. Opinion passed from sobriety to self-confidence and from self-confidence to fantasy, reaching a somewhat absurd level in 1973." Of course, this goes against what we learned in Sunday School in that Israel always wanted to negotiate, but there was no one to talk to.

Shlaim documents seven different times, beginning in December 1969 and ending in March 1972 when the Israeli Cabinet, under the leadership of Golda Meir, rebuffed legitimate peace offers.

First, Secretary of State William Rogers proposed a return to the 1967 Egyptian-Israeli borders. Meir answered this peace plan the next month by deep bombing into Egypt, intending to topple Nasser. Israel sent 3,300 sorties and dropped 8,000 tons of ordinance on the Egyptians. Eban commented: "This episode illustrates the difficulty of being a foreign minister in a cabinet that had an exaggerated vision of the role of war in international politics."

Egypt answered this Israeli military might by inviting the Soviet Union into its country. Russia sent 15,000 soldiers and 200 pilots to Egypt. Buttressed by this defense, Nasser made a second attempt to discuss peace. He invited Dr. Nahum Goldmann, President of the World Jewish Congress, to Egypt. Golda refused to allow Goldmann to travel there.

In September of 1970 the 52-year old Nasser died of a heart attack. His successor Anwar Sadat in February 1971 proposed returning to the 1967 border between Egypt and Israel, offering for the first time a total peace between the two countries. Eban proposed an optimistic but vague response, but Meir insisted on this short but significant sentence being added: "Israel will not withdraw to the pre-5 June 1967 lines." Meir's response killed the initiative. (Of course, that is what did happen in 1978 under Menachem Begin.)

Assistant Secretary for Near Eastern Affairs Joseph Sisco made a fourth attempt at peace in March 1971. Working with Egypt, he proposed to the Meir Cabinet that Israeli troops should withdraw 40 kilometers from the Suez Canal, thereby allowing it to reopen. Israel would have the right of passage through the newly reopened canal. Israel responded by first demanding that Egypt renounce a state of belligerency. Yitzhak Rabin, in his memoirs, wrote that Kissinger went ballistic in his anger over that stance. The initiative died an early death.

Then in May 1971 Rogers and Sisco proposed an Israeli withdrawal to the Gidi and Mitla Passes, which even the hawk Moshe Dayan supported. But Dayan refused to push this in the Cabinet unless Golda would support it. She didn't. Both Dayan and Eban later wrote that they believed that this would have averted the Yom Kippur War, and both blamed Meir for missing the opportunity. In frustration, the United States suspended the supply of phantom jets to Israel.

Sixth missed opportunity: In October 1971 Rogers suggested "proximity talks" in New York City. Golda rejected this and went directly to Nixon and convinced him to resume the supply of phantoms. The talks were dead in the water and Kissinger never even offered the plan to the Egyptians.

Finally, in March 1972 King Hussein of Jordan offered a Federal Plan whereby there would be two Arab entities, Jordan and Palestine (in the West Bank and Gaza) that would be federated loosely as one country. Egypt, the PLO and Israel immediately rejected it. Arafat regarded this plan as "an attempt to put the PLO out of business." He told his biographer, "and the PLO would have been finished. Sometimes I think we are lucky to have the Israelis as our enemies. They have saved us many times."

There is no historical doubt that the Yom Kippur War could have been averted if Israel had not been intoxicated with its dramatic Six Day War victory. Instead, after 2,838 Israeli deaths and 8,800 wounded in the Yom Kippur War, after 8, 528 Arab deaths and 19,549 wounded, both sides finally came to a peaceful conclusion.

There are some verities that can be culled from this sad history. Beware of leaders who think in black and white. This includes both Bush and Sharon. Beware of leaders who have burning convictions that they are always right. This includes both Bush and Sharon. Beware of leaders who rely on strength or supposed strength instead of diplomatic solutions to complex problems. This includes both Bush and Sharon. Beware of demonizing the enemy. Sometimes it is more inclined to compromise than our own leadership, although we never get to know this until the historical records are opened many years later.

Beware of strongmen (or in Golda's case, strong women) with simple answers. We need the sophistication of an Abba Eban or a Yossi Beilin or a Shimon Peres or a John Kerry. The question is: Is the electorate in either nation sophisticated enough to realize this? The next few months should give us the answer for both countries.

The Soul of Israel is at Stake
4/12/05

I have been accused of being overly harsh in my criticism of Israel, but I assure you that it is out of love, out of a deep concern that if peace is not found in the near future the very soul of Israel will continue to deteriorate so that we Jews will have lost the Zionist dream. Yes, a state will exist, but it will not reflect the high ideals of our Jewish tradition.

My fears were buttressed in a series of articles in the Israeli newspaper *Maariv*. It's an unlikely source, since Maariv, which is Israel's second largest daily, is known as leaning toward the right of the political spectrum.

First, the newspaper printed an essay by Yonatan Gefen, an ex-Israel Defense Force officer, who accompanied his daughter to a roadblock in the West Bank as part of Machsom Watch. This is a movement of young Israelis who monitor the Israeli soldiers at these roadblocks in the hope that their presence will elicit more humane treatment of the Palestinians who have to pass through them. It is important to remember that these roadblocks are not stopping bombers from entering Israel. They are spread throughout the West Bank and prohibit Palestinians from going from one Arab town to the next.

Gefen writes: "At 4:00 in the afternoon, a line of more than 100 people has formed outside Hawara roadblock. Some are old, others are babies, some are dressed like Europeans, some of the women wear traditional gowns and veils. They push one another in the line that isn't moving, but which has rules of its own. The worst in the process is that it occurs in exemplary order. Those who don't have the right documents, and they are the majority, are sent out to an open concrete cube that is named the detainees' courtyard. No one tells them how long or why exactly they are being detained. It looks like collective punishment. People are huddled together like sheep to the slaughter. The first in line enter a revolving steel door that shuts behind them by remote control. Now they are trapped in a small cage, like in a chicken pen. When the soldier is in the right mood, he opens the gate and lets one person out, at which point the process of document inspection begins. I look at these people and feel ashamed. Here, that man with the mustache could be my grandfather, that one over there with the long red coat and the sharp toed high heels could be my wife, the kid with a runny nose who is sitting in the middle of the line could be my son or grandson. It hits me suddenly, just like it probably hits every one of the volunteers who come between one and three times a week to the roadblocks: Something inhuman, bereft of any ethics and bereft of any moral code is being done here. And the worst of it all, as I said, is the exemplary order in which this bestial selection is performed. Suddenly I stop being angry with the roadblock, and start to mourn the future. The Israeli standing army troops cannot humiliate an entire population that was declared inferior without developing a certain obtuseness and indifference to human life."

Gefen's conclusions are brought home in the "Breaking the Silence" movement. These are ex-Israeli soldiers who are speaking out on the brutalization of Israeli society as a direct result of their experiences as part of an occupation army to the Palestinians. Back in November *Maariv* reported on some of the testimonies of these soldiers. A First Sergeant in the Armored Corps: "One of the officers wanted to maintain order …he fired once into the air…the second time he just beat the (Palestinian) to a pulp. He struck the butt of his rifle in his face, kicked him in the balls, spat at him, cursed him. He did this in front of his little boy."

First Sergeant in the Nahal Unit: "To scare the Arabs we would walk through the streets in Abu Sneina and just shoot. My job was to shoot at the street lights. I shot at car windows and one of the soldiers with me fired bombs into a store, to blow it up. And all of this for no reason. I remember that night we were all happy…there's nothing cooler than hearing a street light explode that you aimed at, and we did this with great determination and a big smile."

A soldier with Nahal: "There was a sniper… The orders for opening fire were if someone has a firebomb in their hand, you're allowed to shoot to kill, because this is a case of your life being in danger. They would hold firebombs and never throw them. Once, to get them to throw them, one of the platoon commanders had an idea. He told the sniper to be ready and we deliberately made a distraction… and then he threw the bottle and the sniper hit him. It was a kid, ten years old… he didn't kill him. He injured him badly I think…a ten-year-old kid…it was just to fire at something…just to do something."

Armored Corps officer Lt. Ziv Maavar is one of the central activists in the "Breaking the Silence" movement. He maintains that the abuse, the destruction of property, the disobeying of orders for opening fire, the looting, all is the norm, not the exception. He is quoted in *Maariv*: "We are an entire generation of discharged soldiers. We are here to say, 'look what happened to us.' You've ruined an entire generation of fighters, the best of Israeli society, the most ideological, those who were to be the spearhead of society. We all underwent moral corruption. When we went to the induction center to be discharged, we couldn't unload what we went through along with our uniforms. We took it with us, and this is what we've become, violent on the roads, apathetic, insensitive to our surrounding, the value of human life for us has reached rock bottom. This is Israeli society, this is who we are. We are not against the army; we are not saying the army is bad. We are talking about a situation. We are bad. An entire generation was sent on a mission, and this is its moral price."

These are sobering thoughts that should give pause to militant American Jews who urge the Israelis to fight on for every last inch of land, be it on the West bank or in Gaza. Another 50 years of conflict will surely destroy the Jewish character of Israel. The truth is that the occupier ultimately pays a higher price than those who are occupied. Next Shabbat go to *shul* and pray for peace and an Israeli government that understands compromise. After Shabbat, make a resolution to stop supporting right wing American Jewish organizations that prolong the agony, which may help more than the prayers. Do it for the sake of Israel's soul.

Koran and Bible --- Irrelevant to Peace Process
7/15/03

It was recently argued in a *Jewish Journal* opinion piece that Israel couldn't sign onto the Road Map or any peace agreement with the Palestinians due to the fact that they are Muslims. The writer opined about the Muslim hatred of infidels, citing the Koran, Sura 76,4, "For the infidels, we have got ready chains and collars and flaming fire." He also discussed Mohammed's breaking of the Hudaibiya Treaty in 630 C.E. as proof that they do not respect any contract between Muslims and infidels.

Of course, the year is not 630 but 2003, and the question before us is, how relevant are these ancient documents when dealing with a modern political problem? By the term "ancient documents" I mean to include the Christian New Testament as well as the Jewish Bible. The fact is that all three documents (Koran, New Testament and Bible) contain passages that make any modern reader cringe. They were products of their times, and all three include fabulously uplifting messages as well as depressingly vindictive diatribes.

Looking at the New Testament, you really do not want to read the anti-Jewish passages in the Gospel of John. An Episcopalian Priest once confided in me that he would expunge the book from the canon if he had the power. Even the beautiful Good Samaritan story in the Gospel of Luke (Chapter 10, verses 25-37) compares the Samaritan's goodness to the indifference of both a Cohen and a Levite, thereby casting aspersions on Jewish ethical conduct. Does this mean that we can't trust or relate to Christians in the twenty-first century? Of course not. We as Jews accept the uplifting parts of the New Testament as genuine contributions to humanity and we forgive the portions that were captive to the polemics of the tumultuous religious infighting of the first and second centuries C.E.

But before we Jews become too smug, let us face up to the portions of our Bible that are truly embarrassing. The most egregious example is found in Deuteronomy, Chapter 25, verses 17-19. They enjoin the Jews to "Remember what Amalek did to you on the way as you came out from Egypt, how he attacked you on the way, when you were faint and weary...(therefore) you shall blot out the remembrance of Amalek from under the heaven..." First Samuel, Chapter 15, verses 1-34 extends these orders to the point of genocide (We can't avoid the word – it's genocide): "Now go and smite Amalek, and utterly destroy all that they have; do not spare them, but kill both man and woman, infant and suckling, ox and sheep, camel and ass." (Verse 3)

To prove that God is serious about this prescription for genocide, when King Saul defeats the Amalekites but allows Agag, their king, to live, as well as some choice cattle (he evidently spared no women or children) God decrees that the crown is not to pass to Saul's children, paving the way for David to found a new dynasty. The Deuteronomy passage is read on *Shabbat Zachor*, the Sabbath before Purim, because in the Megilla (the Book of Esther) Haman is a descendent of Agag, thus an Amalekite.

This justifies the rampage in chapters eight and nine of Esther where the Jews murder over 75,000 non-Jews on the assumption that they would have done the same had Haman lived. In Jewish tradition, if an enemy can be branded synonymous with Amalek, then that enemy can suffer the same end. It was the amalgam of the Amalek story in Deuteronomy, First Samuel and Esther that allowed a Baruch Goldstein on Purim to slaughter twenty-nine Muslims while they were praying in a Hebron mosque.

I am aware that there are commentaries in Judaism that later soften the transgressing passages in the Bible and in many cases literally overturn their meanings. But there are also Muslim and Christian commentaries that do the same for their early texts. What is important here is that all three major monotheistic religions have imperfect ancient texts when read from the perspective of a liberal humanistic twenty-first century reader. But the crucial point is that it is unfair to the Muslims (read Palestinians), Christians or Jews to cite these texts to prove that any of the three are untrustworthy or bloodthirsty. It is intellectually dishonest in the context of the Middle East conflict to quote militant passages from the Koran as proof that Muslims are not to be trusted to make peace. We would certainly not want them to quote, in turn, the Amalek passages.

If you don't want to cede land to the Palestinians, that is your prerogative, even if I disagree with you. But don't clothe your opposition to the Road Map on pseudo-religious grounds. Let's leave the ancient texts out of this fight.

The Temple Mount and False Prophecies
7/6/04

Reading the opinion pages of the *Jewish Journal* is always a pleasure for me because it reflects the full spectrum of Jewish thought, not just my own liberal bent. About a month ago a piece by a Jewish fundamentalist caught my eye concerning the Temple Mount. He spoke in mystical terms of prophecies under God's direction. Concerning the capture of the Old City of Jerusalem in 1967 he wrote:

"Soon the nation would hear those words that still send ripples of joy to Jews. Motta Gur, commander of the front, announced via his army radio the third prophecy: 'Har HaBayit B'Yadenu, the Temple Mount is in our hands.' They had liberated the Old City of Jerusalem…Who still can't hear those words of prophecy without being moved? The full weight of 19 centuries was lifted off the backs of the Jewish people. 'The Temple Mount is in our hands!'"

The writer then argues that to give the Mount back to the Palestinians either through the Road Map as proposed by the United States and accepted by Sharon or through a comprehensive settlement such as the Geneva Accord would be "a slap in the face to the God of Israel." He concludes, "How could they spurn the blessings of God? How could they try to reverse Jewish history? How could they ignore the prophecies?"

Where does one begin to critique such fundamentalism? It is most difficult to argue with someone who is convinced that a military victory was the direct result of the will of God, actually a prophecy, an instance of God talking to mankind through the triumphs of the Israeli army. But it is this kind of thinking that is represented in the current Sharon coalition.

Let's start with the concept that God has a special relationship with approximately one acre of land on this vast planet. That is as primitive as the concept that God has a special relationship with 15 million people out of the 6 billion that inhabit the earth. Why would a loving God choose to play favorites with His children? Certainly a human loving parent would not do so. It is difficult to dissuade a fundamentalist that his direct line to the Almighty might not exist, for that admission destroys the very core of his belief system. It undermines his surety that God protects him and that God always approves his actions. It is this very surety that makes him a dangerous person to the rest of mankind.

And what would make this Temple Mount so holy? It is not a natural mini-mountain created by God. Building a series of retaining walls to lift it above the surrounding terrain created the Mount. The Western Wall is part of that retaining wall complex. It was built by a very human ruler named Herod, a Jewish puppet king of the Romans, who was anything but godly. In securing his control of the crown he killed his wife and mother-in-law, both direct descendants of Maccabean rulers. Maybe we could understand the mother-in-law situation, but it was no way to treat a wife. He also killed two of his five children in a power struggle. So, it was this Herod who created the Temple Mount, not God himself. We are asked to believe that this Mount, the creation of very human hands, is a chosen and sanctified place for God Himself (or Herself, in deference to my liberated wife).

Finally, the writer pulled a sleight of hand on his reader. When Motta Gur proclaimed that the Temple Mount was in our hands he was not referring to the top of the Mount where the two mosques now sit and where the ancient Temple once stood. He was referring to the retaining wall once called the Wailing Wall, now called the Western Wall. First, when he radioed his message he was standing at the Wall, not on top of the Mount. Second, when the war was completed a few days later Jews flocked to the Western Wall, not to the top of the Mount. Immediately, the Israeli authorities cleared away Arab homes that faced the Wall to create the broad plaza that we see today. Nothing was done to the top of the Mount. In fact, Israel consigned the top of the Mount, what we call today the Temple Mount, to the custody of Arab guardians, where it remains to this day. Israeli police do not patrol the Temple Mount. This has been true with one exception – September 28, 2000 when Ariel Sharon invaded the Mount with 1000 Israeli policemen in riot gear, the event that instigated the current intifada.

Most Israelis and American Jews rarely think about the Temple Mount. I know many Israelis who have never even bothered to visit the place. A vast percentage of American Jewish tourists visit the Wall, but rarely ascend the Mount. It has little emotional pull for us. This was true until the year 2000 when Barak was negotiating with the Palestinians under Oslo. Right-wing religious parties were part of his coalition and they insisted that the Temple Mount be under Israeli sovereignty in any peace agreement. Until that time it was not even a consideration. Barak, a secular Jew who rarely thought about the Temple Mount, capitulated for the sake of maintaining his coalition, i.e. his power. Power creates interesting theological positions.

This right-wing Jewish fundamentalist attachment to the Temple Mount is also mirrored by Christian born-agains. For them the prerequisite for the second coming of Christ is the rebuilding of the Temple on the Temple Mount, the same rebuilt Temple that inspires a cadre of Jewish fundamentalists. So we see that the Temple Mount is important if you want to re-institute sacrifices to God in place of the modern synagogue. It is this joint movement by the coalition of Christian and Jewish fundamentalists that places the Temple Mount as a top priority in any peace settlement. I recommend a book written a few years ago by Gershom Gorenberg, entitled "The End of Days – Fundamentalism and the Struggle for the Temple Mount." It explores in depth the unholy (or should I say holy) alliance between fanatical Jews and Christians. One thing is for sure, if they were to prevail, the two mosques on the Mount would have to be removed and there would be a war with the1.3 billion Muslims in this world.

The sum of this discussion is that we should be wary of fundamentalism whether it is packaged in Christian, Muslim or Jewish garb. We should be wary of letting them set the agenda for peace. If we allow that, there will be no peace -- just more false prophecies in the name of God.

Arafat and the Myth of Camp David
10/7/03

This is the first installment in a two-part series on the search for peace at Camp David and Taba, so *fabrente* Palestinian haters may want to wait another week before they write indignant letters to the editor. After all, why be discomforted twice – wait a week and do it all at once.

Since the Sharon government announced its decision to remove Arafat and in the words of the *New York Times* "threatening the Palestinian leader with expulsion, jail or possibly death," it is time to face up to the myth that the current disastrous situation is Arafat's fault, that he is a man who never wanted peace. We are told that is the truth not only by Israeli leaders but also by our president who seems to have adopted Sharon's line as gospel truth, an apt phrase for our born-again leader.

Here's the myth: Ehud Barak offered Arafat 98% of the West Bank and a chance for real peace at Camp David in July of 2000, and Arafat turned it down because he did not want peace, after which the Palestinians turned to violence.

If we can put aside our own natural desires as committed Jews to defend

Israel, let us look at the real facts. Robert Malley was at Camp David in his capacity as special assistant for Arab-Israeli affairs to President Clinton. He reports a different picture: Barak offered 91% of the West Bank and a land swap of one percent back to the Palestinians in exchange for the confiscation of the 9% remaining with Israel. Malley wrote, "How would Mr. Arafat explain the unfavorable 9-to1 ratio in land swaps to his people?" On top of that Israel was to control a further 10% of the West Bank on "long term lease."

Percentages aside, Barak's offer cut the West Bank into three non-contiguous cantons, which means that super highways would cut across the West Bank, connecting Israeli outposts to Israel proper, and these highways partitioned the Palestinians into three small enclaves. For a Palestinian in his or her new nation to visit a relative or friend in one of the other two enclaves he would have to go through Israeli military check-points, a configuration not unlike the Bantustans created by the South African apartheid government. Israel also demanded control of all borders for the proposed new Palestinian government, thereby controlling international movement as well. From the Palestinian perspective this looked like a re-packaging of military occupation, not an authentic birth of a new Palestinian nation.

For the Palestinians the refugee problem is crucial, or put another way, the right of return to Israel is a major emotional factor in their own sense of peoplehood. As Jews we know that Israel could never allow the right of return for the Palestinian masses, for that would demographically destroy the Jewish character of Israel. We know this, and so did the Arab negotiators. But this did not preclude a delicate compromise, which would include some small family reunification and monetary compensation for lost property, etc. So what did Barak propose? Nothing. Absolutely nothing. According to Malley, and he was there as they were speaking, Barak merely spoke vaguely of a future "satisfactory solution." On this crucial point Israel asked Arafat merely to trust them. Israeli gobbling up West Bank land for illegal settlements immediately preceding Camp David did not auger well for a request of simplistic trust.

Barak also insisted upon Israeli sovereignty over the Muslim quarter of the Old City as well as the Temple Mount. As a Jew and a rabbi, let me propose an analogy. Suppose Arafat agreed to everything Israel wanted, but with one proviso – the Western Wall would have to be under Palestinian sovereignty. Oh, you Jews can have day-to-day de facto control, but philosophically you must admit that sovereignty is in Muslim hands. What Israeli government could accept that proposal? Obviously none. I would be the first American Jew to protest giving sovereignty over the Wall to the Palestinians.

Contrary to right-wing Jewish propaganda, the Temple Mount is to Islam what the Western Wall is to Judaism. The Koran describes how Mohammed ascended to heaven from the Temple Mount. Palestinians aside, the over one billion Muslims world-wide would not allow any Muslim to concede sovereignty over that holy spot. Barak demanded the impossible from Arafat and then labeled him an obstructionist when he could not comply. And the myth began its course.

It was a short step from accepting the myth to the complete demonization of Arafat. Yes, he is a corrupt despot, albeit democratically elected; but he is not another Osama bin Laden. To kill or exile him would be the blunder of the century – for Israel, not the Palestinians. A country does not reach peace with an adversary by hand picking its leadership. Only those as obtuse as Sharon and Bush could believe that. But it does not surprise me. One helped create the myth, and the other bought it.

The prolific author and former Deputy Mayor of Jerusalem Meron Benvenisti has written about the nature of this Arafat myth: "Like all myths, once it has caught on, it becomes more real than reality itself. Israeli society needs the myth, because it is unifying and justifies all actions, clears the conscience, defines the enemy as bloodthirsty and allows society to cope with the tough reality of 'no alternative.'… Anyone who tries to present a more complex and balanced view …is immediately branded an enemy, or 'extreme leftist.'"

Benvenisti ruefully writes: "It's sad to see that some of the best of the intellectuals and historians, who handle the myths of the past so well, don't have the courage to do it in real time." Knowing that myths create an image that a society wants to show to the world, Benvenisti comments, "God help anyone who dares to doubt them."

May God help me.

PS Next week – Sharon picks up the mantle from Barak.

As We Jews Walked Away From Peace
10/14/03

Last week I wrote about the myth that it was Arafat alone who was responsible for the breakdown of the July 2000 Camp David peace talks. Now I want to chronologically follow the downward spiral into the intifada by focusing on the actions of Ariel Sharon.

But first let us clear up one important religious point: In the larger scheme of things the Temple Mount is only tangentially important to modern Judaism. The Western Wall is our emotional bedrock. To prove this point I ask the reader who has been to Israel, how many times have you visited the

Temple Mount? Most will say never; yet very few Jews would visit Israel without a visit to the Wall.

It is true that the Ancient Temple stood on the Mount, but, except for a very lunatic fringe of Jews who want to tear down the Mosque of Omar and rebuild a temple, Jews are not particularly interested in the Temple Mount. I know that I have been to the Wall well over 40 times in the last 35 years, but have only visited the Mount once, and that was with an archeologist.

In contrast, the Temple Mount is exceedingly holy to Muslims, representing the spot from which Mohammed ascended to heaven. As I wrote last week, the Temple Mount is to Islam what the Wall is to Judaism. Which brings us to September 28, 2000, the day that Ariel Sharon, with the approval of Ehud Barak, invaded the Temple Mount.

What follows is not my "interpretation." I footnote each report. I urge the reader to go to the library and check my references and read for him/ herself the very same reports upon which I rely.

Most people believe that Sharon innocently walked onto the Mount. But the *New York Times* reported: "Mr. Sharon entered as a police helicopter clattered overhead and a thousand armed policemen were positioned in and around the Temple Mount, including antiterror squads and ranks of riot officers carrying clubs, helmets and plastic shields. Throughout the tour Mr. Sharon was ringed tightly by agents of the Shin Bet security service." (NYT, 9/29/00) How would Jews feel if a thousand Arab battle-dressed armed policemen were to descend upon the Wall.

The Arabs responded accordingly. In the riots that followed the next day, four Palestinians were killed by Israeli security forces (NYT 9/30), The day after that, October 1, there were twelve dead (NYT10/2). And so the Al Aksa intifada began. Lest you think that Sharon's visit was not a frontal attack on Islam, pay attention to the name of the current intifada. The Al Aksa mosque, which sits upon the Temple Mount, is the third most holy site for Islam. Dennis Ross (incidentally a Jew), President Clinton's Middle East negotiator, when reflecting on Sharon's visit, commented that, "I can think of a lot of bad ideas, but I can't think of a worse one." He concluded that it was Sharon's visit that turned "into a dawning certainty that the moment for attaining Middle East peace on Mr. Clinton's watch had slipped away." (NYT 1/29/01)

Six weeks later, on December 9, 2000, Barak resigned and called for new elections to be held the following February 6th. In late December of 2000 President Clinton called upon both parties to resume the discussions started at Camp David the previous July. He urged the Palestinians to give up their right of return and the Israelis to give up sovereignty over the Temple Mount. (NYT 1/21/03) In response, on January 19, 2001 Arafat proposed "urgent talks." In turn, the Israelis agreed and both sides met at Taba, an Egyptian resort immediately adjacent to Eilat, from January 22nd to the 28th. Both sides had high-level negotiators. For Israel: Foreign Minister Shlomo Ben-Ami, Justice Minister Yossi Beilin and Tourism Minister Amnon Lipkin-Shahak (an ex-general). For the Palestinians: Ahmed Qurei (who is known as Abu Ala), the current Prime Minister of the Palestinian Authority, Saab Erekat and Yasir Abed Rabbo. (NYT 1/21)

While these talks were in progress, on January 24th Sharon declared that he would consider any agreement that would emerge "null and void." He declared that the government should not be conducting peace talks. (NYT 1/25) He reiterated this position the next day and promised to repudiate any accord reached at Taba if he were elected. (NYT 1/26)

At Taba they discussed refugees, security, borders and Jerusalem. The only outsider at the Taba talks was the European Union envoy Miguel Moratinos. He wrote a private summary of the points of agreement that was verified by both sides and was subsequently leaked to the Israeli newspaper *Haaretz* in March of 2002. It is too long for a detailed discussion in this column, but you can find it on the Internet as the "Moratinos Document." (*Haaretz*, March 2002) What we do know for sure is the evaluation of the participating parties as to how close they were. The following are excerpts from the Joint Statement of the negotiators.

"The sides declare that they have never been closer to reaching an agreement and it is thus our shared belief that the remaining gaps could be bridged with the resumption of negotiations following the Israeli elections...

"As stated above, the political timetable prevented reaching an agreement on all the issues. However, in light of the significant progress in narrowing the differences between the sides, the two sides are convinced that in a short period of time and given an intensive effort and the acknowledgement of the essential and urgent nature of reaching an agreement, it will be possible to bridge the differences remaining and attain a permanent settlement of peace between them." (Associated Press 1/28/01)

A week later, on February 6th Sharon was elected. True to his word, he immediately repudiated the peace talks. The English paper the *Guardian* reported: "Ariel Sharon has rejected Palestinian demands to resume peace talks where they left off with the outgoing administration of Ehud Barak." The *Guardian* also reported that Sharon's diplomatic advisor Zalman Shoval said, "There was no accord concluded in Taba and what was discussed does not commit the government that Mr. Sharon will form." (*Guardian* 2/8/02)

From that point it has been all down hill. I have lost count, but Israeli dead number approximately 850 and Palestinian dead number about 2600. It all could have been avoided if Sharon cared more for peace than he did for West Bank settlements. What is sure is that, if you read the documents, it wasn't the Arabs who walked away from the bargaining table; it was the Israelis under Sharon's leadership. It's time that American Jews stop repeating the myth that where we are today is the result of Arafat alone, in that he walked away from Camp David. In truth, the Palestinians continued the negotiations at Taba, but we Jews walked away. Jewish history will ultimately condemn Sharon for this un-Jewish act. It will also condemn American Jewry for ignorantly supporting this catastrophic decision.

Israel's Fatal Flaw
8/9/05

Next Monday is officially D-Day for Israel -- disengagement from the Gaza Strip. Rather than delving once again into the nitty-gritty of what will possibly happen, I want to reflect on why I feel that in the end it will not lead to peace unless Israeli society learns to understand and appreciate the Palestinian narrative as well as their own. In non-academic English, Israelis have to learn to stop looking down on Arabs and Israeli leaders have to stop humiliating Palestinian leadership.

At the end of June and early July I participated in a week's mission to Israel. During that time we had in-depth interviews and dialogue with 23 Israeli and Palestinian leaders, including politicians, academics, generals, a politician-rabbi, government bureaucrats, peace workers and prominent Israeli journalists. Walking away from this it's easy to get mired in the minute particulars of the disengagement and the peace process, if there is still one really in existence. But from a Gestalt point of view today I want to look at the concept of understanding the humanity of the other as a prerequisite to finding peace. This I find lacking in Israeli society and its total disregard by the Sharon government.

When we met with Palestinian President Mahmoud Abbas (Abu Mazen) he reported that he said to Sharon, "Treat me as a friend, not an enemy, otherwise there is no use for talks. I will put my foot in your shoes, and you in mine. We shall talk and reach peace." It is this putting the foot in the other person's shoes that Israeli leaders and public have trouble with.

We met with Israeli Housing Minister Itzhak (Buji) Herzog (member of the Knesset from the Labor Party and son of former Israeli president Chaim Herzog). I found him young and arrogant. He had just published a column in the *New York Times* explaining how traumatic the disengagement was for Israelis, pitting Jew against Jew. He made reference to the Altalena, a ship carrying 900 immigrants into Israel in June of 1948. It was also carrying illegal ammunition to the Irgun, which was a separate militia from the Israeli army, the successor to the Hagganah. Ben Gurion ordered the ship fired upon and sunk. It was a case of Jew killing Jew. The trauma of that experience still resonates in Israel. Herzog then blithely suggested that if Abbas were serious he would immediately wipe out Hamas by force. I personally challenged him as to whether that would not constitute a Palestinian Altalena. He had no appreciation for the fact that Palestinians killing Palestinians could be traumatic for Abbas and his supporters.

The Sharon government makes decisions with no regard to the effects they will have upon the Palestinian Authority (PA). Within the last two months, expecting Abbas to keep peace, (and if he doesn't it will prove that they are terrorists) Sharon has: attempted to confiscate Palestinian property in East Jerusalem (stopped by international pressure); announced a plan to put 30,000 more Jews in a West Bank settlement; attempted to annex Arab land east of Jerusalem into the city limits (the E-1 corridor, which was also stopped, primarily by Condi Rice and the Bush administration); and finally announced that the wall will be imminently built cutting through Jerusalem, thereby stranding on the other side 55,000 Palestinians who work and live in the city. All of these moves were made during the crucial period leading to next Monday's disengagement, a period in which he paid no attention to Palestinian trauma. The Israeli government operates on the principle that Arab sensibilities are irrelevant.

Insensitivity leads directly to outright humiliation. When Arafat was alive he would not officially meet with an Israeli official in Jerusalem because it was "occupied territory." This past June Sharon summoned Abbas, and rather than continue this diplomatic formality, he met Sharon for a few hours in Jerusalem. Substance was more important to Abbas than form. But Sharon used this meeting to humiliate him. He lectured the President of the Palestinian Authority as if he were his employee. Nothing was accomplished at the meeting except to weaken the PA in the eyes of Palestinians. In our meeting with Abbas he was most diplomatic in reference to this event. But his National Security Advisor, Jibril Rajoub was less diplomatic, even angry, calling the Sharon administration, "this crazy government." He added, "Israelis are not ready to recognize the needs of the other party. Mr. Sharon wants only to talk about his own needs."

Sharon's indifference to Arab sensibilities merely reflects general Israeli opinion. Tamar Hermann of Tel Aviv University and one of the most respected pollsters in Israel reported to us that Israelis are basically not expecting peace but merely looking for the maintenance of the status quo minus Gaza – a quiet management of violence. And this is the key – she reports that Israelis are not moved at all by the suffering of the Palestinians. It has been said before, but Danny Rubenstein, the *Haaretz* journalist and Arab affairs expert, emphasizes that this humiliation, not poverty, is the main impetus for suicide bombers. You humiliate the father and his son wreaks vengeance upon the occupier. Rubenstein adds, "We preach to them. We patronize them."

Sharon recently commented in the Israeli press that after all we are dealing with "Arabs." This ethnic slur builds upon the commonly held belief in Israel and among American Jews that there is such a thing as the "Arab mentality," as if they belonged to a sub-species. It reminds me of the propaganda in our country during World War II concerning the "inscrutable Oriental mind." Well, the Japanese subsequently showed us that they could think as clearly as we, witness the Japanese cars we drive and the electronics we use. In Israel there is an expression for menial work as "avodah arevim," meaning "Arab work." It is fair to say that for a vast percentage of Israelis the Arabs are looked down upon with the same disdain that Americans looked upon their darkies (not to use the N-word). This mentality is Israel's fatal flaw.

Disengagement will come and go, but peace will not be found unless Israel begins to understand that Palestinians are human – if you prick them, do they not bleed?

On the Palestinian side there is not disdain or condescension for Israelis, but rather hatred – the result of losing every battle in the last 57 years and living under occupation the last 38 years. This is reflected in their textbooks. But this kind of hatred dissipates after peace, as our hatred for the Japanese and Germans was quickly obliterated after World War II. It is not my intention to paint the Palestinians as perfect people. The point is that they are human, just like us. And obviously, the Palestinians will not and should not get all of their desires.

Israel must first protect its own security and existence, but having said that, there is no reason to rub their faces in the dirt, for that is exactly what Sharon has done to Abbas, and thus to the Palestinian people. They are a proud people, an intellectual people. They do not have a separate mentality and their minds are not inscrutable. If Israel does not give them dignity and hope, there will never be peace. It's time that the American Jewish community begins to think in these terms, rather than to continue being apologists for the Sharon government.

Jewish Empathy, Israel and Robert McNamara
4/13/04

If you haven't seen "The Fog of War: Eleven Lessons from the Life of Robert S. McNamara" run to see this riveting documentary that recently won the

Academy Award. Eighty-five year old McNamara, who was Defense Secretary to both John Kennedy and Lyndon Johnson, reflects on the Vietnam War and his role in it.

The movie has been criticized for the fact that it does not present McNamara as the evil mastermind of that debacle. In fact, he comes across as a decent human being trying to explain how they miscalculated. He never exactly apologizes for his role as the strategist of the war, yet at this late date he does admit that it was wrong.

Lesson #1 in the movie is Empathize with your enemy. McNamara discussed how they avoided a nuclear meltdown with the Soviet Union during the Cuban Crisis by putting themselves in the shoes of Nikita Khrushchev. Ignoring the advice of General Curtis LeMay, who wanted to bomb Cuba off the map, they reasoned their way to a solution that gave Khrushchev dignity and a diplomatic cover that allowed him to withdraw the missiles. Empathizing with your enemy was the key to survival.

What is inexplicable to me is that the same Robert McNamara could not apply the empathetic approach to the Vietnamese. Should he not have known, before 1961 when he first ordered U.S. support troops into South Vietnam and before 1962 when he created the U.S. Military Assistance Command, that we were involving ourselves in a civil war that had its antecedents in a thousand year struggle for independence? Should he not have understood that by our actions we were becoming the extension of a French policy that came to a dead-end at Dienbienphu? Should he not have known that the very creation of South Vietnam under the Geneva Accords of 1954 was a temporary demarcation that was preliminary to an agreed election in 1956 to unify the country and that Diem, with American and French support, negated that agreement, thereby denying Ho Chi Minh the democratic electoral victory that was a surety and was his due?

Why? After 58,000 American and over one million Vietnamese deaths from that useless war, we still ask, no we verily shout out, why? Why should these elemental facts that are so apparent today, and were known to the young protestors including myself, have been missed by our brightest leaders? McNamara tries to clear this up in the movie. The bottom line is that their thought processes were constricted by a paradigm that did not allow them to see the world in any other way than the domino theory of communist expansion. This fear of communist domination literally blinded them to local nationalist desires. It blinded them to the fact that the Vietnamese feared the colonial desires of China more than of France. Being tied to a false paradigm literally blocked out the ability to empathize with your enemy. McNamara understands this now, a little too late.

I write this immediately before Passover, the Jewish holiday that celebrates the passage from slavery to freedom for all peoples, not just for the Jews who made the journey from slavery in Egypt to freedom in Israel. It is the holiday that exemplifies empathy. We are expected to place ourselves in the very shoes of those slaves who made the trek. We are also expected to empathize with the legitimate aspirations of all other peoples on this planet.

My favorite midrash on Passover is that when the Jews safely passed through the divided waters of the Red Sea and the Egyptians were drowned attempting to follow them, the angels began to sing with joy over the fate of the Egyptian army. God silences them with the reproof, how dare you sing with joy when my people are drowning! Yes, in this Jewish story, the Egyptians, the slave-masters over us downtrodden Jews, are still God's people. And we must weep over their demise the same as we would over our own. This is the vaulting empathetic statement that we are expected to internalize.

The problem is that the American Jewish community has not applied its own religious standards to the conflict between Israel and the Palestinians. Instead of empathy for the national aspirations of the enemy we have created an iron-tight paradigm that constricts creative thinking as absolutely as the domino theory did to Robert McNamara and the American State and Defense Departments. This new paradigm goes something like this: All the Palestinians want to destroy Israel. The entire conflict is the result of their terrorism and poor leadership. Israel is a poor defenseless little democracy tossed amidst the sea of 22 despotic Arab governments, and finally, even if Israel were to make a mistake, we should not recognize it because we are governed by the credo of my country right or wrong, my country. Read the literature. Listen to AIPAC and the ZOA and these are the paradigmatic conclusions that guide American Jewish convictions.

This thought process continues a brutal confrontation that has produced almost 900 Israeli and almost 3000 Palestinian dead during just this latest intifada. The danger of this thought process was reflected in a recent newspaper article that reported that John Kerry met with Jewish leaders in New York and repaired his "faux pas" in suggesting that former President Carter and James Baker could possibly act as envoys to the Middle East.

This horrified me, not that they would serve, but that American Jewish leaders could consider this a faux pas. Carter brought lasting peace between Israel and Egypt at Camp David. For this American Jewish leadership vilifies him? James Baker demanded that then Israeli Prime Minister Shamir freeze the West Bank settlements before the U.S. supply a $10 billion loan guarantee under the first Bush administration. For this good advice our leaders now demonize him.

This brings us to two other lessons from the McNamara movie. Lesson #8, Be prepared to reexamine your reasoning, and #10, Never say never.

McNamara learned these lessons too late. The question is whether the American Jewish leadership will continue to be blinded to new realities, will continue to support a disastrous Sharon coalition, because it can't think out of the box that is defined by the current paradigm. The question really is whether American Jews will take the message of their religion, the message of Passover, and begin thinking empathetically and recognize Palestinians as God's children along with us. When that begins, maybe we can play a role in helping Israel achieve real peace and security.

In 20 years, if I live that long, I don't want to see a Jewish Fog Of War movie lamenting our lost opportunities.

An Honest Look At Palestinians
10/28/03

The October 14-16 edition of the *Jewish Journal's* opinion pages focused on Israel and the Palestinians. Five columnists represented the spectrum from left to right, including my piece on how the Jews walked away from a peace agreement at Taba in January of 2001.

Reading the two right-wing pieces truly aggravated me, as I am sure that I have aggravated many people with my columns. That, I guess, is why the *Journal* has the most interesting opinion pages in Jewish journalism. Just what bothered me is what I want to discuss now.

My friend Bill Katzberg queried whether any civilized nation could remain unmoved by continuing terror, and Larry Winig commented that one couldn't have civilized relationships with present Muslim Arabs. Both used the key code-word *civilized*, which is to connote that the Palestinians are not civilized, thus a little less human than we Jews. Other less sophisticated ideologues are calling the Palestinians barbarians.

There is a clear and present danger here in dehumanizing one's enemies. Meir Kahane called the Arabs dogs and pigs, which was the ultimate in dehumanization, the first step to ethnic cleansing and genocide. The Nazi dehumanization of us Jews allowed them to effectuate the Holocaust. As long as we were not fully human, they could intellectually accept the Final Solution.

Let's set the record straight. A hundred suicide bombers aside, the 3 1/2 million Palestinians who live in the Occupied Territories and the 3 million Palestinians who live in the Diaspora are a cultured people with a rich history of intellectual thought. In fact the dispersed Palestinians in other Arab countries are the engineers, teachers and doctors of their host countries. The Palestinians are the Jews of the Arab world. Branding a whole people as terrorists or uncivilized or barbarians not only does an injustice to them, but cleverly blocks any attempt at an honest, compromised peace settlement. That is ultimately an injustice to Jews. And that is precisely what Winig in his article proposed. He calls it his Moses Plan – Israel should wait at least 40 years before it begins serious negotiations with the Palestinians.

Winig and Katzberg share one other important point: You can't negotiate with a people who want Israel destroyed. Bill put it succinctly: "Indeed all that the terrorists in Hamas and Islamic Jihad want is that Israel disappear; call an end to the Jewish state ...Finis." Of course, I agree that this is true. But Bill goes on to make the sleight of hand: "The situation has no rational answer when one partner to peace innately requires that you disappear." Come on, Hamas was never a partner in the peace process. The Palestinian Authority, whom Hamas hates, is the partner. The 3 1/2 million Palestinians are the partners, not the thousand or two thousand terrorists.

Which brings us to the main point of this discourse. The Israeli government and its propaganda machine in the United States repeat ad nauseam that the Palestinians do not want peace, that Oslo was only the first step to reoccupying Tel Aviv and Jaffa. If it is repeated often enough, it will be believed. It's called the Big Lie frontal attack, which was perfected by the Germans during WWII. The problem is that there is no scientific evidence to support this statement. On the contrary, there is evidence that the average Palestinian wants his own country in the West Bank and Gaza, not Haifa or Tel Aviv.

Where is this evidence? One has to turn to Khalil Shikaki, the head of the Palestinian Center for Policy and Survey Research (PSR) in Nablus. Shikaki earned his Ph.D. from Columbia University and has been a visiting professor at Columbia, the University of Wisconsin and the University of South Florida (subsequently in 2007 at Brandeis University). He is a world-class academic and public opinion pollster. I spent about three hours with him in Nablus about eight years ago. He is fiercely democratic, dislikes Arafat and is totally intellectually honest. His job as a pollster is to report the truth, not to shape it.

For years Shikaki has reported that from 75% to 80% of the Palestinians accept the fact that Israel is here to stay and that support for Hamas increases only when they feel that there is no hope for a negotiated agreement or when they see their land gobbled up by West Bank and Gaza Jewish settlers.

Last July Shikaki asked more than 4,000 Palestinian refugees whether they would exercise their right of return to Israel, if it were given to them. Nine out of ten said no. This enraged right-wing Palestinians and a mob of 100 invaded Shikaki's Nablus offices and threatened his life. Right-wing Palestinians share a world-view with right-wing Jews: They don't want to face empirical truth. They would rather believe their own myths. The fact is that the vast majority of Palestinians want to live with dignity in their own country. They are not fighting the battles of their grandparents, circa 1948. They recognize Israel's existence and merely ask that in return their national rights should be recognized.

The highly respected American pollster John Zogby has written, "Dr. Shikaki has been in the business for years now of surviving and surmounting all obstacles in his efforts to provide the most honest polling available among Palestinians. Neither Israeli tanks nor Palestinian toughs have ever been able to deter him...sometimes he angers Israelis; other times, he infuriates Palestinians. Great. That is one of the reasons I like him. There has to be someone somewhere where people who want unvarnished truth can go. That someone is Khalil Shikaki."

It's time that Jewish rejectionists stop the mantra that Palestinians want to destroy Israel. That was a previous generation's agenda. It's time that we realize that mainstream Palestinians (not Hamas) want a negotiated peace, something that Sharon and his extreme right-wing coalition are not willing to confront.

It's Time to Talk to Hamas
3/18/08

In response to Qassam missile attacks on the Israeli town of Sderot, earlier this month the Israeli Army invaded Gaza in what an IDF spokesperson called a "pinpoint operation." This involved killing 116 Palestinians, while the Israelis had three casualties, two soldiers and one civilian.

The Israeli military spokesman claimed that 90 percent of the Palestinian dead were terrorists but the Palestinians claim that half were innocent bystanders. B'Tselem, the respected Israeli civil rights organization, counts 54 of the dead as non-combatants.

The *New York Times* reported on a Palestinian father who was looking for his son who was playing with his friends when the Israeli rocket hit. "I couldn't identify the body of my son," he said. "It was very hard until I found the head of my son." The *Times* also reported on the death of four children, two of whom, brother and sister, 11 and 12, died in their beds from shrapnel.

Many things bother me about this operation. First, if 116 Jews were killed by Palestinians in a two-day period, American Jewry would be in mourning. There would be Jewish Federation rallies and sermons from pulpits and no end to our anguish, and rightly so. But where is our *rachmonis* for the father who has to identify the head of his son? Where are our Jewish souls that we can't recognize the humanity of those whom we kill? We chalk up the body count and figure that we won the battle as if it were a lopsided football game. We're talking about human beings here.

When the Israelis do admit to high civilian deaths, they claim that it is due to the fact that Hamas stores its rockets in civilian neighborhoods. This is true. But where is it supposed to store them? Hamas has no military bases, no tanks, and no air force. It is at a distinct disadvantage in its war with Israel. It does what all nationalist movements do when confronted by a superior force, it improvises.

The real question is the chicken and the egg conundrum – which came first? Is the Israeli force justified because Hamas launches missiles or is Hamas's resistance justified because Israel has blockaded the Gaza strip, since Israel and its ally, our own United States, refuse to recognize the legitimately elected Hamas government? As a result of that blockade Israel has brought poverty and death upon civilians in Gaza.

It really doesn't matter which came first. What is important is to find a way out of this box. One was offered this past December, but Israel declined to consider it. Ismail Haniyah, the prime minister of the Hamas government, offered a cease-fire, a short-term calm (*tahdiya*, in Arabic) which could be expanded into a long-term ceasefire (*hudna*, in Arabic) subject to further negotiations between Israel and Hamas.

The Israeli government immediately rejected the offer. Prime Minister Olmert parroted the usual excuse: Israel will not deal with "terrorist elements." Bush and Olmert are one in their stance. When Condoleezza Rice was in Israel immediately after the Israeli incursion into Gaza, she urged the resumption of peace talks with Mahmoud Abbas but studiously avoided reference to holding cease-fire talks with Hamas.

The Israeli newspaper *Haaretz* reports that 64 percent of Israelis are in favor of direct talks with Hamas while only 28 percent are against it. The same poll showed that support for direct negotiations crosses party lines, including 48 percent of Likud voters, 55 percent of Kadima voters and 72 percent of Labor voters.

Writing in the *Jerusalem Post*, Gershon Baskin points out that Israel always negotiates with terrorists. They have negotiated with Hezbollah over captured soldiers and with Hamas over the return of Gilad Schalit, an Israeli soldier. Baskin asks, "Why would negotiating with Hamas for a cease-fire that has the potential to save tens, perhaps hundreds of lives in Israel be any less legitimate than negotiating with Hamas to save one human (Jewish) life?"

Haaretz also reported that many security figures in Israel support direct talks with Hamas. This group includes former Shin Bet head Yaacov Peri, former National Security Advisor Giora Eiland and former IDF Chief of Staff Shaul Mofaz, presently transportation minister in the Olmert government.

Efraim Halevy, a noted hawk, who served three prime ministers as chief of the Mossad recently called upon both the Bush administration and Israel to talk to Hamas. In a recent interview with the American magazine *Mother Jones*, Halevy described the resiliency of Hamas and concluded that it cannot be ignored. He said, "It makes sense to approach a possible initial understanding including Hamas –but not exclusively Hamas – at a time when they are still asking for one. No side will gain from a flare up leading to Israel re-entering the Gaza strip…"

Halevy has it right. Israel must face Hamas with the Palestinian Authority (a unity government) in peace negotiations. The best one sentence summary that I have read came from the seminal Jewish thinker Henry Siegman, writing in the *Herald Tribune*: "You cannot make peace with half a country's population and remain at war with the other half."

Israel's Long Term Outlook
11/15/05

I am more than sad to report that I see no light at the end of the tunnel for Israel. The conflict with its neighbors has now existed for almost 58 years, and I do not see an end until well after the 100 year mark. I say this for the following five reasons:

First, there is no burning desire for peace in Israel. Tamar Hermann of Tel Aviv University, one of the most respected pollsters in Israel, reports that Israelis are basically hoping for the maintenance of the status quo minus Gaza, meaning a quiet management of violence as the Israeli and Palestinian populations are separated by the wall. She further reports that Israelis are not moved by the suffering of the Palestinians.

This should not surprise us. Over 70 percent of Israelis were born after 1967. Factoring in immigrants and youngsters born immediately before 1967, you get over 80 percent of the population that know nothing other than the status quo. They never experienced a time when Israel was not an overseer of an occupation. This, coupled with their acceptance of separation and the status quo, leads to an easy acceptance of bypass roads and a kind of apartheid where the average Israeli doesn't think about the West Bank or the aspirations of the Palestinians.

This past summer, as part of an American peace delegation, our guide to the illegal settlements on the West Bank commented that we American activists have seen more of the West Bank in one day than over 90 percent of Israelis. Basically he claimed that the average Israeli is in denial, i.e. if you don't personally experience the problem there must not be a problem.

Unfortunately, this kind of avoidance will lead to a third intifada, because the problem is very pressing for the Palestinians, if not for the Israelis. As Danny Rubenstein, the astute *Haaretz* correspondent, points out, this third intifada will not utilize rocks or suicide bombers, but will employ rockets. The separation fence or wall will not protect Kfar Saba or Jerusalem from these rockets. And the third intifada will lead to more forms of occupation and apartheid.

Finally after another 50 or 100 years, the Palestinians will forego the two-state solution and demand their rights as citizens of Israel, since they will have lived under Israeli rule for a hundred or so years. And Israel will not be able to give them their rights since at that time Arabs will outnumber Jews in the area between the Mediterranean Sea and the Jordan River. So Israel will then become a full-fledged apartheid state with two classes of people – Jewish citizens and Palestinians who are denied voting privileges and live between a series of check points to control them. I doubt that in the latter part of the 21st century the world will be accepting of this kind of Israel. I shudder to think of its place among nations.

Second, I do not see the Israeli electorate changing its outlook. I foresee a liberal minority being permanently swamped by an increasing conservative and right-wing block. The well educated western-oriented Ashkenazic secular Israeli has been outnumbered by the wave of oriental Sephardic Jews and Russian immigrants who lean to the right. Add to this the rise of Jewish fundamentalism in Israel. The Orthodox, secular Sephardim and Russians will assure that Labor will never assume power again. If there is an accommodation with the Palestinians it will have to come from a Sharon or a Netanyahu, and I personally doubt that is possible.

Third, given the tenor of the Israeli electorate, I cannot see them approving a withdrawal from the West Bank that would entail the removal of 60,000 to 90,000 settlers (depending upon whether Ariel settlement block would be included in the disengagement) in comparison to the only 8,000 who were removed from Gaza. For an undertaking such as that you need an electorate that has a greater empathy for its adversary and a greater desire for peace.

Fourth, Israel does not understand that time is on the Arab side, not theirs. Let me share with you my darkest nightmare. Today a suicide bomber can blow up a café in Tel Aviv and kill 10, 20, even 100 people. Twenty years from now that same suicide bomber will be able to drive a pickup truck with a mini atomic bomb within it and kill a million people.

Does this sound alarmist? We know that an average graduate student in the sciences can tell you how to build such a bomb. The only constraint is obtaining the fisionable material. Just last week the *New York Times* reported that our government removed plutonium from a storehouse in Prague that we did not know existed until we heard an off-handed remark by a Czech official. How many other left-over atomic stockpiles from the Soviet era are floating around Europe and how long will it be until terrorist cells obtain one?

Technology changes faster than most of us can comprehend. I hate to contemplate what technology of destruction will be available to Hamas or Islamic Jihad 50 years from now, if this conflict is not resolved. Of one thing I am sure – the Palestinians are our cousins. Their desire for nationhood is as great as ours. They are as driven and stubborn as Jews. They will be in Israel/Palestine at the turn of the next century. The only question is whether they will be there as peaceful neighbors or freedom fighters/terrorists. That decision lies mainly in the hands of Israeli leaders.

Fifth, my final pessimistic prognostication: Only the United States can negate all of the above by forcing Israel into a compromise with the Palestinians, and I predict that it will not do so. To begin, Bush's born-again religious constituency requires a strong backing of Sharon. Add to this the Jewish lobby. AIPAC is controlled by fat-cat Republican Jews who will not allow the Bush administration to pressure Israel, and the average American Jew follows the establishment line.

I was appalled during the last presidential race when Kerry had to apologize to the Jewish community for his "gaffe" in suggesting he would use ex-President Carter and Ex-Secretary of State James Baker to find a solution to the Middle East problem. These two were anathema to Jews. All that Carter did was to broker an advantageous peace settlement with Egypt. And Baker committed the "sin" of forcing Israeli Prime Minister Yitzhak Shamir to slow down West Bank settlements. If these are supposed enemies, what is the American Jewish community thinking? Do not expect them to allow an American administration to broker an honest compromise. We will brand any president who tries it an anti-Semite. In this manner, the American Jewish community will ultimately destroy Israel in the name of protecting her.

I wish that I could see a brighter future for Israel and her neighbors. The Palestinians make many mistakes, but as I see it, Israel has the real power and the ability to make peace when it decides that compromise is better than territorial expansion. As the weaker partners, the Palestinians can respond well or poorly, but they are relegated to response rather than proactive actions leading to peace. Only Israel can do that. And I don't see them doing it. I pray to God that I am wrong.

Terrorism

Don't Let Terrorism Stand in Way of Peace
2/5/08

Two months ago, in late December, Ismail Haniyah, the prime minister of the Hamas government, phoned an Israeli reporter and raised the possibility of a cease-fire between Hamas and Israel. He was offering a short-term calm (*tahdiya*, in Arabic) which could be expanded into a long-term ceasefire (*hudna*, in Arabic) subject to further negotiations between Israel and Hamas.

The Israeli government immediately rejected the offer. Uri Avnery, ex-Knesset member and Israeli columnist, commented: "The message is…(T)he offer shows that Hamas is about to break, and therefore the war against it must be intensified… A paradox inherent in the conflict since its beginning is at work here: if the Palestinians are strong, it is dangerous to make peace with them. If they are weak, there is no need to make peace with them. Either way, they must be broken."

Israeli Prime Minister Ehud Olmert could not publicly acknowledge this thought process, so he parroted the usual excuse: Israel will not deal with "terrorist elements" and Israeli "counterterrorist operations will continue as they have for months."

Let's look at this terrorist rationale. The definition of terrorism is the targeting of civilians in order to accomplish a military end. What I am about to write will disturb you, as it does me, but it is the truth, and I owe that to you and to myself. All countries use terrorism while fighting a war. And make no mistake about it, the Palestinians are fighting a war for independence. If this were not the case there would be no excuse for Israel holding 9,000 Palestinians in jail without benefit of trials. (It is their version of Guantanamo Bay.)

America has been the most egregious user of terrorism. During World

War Two we fire-bombed 67 Japanese cities killing over a million women, children and elderly, since they were the only ones left there. The young soldiers were off to battle. Of course, we then dropped the atomic bombs on Hiroshima and Nagasaki, killing another 200,000 civilians. We did this to hasten the end of the war and to save American lives.

The Israelis have used terrorism. Ilan Pappe is the Chair of the history department at Haifa University. His new book "The Ethnic Cleansing of Palestine" describes the systematic clearing of Arabs from what is now Israel by the Hagganah, Irgun and the Stern Gang beginning immediately after the United Nations vote on partition in November, 1947. It is one thing to ethnic cleanse an enemy (surely they would have driven the Jews into the sea had they had the ability), but it is another to use terrorism as a weapon in that cleansing.

Pappe reports on many instances of Jewish terrorism against civilian Arabs including the most famous massacre at Deir Yassin perpetrated by the Irgun and the Stern Gang with the approval of the Hagganah. He writes: "As they burst into the village, the Jewish soldiers sprayed the houses with machine-gun fire, killing many of the inhabitants. The remaining villagers were then gathered in one place and murdered in cold blood, their bodies abused while a number of the women were raped and then killed.

"Fahim Zaydan, who was twelve years old at the time, recalled how he saw his family murdered in front of his eyes: 'They took us out one after the other; shot an old man and when one of his daughters cried, she was shot too. Then they called my brother Muhammad, and shot him in front of us, and when my mother yelled, bending over him –carrying my little sister, Hudra in her hands, still breastfeeding her – they shot her too.'"

Pappe then comments: "Zaydan himself was shot, too, while standing in a row of children the Jewish soldiers had lined up against a wall, which they had then sprayed with bullets, 'just for the fun of it', before they left. He was lucky to survive his wounds." Thirty babies were among those slaughtered. At the time, the Jewish leadership exaggerated the number of dead in its successful effort to panic other Arab villages to flee into Jordan or Gaza. Historians have reduced the body count from 170 to 93.

I can remember that as a young college student, president of my Student Zionist Organization, I denied that Deir Yassin or any other Jewish terrorist attacks ever took place. That was the official Israeli line at the time. Today most Israeli historians acknowledge this reality. To deny it would be equivalent to denying the Armenian genocide by Turkey.

One man's freedom fighter is another man's terrorist. It is absurd to deny the reality of the Palestinian struggle for nationhood and to refuse to bargain with the enemy because they are "terrorists." We are all terrorists. When I admit that I agree with General Curtis LeMay's fire-bombing of Japanese cities and President Truman's dropping of the atomic bombs, I join the ranks of terrorists. It's time to put this terrorist excuse to bed and to start serious peace negotiations, or at least a cease-fire with Hamas.

Being Intellectually Honest -- Defining Terrorism
1/27/09

The last two weeks I have been commenting on Israel's shameful decision to invade the Gaza Strip. The stated public rationale for Israel's use of force rather than diplomacy is that you cannot bargain with terrorists. This has also been the Bush administration's disastrous modus operandi in regard to Syria, Iran and a host of other countries. Hopefully it will end under the current administration.

Without emotion let us look at this concept of not talking to terrorists as it relates to the United States and Israel. This is a tough request and I warn you that many will be outraged, but hopefully truth and logic will prevail. Here goes:

To begin, all countries in time of war resort to terrorism including the United States and Israel. Let us define terrorism so that this discussion can remain calm and dispassionate. Terrorism is inflicting harm on civilians to reach a military objective.

During World War II the United States under General Curtis LeMay fire-bombed 67 Japanese cities, killing well over a million women, children and old men in an effort to force the Japanese to surrender before we were required to launch a mainland offensive against them. At the time estimates assumed that we would lose up to a million soldiers if we had to go that route. So we chose another tactic – attack their civilian population to pressure a Japanese surrender. When this did not work, we dropped atomic bombs on Hiroshima and Nagasaki, killing another 200,000 civilians.

There is no doubt that these cities were not military objectives. We targeted civilians to obtain a military objective. Lest you think that I am some left-wing anti-American nut-case, I hasten to add that I defend these acts of terrorism, but I will not be intellectually dishonest – it was terrorism, period. Most Americans would rather see a million Japanese civilians killed than a million American kids in military uniform dead.

During Israel's War of Independence both Israel and the Arabs used terrorism. Both sides attempted to use ethnic cleansing in their attempt to grab a greater portion of land. If the Arabs had won they would have pushed the Jews into the Mediterranean Sea. As it happened the Jews won and they forcibly expelled 700,000 Arab residents from their land, using terrorism as a tool.

Don't take my word for it. Current Israeli historians are pouring over the historical records of that period and are producing insightful books. Even the conservative historian Benny Morris in his opus "Righteous Victims – A History of the Zionist-Arab Conflict, 1881-1999" comments on the Deir Yassin massacre when the Irgun and the Stern Gang slaughtered over a hundred innocent women and children in that Arab village and then proudly paraded the captured males through the streets of Jerusalem before killing them. This example spread fear throughout the remaining Arab villages and hastened their "voluntary" departure, which was the objective of Ben Gurion's Plan D, the secret strategy for ethnic cleansing.

Deir Yassin was not an isolated incident. During Morris' earlier liberal period he catalogued 24 massacres by Israel against indigenous Arabs between April and May of 1948. Palestinians put the number as high as 40. Terrorism was an integral part of the Jewish war against the Arabs in 1947 and 1948 as it was on the Arab side. I recommend a book written by the Chair of the History Department at Haifa University, Ilan Pappe, entitled "The Ethnic Cleansing of Palestine." Pappe has documented 31 massacres from December 1947 to January 1949. The chief Israeli terrorist was Yitzhak Shamir who headed the Stern Gang. He later served as Prime Minister of Israel. The world spoke to him and ignored the fact that he was a terrorist.

Even the Bush administration applied its absurd definitions inconsistently. We brought Muammar Kadaffi of Libya, the architect of numerous acts of terrorism, back into the western fold, not through military action but through diplomacy. We talked to him.

Now let's focus on Gaza. Hamas is at war with Israel as are all of the Palestinians. They want get out from under 40 years of Israeli occupation. They want their own independence, a goal that I believe most moderate Jews and gentiles accept as legitimate. They don't have airplanes, tanks and other accoutrements of a modern army as does Israel. But they have what they call "freedom fighters" and what Israel labels "terrorists."

Yes, they lob missiles into Israeli cities with the intent of killing civilians. It is an act of terrorism, actually an act of lesser terrorism than Americans killing over a million Japanese. But it is terrorism. For the record, I abhor terrorism and condemn it (except when my government did it to the Japanese! – so much for moral consistency). But this is not a valid reason not to bargain with them in order to find a solution to the Israeli-Palestinian war.

Since we realize there are gradations of terrorism, i.e. different ways to target civilians to reach a military objective, the Israeli blockade of Gaza since 2005 is an act of terrorism. Gazan civilians have died for the lack of medical supplies and the entire population has been reduced to pauper status. Inflicting pain and suffering on civilians is just another form of terrorism.

It's time for level-headed, non-emotional people to urge Israel to come to its senses and bargain with Hamas rather than attempting to destroy them, an objective that is an elusive delusion.

Settlers and Fanatics

West Bank Settlers Destroy Peace Prospects
8/12/08

How long can we expect the ceasefire between Israel and the Palestinians to last if Israel continues to gobble up portions of the West Bank? What would we Jews do if the roles were reversed and the Palestinians were incessantly changing the facts on the ground by colonizing territory that we believe is ours? As an activist Jew I know what I would do, and it wouldn't be to passively accept it.

Two weeks ago Israel's Defense Ministry approved construction of a new Jewish settlement in the Jordan Valley. This is not on the periphery of Israel but is deep into the West Bank. It has yet to be approved by the Defense Minister, Ehud Barak, but chances are that it will be, since he will have to placate the Orthodox party (Shas) that is part of the governing coalition.

What is even more disturbing is the rationale behind the decision. *Israel Radio* reported that the Defense Ministry allowed this settlement as a reward for the settlers' consent to evacuate four illegal settlements on the West Bank. There are currently over 100 Jewish illegal settlements, many on private land owned by Palestinians, and the government has done little to close them down.

So we have come to the point where the government is so feeble that it has to bargain with illegal settlers. The question has to be asked – who really is in control, the settlers or the government ministers? Imagine this scenario in the United States. A fundamentalist religious group decides to create a compound in a national park. Rather than sending in authorities and arresting them our government agrees that if they leave Yosemite it will allow them to relocate to Yellowstone. It's as ludicrous as what's happening on the West Bank.

A few months ago *Israel Radio* reported that law enforcement agencies demolished an illegal outpost built in violation of Israeli law near the West Bank town of Hebron. Several hours after the demolition the settlers returned and rebuilt the outpost. It was reported that this illegal outpost had been destroyed and rebuilt 31 times – that's not a misprint – 31 times. Did anyone ever think of just throwing these religious fanatics into jail?

What kind of a game is being played by the Israeli government and the West Bank settlers? And if you were looking in from the outside, as a Palestinian, what would you think? How can we believe this Israeli government when it assures the Bush administration and the world that it is freezing settlements and desires to reach a two-state solution?

Meanwhile the number of settlers in the West Bank rose by 15,000 in 2007 over the previous year, a 5.5 percent increase in comparison to only a 1.8 percent increase for all Jewish Israelis. Last month Israel's Interior Ministry approved construction of 1800 new housing units in East Jerusalem's Har Homa and Pisgat Zeev neighborhoods and approved doubling the size of the Ariel West industrial zone, deep inside the West Bank.

The settlers' game plan is not only to inhabit the West Bank but to drive out the indigenous Palestinian population through intimidation and violence. Two weeks ago *Ma'ariv*, Israel's second largest newspaper, reported that the settlers have established "battle headquarters" to plan attacks against the Israeli army if it interfered with them and to coordinate attacks on Palestinians.

The paper reported on the ongoing violence, nothing unusual – settlers setting Palestinian olive groves on fire, rampaging through Palestinian villages and smashing cars and windows, cutting electricity lines and the like. *Ma'ariv* editorialized: "The settlers intend to show that they have power on the ground with the goal of blocking any legal mission, such as the evacuation of outposts."

Haaretz, the *New York Times* of Israel, described a typical case of settler violence. A group of settlers attacked a Palestinian shepherd near the settlement of Susya outside Hebron. He and his aunt and uncle, aged 58 and 60, were tending their sheep when the settlers told them to leave. He responded, "This is my land. I'm here to plant trees and feed my sheep." Then the settlers returned with others, now wearing masks, and attacked the family. They were all beaten to the ground. No arrests were made.

Haaretz editorialized that there has been a rise in settler crime "which aims to deprive Palestinians of their land. Jews who presume to be upholding the duty of settling the land openly discuss their intention of making the lives of Arab residents a misery and pushing them out of what they call Judea and Samaria. The law-enforcement agencies, including the prosecution and the courts, must treat Jewish criminal behavior as severely as they do Palestinian crimes."

Until Israel stops West bank settlements and gets tough on the settlers the long-range outlook for peace is bleak. There is no better time to face up to this reality than during the quiet of the current cease-fire agreement with Hamas and the other factions representing the Palestinians.

A Look at Illegal Outposts on the West Bank
10/18/05

Now that the disengagement from Gaza is completed, attention is directed back at the settlements in the West Bank. The vast majority of these will have to be removed before a lasting peace can be achieved with the Palestinians. But there is a subset of settlements that are illegal even by Israeli standards, and it is these that I want to discuss in this column.

There are 105 (and possibly more) "unauthorized outposts" on the West Bank, mini settlements established by zealots without formal government approval. Sharon has promised Bush to dismantle a portion of them, but no action has been taken. The Israeli attorney general summoned a report by an independent attorney (I guess that this would be analogous to our special prosecutors). Talya Sason issued her report and it has become a major document in the legal and political dialogues in Israel. Few Americans have read it. I just completed a 48 page summary, and I want to share it with you.

She reports: "After the High Court of Justice ruling in the case of Elon More, a 1979 Israeli government resolution states that Israeli settlements in Judea, Samaria and Gaza shall be established only on State land...It is absolutely prohibited to establish outposts on private Palestinian property. Such an action may in certain circumstances become a felony." Yet Sason reports that 54 of the 105 outposts are situated partially or fully on Palestinian property.

The Sason Report describes the process: "One way to establish an outpost is first to falsely ask for an antenna to be placed up on a hill. Afterwards comes a request to supply electricity – only for the antenna. Then a cabin is placed, for the guard, and the cabin is also connected to the electricity. Then a road is paved to the place, and infrastructure for caravans (mobile homes) is prepared. Then, one day a number of caravans arrive at the place – and an outpost is established." Amongst other illegal ways, Sason describes "establishing outposts by 'expansions' and 'neighborhoods' in disguise, within existing outposts. The new outpost is named as the old one, as though it were just a neighborhood, even when it is sometimes kilometers away…This enables financing the new outpost by the different authorities: the money supposedly goes to the old settlement, as known to the authorities. In fact, it goes to the new outpost."

Sason implicates two government ministries and the Settlement Division of the World Zionist Organization in theses illegal operations. She clearly states: "The Settlement Division…built many unauthorized outposts, without the approval of the qualified political echelon." This means that Diaspora Jewish money went into this illegal activity, including money given to the UJA that supports the personnel that run the Settlement Division.

She reports that the Ministry of Construction & Housing established public buildings in unauthorized outposts disguising the outlay of money by creating a special budgetary clause named "general development misc." A permit is required for a caravan, which Sason describes as "a house on wheels," to be transported to the West Bank. The assistant to the defense minister has been issuing such permits against the law, without the knowledge of the defense minister (at least that's what the defense minister testified to a Knesset committee). He chastised his assistant with an instruction not to issue any more certificates concerning unauthorized outposts. Period. End of chastisement.

There have been orders by the courts and other government agencies to destroy some of the illegal outposts, but few have been implemented. The Sason Report: "Apparently, these orders can be executed only at the instruction of the Minister of Defense. Ministers of Defense have avoided for years instructing the execution of destruction orders, except for single cases… The conclusion is that, as opposed to Israel, law enforcement in the territories is partially in the hands of the political echelon, especially in the matter of unauthorized outposts. As far as law enforcement is concerned, the political echelon sends a message of no enforcement, when it comes to the territories. Felons are not punished. The overall picture draws the conclusion that no one seriously wants to enforce the law."

Sason reports that the IDF (Israel Defense Force) is dragged into this: "The security concept, that wherever there is an Israeli person – IDF will be there to protect him, resulted in a very sad reality. Therefore, any settler who places his home wherever he chooses, even if unauthorized and against the law –gains the protection of the army. The outcome is that the settlers are the ones who set the army's deployment in the territories, not the army. Everyone is king. In order to protect one outpost, forces must be taken out of other places. The forces are not unlimited, and so the security level goes down."

Sason recommended that the attorney general consider legal measures against the state officials who have broken the law, including the assistant to the defense minister. She concludes, "Democracy and the rule of law are two inseparables. One cannot exist without the other. The reality drawn up in this opinion shows that all of these deeds seriously endanger the principle of the rule of law. Even though the outposts are built in the Judea, Samaria and Gaza territories and not in Israel, the settlers and the authorities who take part in their establishment are Israeli. A continuing, bold, institutionalized law violation undermines the rule of law. When law violations become standard behavior it tends to spread into other areas."

Finally, the Report concludes, "In order to maintain the democratic regime of Israel, urgent measures must be taken to change the reality I have described. It can no longer be accepted. It must be reformed, and I believe you (the attorney general) have the power to do so."

To date there have been no indictments and none of the existing 105 illegal settlements have been dismantled. May I add that every one of them is a violation of the Oslo Accords which required there should be no new settlements after 1993. Some of them exist as testimony to the ineffectiveness of the Israeli Supreme Court, which ordered their removal. All of them are an affront to the United States, in that Sharon promised our government to dismantle them (letter to Condoleezza Rice on April 14, 2004 by Dov Weisglass), but has done absolutely nothing. It is obvious that the settlers and their supporters wield political clout that even trumps the law. Such is the state of law and order and politics in Israel.

Postscript: I write this as a life-long Zionist, not to diminish Israel but to lift her out of the current madness. It's time that American Jews stop blindly supporting the Sharon government and fight for a more just and more Jewish Israel, of which we can all be proud and which will truly reflect the biblical injunction to be "a light unto the nations."

Settler Fanatics and the Jewish Holidays
10/12/04

I write this immediately after Yom Kippur and before Sukkot and Simchat Torah, three holidays that have great meaning for me. I am appalled when I read how West Bank, fundamentalist Jews distort them. On Yom Kippur worshippers at the Tomb of the Patriarchs in Hebron included prayers mentioning those things that should pass from this earth and included were the names of Prime Minister Ariel Sharon and the head of the Disengagement Authority (the government agency preparing for the evacuation of Gaza), Yonatan Basle. It is one thing to think of assassination. It is another to verbalize assassination. But it is a despicable distortion of Judaism to include the call for assassination in High Holy Day prayers.

Talking about distorting Jewish holidays, I also read that the settlers will have a new board game modeled on Monopoly ready to purchase by Hanukah. The players vie to see how many radical right-wing activists they can succeed in recruiting for a violent battle against the Israeli army in opposing disengagement. Another object of the game is to see how many Arabs can be deported from the West Bank and Gaza. A good card in the game would read, "You were silent during police interrogation, you are released from detention," or "195 Arabs emigrate, you receive 242 activists." The game was invented by David Haivri, chairman of the extreme right-wing group, Revava (which means ten thousand, representing the ten thousand activists they hope to pit against the Israeli army.)

Another right-wing activist Nadia Matar of Women in Green wrote an open letter comparing the Disengagement Authority's resettlement of Jews from Gaza to Nazi expulsion of Jews from their homes in Germany. Avner Shaley, the Director of the Yad Vashem Holocaust Museum, condemned Matar's statement, saying: "The use of the Holocaust to manipulatively advance political stands is irresponsible. It deprecates the memory of the Holocaust and perverts historical fact."

Finally this last week the Meir Kahane disciple Noam Federman addressed a letter to "The Jewish Soldier." In it he urged Israeli soldiers to disobey orders to evacuate settlers, calling upon them to desert the IDF (Israel Defense Forces). Security officials said that the letter "looks like an attempt to incite rebellion and mutiny."

All of this activity around the holiday period has a déjà vu feeling for me. I think that right-wing settlers are invigorated by the use of Jewish holidays. Two years ago ultra-Orthodox Jews celebrated Simchat Torah by literally invading Hebron. Not only did they visit the tomb of Abraham, but the Sharon government put 150,000 Palestinians under curfew (read house arrest) so that a couple thousand Jews could wander through Hebron's casbah.

Yossi Sarid, the opposition leader in the Knesset, was outraged: "There is no need that they would celebrate there. It's a shame that for a few thousand Jewish people to celebrate in Hebron, they impose a siege over 150,000 Palestinians, and they arrange tours for Jewish people as if it's a zoo. It's not a zoo. Monkeys are not living there. People are living there."

Along with the Jews were fundamentalist Christian American visitors. The *New York Times* quoted Sharon Spieka, the wife of a light fixture salesman from Loveland, Colorado. Her visit to Hebron "totally changed my life." She called the settlers "the heroes of the land" and "it's the fulfillment of biblical prophecy. God has called us to join in and help." Other members of the

Christian group explained that a Jewish presence in Hebron would speed the return of the Messiah (Christ).

The above-mentioned Naom Federman was also a part of that Simchat Torah celebration two years ago. I remember my own encounter with him and what the *Times* called the "hard-nosed band of a few hundred Jewish settlers" that has rooted itself amongst the 150,000 Palestinians living in Hebron. It was about ten years ago, when I was walking past their small enclave with other peace activists, and they opened their water hoses on us. Rather than stopping their attack, the Israeli soldiers who are stationed to protect them turned upon us and demanded that we evacuate the region.

I refused to move. I had the right to be there. The job of the soldiers was to protect these followers of Meir Kahane against Arab attack and not to side with them when they attacked fellow Jews. A near riot ensued. Police reinforcements were brought in. None was arrested except two photojournalists present. They were taken to police headquarters where their film was confiscated and then they were released. That is how the Israeli government ensured that to the outside world everything seemed calm in the West Bank. Or at least that's how it worked until the outbreak of the current intifada.

We did press charges against Federman. I testified in an Israeli courtroom about two years later. The case was thrown out. Very rarely are the settlers chastised. A few years ago I read that Federman's car was blown up only minutes after his wife and child parked the car and got out. The police reported that the Federmans owned the dynamite. They did not report what they intended to use it for. No arrests were made.

Having recently experienced the High Holy Days, (and by the time you read this, Sukkot and Simchat Torah), I ask myself what I have in common with these fanatics who celebrate the same holidays? Do they really practice the same religion that I and other liberal Jews do? We share the name Jews, but do we share the same religion?

Modern Day Sikarim
8/31/04

The head of the Israeli internal security service, Shin Bet, has recently warned of a double threat from the radical right Orthodox in Israel. He believes that there is imminent danger that they may strike to blow up the mosques on the Temple Mount and/or attempt to assassinate Ariel Sharon and other members of his cabinet. Blowing up the mosques would divert energies from the government's plan to evacuate Gaza, and assassinating Sharon would accomplish the same end. In their minds these acts would protect holy Jewish land from reverting to Palestinian rule.

To understand their thought processes, we have to understand the fundamentalist approach to Torah and Tanach. These would-be assassins rely on the precedent of Amalek. Deuteronomy, Chapter 25, verses 17-19 enjoins the Jews to "Remember what Amalek did to you on the way as you came out from Egypt, he attacked you on the way, when you were faint and weary…(therefore) you shall blot out the remembrance of Amalek from under the heaven…" First Samuel, Chapter 15, verses 1-34 extends these orders to the point of genocide (We can't avoid the word – it's genocide): "Now go and smite Amalek, and utterly destroy all that they have; do not spare them, but kill both man and woman, infant and suckling, ox and sheep, camel and ass."(Verse 3)

To prove that God is serious about this prescription for genocide, when King Saul defeats the Amalekites but allows Agag, their king, to live, as well as some choice cattle (he evidently spared no woman or children) God decrees that the crown is not to pass to Saul's children, paving the way for David to found a new dynasty. The Deuteronomy passage is read on *Shabbat Zachor*, the Sabbath before Purim, because in the Meggila (the Book of Esther) Haman is a descendant of Agag, thus an Amalekite.

This justifies the rampage in chapters eight and nine of Esther where the Jews murder over 75,000 non-Jews on the assumption that they would have done the same had Haman lived. In Jewish tradition, if an enemy can be branded synonymous with Amalek, then that enemy can suffer the same end. It was the amalgam of the Amalek story in Deuteronomy, First Samuel and Esther that allowed a Baruch Goldstein on Purim to slaughter twenty-nine Muslims while they were praying in a Hebron mosque. Today Goldstein is revered in the settler movement and his grave has become a shrine for ultra right wing Orthodox Jews.

A corollary of the Amalek story is the concept of the halachic precept of *din rodef*, which permits killing in defense. It was this concept that Yigal Amir applied when he assassinated Yitzhak Rabin. He struck the first blow to protect the integrity of Jewish soil.

I am aware that there are commentaries in Judaism that later soften these transgressing passages and severely restrict the application of *din rodef*, but they are of no importance to fundamentalist Jews who live a Judaism that reflects two millennia ago. Their Judaism and what we in America consider normative Judaism bear little resemblance.

Jeffrey Goldberg, in a frightening op-ed piece in the *New York Times*, reported on his discussions with West Bank radical settlers. One settler declared, "What Amalek wants to do is swallow up the people of Israel. This is the snake. This is the snake." Turning to a pregnant married teenager carrying an M-16 rifle, he asked if she thought Amalek was alive today. "Of course," she said, pointing toward an Arab village in the distance. She also opined that although Sharon wasn't Amalek, "he works for Amalek." She continued, "Sharon is forfeiting his right to live." Asked if she would like to kill him, she responded, "It's not for me to do. If the rabbis say it, then someone will do it. He is working against God."

And the rabbis are beginning to say it. *The Jerusalem Report* reported that Rabbi Avigdor Nebenzahl, the state-employed rabbi of Jerusalem's Old City (in other words, he is paid by the Sharon government) "blithely stated at a public event with TV cameras rolling, that 'anyone who hands over parts of the Land of Israel to gentiles will be punished according to *din rodef*.'" And the fanatics are beginning to openly talk of destroying the mosques on the Temple Mount, an act that would create a thousand year war between Jews and Muslims worldwide. The *Forward* quoted Yehuda Etzion, a leader of the so-called Jewish Underground, imprisoned for terrorist acts in the 1980s, who said that blowing up the mosques was a "proper" and timely thing to do: "The Dome of the Rock is the wrong structure in the wrong place at the wrong time, because it is right and proper that our Third Temple should stand there."

These are not random observations. Goldberg writes: "Over the past year, I've heard at least 14 young Orthodox settlers – in outposts, and in yeshivas in the West Bank and Jerusalem – express with vehemence a desire to murder Prime Minister Ariel Sharon and his men, in particular the deputy prime minister, Ehud Olmert, and the defense minister, Shaul Mofaz. I've met several more who actively pray –and, I suspect, work – for the destruction of the Dome of the Rock, the Muslim shrine on Jerusalem's Temple Mount. And I have met dozens more who would not sit shiva, certainly not for the Dome, but not for their prime minister, either."

This would not be the first time when zealots would attempt to change the outcome of Jewish history. During the first century the majority of Jews were moderates who wanted to make an accommodation with the Romans, thereby avoiding the war that ultimately destroyed the Second Temple in 70CE.. Fellow Jews in the name of Amalek and *din rodef* murdered them. Josephus, the Jewish/Roman historian, described the sikarim, who assassinated the high priest Jonathan and who terrorized Jews who openly cooperated with the Romans. The zealots received their name from the sicarii, short daggers, that they concealed in their clothing to murder their victims, usually at religious festivals.

The sikarim succeeded in radicalizing the Jewish response, and the outcome was disastrous for Judaism. Two wars later, after the death of countless number of Jews, we finally made peace with Roman domination and entered a period of unparalleled religious creativity.

The question is: will we allow the modern day sikarim to determine our destiny or will we speak out. To date, I hear no normative Orthodox American Jewish leaders chastising these Neanderthal rabbinic sources in Israel. I see unsophisticated Reform and Conservative Jews contributing to the very yeshivas on the West Bank and in Jerusalem that breed this fundamentalism. I see an Israeli government that recognizes the dangers, but refuses to take decisive action in order to preserve its government coalition.

There is a dangerous elephant in the room, and someone had better acknowledge its existence before it tramples the rest of us, i.e. Israel and Diaspora Judaism.

Racism condoned by Israel and U.S. Jewish Leaders
1/20/04

Religion and nationalism can be easily distorted. Both involve immense emotional commitments as well as a certain amount of suspension of disbelief. The combination of religion and nationalism increases the chances of distortion exponentially.

Meir Kahane was an example of the above truism. His brand of Jewish nationalism coupled with virulent hatred of Arabs produced a movement that was outlawed in Israel by the Knesset as a terrorist organization and subsequently designated by the U.S. government as a foreign terrorist organization. Even conservative leader Abe Foxman of the ADL branded the Kahane movement "a cult of violence and racism that violated both the substance and spirit of Jewish tradition."

Now both the *Jerusalem Post* (conservative) and *Haaretz* (liberal) report that the Israeli government is spending one million shekels to pave an access road to a West Bank site that will accommodate a yeshiva dedicated to the teachings of Meir Kahane. Concurrent with this announcement, *Maariv* reported that Kach, the movement that perpetuates Kahane's racist views and is building the yeshiva, held a Hanukkah celebration where it awarded prizes for student essays. The winners received either a framed picture of Kahane or a key chain with a picture of Dr. Baruch Goldstein, who massacred 29 Palestinian worshippers at the Tomb of the Patriarchs in Hebron in 1994.

Kahane was as much an authentic American Nazi and racist as David Duke is today. The shame is that he was not the product of a fringe southern state, but was nurtured within the great Jewish community of New York City.

The essence of nazism was dehumanization. I have visited Auschwitz and contemplated the commandant's home immediately adjacent to the main gate. There a cultured, educated gentleman listened to Brahms and Beethoven while his minions gassed my people and used our remains to process soap and other utilitarian objects.

How could a man who loved his children and the sensitivity of art preside over this human nightmare? The process of dehumanization allowed this. When the Nazis decided that Jews were animals rather than human beings, it became acceptable to treat us accordingly. Even in the United States it is not illegal to kill cats and dogs and other animals. Some we will kill to eat, while others we kill to use their skins (which we designate as leather) as the Nazis used Jewish skins for lampshades.

Meir Kahane was a practitioner of nazism in that he openly labeled Arabs as pigs and dogs. He once began a speech to Arab and Jewish students at Hebrew University with the greeting, "Welcome Jews and dogs." Kahane was taking the first step into a new Auschwitz where Jews would be commandants. We did not survive the Holocaust for that destiny.

It is ironic that Kahane coined the phrase, "Never Again,' and never understood its real meaning. The lesson of the Holocaust is not, "look what the *goyim* did to us Jews," but rather that in each and every human being there is the potential for evil and that we must purge ourselves of such potential.

Talmudic Judaism understood this when it spoke of the evil and good inclinations in every human being. The daily headlines teach us the potential for Hindus to dehumanize Moslems in India, for Catholics and Protestants to dehumanize each other in Northern Ireland and for both Jews and Palestinians to dehumanize each other in the Middle East. It is truly ironic that Kahane was one of the first racists to begin the process of dehumanization after Auschwitz, starting us on the descent into hell. His personal motto should have been "Once Again," not "Never Again."

It is bad enough that the grave of Baruch Goldstein, the Kahane movement's favorite martyr after Kahane himself, has become a shrine for the faithful. Now we have the Sharon government facilitating the opening of a yeshiva that teaches the very racism that produced a mass murderer such as Goldstein. Is there no end to the shame that this Israeli government brings upon itself and upon Judaism?

And the American Jewish establishment must share the shame. The opening of this racist yeshiva with the help of the Sharon government is little reported in our American Jewish press. It is little discussed in the classrooms of our synagogues or in the halls of our Federation offices. As a community we respond by silence, either out of embarrassment, hidden feelings of sympathy with the Jewish racists, or just plain ignorance.

Unfortunately many Jews agree with the moral miscreant who officiated at Baruch Goldstein's funeral when he said that the lives of a thousand Arabs are not worth the fingernail of a single Jew.

As repugnant as this statement is to liberal Jews, we cannot self-righteously condemn it without saying our own *al chet* over the fact that we have allowed racism to be nurtured in our community and that we have countenanced leadership which has been morally lax on this issue. The American Jewish community should protest one shekel spent on facilitating a Kahane racist yeshiva, let alone one million shekels. Where are the voices of our leadership? Ask AIPAC, ask the Conference of Presidents, ask ADL or the AJC. Where are they when we really need them for moral leadership?

The Israel Lobby

The Israel Lobby Unmasked
4/18/06

Oh my God, someone has publicly outed the "Israel Lobby." For those readers who do not closely follow the machinations in academia, let me explain. John Walt, the academic dean of the Kennedy School of Government at Harvard and John Mearsheimer, a political scientist at the University of Chicago, have written a blistering critique of the Jewish lobby, focusing primarily on AIPAC.

Their main complaint is that "the thrust of US policy in the region (the Middle East) derives almost entirely from domestic politics, and especially the activities of the 'Israel Lobby'." There is much with which to disagree in the paper, including their assertion that Israel is not a vital strategic asset (there are many generals who would challenge that assertion). But there is also much truth, if we would only be honest with ourselves.

The usual suspects have jumped on the bandwagon, not merely to criticize but to condemn the paper in vitriolic words. Representative Eliot Engel, a Democrat who represents the Bronx, declared it "anti-Semitic and anti-Zionist drivel." This is somewhat ironic since one of the complaints of Walt and Mearsheimer is that anyone who criticizes Israel is automatically labeled anti-Semitic. The ubiquitous Alan Dershowitz accused the authors of cribbing from neo-Nazi Web sites, which was a sophisticated way of tarnishing them as anti-Semites without using the phrase. The right-wing *New York Sun* called it a "scandal" and warned that if Harvard is not careful, "the Kennedy School will become known as Bir Zeit on the Charles."

The *Forward* was most responsible. Before writing an extensive critical analysis of the paper it acknowledged that "the authors are not fringe gadflies but two of America's most respected foreign-affairs theorists…Though it's tempting, they can't be dismissed as cranks outside the mainstream. They *are* the mainstream."

I agree with Walt and Mearsheimer that AIPAC controls our American government policy toward Israel. But in their paper the two political scientists point out that, "In its basic operations, the Israel Lobby is no different from the farm lobby, steel or textile workers' unions, or other ethnic lobbies. There is nothing improper about American Jews and their Christian allies attempting to sway US policy; the Lobby's activities are not a conspiracy of the sort depicted in tracts like the *Protocols of the Elders of Zion.*"

Coming from South Florida, I am acutely aware that our government policy toward Cuba is dictated by the Cuban Lobby. Why else would we have such an absurd opposition to Castro? If we can make peace with Red China and the "evil empire" of the Soviet Union, why do we continue an embargo against an obscure communist island, if it were not for domestic political pressure? So it is with the Jewish domestic lobby. My complaint is that the self appointed Jewish leaders who control AIPAC and other positions of power within the Jewish community do not represent the best interests of Jews, Israel or the United States in the long run.

Let's zero in on AIPAC. It is controlled by right-wing, rich Jewish neo-conservatives. As one manifestation of the truth of this assertion one merely has to look at its annual meeting this past month. At a time when Vice President Cheney's popularity has dropped below 20 percent the 4,500 delegates to the AIPAC convention gave him a standing ovation for almost a minute before he even opened his mouth and then proceeded to give him 48 rounds of applause in a 35 minute speech. (As my fellow columnist Leonard Fein pointed out, that's once every 43.7 seconds). Considering that 75 percent of American Jews voted for Kerry, it is obvious that these people are out of the mainstream of Jewish thought.

At the same conference, preceding the recent Israeli elections, these delegates were addressed by Ehud Olmert (Kadima), Amir Peretz (Labor) and Benjamin Netanyahu (Likud) by video link from Israel. Olmert and Peretz received polite applause. The AIPAC delegates cheered enthusiastically for Netanyahu, especially when he presented his hard line that was overwhelmingly rejected by the Israeli electorate. Once a great organization, today AIPAC does not even represent the feelings of the average Israeli, let alone the average American Jew.

This American Jewish neo-conservatism is unhealthy not only for America but for Israel as well. A prime example: The Israeli press reports that Israel is trying to find a way to deal with the Palestinians while not dealing with Hamas. Official public statements aside, they realize that they cannot cut off all contacts with the Palestinians and that the world cannot discontinue financial help; otherwise Israel will find a million starving Palestinians on its border, and this will not lead to peace or security for Israel. Privately the Israeli government was against the Palestinian Anti-Terrorism Act (the Ross-Lehtinen-Lantos bill) which recently passed the House of Representatives. It would cut off all American contacts with the Palestinian Authority, even with its president Mahmoud Abbas, who is a moderate seeking peace. Despite Israel's private reservations, AIPAC not only pushed this bill, it was instrumental in writing it. Even though the AIPAC candidate lost in Israel, he won in the US House of Representatives. Hopefully, the Senate and the White House will correct this.

Beware that you are reading treasonable material. If you "out" the Israeli lobby and you are gentile, you're branded an anti-Semite; if you are Jewish, you're obviously a self-hating Jew. The Jewish establishment abides no criticism of Israel. You don't agree with me? Take this example: last month a pro-Palestinian play entitled, "My Name is Rachel Corrie" was to open at the New York Theatre Workshop, a "progressive" company on East 4th Street. The play is based on the writings of a young British girl who was crushed to death by an Israeli bulldozer when she was protesting the demolition of Palestinian homes in Gaza two years ago. Although the play was widely praised in London last year, it never opened in New York. The theatre producers spoke to the ADL and other Jewish leaders, including big-money Jews on its board, and that was the end of that. But, of course, we don't "censor" discussion concerning Israel. We just politely give our opinions and the voice of the other side disappears.

Another example: 400 rabbis, including myself, signed a letter sponsored by Brit Tzedek v'Shalom that appeared in the *Forward* this past month. It was a mildly liberal statement that proclaimed that "we are deeply troubled by the recent victory of Hamas," but went on to urge "indirect assistance to the Palestinian people via NGO's, with the appropriate conditions to ensure that it does not reach the hands of terrorists." Pretty mild stuff. Yet pulpit rabbis across this country who signed the letter have reported a concerted effort to silence them. The letter has been branded a "piece of back-stabbing abandonment of the Jews of Israel." Synagogue boards have been pressured to silence their rabbis by that loose coalition called the "Israel Lobby."

Just another example of the Jewish establishment stifling any discussion of Israel that does not conform to the neo-conservative tenets of AIPAC and its cohorts. Beware of these self-appointed guardians of Israel and Jewish values. In the end they will destroy everything that makes Judaism a compassionate religion, and if in their zeal they do not destroy Israel, they certainly will not make it more secure.

How Powerful is the Israel Lobby?
9/18/07

Last year two respected political scientists, Stephen Walt (Harvard) and John Mearsheimer (University of Chicago) published a 90-page critique of the Israel Lobby in the United States in the London Review of Books. It caused a great stir in the Jewish community with many claiming anti-Semitism. I read their entire report and came to the conclusion that, although I disagreed with many of their arguments, they had some core truths to tell. I shared my opinions in a column in April of 2006.

Now Walt and Mearsheimer have expanded their thesis into a heavily documented 484-page book with 108 pages of footnotes. In response the Jewish community has circled the wagons as if being attacked by wild-eyed, head-scalping Indians (with apologies for the stereotype of Native Americans). Simultaneous with Walt and Mearsheimer's book, Abe Foxman, the self-appointed defender of Jewish political correctness, has published a rejoinder book entitled, "The Deadliest Lies – The Israel Lobby and the Myth of Jewish Control."

It's really hard to deny that the Israel Lobby is effective. In parlor meetings with only Jews present AIPAC raises money on the very claim that it is the most effective lobby in Washington. And then there are the academicians that deny the effective nature of any lobby. George Friedman, writing in the Strafor Geopolitical Intelligence Report argues that "both Israel and the United States are simply pursuing their political interests and that things would go on pretty much the same even without slick lobbying…Beyond its ability to exert itself on small things, the Israel lobby is powerful in influencing Washington to do what it was going to do anyway."

This argument contradicts everything we know about the importance of special interest lobbyists in Washington, from the farm lobby to the oil lobby to the Cuba lobby, (which has certainly changed American foreign policy). Friedman is telling us that money doesn't talk in Washington, which is contrary to everything we have learned in the past decade.

M.J. Rosenberg, who works for the Israel Policy Forum, a pro-peace, pro-Israel think tank, writes: "I spent almost 20 years as a Congressional aide and can testify from repeated personal experience that Senators and House members are under constant pressure to support status quo policies on Israel. It is no accident that Members of Congress compete over who can place more conditions on aid to the Palestinians, who will be first to denounce the Saudi peace plan, and who will win the right to be the primary sponsor of the next pointless Palestinian-bashing resolution. Nor is it an accident that there is never a serious Congressional debate about policy toward Israel and the Palestinians. Moreover, every president knows that any serious effort to push for an Israeli-Palestinian agreement based on compromise by both sides will produce a loud (sometimes hysterical) opposition from the Hill."

Last week my colleague and friend Zel Lurie in his *Jewish Journal* column conceded that "the Israel lobby is strong and effective. It has produced no less than 34 vetoes of Security Council resolutions critical of Israel since 1982." But he pointed out that "when their message contravenes the Administration they lose," implying that it really does not change pre-set American policy, which is a variation of Friedman's argument in the Geopolitical Report.

Zel cites the 1981 AWACS controversy when the Israel Lobby was stifled in its opposition to the Reagan administration's sale of AWACS, sophisticated radar system planes, to Saudi Arabia. He quotes with approval from George Shultz's introduction to the Foxman book: "Jewish groups are influential ... But the notion...that U.S. policy on Israel and the Middle East is a result of their influence is simply wrong." Zel comments, "George Shultz should know. He was President Reagan's Secretary of State. He was a key player in the sale of AWACS to Saudi Arabia." To me the AWACS sale only proves that the Israel Lobby is not omnipotent. When it runs up against other powerful lobbies, such as the industrial-military-complex lobby that wants to sell airplanes to Saudi Arabia, or when other powerful American needs intervene, it occasionally loses.

The Jewish community can attempt to deny Walt and Mearsheimer's contention that there is a powerful Israel Lobby in Washington, but this negates everything we know about how Washington works. If this were really the case, many rich Jews have been wasting their money these past 25 years supporting AIPAC and the lobbying efforts of other Jewish organizations such as the AJC. They earned their money because they're smart. They know reality when they see it.

AIPAC Bares its True Colors
7/29/08

This past month 7,000 Jews attended the annual AIPAC conference in Washington. Without doubt, AIPAC is the most powerful American lobby working on behalf of Israel. The real question is not its power but its wisdom – in the long run is it healthy for Israel or does it hinder the peace process, which is Israel's only guarantee of long-run survival?

There are arguments on both sides of this question, but an easy way to assess AIPAC is to look at the response of its membership to its visiting speakers. The open display of emotion tells us where these people are coming from. Sometimes the leadership tries to hide its real feelings in an attempt to protect its political access in Washington.

Behind closed doors the AIPAC leadership lectured the delegates to receive both McCain and Obama warmly since they want to protect access to either man when he resides in the White House. Despite this warning it was evident who the 7,000 delegates preferred. Their repeated standing ovations for McCain indicated that if it were up to this group of Jews McCain would be our next president. It would be fair to say that AIPAC supporters are out of step with the Jewish community since 75 percent of Jews voted Democratic in the last presidential election and the expectation is that will be the same this coming November.

McCain's message was frightening. He attacked Obama for his refusal to support a congressional resolution declaring the Iran Revolutionary Guard a terrorist group. Most observers believe that this is a neocon strategy preparing this country for an attack on that country. Indeed, the conservative columnist George Will stated on Chris Matthew's MSNBC program that if elected he expected McCain to attack Iran. The AIPAC delegates ate this up with a standing ovation.

McCain also indicated that he was against a quick withdrawal from Iraq, again to a standing ovation. This does not surprise me. I would venture that not one delegate present had a child or grandchild in harm's way in Iraq. We leave the war to be fought by poor rural whites and ghetto African-Americans. No Jewish blood at stake there.

In contrast, there was only scattered applause when Obama stressed that Iran should be handled with economic sanctions and diplomacy (something that seems to be working for North Korea). When Obama called for a West Bank settlement freeze he was met with total silence – repeat, total silence -- this in spite of the fact that a majority of Israelis support a settlement freeze and an overwhelming majority of American Jews believe that continued settlement of the West Bank will doom the prospects for peace.

The AIPAC delegates did give Obama a standing ovation when he pandered to them and spoke of the need for an undivided Jerusalem, in spite of the fact that every knowledgeable Middle East expert asserts that unless there is a Palestinian presence in a city that is as holy to them as it is to us there will never be peace. Without a compromise on Jerusalem we Jews will make history by outlasting the Hundred Year War.

Two hundred years from now my great-great grandchildren will be discussing how to reach peace, assuming that Israel isn't wiped out by an errant nuclear bomb before that time. The next day the Obama camp softened his stance, declaring that the status of Jerusalem is up to the Israelis to decide. But pander he did, which shows that even good men make mistakes in their grasp for power.

Little noticed by the mainstream press, the AIPAC executive committee, which includes representatives from major Jewish groups, made 14 changes to their Action Agenda introduced by Zionist Organization of America (ZOA) president Mort Klein. Klein believes in a Greater Israel which excludes the existence of a Palestinian state. The *Forward*, which covered the conference in depth, commented that the changes "were minor, but gave a right-wing tint to the platform."

How much more right-wing can they go? Pastor John Hagee, an ardent Christian supporter of Israel who received a standing ovation at last year's AIPAC conference when he proclaimed that Israel should not relinquish land for peace ("not one inch, not one inch"), was absent this year. He is the minister that McCain had to disavow because he called the Catholic Church "the whore of Babylon."

It has come to light that Hagee also stated in one of his past sermons that the Holocaust was brought upon the Jews by God as punishment for their coming to America after Herzl promulgated his Zionist platform, rather than going to Israel. But when his name was mentioned at the convention he, also, received a standing ovation.

Do these Jews not have any consideration for our Catholic friends or for the memory of the Holocaust? Does Hagee's support of a right-wing Israeli agenda trump common decency and morality? If you belong to AIPAC the answer is obvious.

PART THREE – UNITED STATES
Right of Privacy

Jubilee Year for Louis Dembitz Brandeis
2/13/07

Brandeis University has announced a year-long Jubilee in recognition of the 150th birthday of Louis Dembitz Brandeis. I want to add my praise and comments.

Brandeis was born in 1856 to a prominent Louisville, Kentucky family. His uncle, Lewis Dembitz, a lawyer and scholar, presented one of three nominating speeches for Abraham Lincoln at the Republican Party Convention of 1860. Brandeis' middle name was originally David, but he changed it to Dembitz as part of his tribute to his uncle.

At a very young age it became apparent that Louis Brandeis was destined to make his mark. He graduated high school at age 14, studied in Europe and then graduated from Harvard Law School before he reached his 21st birthday as number one in his class with the highest marks ever recorded at that institution.

He was "Jewish" but not observant. He was married by his wife's brother-in-law Felix Adler, an ex-rabbi who founded the Ethical Culture Society. Brandeis traced his real connection to the Jewish community to two events. In 1910 sixty thousand Eastern European immigrant Jewish workers, members of the New York Cloak Operators Union Local of the ILGWU (International Ladies Garment Workers Union), went on strike against the German Jewish manufacturers. The strike was a two-month bloody affair that tore the Jewish community apart, more than a book by an ex-president. Finally both sides turned to Louis Brandeis, by then a well-known Boston attorney, to mediate a settlement.

On Friday, September 2nd Brandeis announced his "Protocol of Peace" that gave the workers a 50-hour work week, wage increases and a preferential union shop. Irving Howe in "The World of Our Fathers" describes the intensity. As soon as word of the agreement reached the East Side, people started streaming toward the square in front of the *Forward* building on East Broadway. That paper reported: "Everywhere men and women, old and young, embraced and congratulated one another on the victory. It was early morning, Saturday, September 3, before the streets were emptied of the masses of humanity ... Saturday afternoon, trucks decorated with flags, with bands of music, and carrying crowds of cloakworkers drove through the streets, announcing the strike had been settled."

It was in this milieu that Louis Brandeis, the wunderkind from Kentucky, forged his identity with the Jewish masses newly arrived from the *shetl*. The second event that helped cement his Jewish identity was his meeting Jacob DeHaas, then editor of the *Jewish Advocate* in Boston, who had served as Theodore Herzl's secretary in London. DeHaas was the catalyst who turned Brandeis into a life-long Zionist. Brandeis served as the president of the Zionist movement in the United States from 1914 to 1918. He resigned his leadership role in 1921 in a power dispute with Chaim Weizmann (who later became the first president of the newly formed State of Israel in 1948). Brandeis retained his membership if not leadership and left bequeaths in his will to the movement.

Of course, we celebrate Louis Dembitz Brandeis as the first Jew to serve on the Supreme Court. President Wilson made that appointment in 1916, not without great controversy. Conservatives opposed him not so much because he was Jewish but because he was an acknowledged social progressive who opposed monopolies and big business control of the legal system. (Those were the times when the Supreme Court ruled consistently against regulation of business and in favor of unfettered property rights.) After a four-month battle he was finally confirmed by the Senate on a 47-42 vote.

But his significance to the Court is not his "firstness" but his brilliance. Brandeis is remembered in legal circles for two outstanding contributions. In 1908, arguing before the Court he submitted a brief that contained merely two pages of legal reasoning and over 100 pages of sociological data on the harm of long workdays to women. It was the first time that empirical evidence of this kind was presented to the Court. Today it is common. It was on such evidence that the famous *Brown v. Board of Education* case in 1954 was decided, outlawing segregated school education. But it was radical in 1908 and in legal circles such an approach is still called the "Brandeis brief."

Brandeis' second legal contribution is the constitutional protection of the Right to Privacy. Such a right is not explicitly stated in the Constitution.

In 1890 Brandeis co-wrote an article in the *Harvard Law Review* making the claim that the Fourth Amendment, which protects people from unreasonable search and seizures, was a personal as well as a property right. In a famous dissent in the *Olmstead* case in 1928 he wrote that the Constitution guaranteed "the right to be left alone – the most comprehensive of rights and the most valued by civilized men... Every violation of the right to privacy must be deemed a violation of the Fourth Amendment."

This Right to Privacy was finally accepted by the Court in 1965 (*Griswold v. Connecticut*) and in 1967 (*Katz v. U.S.*) where Justice Potter Stewart wrote for a nearly unanimous majority (7-1, Justice Thurgood Marshall not participating) that, "The Fourth Amendment protects people, not places," vindicating Brandeis' position back in 1890. It is this privacy right that is the foundation of abortion rights (*Roe v. Wade*) and the right of sexual freedom for gays (*Lawrence v. Texas*). It is also the basis for our protection against illegal wiretapping in the name of national security.

In that famous 1928 dissent Brandeis wrote: "Decency, security, and liberty alike demand that government officials shall be subjected to the same rules of conduct that are commands to the citizen. In a government of laws, existence of the government will be imperiled if it fails to observe the law scrupulously. Our government is the potent, the omnipresent teacher. For good or for ill, it teaches the whole people by its example. Crime is contagious. If the government becomes a lawbreaker, it breeds contempt for law; it invites every man to become a law unto himself; it invites anarchy." Attorney General Gonzales and President Bush should read Brandeis. Louis Dembitz Brandeis' writings are as relevant today as they were almost a century ago.

Brandeis served on the Supreme Court from 1916 to 1939 when he was succeeded by William O. Douglas, another liberal giant. Brandeis died in 1941 at the age 85. He will remain one of the most important American Jews significantly to contribute to this country. As a community we have the right to be proud and to *kvell* during this year of Jubilee commemorating his birth.

Roe v. Wade
5/10/05

I'm beginning to think that I'm reverting to my lawyer persona, having once practiced law. Last week I wrote about the balance of power inherent in the filibuster and two weeks before that about the concept of balance of power vis-à-vis the courts and the legislative and executive branches. I had hoped to leave all of this legal and governmental talk behind, except that I made the mistake of reading David Brooks, the *New York Times* resident conservative columnist (replacing Bill Safire).

Brooks is always challenging if not correct. He calls for the overturning of *Roe v. Wade* claiming that it "set off a cycle of political viciousness and counter-viciousness that has poisoned public life ever since, and threatens to destroy the Senate as we know it."

Brooks argues that he whole abortion issue should have been left to the state legislatures, where "legislative compromises wouldn't have pleased everyone, but would have been regarded as legitimate. Instead, (Justice Harry) Blackmun and his concurring colleagues invented a right to abortion."

He's wrong on two points. If the right of a woman to control her own body is a legitimate personal right, then the Court has an obligation to protect it. Majority rule through the legislature is not the sole criterion of a democracy. If that were so, we would still have laws favoring segregation and slavery in many parts of this country. The courts are there to protect us against majority rule.

Brooks is wrong on count number two – Justice Blackmun did not invent the right to abortion. *Roe v. Wade* was based on a much broader concept called the Right of Privacy. I'll try to describe the evolution of this right without sounding like a lawyer and boring the reader.

The Fourth Amendment to the Constitution provides for, "The Right of the people to be secure in their persons, houses, papers, and effects, against unreasonable searches and seizures..." The early courts considered this a property right, ignoring the phrase "secure in their persons." Thus the Fourth Amendment protected privacy in your home, but not other intrusions concerning your body. In 1890 Louis Dembitz Brandeis (later the first Jew on the Supreme Court, thus Brandeis University) co-wrote an article in the *Harvard Law Review* making the claim that the Fourth Amendment was a personal, not a property right.

In a dissent in the *Olmstead* case in 1928, then Supreme Court Justice Brandeis wrote that the Constitution guaranteed "the right to be left alone – the most comprehensive of rights and the most valued by civilized men... Every violation of the right to privacy must be deemed a violation of the Fourth Amendment." The Court was so distant from Brandeis' reasoning that from 1923 to 1939 it was constitutional to sterilize people against their will after declaring them imbeciles, morons or unfit, thus "protecting" society by taking away their ability to reproduce.

Finally, in 1965 in *Griswold v Connecticut* the Supreme Court recognized a "Constitutional" right of privacy for the first time. The Court decided that the State of Connecticut could not make it a crime to distribute birth control devices. The Court's position was further clarified in 1967 in *Katz v.*

U.S., where Justice Potter Stewart wrote for a near unanimous majority (7-1, Justice Thurgood Marshall not participating) that, "The Fourth Amendment protects people, not places," vindicating Brandeis' position back in 1890. (Another case of a nice Jewish boy making good.)

It is in this context that *Roe v. Wade* was decided in 1973. It applied the Fourth Amendment protection that the government could not take control of our bodies, that we had the right of privacy against government telling us that we could not use condoms or that we had to carry a child against our will. "Hands off the person" was the message, unless it spilled over into the public arena. We have the right to fornicate as we like, but not in the public square. Carrying a child is a personal thing, not a public enterprise.

Here in Florida, this concept was supported by a conservative majority in 1980 when they wrote the Right of Privacy into our state constitution (Section 23) concerning people, as distinct from the privacy of our homes, which is protected by an entirely different section (12). It's really a libertarian, conservative concept – keep the government off our backs, except when absolutely necessary. It also keeps people from using government to foist their particular religious beliefs on others.

The Right of Privacy has been applied by the Supreme Court to protect a person's right to deny unwanted medical treatment (*Cruzan* case, 1990). The next logical step could be the Court's review of a person's right to check out when he or she desires – end of life issues, which are really private decisions. In 1993, to the great consternation of the religious right, the Court ruled in *Lawrence v. Texas* that what homosexuals do in the process of expressing theirs sexuality is protected by the right of privacy, thereby striking down Texas' sodomy laws.

Brooks is dead wrong. Justice Blackmun did not invent a right to abortion. It is merely one decision in a line of reasoning that protects our precious right of privacy. And it was not this case that activated the cultural war that is playing itself out in the fight over the Senate filibuster and judicial appointments this month. It is the whole reasoning behind the right of privacy. The religious right wants to void any right of privacy as relates to the body, even in the privacy of our bedrooms. They want to tell us how to die, how to have sex, how not to protect ourselves against pregnancy (their fight against the morning-after pill) and generally what is moral and immoral. They want to use the government to legislate their religious beliefs. Their great crusade is a subtle Inquisition – they will control our conduct through government fiat. We won't have to convert to Christianity; we'll just have to live the way they do.

Shmuel Ginsberg, Shirley Shapiro & an Unborn Fetus
4/27/04

The mother and stepfather of Laci Peterson stood behind President Bush as he signed the Unborn Victims of Violence Act in the East Room of the White House. For those readers who have been hibernating the last few months, Laci Peterson was the murdered pregnant young woman whose husband has been indicted for the crime.

The religious right has used the anger engendered by this heinous murder to propose laws that protect an unborn fetus both on the state and federal levels. Three more states are in the process of passing legislation, adding to the 30 states that already criminalize the harming of a fetus. Many of these states, including Bush's home state of Texas, define the fetus from the moment of conception.

The momentum in this country has definitely moved toward the right. The feticide bill in Mississippi passed that House of Representatives by the margin of 99-3. The national act signed by Bush received approval in the Senate by the comfortable margin of 61-38 and in the House by an equally comfortable margin of 245-163.

Proponents of these laws deny that they are a veiled attack on the right of free choice protected by Roe v Wade. This dissembling is belied by the prominence that Bush placed on this legislation which covers no more than 10 people out of our population of 280 million. You read it correctly – 10 people. Federal criminal law covers 68 specific crimes, such as drug related drive-by shootings, interstate stalking or an assault on federal property. Annually there are approximately 200 such cases filed. It is estimated that no more than 5 percent would involve a fetus, and possibly even less. Yet this was important to the president and his advisors simply because of its symbolic significance. It was one more step toward the drive to undercut abortion rights.

In signing the national law Bush made it clear that he was "building a culture of life." Senator Barbara Boxer of California offered an alternative to the bill that would have increased criminal penalties for killing a pregnant woman, rather than extending legal status to the fetus. It would   have accomplished the same result and not forged into new legal territory. Currently in many states a hate crime receives increased penalties as compared to the same act if there was no racial or religious motivation. But this did not satisfy the president or his followers, since they were not so much repelled by the crime, as they were interested in creating new legal rights for a fetus.

The ramification of this type of legislation can be seen in the Melissa Rowland case in Utah. Mrs. Rowland refused to have a Caesarean section against the advice of her doctor, resulting in the death at birth of one of the twins that she was carrying. This past month she was charged with murder because of her "depraved indifference" to the rights of the fetus. This is not an isolated case. Over the last 15 years more than 275 similar cases have been brought against women in various states. Most of them have involved drug use during pregnancy thereby endangering the fetus. Higher courts overturned many, but not all, of the convictions, but that can also change.

Now let us ponder a few hypothetical scenarios, as we were wont to do way back in law school. Shmuel Ginsberg is driving his Mercury Marquis down Federal Highway in Fort Lauderdale while talking to his wife, Esther, on his cell phone. She was *hocking* him to stop at Publix for some Metamucil on his way home. In the midst of this conversation, traffic abruptly stops and Shmuel lightly rear-ends Catherine O'Reilly in her BMW Z-3 sports car. Catherine gets out of her car and assesses the damage which is minimal. The policeman duly writes up the accident and they all part on good terms. But Ms. O'Reilly was more upset by the accident than was apparent. When she returns home she has a miscarriage of a month old fetus. Under a state law that defined the rights of a fetus from inception, Catherine, who is now outraged over her loss, presses the prosecutor to indict Shmuel for vehicular homicide, a crime that carries up to 15 years in jail. To make things worse, Shmuel forgot to pick up the Metamucil because he was so upset over the minor accident. Esther was upset, but she was even more upset when they came the next day to arrest her husband. (Lucky for Shmuel, in Florida under Section 782.071 of our state statutes a "viable" fetus is required for vehicular homicide. But this is still a reasonable scenario in many other states that define feticide from inception)

Alternative scenario: Shirley Shapiro, mother of three children and wife of a successful attorney, has a slight problem. She is not quite an alcoholic, but she does drink a little too much at cocktail parties. She claims that this is her release from the burdens of rearing three children, of whom one is autistic. Her drinking is a slight embarrassment to her husband, but her "problem" has not seriously affected their relationship. One Saturday night (after sundown, because Shirley is an observant Jew) she attends a party at a friend's house without her husband since he is out of town on a very important case. While driving home she is involved in an accident that causes serious physical damage to her and the loss of a seven-month old fetus that she was carrying. The policeman administered a Breathalyzer test that showed that Shirley was legally drunk, since she registered .09, just above the legal limit of .08. Shirley did not think that she was drunk, but according to the law she was. The upshot was that Shirley was charged with the murder (second degree) of her unborn fetus, and under Florida law, section 782.071, she can go to jail. The reasoning is that drunken women should not kill their children.

You protest that these are merely hypothetical scenarios that would never actually occur. Don't bet on it. Remember those 275 cases that have already been filed against women who "abused" their fetuses. Ask Melissa Rowland in Utah, who faces life in jail, whether it could happen. The fact is that most cases involving feticide have not been prosecuted, but those that will be prosecuted will involve undesirables, outcasts, illegal residents and other disadvantaged. Suppose that Shmuel Ginsberg were not Jewish but African American and living in some rural county of Mississippi. What if Shirley Shapiro lived in Sh'mini Atzeret, Texas, where there was an anti-Semitic local prosecutor?

The point is that the existence of these laws puts a vast amount of discretion in the hands of local prosecutors. Some of them may belong to certain religious groups that believe that abortion equals murder, and these prosecutions would help in the fight against Roe v Wade, assuming that it wasn't already overturned by the new justices that President Bush appointed to the Supreme Court in his second term.

The bottom line is that giving legal status to a fetus, whether at inception or at a later date, opens the way for a social and ethical revolution that may not be healthy for the Shmuel Ginsbergs and Shirley Shapiros of this world.

Gay Marriage is a Jewish Issue
10/31/06

In the last few months preceding the upcoming national elections for Congress we have seen resurgence in the polemics involving gay marriage. President Bush has once again called for a federal Constitutional amendment to outlaw this. Although it had no chance to pass, it was approved by the Judiciary Committee along party lines. Every Republican voted to bring it before the Senate, including its chairman Arlen Spector. His rabbi should be talking to him. Thirteen states presently ban gay marriage, including Florida. Our state allows homosexuals to be foster parents, but prohibits them from adopting children -- so much for consistency.

This is an issue that will not fade away. Local courts in the states of Washington, California and Maryland have ruled in favor of gay marriage. These decisions will find their way to their respective supreme courts. In New York the highest court ruled in August that the legislature has the right to ban gay marriage. I will comment on that peculiar decision later in this column. Vermont and Connecticut have legalized civil unions, the first step toward full equality. And we all know that the Massachusetts Supreme Court legalized gay marriage in 2003, and to my knowledge civil order in that state has not collapsed, even if the tunnel under the bay did -- maybe it's God's punishment to the liberals in that decidedly blue state.

Let me make two confessions before I delve into this issue. First: I, like most people my age, was reared in a homophobic society. I was taught to deride "sissies" (maybe I should use Arnold Schwarzenegger's term, "girlie boys"). I thought them deviant and I repeated the homosexual jokes that were common to mid-twentieth century, along with ethnic jokes that today we would be ashamed to even think in private. I am no different than the vast majority of Americans who just didn't know better.

Second confession: When the Lambda Legal Defense and Education Fund pushed the original case in front of the Massachusetts Supreme Court I had great doubts about the timing. I worried about a backlash that would give the presidency to George Bush in 2004. And there may be some evidence that this issue helped get him reelected. But that is water over the dam. The struggle has gone too far to have reservations today. We are past the time for gradualism or procrastination. Now is the time to stand up and be counted.

I wonder whether anyone can believe that God would create a human being with an orientation that damns him from birth. Granted that homosexuality is a minority occurrence in nature, but so is left-handedness. We must remember that medieval man considered this an evil affliction, thus the word sinister originally referred to this minority occurrence in nature. But just as left-handedness comes from the genes, so does homosexuality. It is not a choice.

Personally it makes no difference to me whether it is or is not a choice, for I take my stand on the concept of privacy. One can do in private what one wants and the state should not have the right to interfere as long as it does not affect public decorum, health or safety. A marriage contract is a personal, private contract that does not impinge on public decorum, health or safety.

Modern day Judaism has come to the conclusion that the time has come to understand, not to judge, to accept, not to condemn. Both the Reform and Reconstructionist movements now ordain openly gay and lesbian rabbis and approve of gay marriage. The Conservative movement is struggling with this, but it is only a matter of time until it reaches the same conclusion, led by rabbis such as Harold Schulweis and Elliot Dorff. On this issue Orthodoxy is still mired in the Middle Ages or earlier, in Talmudic times. The Talmud declared that homosexuality was the cause of the flood, not a flood, but Noah's flood that destroyed mankind except for Noah and his family. (A nice story, but it shouldn't be taken literally.)

From my perspective as a Reform rabbi, believing that the bible was written by man, I have no trouble saying that the writer of Leviticus 18, verse 22 struck out when he declared homosexuality an abomination. That's the end of the argument. But from the perspective of someone who lives by Halacha, there has to be a way to justify homosexuality within the Talmudic legal tradition. It turns out that there are a couple of ways which, because of space limitations, I will not discuss here.

Again, from my perspective I care not what tactic is used. Halacha, the continuing Jewish legal system that is so prized by the Conservative and Orthodox movements, figured a way to get around other objectionable parts of Torah. Just a few examples: If a child is disrespectful to his parents, he is to be put to death; there should be an eye for an eye in retribution; if one marries a woman and finds that she is not a virgin, she is to be put to death; and slavery is totally accepted in the bible. If the Jewish tradition can undo all of these prescriptions, then it can find a way to undo one simple statement in Leviticus concerning a supposed abomination. As Rabbi David Ellenson, President of the Reform seminary, Hebrew Union College, wrote: "A tradition that demands 'You shall do that which is upright and good' can surely be construed in such a way that the ethos of Jewish tradition can be said to trump a single statement in Leviticus…"

If we want to hold on to our prejudices we can contort logic and reality. The recent decision by New York's highest court (the Court of Appeals) did that in a case upholding the Legislature's ban on same-sex marriage. The Court ruled that (hold on to your seats, for this is a convoluted argument) the institution of marriage is needed to protect children because heterosexuals indulge in reckless procreation, creating children without intention, while homosexuals do not need this institution because they carefully decide to either adopt or to have artificial insemination. Thus gays are more responsible than straights. Therefore the institution of marriage is for the irresponsible straights of this world to protect the unintended children. This is a very weird argument that turns the stereotype of the promiscuous gay on its head. Further, logically it does not require the institution to be limited to straights. As the Chief Justice Judith Kaye wrote in dissent, "There are enough marriage licenses to go around for everyone."

Rob Eshman, the editor of the *Jewish Journal* in Los Angeles, has written: "For centuries non-Jewish law treated Jews as inferiors, and for centuries white people discriminated against blacks, and for centuries straight people have looked upon gays as flawed and fallen and has scape-goated them as well. Gays are now stereotyped as Jews once were, but someday we will look back on our blithe acceptance of discrimination against gays and marvel at our shortsightedness. We who were once Marranos in Madrid, we who clung to the closet of assimilation in order to live without molestation, we should not be the ones who reject the rights of others to be visible."

This is the civil rights movement of our times. We American Jews, who led the fight for equality no matter the color of one's skin, must now lead this nation in the fight for equality no matter the sexual orientation of one's body.

Sexuality and American Law
12/21/04

In our recent elections, besides reelecting President Bush, in their wisdom the electorate in eleven states passed constitutional amendments that barred same-sex marriage. This is a reflection of fundamentalist fervor in opposition to changing sexual mores, a process that started in the sixties and continues unabated. They have stalled the progress on gay marriage, but I doubt that they will stop the trend toward liberality and away from repressive Victorian Christian sexual ethics.

Both the Reconstructionist and Reform movements endorse gay marriage. Generally the Orthodox oppose it, while the Conservative movement is predictably agonizing in the middle. They are desperately trying to find a way to accept what the vast majority of their adherents believe (If God made them gay, it's all right with them), while finessing *halacha* to find a way to say it's in the Jewish tradition. One thing is for sure—neither the bible nor Jewish tradition explicitly prohibits oral sex acts, the foundation of gay and lesbian sexual relations.

The keystone Supreme Court decision that validates the changing sexual morality was the Lawrence case decided in 2003. By a 6-to-3 majority the Court overturned the Texas sodomy law based on adults having a "right of privacy." The police invaded Lawrence's bedroom while he was having homosexual relations and arrested him and his partner. The Court ruled that private sexual acts between two consenting adults are out of the purview of government.

This is an important breakthrough. The distinction between private and public acts is crucial. It applies to heterosexuals as well as gays. What is legal in your home is not necessarily legal in public. One can't decide to have sexual relations in the rotunda of the Town Center Mall, be it hetero or homo. Likewise with free speech. You can shout what you want in your own home, but you can't shout "fire" in a movie theater (assuming there is no fire). The sense of the Lawrence decision is that there are areas of conduct that government should keep its nose out of.

In his uncontrolled and hyperbolic dissent in the Lawrence case Justice Antonin Scalia wrote that the majority decision would ultimately negate state laws against "bigamy, same-sex marriage, adult incest, prostitution, masturbation, adultery, fornication, bestiality and obscenity."

Let's review this list. I was not aware that there were laws against masturbation. I thought that the punishment for that was loss of eyesight from the Almighty. If there are still laws against fornication and adultery, I am not aware of their being enforced. For the record, adultery is always, always immoral. It involves cheating on a spouse. But remember that everything that is personally immoral should not be illegal. The problem with legislating morality is: Who is to determine what is immoral? I don't want to live under a system where other people have the right to tell me what is immoral in private. Society has the right to regulate public conduct (no fornicating or masturbation in the streets) but not in private. They can save their sense of decorum in public but not my soul in my private quarters.

Adult incest affects the public for obvious biological consequences and I know of no one who advocates it or worries about it except Justice Scalia. Bestiality involves regulation of human conduct toward animals that is already addressed in our laws. Animals, like children, must be protected by the law. Obscenity. What is he talking about?

This leaves three categories on Scalia's list: same-sex marriage, bigamy and prostitution. For once, he is correct. If we follow the logic of the Lawrence case to its logical conclusion, all three of these things would be legal.

If you have a legal right to have gay relationships, then it logically follows that these relationships should have the same standing as their heterosexual counterparts, absent proof that they present a burden on society in the public realm. But it was not to protect public space or finances that the laws against same-sex marriage were passed. The motivation was strictly religious -- Christian sexual ethics consider them sinful. But our laws are not supposed to promulgate the morality of any religion. I can see a day when these state constitutional amendments could be ruled unconstitutional (assuming that George Bush doesn't have too many appointments to the Supreme Court).

You don't have to have a doctorate in cultural anthropology to understand that our abhorrence of bigamy or polygamy is totally culturally bound to the European Christian experience. There is nothing inherently moral or immoral about it. Polygamy is rampant in the bible and still legal today in Jewish Sephardic communities. Rabbenu Gershom issued an edict against it in the ninth century, but this was only accepted by European Ashkenazi Jews. Even today in Jewish law (*halacha*) there can be a release from this edict to allow a second wife if the first is insane, adulterous or barren after ten years (you have to fulfill the mitzvah of "be fruitful and multiply.")

About three months ago George Washington Law School professor Jonathan Turley wrote a provocative column in USA Today (of all places) where he challenged the legality of our laws against bigamy and polygamy. The 1878 Supreme Court case (Reynolds v. U.S.) that declared it illegal reeked of cultural condescension, describing polygamy as "almost exclusively a feature of the life of Asiatic and African people." But Turley points out that polygamy has been present in 78% of the world's cultures, including Nepal and Tibet, where one woman has multiple male spouses, and as many as 50,000 polygamists live in the united States Don't get me wrong, I am not advocating polygamy (nor is Turley). I am advocating letting people live their lives and contract with whomever they choose, as long as it is a private matter not affecting the good order of society.

As for prostitution, I'm not advocating that either. But I believe that a woman can do whatever she wants as long as it is in the privacy of her own premises. This would outlaw prostitutes soliciting on the street, but not accepting guests (customers) in her home. This is precisely the British system. It is also the system that is presently legal in certain counties of Nevada where the customer must come to the establishment. I don't think that sex for money is either aesthetic or emotionally enriching, but who is to say that it is immoral (cult prostitutes existed in the bible – Judah thought he was frequenting one of them when he impregnated Tamar). If you believe that it is immoral, don't do it; but the job of government is not to legislate your morality.

Finally, in Scalia's dissent he lamented that, "This (the Lawrence majority opinion) effectively decrees the end of all moral legislation." Good Lord, I hope he's right. It is usually fundamentalists of all religions, in all countries, who attempt to foist their own particular morals upon the rest of us. In this country, given the demographics, it is a born-again Christian ethic. Save me from them and anyone else who wants to invade my right of privacy.

Gay Marriage, Ignoramuses and Brilliant Dilettantes
3/23/04

Sometimes I think that I should not read the newspapers (and I read a lot of them) because it is not good for my blood pressure. God save me from ignoramuses and brilliant dilettantes. The case of the former is Cal Thomas, a nationally syndicated columnist who appears in the *Sun Sentinel* and the latter is the ubiquitous Alan Dershowitz.

The focus of my ire is their stands on gay marriage. It is not so much that they are against it, but their reasoning.

Let's start with Thomas. I should not be so disturbed, because he is to a serious conservative like William Safire or George Will what the *National Enquirer* is to the *New York Times*. Yet I am told that he is one of the most popular columnists carried by the *Sun Sentinel*. I guess that I should not be surprised, for mud wrestling and Nascar racing are also favored by a great many Americans.

Cal Thomas writes: "If you tell me you do not believe in God…then what you are asking me to accept is an idea that has taken hold in your head but that has all of the moral compulsion of a bowl of cereal…The idea of marriage did not originate in San Francisco or Massachusetts…Like it or not, it came from the book of Genesis. The problem is that too many people…no longer accept this historical view of marriage…"

First off, Thomas thinks that all morals come from God, as we in the West understand religion. This would exclude the billion Buddhists and other righteous atheists among us from the family of moral human beings. I'm a believer in God, but I believe that men seeking to find God wrote all of the testaments. Morals rise toward God; they do not come streaming down from him (or her). I don't mind if Thomas and his followers exclude me from heaven because I don't believe in their salvation, but I get very angry when they exclude me from the circle of moral creatures here on earth.

Let's look at marriage in the book of Genesis. Abraham was married to Sarah, but bore a child, Ishmael, with his concubine Hagar. Sarah, in a fit of jealousy, demanded that he send them into the desert away from her. In one of the more cruel acts depicted in Torah, Abraham does that. Abraham also attempts to sacrifice Isaac to God, one of his more insane ideas. You drive away one kid and attempt to kill the other. Sounds like this family was a prime candidate for intervention from the Florida Department of Children and Families. Jacob had two wives (Rachel and Leah) and two concubines (Zilpah and Bilhah) from whom he had twelve boys and one girl, Dinah, whom we don't know much about except that she was raped. These stories are really R-rated. OK, Cal Thomas, here is marriage as put forth in the book of Genesis. Where's your definition? By comparison, gay marriage seems innocuous, and definitely more monogamous.

Now to the dilettante. I was reading in the *Forward* that Dershowitz supported civil unions but not gay marriage. I understand presidential candidates espousing this position, for to do anything beyond that would be political suicide. But what is Alan Dershowitz running for? However, he has his rights, and it is not for me to criticize him on this point. But his reasoning is what drives me to minor outbursts of ranting.

"Marriage is a religious sacrament," he declared recently to the Jewish Council for Public Affairs at their annual meeting in Boston. That may be true for Catholicism and some other Christian groups, but not for Judaism. A sacrament is a Christian religious rite that involves the direct intervention of God. An example is the Eucharist, where the wine and the wafer miraculously transform to the blood and body of Christ. In Catholicism marriage is also a sacrament, in that God is miraculously present at the joining of two individuals. Catholicism is a very rational religion as long as you accept the basic tenets. If God was a part of putting the couple together, then it should be an eternal coupling; therefore, it is reasonable from the perspective of Catholic theology to oppose divorce.

We do not have sacraments in Judaism. We have rituals, which guide us and evoke emotions that lead us to a better life, but they are man-made tools. God does not miraculously visit our homes every time we light the Shabbat candles or say the *kiddush* or participate in a marriage ceremony. In Judaism marriage is a simple contract between two people. Specific rights were spelled out in the traditional *ketubah* (marriage contract). Marriage is called *kidushin*, meaning holy, because a relationship becomes sanctified through a common devotion to the welfare of the partner. It is a contract that enriches one's life through love, as I can attest after almost 44 years of marital bliss, but it is still just a contract and nothing more. That is the reason that divorce was always relatively easy to obtain in Jewish tradition.

I see no reason that we should deny the rights and value of such a contractual arrangement to gays and lesbians. Would we deny them the right to contract for a business or other non-marital relationship under our laws? Why single out this one kind of contract, unless basic Christianity has rubbed off on you as it has on Dershowitz.

What bothers me the most about Dershowitz is that he is a brilliant lawyer. We were classmates at Yale Law School. He was number one in the class. I was not. I truly respect his legal acumen. There is a reason that he teaches at Harvard Law School. But he is a dilettante where Judaism is concerned. He writes about Judaism without formal training or scholarly insight. He produces shallow books that are gobbled up by unsuspecting Jews, simply because he is a celebrity. And he is a real celebrity. He was one of O.J. Simpson's lawyers, and Ron Silvers played him in the movie "Reversal of Fortune" when he was the hero who saved Claus von Bulow from the electric chair. I thought it was a pretty good flick.

But his books do Judaism a disservice. In "Chutzpah" (a #1 *New York Times* Best Seller) his obsession with the Holocaust essentially obliterates meeting God at Sinai as the Master Story of Judaism. His latest book, "The Case for Israel", is a simplistic regurgitation of official Israeli propaganda, mixing truth with historical myth. It negates sophisticated criticism and honest self- appraisal.

What really, really bothers me is that there are serious rabbis and scholars (and rabbi scholars) who produce thoughtful books that are scarcely read because they do not have Dershowitz's notoriety. Good time is wasted reading his trifles instead of these important works. But all of this is an excursus from the topic of gay marriage.

Suffice it to say, God save us from the ignoramuses and brilliant dilettantes of this world.

Church and State

Jefferson & Madison on Church and State
10/21/03

Daily we see attacks on the wall separating church and state. The Bush administration is pumping money into religious organizations under its faith-based initiative program. A demagogic judge in Alabama has found his fifteen minutes of fame by invading the courthouse with the Ten Commandments. But what is even more ominous is the argument of the religious right that the foundation of this country was based on Christianity, i.e. the separation of church and state is a false tradition. To assess this claim we have to look to our founding fathers.

Thomas Jefferson and James Madison were the primary architects of the separation of church and state. Both worked together on the "Virginia Bill For Establishing Religious Freedom." Jefferson wrote it, but was in France when it was debated. Madison shepherded it through the Virginia Assembly. Madison went on to be the father of the Constitution and the Bill of Rights, where the separation of church and state is ensconced in the First Amendment.

Jefferson was a Deist, meaning that he believed in God, but in no established religious dogma. There is a telling incident involving the prominent Jew Colonel David Salisbury Franks that illustrates this point. (Franks was a proud Jew who was president of his synagogue in Montreal before coming to the colonies.) The noted historical painter John Trumbull relates it in his autobiography. The setting was a dinner party with Jefferson, Franks, Virginia Senator William Giles and Trumbull, among others. Giles twitted Trumbull for his Christian beliefs. Trumbull reported that Christianity was "powerfully ridiculed...promising amusement to a rather free-thinking dinner party" and that Giles ridiculed "the character, conduct and doctrines of the divine Founder of our religion."

Trumbull then wrote: "Mr. Jefferson (was) in the meantime smiling and nodding approval on Mr. Giles, while the rest of the company silently left me and my defense to our fate, until at length my friend David Franks took up the argument on my side … I turned to Mr. Jefferson and said, 'Sir, this is a strange situation in which I find myself…at a table with Christians, as I supposed, I find my religion and myself attacked with severe and almost irresistible wit and raillery and not a person to aid in my defense but my friend Mr. Franks who is himself a Jew."

In contrast to Jefferson, Madison was a traditional Christian believer who held religion and particularly Christianity in high regard. He was a graduate of Princeton University, which was founded by the Presbyterian Church. While there he attended morning prayers at six and evening prayers where students took turns singing psalms. All of his teachers were Presbyterian ministers. Religion resonated within him his entire life.   Precisely because he cherished Christianity, he fought for the separation of church and state.

In the Virginia Assembly Patrick Henry introduced a bill to support "teachers of the Christian religion" by a general tax. Madison killed that bill, arguing strenuously that an "ecclesiastical establishment" far from promoting religion had nearly always corrupted and stultified it: "The policy of the bill is adverse to the diffusion of the light of Christianity."

As President, Madison opposed having the government pay military chaplains. He would not issue presidential proclamations for religious holidays and he vetoed a Congressional grant of land to a Baptist church in Mississippi because it comprised "a principle and precedent for the appropriation of funds of the United States for the use and support of religious societies." Unlike Jefferson, it must be remembered that Madison did this in defense of religion, as a devout believer.

To understand Madison's reasoning on the separation of church and state one must understand that he feared the unfettered rule of the majority. That is why, as father of the Constitution, he developed the checks and balances that guide our nation. He also believed that the more religious sects (including non-Christian religions) in America, the greater chance for religious freedom for all. He wrote: "Freedom arises from the multiplicity of sects, which pervades America, and which is the best and only security for religious liberty in any society. For where there is such variety of sects, there cannot be a majority of any one sect to oppress and persecute the rest."

Madison often quoted Voltaire's comment that, "if one religion only were allowed in England, the government would possibly be arbitrary; if there were but two, the people would cut each other's throats; but as there are such a multitude, they all live happy and in peace." When you think about it, that is the basis for the astounding strength of our polyglot nation. Madison expounded this thesis in the 10ᵗʰ Federalist Paper.

A couple of simple conclusions can be drawn from the above. With surety we can say that the two founding fathers of the separation of church and state did not envision this country as being founded on religious tenets, Judge Moore and his Ten Commandments aside. One was mildly antagonistic to religion while the other was a believing and practicing Christian, but both were adamant that religion is a private matter that should not be entangled with the state.

Also, following Madison's logic that the more variety of sects provides the greatest protection, we should welcome Muslim, Hindu, Buddhist, atheist and all other immigrants to our shores. They will strengthen our democracy and the fabric of our society. Unfortunately, we are doing just the opposite in reaction to 9/11. It's time that we begin again to listen to the wisdom of our founding fathers.

I Pledge Allegiance to the Flag…Under God?
4/20/04

An atheist doctor/lawyer recently pleaded his own case before the Supreme Court in an attempt to remove the words "under God" from the Pledge of Allegiance. The Ninth Circuit in San Francisco has already ruled that "under God" turned the pledge into a "profession of religious belief." Still, not many people give the good doctor a chance of winning in the Supreme Court.

Before we begin this discussion it is important to remember that we are not talking about a long-standing American tradition. A schoolteacher wrote the pledge in 1892 for the 400ᵗʰ anniversary of the landing of Columbus. It was not until 1954 that the Eisenhower administration added the words "under God" as part of the McCarthy era hysteria to distinguish us from godless communism. Personal confession: For 50 years I have never uttered "under God" when I proudly recite the pledge. I don't mix my religious beliefs with my patriotism. I consider it an unhealthy exercise.

The Court's decision will depend on its answer to the crucial question as to what "under God" really means. Solicitor General Ted Olson argued before the Court that the pledge is merely a benign form of "ceremonial deism", that it is akin to "In God We Trust" on our coins and currency. But as the writer on religion, Peter Steinfels, has pointed out, "No one is asked to say 'In God We Trust' when counting cash."

An open recitation of the belief in God means a great deal more than "ceremonial deism" to President Bush. In a form letter sent to those who wrote the White House about this case he declared that reciting the pledge is a way of proclaiming "our reliance on God ...humbly seeking the wisdom and blessing of divine providence." He concluded with the wish that "the Almighty continue to watch over the United States of America." To me this is not benign deism, but rather practicing religion and tying God's beneficence particularly to this country. This is the Chosen Nation as distinguished from the Chosen People concept.

Supporters of "under God" point to the fact that it merely reflects our historical tie to the belief in God. God is mentioned in the Declaration of Independence, national anthem, and on our coins. In one respect they are correct. Going back to the colonial period, God played an important role in our society. From the Salem witch trials to the extensive discrimination in practically all the colonial constitutions, God was present. (Maybe not God himself, but the colonial approximation thereof.)

Religious discrimination took many forms. In Maryland, founded by the Catholic Lord Baltimore, when the Protestants gained numerical superiority they disenfranchised Catholics. Georgia also discriminated against Catholics because of its proximity to Spanish Catholicism in contiguous Florida. None of the states allowed Jews to serve in office. This right was secured state by state over time, as late as 1868 in North Carolina.

It was precisely this mixing of church and state that the founding fathers, who wrote the Constitution and the Bill of Rights, repudiated. God is not mentioned in either document, not by happenstance, but by design. Even an opening prayer at the Constitutional Convention was almost unanimously rejected after Benjamin Franklin made the suggestion. Make no mistake about it; our federal government under our Constitution is consciously secular. It was not that the founding fathers were anti-religious. In fact, James Madison, the chief architect of the Constitution, was a deeply religious Christian. But they knew something that the Eisenhower administration ignored: Religion and government should not mix, for the long-run benefit of religion as well as the nation.

Apropos to this, a group of Jewish and Christian clergy oppose having "under God" in the pledge because it invites a kind of civic blasphemy. If God is really not involved in the pledge, as our solicitor general has argued before the Court, then the daily recitation using God's name, "asks millions of schoolchildren to take the name of the Lord in vain." In short, it cheapens religion and God and is as offensive as using God's name as an expletive.

During the oral arguments of this case Justice Sandra Day O'Connor commented (concerning the 9-year old child in question), "Well, she does have a right not to participate." The father responded that opting out was a "huge imposition on a small child." Indeed it is. Sixty years later I still vividly remember my own experience of opting out as a 7-year old. As the lone Jew in a class of Catholics at Roosevelt Primary School (named for Teddy), every Wednesday afternoon I sat alone in an empty classroom when my classmates were excused to attend catechism at the local church (a practice since declared unconstitutional). I remember staring at the teacher, who could not leave for home simply because she had the only Jew in the school in her class. This experience did not enrich my life. Neither did the fact that my high school graduation ceremony ended with the senior class singing Onward Christian Soldiers, during which I stood mute. Has all of this scarred me? Who knows, maybe it was the foundation for my contrariant personality. I do know that it was unpleasant and unnecessary in a country that is supposed to be committed to the separation of church and state.

But how important is "under God" in the scheme of things? How many little atheist children or children of atheists will be affected by this decision? I believe that is irrelevant. It is the principle that counts. We can learn from one of my heroes of colonial America. Thomas Kennedy served in the Maryland legislature in 1822 when he championed his "Jew Bill" that provided equal political rights for Jews in that state. He was defeated for re-election based on this issue in 1824, but two years later he was triumphantly re-elected and his bill was passed. He wrote: "There are no Jews in the country from which I come, nor have I the slightest acquaintance with any Jew in the world…there are few Jews in the United States; in Maryland there are very few, but if there were only one, to that one we ought to do justice."

I believe we owe the same justice to the very few little children or their parents who object to mixing God and nation in the Pledge of Allegiance.

"Public Religion" and the Separation of Church and State
5/16/06

Jon Meacham, managing editor of *Newsweek*, this month published a new book entitled "American Gospel" in which he discussed the separation of church and state. It's an interesting book that really doesn't live up to the glowing endorsements from the likes of David McCullough, Tom Brokaw and Jonathon Sarna that are emblazoned on its back cover. However, he has one major theme that is well worth reviewing and justifies the price of the book.

Meacham writes, "From appointing chaplains, opening legislative sessions with prayer, and declaring days of fasting and thanksgiving, the Founders' public piety has fueled a conservative view that the 'wall' between church and state was erected only recently, in the more secular twentieth century." He goes on for 250 pages to refute the growing religious right's view that the separation of church and state is some new, secular attack on religion and that as an errant Supreme Court decision in 1892 said, "(We) find everywhere a clear recognition of the same truth…this is a Christian nation."

In response, Meacham points out the key distinction between what Benjamin Franklin called "public religion" (opening prayers at public meetings, etc.) and a serious commitment to Christian (or for that matter, any other religious) beliefs. It is well known that Jefferson, Hamilton and Franklin were deists, as distinct from Christians. As Meacham states, for Jefferson and Franklin "the Holy Trinity was seen as an invention of a corrupt church more interested in temporal power than in true religion." Washington, although no deep philosopher, was basically on the same wave length. Bishop William White, who knew Washington well, said, "I do not believe that any degree of recollection will bring to my mind any fact which would prove General Washington to have been a believer in the Christian revelation."

Although Franklin was fond of opening prayers at public meetings, his suggestion that the Constitutional Convention open each session with a prayer was roundly defeated. Yet the Founders had no qualms about establishing the seal of the United States that proclaimed, "*Annuit Coeptis* – God (or Providence) has favored our undertakings" Pull out a dollar bill and you will see the "Eye of Providence" staring out at you. But this phrase comes from the Roman poet Virgil, not from the bible or from the Christian tradition. Such is the sense of "public religion." It praises some amorphous concept that there is something beyond this mortal existence without ever getting into the real realm of religious dogma. This is not satisfactory to the absolute atheist, but it is a far cry from the religious state involvement that Jerry Falwell would want.

The Founders purposely kept the word "God" out of the Constitution. Their determination to keep government separate from religious establishments was reflected in the adoption of the First Amendment. The original Senate version read: "Congress shall make no law establishing articles of faith or a mode of worship, or prohibiting the free exercise of religion." This would have allowed the government to subsidize religious organizations on a non-discriminatory basis as long as it did not prescribe any one article of faith or mode of worship.

In conference with the House, the final version stated, "Congress shall make no law respecting an establishment of religion, nor prohibiting the free exercise thereof." This clearly goes beyond a prohibition against promulgating articles of faith. It clearly says that the state cannot establish, i.e. subsidize, encourage or in any way give special favor to, religion. That created what Jefferson later described as the "wall" that separates church and state. This does not mean that government is antagonistic to religion. It merely means that our Constitution separates these two realms of existence for the benefit of civil authority and for the ultimate benefit of religion.

This was crystal clear to the Founders. President George Washington entered into a treaty with the Muslim nation of Tripoli off the Barbary Coast which stated, "The government of the United States is not in any sense founded on the Christian religion." This treaty was completed under President John Adams and was ratified by the Senate in 1797. There is no record that this statement that defines our government as secular was even debated in that chamber.

In later years, recurrent religious revival leaders have attempted to change this separation. In 1864 the "Christian Amendment Movement" was founded. It appealed to President Lincoln to amend the Preamble to the Constitution to read, "We the people of the United States, humbly acknowledging Almighty God as the source of all authority and power in civil government, the Lord Jesus Christ, as the Ruler among the nations, and His revealed will as of supreme authority, in order to constitute a Christian government, and in order to form a more perfect union…"

This was not only rejected by Lincoln, but by his successors for the next half century, until the movement petered out in the early twentieth century. Such fervor did produce that errant statement by the Supreme Court in 1892, the same Court that four years later declared in Plessey v. Ferguson that racial segregation in public schools was acceptable because separate is equal. Of course that was unanimously repudiated in 1954 by Brown v. Board of Education and if this Christian phrase were to arise today, it, too, would be repudiated (with the possible exception of Scalia and Thomas).

I cannot stress enough that I write as a rabbi, a practicing religionist, and that I believe that this separation of religion and state is not only good for the civil authority but is crucial for the healthy exercise of religion. James Madison, the father of the Constitution, in contrast to Jefferson, Franklin, Hamilton and Washington, was a believing and practicing Christian. Yet it was he who kept the wall of separation high. He wrote in the "Memorial and Remonstrance against Religious Assessments," that government support of religion, far from promoting religious purity, nearly always corrupted and stultified it.

Meacham and most citizens have no problem with "public religion," although I am wary of encroaching religious affirmations in the public dialogue. But I recognize that an opening prayer at an adult function (not in public schools where peer pressure is at its height) is innocuous. Public religion was totally acceptable to the Founders and is not really involved in the current struggles to co-opt our government in strengthening religious establishments. But I also recognize the truth of Meacham's warning: "The line between theology and theocracy, between public religion and consuming religious fervor that could distort the delicate American balance between religious and civic life, is a very thin one."

That is why his book is important, and that is why we cannot for a moment let our guard down against the religious right that is now dominating the Republican Party. Our religious freedoms are at stake.

Save Me -- From Government Support of Religion
2/19/08

Mike Huckabee is running for president and I'm scared. I know that statistically he can't overcome McCain, but I also know that as of this writing he has won five states and that he represents a significant portion of the Republican constituency and that he may end up a vice presidential candidate.

Why am I scared? In 1998 Huckabee preached at a Baptist convention: "I hope we answer the alarm clock and take this nation back for Christ." He said that he had not entered politics "because I thought government had a better answer. I got into politics because I knew government didn't have the real answers, that the real answers lie in accepting Jesus Christ into our lives."

The conservative columnist Robert Novak reported that Huckabee held a fundraiser in December at the Houston home of Dr. Steven Hotze who is "a leader in the highly conservative Christian Reconstructionist movement." This movement believes that America is an agent of God and all political opponents of Christian leadership are agents of Satan.

The separation of church and state is always subject to attack in this country. Last September the First Amendment Center conducted a poll that reported that 55 percent of Americans believe that the Constitution establishes a Christian nation. Only 56 percent of Americans believe that freedom to worship extends to all religions. (You can see why the beleaguered American Muslim community feels insecure.) Finally, the poll showed that fully 28 percent of Americans believe that religious freedom does not apply to groups that the majority of people consider extreme or on the fringe.

Thirty two Republican Congressmen recently introduced a bill honoring American Religious History Week. In its preamble it declares that the Fourth of July was designed as a Christian holiday. I also know that it has no chance of passage, but the very fact of its existence sends chills down my spine.

A reader should not misunderstand my intent in writing this column. I am not anti-religion (C'mon, I'm a rabbi) and I'm not anti-Christian or anti any other religion. I have a deep respect for the theology of Christianity. Obviously I don't believe it, but that does not mean that I don't respect its sophistication. To me religion is a very private thing. Our beliefs are absolutely true for each of us, but not necessarily true for another person. I believe in multiple truths when it comes to the meaning of existence and personal salvation. This is a sophisticated process and no state should intrude into our private journeys.

Americans do not understand that our founding fathers created the separation of church and state to protect religion as well as the state. The "father of the Constitution," James Madison, a devout Christian, understood this well. He remembered his struggles in Virginia where the Anglican majority attempted to stop the Baptists from praying.

In arguing against a Virginia bill that would use tax money to support "teachers of the Christian religion" Madison wrote that an "ecclesiastical establishment," far from promoting religious purity, had nearly always corrupted it. He further wrote: "The policy of the bill is adverse to the diffusion of the light of Christianity." That is why our Constitution does not even mention the word "God." It is pro-religious in the best way – it keeps government out of our religious lives.

But under the faith-based spending program of the Bush administration, this separation is eroding. One example: The government funded Chuck Colson's Inner-Change Freedom Initiative to work with inmates in state prisons. (You may remember Colson as one of Nixon's operatives who then found Jesus when he was incarcerated.) A lawsuit challenged the constitutionality of the program. At trial, inmates testified that they were pressured to convert to evangelical Christianity and that Roman Catholicism and other faiths were ridiculed. Non-Christians were frequently referred to as "lost," "pagan," and "sinful."

The trial judge ruled that the program offered help to converts and eliminated rehabilitation programs for inmates failing to show deference toward the evangelical faith. Judge Robert Pratt wrote: "For all practical purposes the state had literally established an Evangelical Christian congregation within the walls of one of its penal institutions, giving the leaders of that congregation, i.e., Inner-Change employees, authority to control the spiritual, emotional, and physical lives of hundreds of Iowa inmates."

The Court ruled that this was a violation of the separation of church and state as required under the Constitution. This past December the trial court's decision was upheld by the 8th U.S. Circuit Court of Appeals. This particular program was shut down. The question is: how many other faith-based programs in jails and throughout society are operating under the radar, using government money for proselytizing?

I am sure that our born-again president is not too worried about this, but I am.

Church-State and Liberal Religion Issues
4/24/07

Three weeks ago Stanley Fish (a Delray Beach resident and professor emeritus of law from FIU) wrote a guest column in the *New York Times*. He reflected on *Time* magazine's April 2 cover story on "The Case for Teaching the Bible." I concur with his reluctance to allow bible studies in public schools under the guise that the bible can be taught as a secular text, but I disagree with his reasoning.

First, let me comment on that with which we agree. It is folly to allow the camel's nose under the tent. Teaching bible with a secular approach would lead inexorably to proselytizing in the heartland of America. One must understand the mind set of the evangelical Christian movement. They consider this a "Christian country" and deny the concept of separation of church and state. They want to return to the good old times when they ran the public schools as Protestant religious establishments.

They want to return to what I experienced in the mid-fifties as a teenager in West Pittston High School, in the coal regions of Pennsylvania, when I attended "Chapel" (not merely morning assembly) at the beginning of each school day. We sang three Christian hymns, recited the Lord's Prayer (The Lord referred to was Jesus) and listened to a New Testament bible reading. No one asked this little Jew boy what he thought about all of this. It was their Christian country; it was their school. At my high school graduation ceremony, the invocation was by the minister of the First Presbyterian Church and the benediction by the minister of the Immaculate Conception Church. Between these bookends we sang a "Commencement Hymn" (Psalm CXXII) as well as "Onward Christian Soldiers." This happened in my lifetime and it could happen again if we let our guard down.

You may think that I am an alarmist, but I remind you of what happened just this past year at the Air Force Academy. Cadets were pressured by faculty members and chaplains in command to accept Jesus. The football coach displayed a banner proclaiming "Team Jesus Christ." Pressure was put upon cadets to view Mel Gibson's movie, "The Passion of Christ." When a Lutheran Air Force chaplain complained that the cadets were being abused by "systematic and pervasive" proselytizing she was immediately transferred to

Asia. Finally the superintendent of the Academy acknowledged the problem and predicted that it will take years to rid the campus of religious intolerance: "If everything goes well, it's probably going to take six years to fix it," he said. If this is what happened at the prestigious Air Force Academy, what can we expect at nondescript and anonymous local high schools in mid-America if we allow the camel's nose under the tent through "secular bible studies?"

Actually, I don't understand the term "secular bible studies." There is nothing secular about the bible. I also don't understand how the bible can be taught as "literature" as is done in many colleges. Of course, it is literature in that it tells stories. But all of these stories are religious in nature. The underlying premise of the bible is that God controls history. Each and every story is told with the understanding that God is directing the outcome, or short of that, that the moral of the story shows some aspect of God's being, either retribution, forgiveness, omnipotence or omniscience. There are no neutral stories in the bible.

Take as one example the beautiful love story in the Book of Ruth. This was included in the bible to buttress a rising proselytizing movement in Judaism. Remember that in the end Ruth converts to Judaism. Even the prophets, who are seen as the most secular spokespeople in the bible, were speaking out because they believed that God communicated to them. What we consider good social action on behalf of the poor and downtrodden was to them the word of God in action. Today we can draw upon biblical sources as individual inspiration for *Tikun Olam* (the repair of this world) and we can use this motivation in the secular world, but it is religious literature and cannot be taught in a public school in a secular context.

Now to my disagreement with Stanley Fish's reasoning. He comes to the same separation-of-church-and-state conclusion as I, but I believe that he does not recognize that the practice of religion can change over time. He writes: "The truth claims of a religion – at least of religions like Christianity, Judaism and Islam – are not incidental to its identity; they are its identity... Take them away and all you have is an empty shell" (which is a reference to rituals without core beliefs).

That may be a description of fundamentalist religion, whether Jewish, Christian or Muslim, but it denies the reality that religions, like all things in this Darwinian world, evolve. Liberal Judaism (along with liberal Christianity and Islam—and there are liberal forms of Islam) practice the rituals in seeking truth and meaning and some presence of God, or minimally, a definition of God. The rituals of all three religions are then tools in seeking truth, but are not truth claims in themselves. They are not incidental to the religion; they are its identity. They are the tools by which we quest. They are certainly not empty shells.

Fish's contention that truth claims form the basis of all three religions is true for orthodoxy, but certainly not for liberal Judaism. Only personal truths can be found in liberal religions (a truth to sustain our personal existence, but not a truth that we insist all people live by), and that truth for the individual is found at the end of the quest. The only given is the inherited rituals that help us along the searching path. It is also important to realize that these rituals are not dogma in that each generation can accept the inherited rituals, discard them or modify them. In the practice of liberal Judaism, the rituals are tools, not laws of God.

But this is an academic carp. Fish is absolutely correct that the bible should not be taught in public schools. Keep the door tightly shut or we may end up back in West Pittston High School.

The Supreme Court and the Ten Commandments
12/14/04

We can thank or damn the former Alabama Chief Justice Roy Moore for the fact that the Supreme Court is about to rule on the legality of having the Ten Commandments displayed in the courtroom or on government property. Although the Court refused to hear his case, he inspired local officials across the country to display the commandments, thereby engendering over 30 lower court opinions. Slightly more than half of these ruled them unconstitutional. The rest agreed with Moore and company.

Finally the Supreme Court has agreed to hear two cases together. One from Texas involves a Ten Commandments monument that was given to the Texas Legislature in 1961 by the Fraternal Order of Eagles and has been on display on public property since then. The Eagles thought that the commandments offered a personal code of behavior that would reduce juvenile delinquency. The Fifth Circuit Court of Appeals stated that this was evidence of a lack of religious purpose, but in upholding the constitutionality of the monument commented that, "religion and government cannot be ruthlessly separated." Of course, many of us firmly believe that is precisely what is required, for the well-being of religion as well as government.

In the Kentucky case the Sixth Circuit ruled that a plaque of the Ten Commandments in the courthouse was unconstitutional even though it was surrounded by plaques of the Declaration of Independence and other public utterances. The Court cut to the chase and declared that the "predominant purpose for the displays was religious."

The last time the Supreme Court ruled on the Ten Commandments in 1980 it declared in a 5-to-4 decision that they could not be displayed in a public school classroom. Even the Texas solicitor general, arguing in favor of the Eagles monument, distinguished his case from that earlier decision by admitting the possibility of "a potentially coercive schoolroom setting," something that we do not have in the two cases before the Court at this time. In the 1980 decision Justice John Paul Stevens voted with the majority that held that the commandments could not be displayed in the classroom while Justice William Rehnquist voted in the minority. This gives us a clue as to how they will vote in the present case, but there are seven other justices that are unknowns.

Let's take a close look at the Ten Commandments. First, there are really 13 statements (they are not commandments in Hebrew *–aseret hadevarim* translates as "the ten utterances or things"). For traditional Judaism the whole of Torah was revealed by God, not just these utterances. The genius of our religion is not in broad philosophical statements but in the nitty-gritty of following 613 commandments. Actually, even wtihout the Ten Commandments Judaism would still be a highly moral religion based on extensive laws of ethical conduct found both in Torah and Talmud.

Getting back to the 13 statements, religions codify them differently. Roman Catholics and Lutherans combine the first two statements into one, while other Protestant groups and Judaism consider them separate commandments. The question is, will we have different versions of this "sacred" text in different courthouses, depending on whether we are in Catholic or born-again Protestant territories?

Please tell me what is so uplifting in the second commandment (by the Jewish count): "You shall have no other gods before me…You shall not bow down to them or serve them. For I the Lord your God am an impassioned God, visiting the guilt of the fathers upon the children, upon the third and upon the fourth generations of those who reject Me…" Is this exalting religion? The prophet Ezekiel felt compelled to correct this at a later date when he says that God does not punish children for the sins of their fathers.

The last commandment is also problematic. It proscribes coveting your neighbor's wife. Although this is found in our Torah, rabbinic Judaism went on to define sin as acts, rather than thoughts. You can covet all that you want, as long as you don't act deceitfully and commit adultery. Human sexuality is understood and maturely accepted by Judaism. It is Christianity in the New Testament that has Jesus proclaiming that he who thinks as an adulterer is an adulterer. There goes the human race down the road of sinning. This was President Jimmy Carter's confession in his famous *Playboy* interview. He admitted that he had thoughts of adultery, but then said that Jesus died for his sins and that his belief in Jesus wiped clean his unclean thoughts. Judaism basically says that you can think what you want, just don't act. When religion brands thoughts as sin we move into a Christian realm that produced the Inquisition and the Salem witch trials. When you ponder these things, it makes you wonder what's so great about the Ten Commandments.

There are many other philosophical problems with the Ten Commandments that I cannot discuss without turning this column into a book. But what is really at stake before the Supreme Court is whether fundamentalists, Jewish and Christian, can project the concept that our laws are based on revelation from God. A Jew, David Klinghoffer, writing in the *Forward*, comments, "as the Talmud realizes, there are two ways to keep a country ordered and peaceful: The people might be restrained either by fear of the government, or out of respect for an unseen lawgiver – God."

The problem with this kind of reasoning is that you then turn to the bible to determine what God really thinks. Is God for or against free choice, gay rights, capital punishment etc.? This is what is happening in the born-again Christian community when they use the shorthand, WWJD. That stands for What Would Jesus Do? You look for answers to complex problems by running to scripture or your local minister. This is a road that leads to a Taliban state.

And let me be perfectly clear. I fear Jewish fundamentalists as much as I do the Christian and Muslim variety. Whenever religion begins to break down Jefferson's wall of separation between church and state, basic human rights are in jeopardy. If you don't believe me, look at Israel. The lack of church-state separation there has produced a stagnant variety of Judaism, but equally important, it has oppressed all forms of our religion that are not fundamentalist.

We must not forget that the mixture of government and religion is not only bad for dissenters and members of non-recognized religions, but it is bad for the dominant religion. Who today thinks that the Inquisition or the Salem witch trials were good for Christianity? James Madison, the father of our Constitution, a practicing and believing Christian, knew this and he consciously crafted a document that has no mention of God.

It is this greater consideration of how we keep religion, any religion, from imposing its beliefs into settings that should be reserved for governmental functions that the Supreme Court will have to decide in these cases. It is not just the ten utterances, or the Ten Commandments, if you insist, that are at stake. This decision will give us a look at where this country is heading in the constant battle to keep religious practice in the homes and houses of worship and out of the faces of fellow citizens.

Footnote to the above in 5/31/05 column:

The arguments in these cases and the give-and-take by the Supreme Court Justices back in March starkly presented the issues. To begin, Justice Antonin

Scalia expressed the conservative view. He called the Ten Commandments "a symbol of the fact that government derives its authority from God. That seems to me an appropriate symbol to put on government grounds." I take exception to this argument. Someone should remind Justice Scalia that the word "God" was purposely omitted from the Constitution by our founding fathers. It was not an anti-religious decision. Most of the framers were devout Christians, including James Madison, the "father of the Constitution." The deliberate deletion of a reference to God reflected that our legal system is based on a social contract between the people and those governing. God does not play a role in civil government. If God did play a role we run the danger of ending up with an Orthodox establishment akin to the Israeli model, an Afghanistan Taliban rule, or some form of Christian oppression. Our founding fathers consciously kept God far away from power.

The real question with which the Justices wrestled was where the line is between minimal public reference to religion, which has always been with us (In God We Trust on currency, and other passing references) and endorsement of religion sufficient to constitute an establishment, which would be patently illegal under the First Amendment. Justice Sandra Day O'Conner challenged the Duke University law professor arguing the case against the public display of the commandments. She pointed out that the Supreme Court has upheld the practice of beginning a legislative session with a prayer. The lawyer responded, "It can't be that just because a prayer is permissible, everything becomes permissible." He added that a legislature could not affix a large cross on top of a state capitol. Justice O'Conner exclaimed, "It's so hard to draw the line!"

Indeed it is hard. For that reason I have always argued for a complete separation. Many times over the years I have been asked to present the opening prayer at either the Florida Senate or House. I have refused, believing that although this is legally acceptable according to Supreme Court standards, it does not pass muster for me. I have always been afraid that it was only the beginning of the slippery sliding board upon which we will slither toward religion infusing our government institutions. The fact that we are still arguing this in front of the Supreme Court vindicates this position.

The Texas attorney general made an end run around the issue by declaring that the Ten Commandments were not really a religious symbol. He described them as merely a "recognized symbol of law" which has the secular purpose of "recognizing historic influences" on the legal system. This is an argument commonly used by conservatives to pass off their religious symbols on the general public. Haven't you heard that the manger scene at Christmas is really not a religious symbol? Ironically, this argument was destroyed from the ultra conservative Justice Scalia when he responded, "You're watering it down to say the only message is a secular message. I can't agree with you. 'Our laws come from God.' If you don't believe it sends that message, you're kidding yourself." He then added, "I would consider it a Pyrrhic victory for you to win on the grounds you're arguing."

Religious symbols of all kinds should be kept off public property, even though certain kinds of Christmas and Hanukkah symbols are legal under current Court decisions. Even if we have the legal right, we should abstain. Unfortunately there are some Jews, primarily Chabad and the ultra Orthodox who are as eager to tear the wall of separation down as their Christian counterparts. While our neighbors are attempting to put manger scenes on public property, the Chabadnicks are running around placing Hanukkah menorahs on the same public property. If you don't believe that the menorah is a religious symbol, then you may not understand the holiday. We must be consistent. If we want to keep fundamentalist Christians from the destroying the wall, then we Jews should refrain from doing likewise.

Final comment: The Court split the baby in half. It ruled that the display of the Ten Commandments in Texas was legal because the original intent of the gift to the state was not religious in nature. In the Kentucky case the Court ruled it was unconstitutional since, no matter many other symbols accompanied the Ten Commandments, the intent of the state was to support religion. Thus the ruling left the waters muddy and open for future litigation.

Capital Punishment

Capital Punishment and Judaism, Part One
1/27/04

In early January New York Times columnist Bob Herbert wrote two pieces about a teenage black youth who was convicted of murder. Narrowly avoiding death row, he had been incarcerated for 20 years until recently being declared innocent as a result of DNA testing. This is just another incident in the continuing saga of mistaken executions and near misses in the only western civilized country to still countenance capital punishment.

Both this week and next week I want to take a minute of your time and think about this important issue. It will be a welcome relief from agonizing over what will happen in Israel and will actually validate the concept that Judaism really cares about something other than Zionism, albeit that is important.

This is not intended as a *dvar Torah*, but as a rabbi I do have a tendency to arrive at moral conclusions by turning to our ancient documents. It's not a bad habit, and I recommend it to the reader. So let's start with Genesis.

In a fit of jealousy Cain killed Abel, the first murder recorded in the bible. After the killing, the bible states: The Lord said to Cain, "Where is your brother Abel?" And Cain said, "I do not know. Am I my brother's keeper?" Then God said, "What have you done? Hark, your brother's blood cries out to me from the ground! Therefore you shall be more cursed than the ground, which opened its mouth to receive your brother's blood from your hand. If you till the soil, it shall no longer yield its strength to you. You shall become a ceaseless wanderer on earth."

It is interesting that God, the final judge of righteousness did not proclaim a sentence of capital punishment on Cain. In fact, to the contrary, God protected Cain's life. The bible continues: Cain said to the Lord, "My punishment is too great to bear! Since you have banished me this day from the soil, and I must avoid your presence and become a restless wanderer on earth -- anyone who meets me may kill me!" It is at this point that God promises seven-fold vengeance upon anyone who would kill Cain and puts a mark upon Cain to distinguish him, literally to protect his life.

Not only does Cain live, but he goes on to be rehabilitated, living a productive life. He marries, begets children and becomes a builder of cities. In fact he ceases to be a wanderer. Cain becomes the poster boy for the concept of rehabilitation, rather than punishment. It is true that other sections of the bible are not as forgiving. There is the famous Exodus, Chapter 21 passage that proclaims that the penalty shall be a life for a life, an eye for an eye, tooth for tooth, hand for hand, foot for foot, etc. But Jewish law, as expanded in the Talmud, made it eminently clear that this refers to the value of a life, or eye or tooth. This passage was transformed into what is comparable to a modern legal compensation program.

Our sources are never black and white, and it is true that in the specific case of intentional homicide that the bible in Numbers, Chapter 35 allows the death penalty. But then again Jewish law went on to circumscribe this judgment by requiring not one but two witnesses to the actual murder. Even the strongest of circumstantial evidence would not warrant a death penalty.

The Mishna records the famous statement about the Sanhedrin (the High Rabbinic Court from about the first to the fourth centuries): A Sanhedrin that executed more than one person in a week is called a 'murderous" court. Rabbi Elazar ben Azariah states: More than one person in 70 years would be denoted as a murderous court. Rabbi Tarfon and Rabbi Akiva state: If we had been members of the Sanhedrin, no defendant would ever have been executed. This seems to have been the dominant feeling, yet Rabbi Shimon ben Gamiliel responded that if the death penalty would never have been carried out, then Rabbis Tarfon and Akiva "would have been increasing the murders in Israel." This refers to the deterrent effect of capital punishment, something that we will discuss later in this column. But Rabbi Gamiliel is in the definite minority in Jewish tradition. Rabbis Tarfon and Akiva represent the general abhorrence to capital punishment.

Getting back to Cain and Abel, the Midrash Rabbah, written in the early centuries of the Common Era, expand on the story. After God speaks to Cain, Adam (Cain's father) asks him, "How did your case go?" Cain replied: "I repented and am reconciled." Thereupon Adam began beating his face, crying, "So great is the power of repentance and I did not know!" (Genesis Rabbah 22:13) This speaks to the very core of Judaism and to Yom Kippur in particular. If we cannot believe in the power of repentance, why go to *shul* on the High Holy Days?

Surely, the basis of our prayers, the foundation of our commitment to a moral life, is our belief that, although we are imperfect, that we will inevitably falter, that we will sin, yet we are capable of purifying ourselves by asking God for forgiveness, by looking at ourselves not merely in the mirror but into the reflections of our souls – and emerging a new, better person, made in the image of God.

If we allow for ourselves the concept of repentance and spiritual rebirth, can we deny this to others? Yet capital punishment forever negates this potential for moral regeneration. You cannot repent and receive God's reprieve if your life is ended by the death penalty. Putting it simply, dead men cannot be spiritually reborn.

Going from the spiritual to the practical, it is time to confront the argument that capital punishment is needed as a deterrent: Without the knowledge that the killer will pay for his crime with his own life, he will kill with abandon. This is an old argument. It was Rabbi Shimon ben Gamiliel's argument against Rabbis Tarfon and Akiva in the Third Century. If there were really deterrence, we would have to acknowledge society would have a legitimate stake in ignoring the concept of repentance and forgiveness. In other words, deterrence would trump repentance. Unfortunately, deterrence does not work. Most crimes are the result of passion, be it a barroom brawl or a fit of jealousy (as in "what are you doing in bed with my wife!"). The killer does not stop to weigh the consequences of his actions.

Stuart Banner, in his book "The Death Penalty: An American History" points out: In colonial America criminals were regularly sentenced to death not only for murder or rape, but also for less serious offenses such as burglary, forgery and smuggling. The preferred method of capital punishment was hanging, and executions were usually carried out before large crowds and accompanied by a dramatic public ritual that included the delivery of religious sermons. I hasten to point out that they were Christian, not Jewish, sermons. But what was the outcome? Crime was rampant, especially on the frontier, and if public hangings accompanied by religious sermons were not a deterrent, how could private antiseptic injections of lethal poison in an isolated prison act as a deterrent?

Maybe we should telecast the executions on CSPAN or better yet, CBS. But, *gournisht helfen*, there is not deterrence. History has taught us that. Deterrence depends on the fear of dying. Modern day suicide bombers show us that if one believes in his cause, be it legitimate or grotesque, the fear of dying will not deter the act. Capital punishment would not have deterred the atrocities of September 11, 2001.

Next week: Vengeance and the Innocent

The Death Penalty, Vengeance and the Innocent
2/3/04

Last week we reviewed capital punishment from the perspective of Torah and Talmud, as well as the fact that putting someone to death is not a deterrent to others, although we wish it were. Today we review other problems with the death sentence.

The most potent argument against capital punishment is that under a death penalty system innocents are inevitably killed. The novelist and attorney Scott Turow served on the State of Illinois governor's commission that reviewed death-penalty reform. He reported that in that state alone, in recent times 17 men were sent to death row who were later exonerated. He wrote: "The 14-member commission on which I served found persistent problems: false confessions that has been coerced or dubiously reported by the police; mistaken eye-witness identifications; murderers who portrayed innocent people as accomplices; jailhouse informants who became witnesses in exchange for the kinds of favors that clearly tempted lies; and a statutory structure that provided an obvious pathway to arbitrariness in deciding who was to die… Again and again, the cases that seem to present the most compelling facts favoring execution prove, under scrutiny, to contain elements raising doubts."

And this was in Illinois, not Texas or Alabama. The system was so broken that Governor George Ryan commuted the remaining 167 prisoners on death row to life sentences, not without a public outcry. The fact is that we can and do make mistakes, and once you execute someone, you can't say I'm sorry, at least not to him personally. My son Michael put this argument to me when he asked: How many innocent people are you willing to kill to wreak vengeance upon the truly guilty? Ten? Nine? Eight? My answer had to be – not one. I cannot justify killing one innocent person to satisfy my desire for retribution or vengeance, when there are alternative ways to protect society and punish offenders, such as life in prison without the possibility of parole. And certainly a life spent isolated in a 6x8 cell is a living death that many would say is worse than actual death.

The most potent argument for capital punishment is the concept of retribution, or put more bluntly, vengeance. Society, especially those relatives and friends of the victims, deserve to have the closure that capital punishment provides. The hundreds of relatives of the victims of Timothy Mc Veigh were not only relieved, but were fulfilled the day of his execution. I do not fault them. I understand, even if I don't feel, their anguish. This is the only argument for capital punishment that holds a modicum of water in my estimation.

I want to clarify that. It certainly does have emotional validity, in that it is hard to argue that an Eichman or a McVeigh or a Jeffrey Daumer deserves to live. I did not say *kaddish* for any of them, nor did I anguish over their fate. Yet, I understand that to satisfy our longings for their deaths we must keep a system that guarantees that other innocent people will die. To keep the death sentence to satisfy the few unambiguous instances at the expense of the many injustices is just too high a price to pay.

I have to squelch my desire for vengeance for the greater good. I do not have to deny my desire for vengeance, for there are times when it is justified, and I am human and have emotions. But I do have to stop and remind myself that I am a civilized person who can control my emotions for the greater good. The price is just too high for society. After all, the ability to control our emotions is what distinguishes us from the animals. We are made in the image of God, and we should strive to perfect that image.

It is interesting to note that in 1965 forty seven (47) percent of Americans opposed the death penalty while only 38 percent supported it. But by 2001 fully 67 percent supported capital punishment and only 26 percent opposed it. More startling, Jews favor the death penalty by the same 67-27 percent margin. Given our tradition and teachings on this, we can do no better than the rest of the country.

Why this dramatic turnaround? I believe that it is fear. Fear of rising crime rates (which actually are not rising). Fear of a changing society where a lot of people look different than we – they are yellow and black, and speak different languages. It is the same fear that Wasps had of the unwashed immigrants to the East Side who spoke a strange language called Yiddish. Fear for our personal safety. I admit that some of this fear is legitimate. We live in a violent society. But it is no more violent today than in 1965. It is certainly less violent than the colonial period or the nineteenth century, when violence ruled the streets of New York as well as the frontier west.

So why the increase in the support of the death penalty? It is not just fear, but fear coupled with the resurgence of the political conservative right. As "liberal" became a dirty word in American politics, support for capital punishment increased. To be "soft on crime" became a political death sentence, certainly a lesser sentence in the context of losing one's life, but a death sentence for a politician nonetheless. In fact, the death sentence has become a tool for the radical right in its frenzy to reconstitute our society in its narrow image.

The arguments for or against the death penalty are not really important to those who blindly oppose the licentious, permissive liberal ideology that they mistakenly perceive. To them the world is black and white. You are either for or against them. You are either worthy of living or dying. Grays are hard for them to understand. The gray world of life without parole is not satisfying to their palate.

Alas, we are the last civilized, western nation to still impose the death sentence. So the question arises, what are we to do? First, as practicing Jews we should begin perfecting our image of God by making a commitment to contain our own desires for vengeance and to protect society from its own worst instincts. Second, we can follow the lead of the Reform movement by publicly working toward the eradication of capital punishment in our system.

It is about time that we join the rest of the civilized world.

The Odds for Error with the Death Sentence
6/19/07

It happened 22 years ago. The crimes were really heinous. Seven-year-old Tina Urquhart was raped and strangled and her 8-year-old brother, Tyrone, died after four nails were hammered into his skull with a brick. The children's bodies were found in a basement of a rooming house in Plainfield, New Jersey where Byron Halsey lived with their mother.

Halsey, who has a sixth-grade education and severe learning disabilities, signed a confession after 30 hours of interrogation. Miraculously, he was not sentenced to death because a member of the jury did not believe in capital punishment. After 22 years in jail, a month ago Halsey was released from prison when DNA evidence proved his innocence and pointed to a neighbor who testified against him who is currently in prison for sexual assault.

Byron Halsey is alive and free because someone did not believe in the death sentence and because his case was investigated by the Innocence Project created in 1992 by Barry Scheck and Peter Neufeld. It is affiliated with the Benjamin N. Cardozo School of Law at Yeshiva University. As a clinic, students handle the case work while supervised by attorneys.

This is just the latest case in a series of literally hundreds that prove that under a system of capital punishment it is inevitable that innocent people will die for crimes they did not commit. Human frailty guarantees that mistakes will happen. There are basically three reasons for conviction, all of them susceptible to error. They are: confessions, eyewitness identification and scientific evidence (I should say fraudulent science, which is always wrong).

Concerning confessions: John Grisham in his book "The Innocent Man – Murder and Injustice in a Small Town," discusses the case of Jeffrey

Deskovic. In 1990 he was convicted of rape and murder in Peekskill, New York. He was a 16-year-old high school sophomore. He spent nine hours in police custody without his parents or attorneys and without access to food. At the end of the interrogation he was curled up under a desk in the fetal position, sobbing. He signed a confession. Sixteen years later, this past year, he was exonerated based on DNA evidence. Barry Scheck of the Innocence Project reports that in about a quarter of the 201 wrongful convictions that have been overturned with the use of DNA evidence, people had confessed to the crime.

Concerning eyewitness identification: Eyewitness error is the leading cause of wrongful convictions where defendants have been exonerated by later DNA evidence. Human frailty is genetically built into our capacity for observation. Daniel Gilbert, a professor of Psychology at Harvard, in his best-selling book 'Stumbling on Happiness" discusses at length our inability to see things as they really happen. One study that he reports is both humorous and profound. The following is his description of that study:

Even dramatic changes to the appearance of a scene are sometimes overlooked. In an experiment taken straight from the pages of *Candid Camera,* researchers arranged for a researcher to approach pedestrians on a college campus and ask for directions to a particular building. While the pedestrian and the researcher conferred over the researcher's map, two construction workers, each holding one end of a large door, rudely cut between them, temporarily obstructing the pedestrian's view of the researcher. As the construction workers passed, the original researcher crouched down behind the door and walked off with the construction workers, while a new researcher, who had been hiding behind the door all along, took his place and took up the conversation. The original and substitute researchers were of different heights and builds and had noticeably different voices, haircuts and clothing. You would have no trouble telling them apart if they were standing side by side. So what did the Good Samaritans who had stopped to help a lost tourist make of this switcheroo? Not much. In fact, most of the pedestrians failed to notice – *failed to notice that the person to whom they were talking had suddenly been transformed into an entirely new individual.* (Gilbert's original emphasis)

Wow. These are the very same people, including you and me, who can put someone on death row based on our powers of observation. There are some procedures that can help protect us against error. The Innocence Project suggests that the traditional line-up be replaced with a series of suspects shown individually and that the administrators of the line-up not know who the real suspect is. Some police departments have voluntarily switched to this and others have been spurred to do so by legislation and court decisions. But human error cannot be eradicated. The problem with capital punishment, unlike life imprisonment without parole, is that the error can never be reversed. The object of the error is dead.

Finally, Fraudulent Science: Stephan Cowans was convicted in Massachusetts of assault and intent to murder and given a 30 to 45-year sentence. The conviction was based on faulty eyewitness identification and on a fingerprint that had been left on a glass used by the assailant. After he was exonerated based on DNA evidence, the District Attorney re-analyzed the fingerprint and found that it, in fact, did not actually belong to Cowans.

In Montana Jimmy Ray Bromgard was convicted of rape of an eight-year old girl based on fraudulent science. The forensic expert testified that the head and pubic hairs found on the sheets were indistinguishable from Bromberg's hair sample. He further testified that there was less than one in ten thousand chances that the hairs did not belong to Bromberg. There has never been a standard by which to statistically match hairs through microscopic inspection. The expert took that impressive number out of thin air. After over 15 years in prison Bromgard was exonerated based on DNA evidence, which did not exist in 1987.

The Project Innocence report on this case stated: "The forensic scientist that testified against Bromgard was, at the time, the director of the Montana Department of Justice –Forensic Science Division. He testified in hundreds of other cases and is now working for a state crime laboratory in Washington. A report by a peer review committee of top forensic scientists was issued which characterized the statistical evidence as junk science and urged the Montana Attorney General to conduct an audit of the witness's work in other cases." If this had been a capital offense, Bromgard would be dead and forgotten.

Some "errors" are not errors, but the product of overzealous prosecutors, a factor that cannot be ignored, but, for lack of space, will not be discussed here. But assuming innocent error, there are numerous confessions that are elicited from sick individuals who are self self-destructive, faulty eyewitness identifications and honest mistakes in crime laboratories.

It may even be true that the cases of error are a small percentage of the above categories. But what percentage of mistakes, when the state legally kills people, are you willing to live with? My answer is none. That's why I opt for life imprisonment without parole as the ultimate punishment. Sitting in a 6 x 8 cell for a lifetime may very well be worse than death, but it does give us the opportunity to rectify errors.

The Death Penalty is Fading Away
2/26/08

There's good news concerning capital punishment. In late December New Jersey was the first state to abolish the death penalty since the Supreme Court reinstated it in 1976. In its place it substituted life without parole. The legislature and Governor Jon Corzine relied on the findings of the New Jersey Death Penalty Study Commission, which consisted of a wide range of perspectives, including law enforcement, victims and attorneys.

That report stressed three points: First, the abolition of the death penalty will eliminate the risk of disproportionality in capital sentencing. That's a fancy way of saying that if you are a poor white person or African American your chances of receiving the death sentence are astronomically higher than if you are middle class white or white and rich. The Torah tells us that justice should not favor the rich or the poor, but that is not the case in the real world of America today.

The Commission also decided that executing the guilty did not justify the risk of making an irreversible mistake. When new evidence shows up, such as DNA, you can't go back and revive the dead. The Commission also found that life without parole was better for the families of murder victims. With the death sentence there is no closure for the family as they wait interminable years for court reviews. With life without parole there is instant closure.

A mother of a murdered child stunned prosecutors when she testified at a New Jersey legislative hearing. She said, "The death penalty is a harmful policy that exacerbates the pain for murdered victims' families." Later the County Prosecutors Association of New Jersey supported the legislation and concurred in the Commission's finding that "There is increasing evidence that the death penalty is inconsistent with evolving standards of decency."

It's not just New Jersey. For all practical purposes New York has outlawed capital punishment. Its death penalty law was declared unconstitutional in 2004 and the legislature has rejected all subsequent attempts to reinstate capital punishment. Illinois is now in its eighth year of a death penalty moratorium and there is no movement to change it.

Death sentences in the United States have dropped by 60 percent since 1999 and public opinion polls show that life without parole is replacing the death sentence as the preferred punishment for murder.

In the near future the Supreme Court will rule on a Kentucky case to determine if lethal injections are cruel and unusual punishment prohibited by the Constitution due to failures with the drugs utilized. In the interim there has been a national moratorium on executions. But this is a temporary thing. The most that the Supreme Court will do is clean up the procedures used to put someone to death.

There are important Supreme Court decisions that ultimately may do away with capital punishment. The Court ruled in 2003 and 2005 that a state cannot execute someone if he or she had not received an adequate defense. This was in response to instances where the court assigned divorce lawyers as defense counsel and cases where the defense lawyers actually were sleeping through trials.

But an adequate defense in a death penalty case requires an immense outlay of money. In Atlanta the prosecution of the person indicted for murdering a judge and others in a courtroom gave the defense counsel 32,000 pages of documents and 400 hours of taped telephone calls. The defense team has the legal obligation to review every document. The problem is that the state refuses to pay the cost of this process. Yet if this is not done, then the Supreme Court will inevitably overturn the conviction on the basis of inadequate defense.

Here's the key point: The Supreme Court does not require the same degree of completeness on the part of the defense counsel if the death sentence is not in play. In the Atlanta case the judge stopped the trial until the defense lawyers are paid, which the state refuses to do. Everyone knows the accused is guilty. In fact, he has offered to plead guilty if the sentence were life in prison without parole. The Georgia authorities want blood and refuse to take this plea bargain. The bottom line is Georgia wants the execution but refuses to pay the costs of getting it.

It is precisely the growing expenses of a death sentence trial that is driving many prosecutors and state legislatures to look at life in prison without parole as the reasonable alternative. Obviously, I take my stand on moral grounds, but if another does it for economic reasons, I shall not protest. Yes, things are looking better and we are rapidly ascending to a higher standard of decency.

Legacy of Guantanamo

Habeas Corpus – It is Not Merely a Latin Phrase
4/8/08

It's hard for Americans to get excited about habeas corpus. Habeas what? Or even worse, Habeas who? It's a Latin term which refers to the right of a person to have a speedy appearance before a civil court of law. It protects a person from being arrested and thrown in jail and remaining there, never to see the light of day in an open courtroom.

Slate Magazine's law guru, Dahlia Lithwick, succinctly put it in perspective when she wrote: "If the rule of law were a religion, habeas corpus would be the first commandment." The right not to be held in confinement without a civil trial goes back to the Magna Carta and British common law.

Our Constitution provides that "habeas corpus shall not be suspended unless when in cases of rebellion or invasion the public safety may require it." President Lincoln suspended it when there was a rebellion called the Civil War and Confederate soldiers were a mere 40 or 50 miles from the White House. Even then this dire act nearly cost him his reelection in 1864, so angry was the electorate over the lack of this basic civil liberty.

This past December the Supreme Court heard an important habeas corpus case (Boumediene v. Bush). It should be delivering its opinion sometime in the next two months. Boumediene is suing on behalf of the over 300 remaining detainees at Guantanamo Bay who have been incarcerated for over five years without a trial in a civil court. Their argument is that they are covered by the right of habeas corpus as provided in the U.S. Constitution.

During the oral arguments Justice Scalia challenged the proposition that the right to habeas corpus covers non-citizens. He went even farther, commenting that "prisoners on a tropical island we rent but don't own" have no right to habeas corpus. Never mind that the lease for Gitmo is perpetual, thereby making it an integral part of our country, the question must be answered – does habeas corpus as protected in our Constitution apply to all people under our jurisdiction or just citizens. My answer is simple: the mark of a truly civilized nation is how it treats the stranger in its midst. Legal norms should be universal and not restricted by one's passport.

The government also argued that habeas corpus requirements are met because, although these detainees do not have the right to a civil court trial, they do have the right to a trial under the 2006 Military Commissions Act. This sounds impressive until one realizes that venue allows hearsay evidence and secret sessions; the government has the right to decide whom the defense can call as witnesses; the defense attorneys are appointed by the prosecutors who owe their future careers to the government; and confessions obtained through the use of torture are allowed as evidence.

Apropos of habeas corpus, the *San Francisco Chronicle* reported that beginning in 1999 the government has contracted with a Halliburton subsidiary to build detention camps at undisclosed locations within the United States and with other companies to build thousands of railcars, some reportedly equipped with shackles, ostensibly to transport detainees.

We know that the 2007 National Defense Authorization Act (NDAA) gives the president the power to invoke martial law for the first time in more than a century and the Military Commissions Act of 2008 suspends habeas corpus and allows for indefinite imprisonment of anyone who donates money to a charity that turns up on a list of "terrorist organizations." And the National Counterterrorism Center holds the names of 775,000 "terror suspects" with the number increasing by 20,000 per month.

It can't happen here? It already has. In 1920 Attorney General Palmer in the now famous "Palmer Raids" imprisoned thousands of Americans because the government merely suspected them of being radicals or communists, habeas corpus be damned. The Palmer raids were directed by J. Edgar Hoover, then the head of the intelligence division of the Justice Department, later to morph into the FBI.

In 1950, twelve days after the Korean War began, Hoover wrote a letter to President Truman suggesting that he suspend the right of habeas corpus and that he imprison 12,000 American citizens whom Hoover suspected of disloyalty. Hoover noted that the preponderance of his suspects were from New York and California. So what's new?

Fortunately Truman ignored Hoover. But can we be sure that a future president, not a Truman but maybe a Bush, would not ignore such a request? In 1943 Winston Churchill wrote: "The power of the Executive to cast a man into prison without formulating any charge known to the law, and particularly to deny him the judgment of his peers, is in the highest degree odious and is the foundation of all totalitarian government whether Nazi or Communist."

Much is at stake in this upcoming Supreme Court decision. We're a long distance from the Constitutional requirement of rebellion or invasion that would undermine public safety. Let's pray that the Supreme Court agrees.

Comment: The Court ruling is discussed in the next column written on 9/2/08

The Show Trials Begin With a Surprise
9/2/08

At the end of its last session the Supreme Court ruled that the prisoners in Guantanamo deserve habeas corpus, the right to a speedy trial. Unfortunately, the Court did not specify that such a trial should be in a civil court. This past month the first detainee, Salim Hamdan was tried before a military tribunal at the prison with surprising results.

But first, let us review the rules under which he and future prisoners will be tried: Hearsay evidence is allowed (meaning, "I didn't see him do it, but my friend told me he did it); secret sessions are permissible; the judge has the authority as to whom the defense can call as a witness; confessions derived from torture are admissible; the defense counsel is chosen by the prosecution; and the jury pool is also chosen by the prosecutor.

In Hamdan's case 13 senior Army, Air Force and Navy officers, all of whom had friends and colleagues involved in the September 11, 2001 attack, were assigned to the jury pool. From them six, plus a single alternate, were chosen in less than half a day. Compare this to the civil trial of Jose Padilla, in a real court of law, where it took six months to choose a jury of 12 from 500 potential jurors, who, of course, were not hand-picked by the prosecution. Yeshiva University law professor Ellen Yaroshefsky best summarized the legitimacy of these military tribunals: "It's Alice in Wonderland. It looks like a court and sounds like a court, but in fact it's 'Heads I win, tails you lose.'"

In spite of the above, the trial had a surprise happy ending, at least for the defendant. We will get to that in a moment. Hamdan was in his early thirties when he was arrested and transported to Guantanamo. He is from Yemen, married with two daughters, and has a fourth grade education. He was bin Laden's limo driver for $200 a month. He was not exactly a master criminal. A Huffington Post blogger put it in perspective: "We finally got him...Osama bin Laden's limo driver. Move over Hermann Goering and make room for Ahmad Hamdan." Even Hitler's driver, Erich Kempka, was not prosecuted as a war criminal.

Hamdan was charged with two counts: conspiracy (which means that he was one of the masterminds that plotted to destroy the Twin Towers) and material support for terrorism (which means that he was a limo driver). The prosecution asked for 30-years to life. Here's the surprise: The six military officers on the jury threw out the conspiracy charge and convicted him on the second charge, giving him only 5 ½ years, with credit for the five years that he has been held at Gitmo. This means that in six months Hamdan should be free to return to his family.

This decision doesn't validate the fairness of the military tribunal system. It is still extremely flawed, having absolutely no protections for a defendant. What it does show is that even in a kangaroo court common decency can prevail. The people who set the system up did so in order to get convictions, not truth. But six senior officers bucked their own government. However, they covered their behinds by not throwing out the whole case and making sure that Hamdan serves six more months, allowing the Bush administration to figure future plans.

The case was so flimsy that at the end of the trial the presiding judge said, "Mr. Hamdan, I hope the day comes that you are able to return to your wife and daughters and your country." It appears that the judge and Hamdan had established a warm relationship in the months leading up to the trial. That's fine, because it introduces a humane aspect to an inhumane environment – but what does it say about a legal system where there is no distance between a judge, who is supposed to be impartial, and a defendant? It is Alice in Wonderland.

The happy ending is not assured. President Bush maintains that he still has the right to keep Hamdan incarcerated as an "enemy combatant" for the duration of the War on Terrorism, which means for the rest of his life. Under normal military rules that apply to a court marshal a Pentagon official has the authority to reduce a sentence, but not to increase it.

Hamdan was not tried under court marshal military rules but under a different military court system invented by the Bush administration. If Bush continues to keep Hamdan in Guantanamo after he finishes the six months left on his sentence, why have the trial in the first place?

The answer is that our president isn't interested in justice and that this is merely the beginning of many show trials. Isn't it curious that after five years the Bush administration is beginning this process before the November elections? It could be a coincidence, but if you believe that I have a certain bridge in a certain borough that I want to sell you.

God, or Barack Obama, Save our Judicial System, Please
12/2/08

In July of this year the Supreme Court ruled that "enemy combatants" held in Guantanamo have the protection of habeas corpus as provided in the Constitution. Habeas corpus is a legal term which refers to the right of a person to have a speedy appearance before a civil court of law. It protects a person from being arrested, thrown in jail and remaining there, never to see the light of day or a fair trial in an open courtroom.

This past month, under pressure from the Supreme Court ruling, the Bush administration initiated its first habeas corpus hearing before federal Judge Richard J. Leon, a Bush appointee who previously ruled in 2005 that Guantanamo detainees have no habeas corpus rights. The case involves six Algerian men, who lived in Bosnia, who supposedly were planning to go to Afghanistan to fight against the United States. The prosecution also alleged that one of them was a member of Al Qaeda.

To the amazement of the Bush administration and the liberal community that is critical of these kangaroo courts the judge ruled that five of the six should be released immediately for lack of evidence; however, we should not be too optimistic since he stressed that, "This is a unique case. Few if any others will be factually like it. Nobody should be lulled into a false sense that all of the...cases will look like this one." Thus it behooves us to take a look at the procedures under which the remaining 250 or so will be tried. These rules of the court were reported by the *New York Times* in discussing the current case.

Judge Leon accepted classified evidence against the defendants, but the *Times* reported, "The detainees' lawyers have not been permitted to discuss the classified evidence with their clients." *With their clients.* How can a detainee defend himself if he has no access to the evidence against him? How can a lawyer fulfill his legal obligation to be part of a fair judicial system if he cannot discuss evidence with his client?

The *Times* reported that "A Justice Department spokesman said lawyers in the case had no role in classifying evidence, adding that it had been classified by intelligence agencies 'for valid national security reasons – well before preparation for this case even began.'" Perchance these were the same intelligence experts who rounded up over 500 other prisoners at Guantanamo, kept them there for years, and finally released them without ever admitting that they were wrong, leaving the remaining approximately 250 prisoners to face these trials. Here we have the absurd legal scenario that a prosecutor has to rely on evidence that his own department has not gathered and over which he has no control.

Finally the *Times* reported: "They (government lawyers) filed a sealed envelope of evidence with Judge Leon, which the detainees' lawyers have not been permitted to see. In court filings the government lawyers said that if the evidence in the closed hearings was not enough to justify the detention, then the judge should open the envelope. Judge Leon, the filing said, 'may very well ultimately face the circumstance where the information justifying detention is too sensitive' to share not only with the detainees but with their lawyers."

Too sensitive to share with their lawyers. The cat is out of the bag. If you can't prove that these detainees are not deserving of a trial in a courtroom that is closed to the public by withholding evidence from the detainees (which obviously affects their ability to defend themselves), then you supply an envelope which contains whatever, we will never know and the defense attorneys will never know, and that will suffice to keep these people locked up in the American Gulag.

I just cannot take this anymore. As a citizen I am outraged. As a lawyer I am ashamed of my country. As a rabbi I repudiate this kind of immoral behavior. Upon assuming leadership the first thing that Moses did was to establish a just legal system. This is not just. It's not even arguably within miles of being just.

Judge Leon opened the envelope and found that the evidence against these men was based on information obtained from a single unnamed source. After seven years of incarceration, five in Guantanamo, even a conservative judge, who believes that there should not be any habeas corpus trials, could not stomach the injustice. But what will happen in the trials of the remaining detainees? What will be in their envelopes? We and their attorneys will never know. I do not expect to see many outcomes as in the current case. Something must be done to cleanse our justice system.

Is this America? God save us. Barack Obama save us.

Guantanamo Bay – Have We No Sense of Decency?
3/11/08

There is much wrong with Guantanamo, but the most egregious sin the use of torture, what the Bush administration has called "enhanced interrogation" or "special interrogation techniques." The press and Congress have focused on waterboarding, a technique that simulates drowning. It sounds innocuous, a little water in your nostrils and lots of fear. But it's far more. It is so fearsome that it was practiced by the inquisitors under the Inquisition (i.e. we Jews were the first to experience waterboarding), and Japanese officers in World

War II were prosecuted for using the technique on American prisoners. Who will prosecute us?

President Bush has reiterated his stance that waterboarding is legal and that he could authorize it in the future; this despite the fact that the State Department has outlawed it, the Army Field Manual forbids it, the FBI Director Robert Mueller intimated that it was not needed to extract information and the United Nations special rapporteur on torture has declared it "unjustifiable" and "absolutely unacceptable under international human rights law."

But it's much more than waterboarding. Majid Kahn is a 27-year-old former suburban Baltimore high school student seized in Pakistan where he says he was visiting his brother. After spending three years in a secret CIA "black site" in an undisclosed country he was recently transferred to Guantanamo Bay. Khan claims that he has been tortured. He has written letters to his lawyer and relatives on the outside and they have been censored by the military. One of his letters begins: "In this letter I am going to mention some of the things that I have been through." The next 19 lines of the text are blacked out by the Gitmo censors. We are left to imagine what techniques of torture he endured.

The 2002 Bush Justice Department memo on torture written by the now infamous John Yoo (who still teaches at the law school at Berkeley) stipulated that interrogation methods were not torture unless they produced pain equivalent to that produced by organ failure or death.

It is a long, painful and inhumane trek from probing questions to organ failure and death. And along the way there are torture techniques, excluding waterboarding, which Bush and the CIA do not want us to know about. But they are doing these things in the name of America. We are America, not Cheney or Bush or their minions. We, the people, are besmirched by our leaders and it is our country that stands before the world as the heirs of the commandants of the Soviet Gulag. If I sound outraged, you bet I am.

Gitmo is a cesspool and a moral embarrassment. The Bush administration contends that U.S. laws do not apply there because it is not part of the United States in spite of the fact that we have an eternal lease (it never ends) on this enclave in Cuba. It is America, whether we admit it or not.

There have been as many as 600 prisoners held at Guantanamo over the past six years. Originally we were told that all were dangerous Al Qaeda operatives. Now there are 277 left. None received trials and many were tortured, but over 300 were released. The Bush administration never declared them innocent. It merely said that they were no longer "enemy combatants."

Surely there are some dangerous and guilty criminals left there, but we will never know how many if fair trials (not the sham trials I described last week) are not held. Gitmo is such an embarrassment that the recently appointed chairman of the Joint Chief of Staff, Admiral Mike Mullen, has declared, "I'd like to see it shut down."

The *New York Times* columnist Nicholas Kristof recently discussed the case of one Gitmo prisoner, Sami al-Hajj, an Al Jazeera cameraman who was picked up in Afghanistan doing his job. Remember that George Bush hates Al Jazeera and he once proposed to Tony Blair that they bomb their studios.

The government initially confused al-Hajj with another cameraman, but this did not stop them from torturing him. Realizing his innocence they offered him freedom if he would spy on Al Jazeera. He refused and continues to be imprisoned at Guantanamo where he is on a hunger strike and is being force-fed twice daily. He is allowed a Koran, but his glasses have been confiscated so he can't read it.

Kristof wrote: "Suppose the Iranian government arrested and beat Katie Couric, held her virtually incommunicado for six years and promised to release her only if she would spy for Iran." I suspect that it would be Bush's pretext for another preemptive war.

My question: Where is the soul of the American people? To paraphrase Joseph Welch, have we no sense of decency?

Comment: The Obama administration has explicitly stated that waterboarding and other techniques of torture are outlawed, but it remains to be seen whether anyone connected with the Bush administration's use of torture will be criminally prosecuted.

President Bush as a Moral Failure
1/4/05

This past year we have had to face the incontrovertible evidence of American cruelty, torture and blatant murder of prisoners in Guantanamo and the Abu Ghraib facility in Iraq which included 40 deaths, 20 of them homicides, almost 100 documented cases of prisoner abuse, and God only knows how many undocumented cases of torture and death. We ask ourselves, how could Americans, reared in our liberal culture, schooled in our western educational process, subject to the same cultural parameters we have experienced, do such a thing?

To answer this we can turn to the most famous and widely recognized experiment in the history of psychology. In 1963 Stanley Milgram of Yale University decided to test the capability of average people to carry out great harm to others, simply because they were ordered to do so. The theoretical proposition was that humans have a tendency to obey other people who are in a position of authority, even if, in obeying, they violate their own codes of moral and ethical behavior.

Milgram created a bogus shock machine with voltage levels starting at 30 volts and increasing by 15-volt intervals up to 450 volts. The subjects of the experiment were told by an official looking person in a grey lab coat (the experimenter) to increase the voltage on another person (the learner) every time he answered a question wrongly. The subjects did not know that the learner was an actor and was not actually receiving the electric shocks.

As the voltage increased the learner began to shout his discomfort. He began to writhe in pain and complain of heart problems. At the 300 volt level the learner pounded on the wall and demanded to be let out. At this point the subjects would turn to the experimenter (the official looking man in the gray lab coat) for guidance on whether to continue the shocks. The experimenter sternly told each subject to continue up to the highest level, 450 volts. (Google Stanley Milgram on the Internet and read about the experiment in depth.)

The question now is what percentage of the subjects would you think would deliver shocks all the way up the 30 levels, all the way up to 450 volts? Milgram asked that question to a group of Yale University seniors, all psychology majors, as well as various colleagues. The estimates ranged from 0% to 3% with the average of 1.2%. That is, no more than 3 out of 100 were predicted to deliver the maximum shock.

Here are the actual results. Although 14 subjects defied orders and broke off before reaching the maximum voltage, fully 26 of the 40 subjects, or 65%, followed the experimenter's orders and proceeded to the top of the shock scale. True, the subjects were not calm or happy about what they were doing. Many exhibited signs of extreme stress and concern for the man receiving the shocks, and they even became angry at the experimenter (the man in the official looking lab coat). But the point is: They still obeyed.

Please remember that these subjects were average, normal people who agreed to participate in an experiment about learning. They were not cruel or sadistic people in any way. Over the years this experiment has been replicated using women and people of other cultures and nationalities. Obedience rates did not change significantly. Most interestingly, there was no difference in obedience rates for males versus females.

So what can we learn from the Milgram experiment and apply it to Abu Ghraib and Guatanamo? First, ordinary, decent people are capable of extreme acts of cruelty and inhuman behavior if ordered to do so by people in authority. The ordinary-ness of evil is precisely what Hannah Arendt highlighted when she subtitled her study of Eichmann "The Banality of Evil".

A recent film by a survivor of the Khmer Rouge genocide in Cambodia makes this same point. 1.7 million of his countrymen (nearly one quarter of the population) were murdered between 1975 and 1979 in the Killing Fields of that country. The conclusion of this documentary shows that those who perpetrated this genocide were ordinary people just following orders. People who loved their wives and children. People who under other circumstances would be anonymous accountants, housewives, teachers and laborers. That is why evil is such a terrible presence. We don't need psychopaths and sadists and other miscreants to fulfill evil ends. All we need is a properly conditioned population.

This leads us to the second conclusion. Leadership is most important, because leadership conditions the population. The subjects in the Milgram experiment would not have progressed to the 450-volt level without the prodding and commands of someone in authority. For 65% of the population an authority figure will predominate over one's own conscience. This is a scary thought, but it is reality.

This brings us back to the atrocities at Gauntanamo and Abu Ghraib. We can prosecute a few underlings and convict them as we have done these past months and declare to the world that what happened was an aberration, not representative of America or American ideals. But this is not really the case. At least subconsciously and possibly in reality these soldiers were only following orders, just like the subjects in the Milgram experiment. Leadership at the very top of this government sent clear messages that we tolerate torture.

There is by now the very famous January 22, 2002, 56-page confidential memorandum within the Bush Administration as evidence of culpability by our highest leadership. The memorandum declared that international treaties and our own federal laws that prohibit torture do not apply to our handling of "enemy combatants" if the president deems so. This memo was written to protect American officials from being charged with war crimes for the way prisoners were detained and interrogated. Lawyers for the Defense Department, the Justice Department and the White House as well as counsel for Vice President Cheney approved this memo, which set the tone for government and military action for the subsequent aftermath of the Iraq war.

There is no doubt that leadership created the conducive environment if not the actual orders for torture. Our top leadership, going up to and including the president – let me repeat that, including the president – approved of torture. They were the counterparts of Stanley Milgram's experimenter, standing there in his grey lab coat as a symbol of authority. The result has been death to prisoners and diminution of American standards of decency that we hold dear.

The supreme irony is that a good portion of the American electorate voted to re-elect our president because they saw him as the exemplar of old-fashioned American morality. The truth is that he countenanced torture and cruelty in the name of security and he diminished America's moral standing in the world. His leadership was the real cause of the moral lapses at Guantanamo and Abu Grhaib. We convicted a few underlings, but we left the president off the hook. He will never be charged, but, nonetheless, he failed his moral test.

The Electoral Process

It's Time to Abolish the Electoral College
12/7/04

In reflecting on the trauma of the recent presidential election, (anxiously waiting for the results of key swing states and playing with the magic number of 270 electoral votes, not giving a darn about the popular vote, since it doesn't count) it is time to seriously consider amending the constitution to abolish the Electoral College and to provide a direct popular vote for president. It is the democratic thing to do.

The Electoral College is not sacrosanct. It was a compromise at the Constitutional Convention. One faction wanted the president to be elected by state senates while another wanted the president to be chosen by direct popular vote. The Electoral College emerged as the compromise. It is a peculiar institution that is found nowhere in any other democracy. To the rest of the world it is a perplexing phenomenon since they cannot fathom the possibility of a person being elected president without winning the popular vote, as was the case with George W. Bush in 2000.

Three times in our history (not including the 2000 election that was decided by the Supreme Court) the Electoral College has produced a crisis. It is worth reviewing this history. The first instance was in 1800 before the passage of the Twelfth Amendment, which required a president to run on a joint ticket with his vice-president. In that year Thomas Jefferson and his supposed vice-presidential candidate, Aaron Burr, were tied with 73 electoral votes apiece. The election was thrown into the House of Representatives where Jefferson was finally elected after 36 ballots. The key player was Alexander Hamilton who despised both Jefferson and Burr. Fortunately for the country, he loathed Burr more than Jefferson, and he threw his weight to

Jefferson. Of course, Burr never forgot this, and eventually killed Hamilton in a dual a few years later.

The second crisis occurred in 1824 when Andrew Jackson outpolled John Quincy Adams 153,000 to 108,000 votes. Jackson also beat him in the electoral votes, 99 to 84. But Henry Clay and another candidate received almost 100,000 votes. Clay controlled 41 electoral votes. Clay instructed his electors in the Electoral College to switch to Adams, electing him president. Upon assuming the office, Adams appointed Clay Secretary of State. Charges of a stolen election haunted Adams throughout his four years as president and may have played a role in producing what is generally considered a failed presidency.

The last time the Electoral College produced a crisis was immediately after the Civil War in 1876. The Democratic candidate, Samuel Tilden, outpolled the Republican, Rutherford B. Hayes, by 250,000 out of over eight million votes cast. Tilden was also leading in the Electoral College when the Republicans challenged the results in three states, South Carolina, Florida and Louisiana. There was no doubt that there was vast corruption in South Carolina and Florida, not the least being Democratic pressure to keep the newly enfranchised blacks from voting. History seems to conclude that the Democrats won Louisiana more fairly. Both the Democrats and the Republicans sent separate electoral ballots to the Senate for certification. Hayes needed all three states to be elected. After much maneuvering, outgoing President Ulysses S. Grant appointed a special electoral commission, approved by Congress, to decide the question. It was comprised equally of seven Democrats and seven Republicans with a non-partisan Supreme Court Justice as the deciding vote. After the formation of this commission, that Justice could not serve. He was replaced by another Justice who was an acknowledged Republican. All three states were counted in the Republican column by an 8-7 vote. It was a stolen election. Without the Electoral College, Tilden would have been president.

We can not afford another stolen election and the existence of the Electoral College puts us at risk.

There are other good reasons to abolish this peculiar institution (that's also the phrase our Colonial forefathers used to describe slavery). Its existence negates the concept that every vote counts. If you live in a heavily Democratic state, your Republican vote does not count, and vice-versa. What motivation is there for a Republican in Massachusetts or a Democrat in Mississippi to vote, knowing that he/she cannot really change the outcome of the electoral votes from those states?

The Electoral College also distorts the true vote by favoring small states. Each state gets three automatic electors (one for each senator and a House member). Based purely on population there are small states that would receive only one or two electoral votes. We have to live with this inequity in the Senate where Rhode Island has the same representation as New York, but there is no reason to compound the inequity through the Electoral College.

Here's a scary thought: Once the electors are chosen they are not legally required to vote for the person to whom they are pledged. That means that in a close election one person in the Electoral College can change his or her mind and change the outcome, in spite of approximately 120 million combined votes or 538 electoral votes. There could come a time when we are jolted into this reality, and, depending on who sits on the Supreme Court, the final changed vote will be upheld (strict constitutional construction).

If there were a 269-269 tie in the Electoral College (and this is not a far-fetched premise – it easily could have happened this last time around), then the election is thrown into the House of Representatives where the vote is counted state by state, one vote for each state, which could also produce a tie since we have an even-numbered amount of states. But even discounting this factor, such a vote in the House gives one vote to Alaska, with a population of 640,000 and one vote to California, with almost 36 million people. Is this a way to run a democracy?

I am aware that abolishing the Electoral College will take leverage away from special interest groups. No longer would Cuban-Americans be able to control foreign policy because they are a voting block in a key swing state where the winner takes all of the electoral votes. No longer would Jews be able to lobby on the basis that we may affect the outcome in Florida and Pennsylvania.

I say this to all special interest groups, especially Jews: Your commitment to American democracy far outweighs any special interests. This country is evenly divided on many moral and political issues. In a democracy you have to live with that, and it may even be beneficial since unanimity of opinion can produce a repressive society. But on one thing we cannot be divided: We must all have faith in the fairness and honesty of the political process. Without that we will ultimately slip into chaos. I believe that it is good for Republicans and Democrats alike that the Electoral College be abolished. This is not a partisan issue. It is an American issue.

Footnote written on 10/7/08:

Each evening I listen to CNN or MSNBC to receive the latest poll results. One day Obama and McCain are tied, on another day one or the other is leading by a percentage or two. The problem is that all of this polling does a disservice to the American people in that it obscures the fact that we do not have a race involving all Americans. It matters not whether one candidate or the other wins the popular vote because presidents are elected by 538 members of the Electoral College.

In reality we have a five or six state contest: If Pennsylvania flips to the Republicans, if Ohio can go Democratic, if Florida goes either way, etc. Throw in Colorado and Michigan and one or two other states and you have the whole election in a nutshell. It's an absurd system. It's time for a change.

I seem to write this same column every four years and nothing much happens. But there is some movement. There are only two ways to abolish the Electoral College, either by constitutional amendment, which is very difficult, or by a new concept called the National Popular Vote bill, which may ultimately succeed.

That bill would guarantee the presidency to the candidate who receives the most popular votes in all 50 states, plus the District of Columbia. The bill would take effect only when enacted, in identical form, by states possessing a majority of the electoral vote, enough electoral votes to elect a president (270 of 538). When the bill comes into effect, all the electoral votes from those states would go to the candidate that received the most popular votes in the entire country. Thus the Electoral College would still be in existence, but it would have no value, like an appendix in a human being.

Four states (Hawaii, Illinois, New Jersey and Maryland) have enacted this legislation. They possess 50 electoral votes – 19 percent of the 270 necessary to bring the law into effect. Both legislative branches in California, Massachusetts, Rhode Island and Vermont have also passed it, but it has not yet become law in those states. But progress is being made.

Free Speech and Campaign Spending Limits
3/21/06

Earlier this month the Supreme Court heard arguments on what may be the most important decision of this year or maybe this century. It presents the question whether a city or state can set spending limits on political campaigns. Put another way, does the free speech protection in the First Amendment protect the right of an individual to spend as much money as he or she wants to win an election?

This is not a new question. In 1976 the Supreme Court ruled (Buckley v. Valeo) that the City of Albuquerque could not limit the amount of money spent on a mayoral race. The Court said that the city had the right to limit contributions from a single person to a candidate, but that, under the free speech rights of the First Amendment, a candidate could spend unlimited sums of money.

Now the State of Vermont has passed a law limiting the amount of money that a state candidate can spend, in direct defiance of the Buckley decision. It was immediately challenged by both the state and federal Republican Committees. Republicans, being the party of the rich, want to continue to buy elections with no limits set.

How valid is the free speech argument? Well, we know that free speech is not without limits. It is often pointed out that you can't shout fire in a crowded theater (of course assuming that there is no fire), for that speech would harm others and possibly endanger their lives. You can't wrongly accuse another of immoral conduct, for that would be slander or libel. You have the right to criticize the government and even propose its overthrow, unless you are inciting a mob to destroy a government building. In such an instance your free speech becomes illegal behavior. Free speech is a wonderful concept, but it has its limits

I believe that it is time to realize that the Buckley decision is just plain bad law and should be overturned. It would not be the first bad Supreme Court decision to meet this fate. Along with the Dred Scott decision that extended slavery and the separate but equal decision of 1896 that was overturned by Brown v. Board of Education in 1954, it's time to revise Buckley.

Here are the arguments on both sides. The Republican Party says that money is speech. You have the right to use your money to support whatever cause you want, and to limit that spending is to limit your free expression of what you believe. That's basically the whole argument. You either buy it or you don't.

In response, the State of Vermont and the Second Circuit Court of Appeals that agreed with Vermont argue that unlimited spending destroys democracy and free speech. To begin, it stresses the excessive costs of campaigning. Thirty years ago the average cost of a House of Representatives race was $100,000. Today it's close to $900,000, and millions in media markets like California and New York. In 2002, 94 percent of the candidates that raised the most money won their congressional races. Thus the average House member has to raise more than $2,000 a day, every day from the moment he or she is seated to the next election.

This leads directly into the question of time priority. We elect our officials to concentrate on the tasks of governing, not money-raising. The time and energy spent on money-raising is so onerous that even Senator Mark Dayton, Democrat from Minnesota, who spent $12 million of his own money on his last campaign in 2000, decided not to run again this year because, "I cannot stand to do the fund raising necessary to wage a successful campaign and I cannot be an effective senator while also being a nearly full-time candidate."

All of this money spent on politics raises an even more important consideration. Vermonters held public hearings where lawmakers openly admitted that campaign contributions affected what laws won their attention. Certainly, money brings access to the lawmaker. Show me an office holder who doesn't respond to a call from a major contributor and I'll show you an ex-lawmaker. Where access crosses the line to buying the legislator is a very murky terrain. Many people are convinced, either correctly or not, that we have the best politicians that money can buy. What is important, and courts have taken notice of this, is that this perception, right or wrong, undermines democracy.

Limits on campaign spending would negate the advantage of incumbents who build up huge war chests that inhibit any serious challengers. They would also stop the obscene practice of multi-millionaires funding their own campaigns. Is it good for democracy that Michael Bloomberg could spend $80 million dollars of his own money on a mayoral campaign in New York or that Jon Corzine could spend $60 million of his own money for his Senate seat five years ago and another $40 million for the governor's seat in New Jersey this year? Corzine's Republican opponent spent $30 million of his own money in losing the governor's race. Thus we have come to the point that we see multi-millionaires dominating the political scene. What happened to the free speech of the average person who wants to run for office? We now have free speech for the rich but not for the average person. This is the outcome of equating money with speech.

It's hard to predict how the Supreme Court will rule on the Vermont case. I'm pretty sure that justices Stevens, Ginsberg, Souter and Breyer will rule for Vermont. I'm also pretty sure that justices Thomas, Alito, Scalia and Roberts will rule for the Republican Party. That leaves Justice Anthony Kennedy as the new swing vote, replacing the role played by Justice Sandra Day O'Connor. When the McCain-Feingold Act, which barred certain kinds of political contributions barely received the Court's approval in a 5-4 decision, Justice Kennedy voted in dissent with justices Scalia and Thomas. But in a recent case Justice Kennedy observed, "I would leave open the possibility that Congress, or a state legislature, might devise a system in which there are some limits on both expenditures and contributions, thus permitting officeholders to concentrate their time and efforts on official duties rather than on fundraising." So who knows?

I recommend a book by Justice Stephen Breyer entitled "Active Liberty –Interpreting Our Democratic Constitution." In it he talks about how one interprets a short document that must speak to problems today that the framers of the Constitution could never envision. He proposes that we look to the underlying values of the text. The intention of the free speech amendment was to protect personal liberty and the democratic process. Whatever would destroy that democratic process could not be valuable free speech. Justice John Paul Stevens put it bluntly in a recent decision: "Money is property, it is not speech."

Now let's see if the full Court will agree with him. For democracy's sake, I hope that it will.

Footnote: The Court decided in a 5-4 decision that money equals free speech. It struck down the Vermont law. President Bush's most lasting legacy will be his conservative appointments not only to the Supreme Court but to the entire Federal judiciary.

Another Bad Decision by the Supreme Court
7/15/08

Last week I discussed the 5-4 decision of the Supreme Court in declaring that the Second Amendment applies to individuals and gives them the right to possess handguns. On the same day by another 5-4 majority the Court declared the "millionaire's amendment" of the 2002 McCain-Feingold campaign finance law unconstitutional.

Under the "millionaire's amendment" when a candidate spent more than $350,000 of his or her own money for a House seat the opponent was allowed to receive triple the usual amount of contributions from a single person, $6,900 rather than $2,300. The rationale of the law was to create a level playing field in the political process. It was felt that someone should not be able to buy his way into public office, a practice which is becoming more common, witness Michael Bloomberg spending $80 million dollars of his own money in a municipal election and Jon Corzine putting out $60 million to become a Senator from New Jersey.

This decision was the third in three years by the conservative majority to strike down election reform. In 2006 it invalidated a Vermont law that limited the amount of money that could be spent on state elections no matter the source of the contributions. Vermont attempted to return the political process to a discussion of issues rather than a never-ending series of expensive attack ads on television.

In 2006 the same majority of the Court negated the provision in McCain-Feingold that forbade corporations or unions from paying for television ads that attacked individual candidates for 60 days prior to the general election. This was an attempt to regulate what has been called "soft money."

In all three of these cases the Court ruled that by spending money a person is exercising his free speech rights under the First Amendment, which means that rich people have more free speech than poor people. It reminds me of the variant on George Orwell's "Animal Farm" that declares that all people are created equal, except some are more equal than others. In the latest case the Court ruled that allowing a poor opponent to receive a larger outside contribution than the self-financing millionaire would infringe on the millionaire's free speech. It is their distorted concept of a level playing field.

Justice John Paul Stevens in his dissent wrote: "The millionaire's amendment quiets no speech at all. On the contrary, it does no more than assist the opponent of a self-funding candidate in his attempts to make his voice heard; this amplification in no way mutes the voice of the millionaire, who remains able to speak as loud and as long as he likes in support of his campaign."

The concept that spending money is a form of free speech is an anti-democratic concept. The argument that free speech must be protected is appealing on the surface but does not hold up under further scrutiny. Indeed our founding fathers were very interested in protecting free speech. Their reasoning was that free speech was a protection of democracy for they feared an imminent return of some form of monarchy. Their fears were so great that supporters of Jefferson actually thought Hamilton and Adams secretly wanted to undo the democratic process. For the founding fathers free speech was not an end in itself; it was a tool to protect democracy.

The question that we must ask ourselves today concerning all three of the Court's decisions that stuck down reforms that curtailed the power of money in politics is whether the money, either from personal fortunes or from special interest groups, protects democracy or destroys it.

My personal answer and the position of the liberal four justices in the minority is that it harms democracy. The average person is beginning to understand that we have the best politicians that money can buy. It turns people off of the political process. At its best we end up with a legislature of wealthy patricians who think they know what is best for the average Joe.

One other question must be asked: why do conservatives and Republicans generally oppose election reform while liberals and Democrats support it? The answer is simple. Except in this election cycle when Barack Obama has miraculously been able to substantially out-raise his Republican rival through the use of small contributions on the Internet, Republicans have always enjoyed the luxury of having more money to spend.

No wonder conservatives believe that money equals free speech. Money means that they have more free speech than their Democratic rivals. So the bottom line is that the conservative majority on the Supreme Court, appointed by Republican presidents, is negating the will of the legislature by protecting the Republican advantage. Another description of that is called "judicial activism," the very same sin that conservatives blame on liberal jurists.

Race in America

50 Years Ago -- Brown v. Board of Education
5/18/04

This week marks the 50th anniversary of the Supreme Court ruling in *Brown v. Board of Education*. From the perspective of half a century later we can see that the Court was very cautious. After deciding that separate was not equal in education the Court did not require immediate integration. Instead it set the legal standard and merely required "all deliberate speed" in its implementation. A full decade after the *Brown* decision only 1 percent of black children attended integrated schools in the south.

But *Brown* was vitally important because it set in motion the civil rights movement that ultimately overcame Jim Crow laws, not only in education but also in all facets of American society. There is a direct causal connection between the *Brown* decision and the Civil Rights Act of 1964 and the Voting Rights Act of 1965.

Some personal reminiscences: It was only a year after the *Brown* decision. The precise date was July 22, 1955. Sugar Ray Robinson (pound for pound the greatest fighter of all time) was making a comeback against Rocky Castellani, a middling middle-weight from Pittston, Pennsylvania, a gritty coal town about a hundred miles north of Philly. I, along with sixty other Jewish families, also lived in Pittston. I was then not quite19 years old and Sugar Ray was my idol. (Today, a little older, wiser and hopefully more sensitive, I no longer follow boxing.) But Rocky was from Pittston, a local hero. Whom was I to root for?

Southern bigots who probably never heard of *Brown v. Education* provided that answer. The summer of 1955 I had a job as an advance man for a three-ring circus, not a bad gig for a kid who just finished his first year of college. I preceded the circus into small towns as it worked its way through the midwest, heading south as autumn approached. It was then for the first time I crossed the Mason-Dixon line into alien country.

The night of July 22, 1955 I was in a small southern town. I went to a working class bar to see the fight on television. The fight was evenly matched. The crowd in front of the TV set was shouting, "Kill the N....." (In case someone reading this is from outer space, Sugar Ray was black). "Kill the N....." they continued. Obviously the *Brown* case did not change their orientation. Now it is in the sixth round of a ten rounder, and the fight is in a virtual deadlock. The crowd is still chanting its mantra.

That's when a foolish young Jewish liberal took his stand. I slapped a $20 bill on the bar and proclaimed, "I bet on Robinson. What SOB will cover me?" In current dollars that's about equal to a hundred bucks, not a small wager for a young kid. Four or five hefty laborers together matched my bet. The money sat on the bar throughout the rest of the fight. The first judge gave it to Sugar Ray, the second to Rocky and (here I held my breath) the referee went for Robinson. Robinson by a narrow, split decision. At that very instant I scooped up the money and made a mad dash for the door before I was lynched as a "N..... Lover." To this day I still believe that I heard footsteps behind me as I raced down the narrow street to my hotel room. I never stepped into the south after that experience until my wife and I returned in the early sixties as part of the civil rights sit-in movement.

It's important to remember what this country was like in the fifties to correctly assess the importance of the *Brown* decision and to understand the awesome impact of the civil rights agitation that followed it. One of the legacies of *Brown* was the massive resistance by bigoted whites both in the north and the south. That resistance reached it pinnacle when Eugene "Bull" Connor, the Birmingham, Alabama Police Chief, set his attack dogs on the non-violent protesters. It was a photo-op that changed a nation. At that moment America witnessed a hatred that it could not abide. Public opinion changed, and we became a better people.

But it took us a long time to get there. As late as the early sixties my wife Lynne led a yearlong picket line, throughout the bitter winter, of St. Lukes Hospital in Cleveland, Ohio. This was Cleveland, Ohio, not Cleveland, Georgia. Many will remember that the north was as segregated as the south, except that we did not shout out our prejudices in bars. We were much more genteel. St Lukes did accept blacks, but they would not put black and white patients in the same room. We won that battle, but only after half our bodies were attacked by frostbite.

Since this is a Jewish newspaper, it is important to talk about motivation. In thinking back I ask myself, where did my liberality come from? The simple answer is that it came from my religion. I became a Bar Mitzvah, and like most adolescents did not return to *shul* to *daven* each week. But Judaism, and what it stood for, was a part of my soul. Maybe it was because we were such a small minority in our coal town; maybe it was because I had a very good rabbi at a crucial juncture of my young life; maybe it was because my father was a liberal, compassionate man who taught me to care for the underdog – not maybe, but surely because all of these things were wrapped up into a Jewishness that fostered a humanitarian identity, that I understood the plight of those whom our country excluded.

The challenge today in our assimilated, inviting world is to replicate that sense of Jewish *menschlekite*. As we increasingly turn to Jewish spirituality, let us remember that spirituality is useless unless it is translated into social action. In any case, I have always maintained that if you want to feel spiritual, find a picket line for a good cause and walk it.

All of this has great relevance to *Brown v. Board of Education*. Thinking back to those pre-civil rights days makes one realize how far we have come since the *Brown* decision. I know that we still have a long way to go, as my wife keeps reminding me, and I certainly do not want to become complacent; however, we have come a long way, and there are times such as this 50th anniversary of *Brown* when we have earned the right to pause and to take some satisfaction in our accomplishments as a people and a nation.

Footnote: The above column was written in 2004. Little did I believe that four short years later an African-American would be elected president of the United States. Yes, we have come a long way, but one person's journey does not deny the fact that there are still bigots out there (there always will be) and that we still have a lot of work left toward the end that every person should be judged on his or her own merits and not on race. But it gives me a warm feeling about America to think that a group of white mid-westerners in Iowa, and not some polyglot liberals from the Upper West Side of Manhattan, started Barack Obama on his trajectory. Who could have envisioned this back in May of 2004?

Lessons Learned from French Riots
12/13/05

In late October through mid November riots scourged the French landscape. Over 6,000 cars were torched in 300 cities and towns across France as poor and disenfranchised Muslim youth lashed out against the French establishment. At least one person was killed and scores were injured.

We cannot condone mass violence, but we need not condemn it without looking to its source. There are lessons to be learned here. The ten percent

Muslim minority in France are at the bottom of the economic rung. They live in housing projects that are basically cordoned off from French society. These are ghettos without walls. In the evenings the police, often wearing riot gear, circle the apartment buildings in their cars or sit at the roads leading into them. The *New York Times* quoted one young man: "It's not unemployment, it's the police."

But, of course, the unemployment is a root cause. For ages 50 and older the Muslim unemployment rate is 22 percent compared to 5 percent for the general French population. Muslim unemployment reaches 36 percent for ages 15 to 24. Obviously, mass discrimination exists in France. As one unemployed 38 year old commented, "You're French on your identity card, French to pay taxes and go into the army, but for the rest, you're an Arab." Even college educated Muslims find that they cannot gain acceptance into French professional practices, corporate structures or meaningful government positions. Eventually the lid pops on the pressure cooker and we witness the rage of the disadvantaged.

Lessons to be learned: First, a parochial Jewish perspective. These past years Jewish alarmists have trumpeted an increase in anti-Semitism is France, highlighting the synagogue and cemetery desecrations. These outrages were the product of the same unemployed, angry Muslim youth who were fighting the Middle East war by proxy. I wrote a few columns this past year citing French polls that showed that among the 90 percent of France that is not North African in origin, anti-Semitism is actually decreasing. These recent riots show that the acting out against Jews was merely a subset of the anger present in the Muslim community. Yet Jews, who make a living convincing us that everyone hates us, continue to call for a general boycott of France. Just this past week I received another boycott appeal on my email. The French riots of early November are a clarion call to Jews to put things in context. Jews are not always the primary focus of hatred. In France we are a collateral issue.

Second and more important lesson: The French riots validate the affirmative action movement in our country. In July of 1967 Detroit burned and 43 people lay dead. The riots soon spread to practically all major cities (Chicago was the noted exception) and even trickled down to smaller urban areas as disparate as Tampa and Muncie. It was our wake-up call. We were paying the price of 200 years of slavery and discrimination. It was a pivotal point in our history. We could have either railed against the lawlessness and condemned the hoodlums or listened to the message, which was that people of color wanted to be part of the mainstream and resented the unemployment, poverty and neglect that were their traditional lot in America. Fortunately, we listened and we acted.

Fearing reverse discrimination, many white people distrust affirmative action, both in public and private spheres. This is especially relevant when quotas are used to redress past wrongs. Given our history of exclusion through the use of quotas, we Jews instinctively distrust them. I freely admit that when my wife, Lynne, and I were involved in the civil rights movement of the early sixties we envisioned a color blind society where each person succeeded or failed on his or her own merits. But we were naïve. Society does not work that way. You cannot break the legs of your competitor and then expect him to run an equal race with you. He inevitably will stumble behind. For 200 years we have been breaking the legs of our non-white minorities. As a Jew, it took me a little while to emotionally internalize this reality.

Last year's Supreme Court decisions concerning the University of Michigan put affirmative action in perspective. The Court ruled that the undergraduate college could not use a raw quota system to achieve diversity, but that the law school could use more nuanced and sophisticated tools to reach out to various ethnic and racial sectors in our society. The Court validated the concept of affirmative action while minimizing the discriminatory effect on the majority white population.

The law school won its case primarily on one point. It argued that affirmative action was good for whites as well as blacks because it created a classroom that better educated both races. An integrated classroom helps to "break down racial stereotypes," enabling "students to better understand persons of different races," and produces "livelier, more spirited, and simply more enlightening and interesting" discussions. The argument can be restated this way: Our classrooms should reflect our whole society because that is the world that the student will eventually live and work in.

Our country has come a long way since the riots of 1967. Today we see integrated universities and workplaces. I am proud to say that leading the way is the Tribune Corporation, the parent company of the *Jewish Journal.* We also see lawyers and doctors and other professionals in all shades of color in our daily lives. This is a vastly different country than the one of my youth. This is not to say that we don't have problems and that we can't improve. But despite the continual backbiting against affirmative action by conservatives, it is uncontestable that without affirmative action we would not be where we are today.

France is a good country. Without its help the colonies would not have prevailed against England and Tony Blair would be our Prime Minister today. France was also the first European country to give Jews full citizen rights. It mystifies me why Jews and Americans are so quick to vilify anything French. But all countries are imperfect, and now it's time for France to look at its own blemishes and realize that in the last 50 years it has not lived up to its own ideals of liberty, fraternity and equality, a legacy of their own revolution. It's time for France to draw its own lesson from the recent riots and develop an equivalent to American affirmative action.

Our National Heritage of Slavery
1/24/06

I was reared in a small coal town of 12,000 people in northeastern Pennsylvania, but I have always had an affinity for the great city of New York, so much so that my wife, Lynne, and I have a small pied-à-terre there. A few blocks from our apartment is a cultural jewel with which I believe only a minority of native New Yorkers are acquainted. I refer to the New York City Historical Society at 77th Street and Central Park West, one block south of the Natural History Museum. If you're in New York in the next couple of months, don't miss the current exhibit concerning slavery in New York City during the colonial period. (It closes at the end of March.)

Although I have lived in the south for 30 years, I still consider myself a northerner. We who live in Miami-Dade, Broward and Palm Beach counties know that to reach the real south we have to travel north to central Florida or even to that extension of Georgia called Jacksonville. We still carry a northern superiority complex that says that slavery and bigotry were the products of our southern cousins, the rascals we had to subdue and civilize in what they called the War Between the States. Well, go to the New York Historical Society and get reeducated.

Slavery was part of the fabric of New York society from the very beginning. In 1664, when New York passed from Dutch to British rule, there were 800 slaves in the city, more than were in Virginia. By 1703 fully 42 percent of New Yorkers had slaves. Since it was difficult to recruit European settlers during this period, laborers were in short supply. To meet this need slaves were purchased to toil as dockworkers, domestic servants and farm hands in rural Long Island.

All of the ills that we associate with slavery in the south were present in New York City and were reflected in periodic slave rebellions, primarily in 1712 and 1741. In the latter year the slaves attempted to burn down the entire city upon the heads of their captors, and they succeeded in destroying a substantial part of the city. During the later colonial period New York became a major center of the slave trade. In current dollars, in 1750 a slave could be imported from Africa for $2, 676 and sold in the colonies for $5,180, a neat 94 percent profit. In 1775, the same year that our forefathers fought at Concord and Lexington for freedom from the British, a slave could be imported for $2,292 and sold on American soil for $5,929, a whopping profit of 159 percent.

There is the irony that during the Revolutionary War an American slave could obtain his or her freedom by siding with the enemy, and, indeed, many slaves crossed over to the British lines. The peace treaty that ended the Revolutionary War gave slaveholders the right to reclaim runaway slaves who joined the British. But the English General Guy Carleton decided that slaves who were with the British for one year or more would receive freedom certificates and free passage to Canada. Three thousand ex-slaves escaped to Canada with the British. Among them was one Deborah Squash, a 20-yr-old who was formerly owned by General George Washington. Washington came personally to Carlton to demand her return, but she had already sailed to freedom in Canada. It was reported that Washington was furious that he was powerless to recover his "property."

Although other northern colonies moved to abolish slavery after independence, New York tarried. Vermont was the first to outlaw slavery in 1777. In Massachusetts slavery was abolished in 1783 by a court decision. (Progressive courts seem to be associated with that state, given the fact that gay marriage was validated there in 2004, also by court action.) New York stumbled along with a law in 1799 that began a gradual emancipation process that did not bring full freedom to slaves until 1827.

This history is very relevant for us smug northerners who think we are morally superior to the rednecks who fly Confederate flags. We, too, carry upon our shoulders the burden of history and its effects that are manifested in our society today. This was a lesson that I learned in law school in New Haven, Connecticut back in 1958. I had an African-American student friend from Louisville, Kentucky. When his parents drove from that city to New Haven to visit him they could not find a hotel or motel that would accept them – and a good part of the trip was north of the Mason-Dixon Line. They were reduced to driving 15 hours without a break.

In the early sixties, when Lynne and I were active in CORE (Congress of Racial Equality) in Cleveland, Ohio, definitely a northern city, we were involved in desegregating hotels there. Lynne led a year-long picket line against Saint Luke's Hospital where they accepted blacks but would not mix the races in the double-occupancy rooms. Yes, bigotry was not confined to southern plantations. Unfortunately, it is our national heritage.

In a mid-December column I discussed affirmative action in relation to the wake-up call of the 1967 riots. I also admitted that as a Jew it is most difficult for me to accept quotas, given their pernicious use against my people. But affirmative action need not use strict quotas, except in cases to undo specific acts of historical injustices, such as city-wide school segregation.

Affirmative action, as defined by the Supreme Court, is a process of reaching out to provide school and work-place environments that reflect our multi-cultured society that is America today. This includes Hispanic, African-American, Asian, Native-American and other colors of the rainbow.

Our white-dominated society is a direct descendant of colonial New York City and other centers of slavery and prejudice. Those of us who are white do not start with a blank slate. We have been unfairly helped by this history that has affected our lives, although we have not necessarily realized it. It's now time to truly level the playing field. A little affirmative action and a little understanding of history go a long way.

Strom Thurmond, Thomas Jefferson and Magnanimous Me
12/30/03

I had a personal reason for not liking Strom Thurmond, so it was a bit satisfying to read of his hypocrisy, now that it has been revealed that he sired a child with a black teenager, the daughter of the family maid, when he was but 22. It's interesting to contemplate his thought processes as he advocated separation of the races in his historic bid for the presidency as the candidate of the Dixiecrats in 1948, at which time his mixed-race child was 23 years old.

It was 1963 and Cleveland, Ohio was a deeply segregated city. My wife Lynne and I were active in the local chapter of CORE (Congress of Racial Equality), the cutting edge civil rights organization. Strom Thurmond was to speak in the working class lily-white western suburbs, whereas we Jews and blacks lived on the east side of town. We scheduled a picket line for his appearance.

Three hours before the event my wife received a telephone call informing her that if her husband walked the picket line that evening, "he would not return home alive." Needless to say, it was a disconcerting message. I came to the conclusion that if they really intended to kill me, they would not have been kind enough to warn me. We walked the picket line with extra vigilance. Ol' Strom came, delivered his venomous message, and left, not knowing that a young civil rights attorney (which I was at that time) would remember the event long after he delivered his diatribe at hundreds of other cities across this country.

The Rev. Jesse Jackson was struck by what he considered the similarities between Thurmond and Thomas Jefferson, reflecting "a deep and ugly Southern tradition" of taking advantage of black women in their employ. "By day they are bullies. By night, they manipulate race to their advantage." Referring to Thurmond, he continued: "The point that strikes me the most is that he lived 100 years and never acknowledged his daughter. He never let her eat at his table. He fought for laws that kept his daughter segregated and in an inferior position. He never fought to give her a first-class status. Thomas Jefferson did pretty much the same."

Wait a moment. Jefferson is not my favorite founding father, but Jesse Jackson has done him an injustice. He was not a segregationist and obstructionist in the Thurmond mold. In spite of a 38-year illicit relationship with his black slave, Sally Hemings, or maybe because of it, he was by eighteenth century standards a liberal on racial issues.

In 1784 at the Continental Congress, Jefferson introduced legislation that proposed that after 1800 "neither slavery nor involuntary servitude" would be allowed in any newly created state. Had this passed, the "peculiar institution" would have withered away and the civil war would have been avoided. Jefferson needed the votes of seven states. He received only six. New Jersey would have voted with him, except that its single delegate on site was ill and he did not vote. Such are the little dramas of history. A bad cold changed the course of history. But Jefferson made the attempt.

In 1781 Jefferson wrote his book, "Notes on the State of Virginia" in which he put forth his beliefs on race. Within the context of the eighteenth century he was progressive, so much so that he feared to publish the work. He shared the manuscript with John Adams, a fierce opponent of slavery. Adams wrote to him, "The Passages upon Slavery are worth Diamonds." Jefferson replied, "But my country (meaning Virginia) will probably estimate them differently." Jefferson waited until 1785 to publish the book, and even then he refused to have his name appear on the title page.

So if Jefferson was such a liberal, how could he own slaves and abuse Sally Hemings? First, his relationship with Hemings was long and tender, even though she was a subservient slave. But how could Jefferson continue to own slaves when he knew that it was a pernicious institution? He wrote that it "transports (whites) into despots, and...destroys the morals (of slave owners)." He knew this, but he was a Virginia plantation owner whose primary asset was his slaves. He was also a terrible businessman with a penchant for purchasing the good things in life, whether he could afford them or not, which he could not. To free his slaves would have impoverished him further. This fact does not exonerate him; it only explains his position.

His blot on history is that he allowed his slaves to be sold (thereby breaking up families) while he was alive, and not emancipating his slaves before his death. They were all sold at the block to cover the debts that he accumulated during his life, with the exception of the Hemings family. Monticello was also sold off, ending up in the hands of the Uriah Phillips

Levy family, a leading Jew of his time, there to remain until 1924 (but that's another story).

But the bottom line is that Thomas Jefferson was no Strom Thurmond. Jesse Jackson overstated his case.

Senator Joseph Biden of Delaware, a champion of civil rights, has softened my personal animosity toward Thurmond. Biden became a close friend of Strom Thurmond in the Senate. Thurmond changed course in his later years, supporting the Martin Luther King national holiday, the funding of black colleges, and personally hiring many blacks on his Senatorial staff . Biden believes that this was a true conversion and not merely a political ploy to accommodate the times. The *New York Times* also reported that Thurmond had contact with his daughter throughout his lifetime and that his parentage was an open secret to his family and staffers.

All of this softens my sense of perverse joy at seeing Thurmond's hypocrisy unmasked after his death. In the end, we are all very complex people, neither all bad nor all good. There comes a time for forgiveness, for Jefferson's lapses and for Thurmond's life for the first 75 years. If we live long enough, we can come to the point of forgiveness. Fortunately that anonymous caller in Cleveland never followed through on his threat, which now allows me my magnanimous perch on which I sit. So goes life.

Censorship

Censorship & Media Manipulation
6/28/05

Last month Comedy Central broadcast a special by the comedian D.L. Hughly. I liked him when he appeared on Bill Maher's HBO show and looked forward to his special. He uses the F-word and other examples of innocuous profanity, but he speaks political and social wisdom in the lingo of the "hood," all the while denigrating himself because he has only a GED. I know many PhD's who do not have his wit or wisdom. So this is what happened – every other word was bleeped out by Comedy Central (by Comedy Central, of all places, a cable station aimed at the young). It got so bad that I abandoned the show after a couple of minutes.

What's going on here? Comedy Central is owned by Viacom, the giant telecommunications company that also owns CBS, Infinity radio and Simon & Schuster, amongst other household names. It's pretty obvious that Viacom is petrified of the Federal Communications Commission's intensified policy to police the airwaves. Comedy Central is a channel network, not broadcast over the air, and probably is immune to FCC regulation, but that did not stop Viacom from censoring its program. What we have here is craven fear of the censorship czars in Washington.

I am told that the easiest way to boil a person is to put him in a large pot of cold water and then imperceptibly increase the temperature until it boils and he is fully cooked. That's what's happened to us. Slowly the Bush censors have turned up the heat and we're on their dinner table. How did it all happen?

It started with Bono in 2003 when he accepted a Golden Globe award and commented that it was "f-----g brilliant." Note that this use of the F-word has nothing to do with sex and carries no prurient interest. Also note that this society is so uptight that I hesitate to print the full word in a newspaper that is read by mature and sophisticated readers (our demographics show that our readers are very, very mature, including myself).

It went from there to Janet Jackson and the "The Breast" incident on the Super Bowl halftime extravaganza. How could they do this on a family entertainment show? Hughly asks how they can call this "family entertainment" when every other ad was either for beer, Cialis, Levitra or Viagra.

Then it really got nasty. The FCC fined Clear Channel (the largest owner of radio stations in the country) $495,000 for some comments on their stations about anal sex and some flatulence jokes by Howard Stern. That forced the "shock jock" to abandon his radio show and to soon transfer to satellite radio where a fraction of his millions of listeners will hear him. I have only heard him in bits and pieces a few times, and I find him boring and puerile, but I am enraged that the moral cops of the religious right have triumphed over free speech.

This fight is not only over language, but over political content. The ABC late night show "Nightline" was dropped by the 62 television stations owned by Sinclair Broadcasting when it devoted an entire show to reading the names and displaying the photos of soldiers killed in Iraq. This was believed to be a criticism of the war. Sinclair owners, who are major Bush backers and money-raisers, were falling in line with the media manipulators in our government.

Last month there were two incidents of media manipulation. *Newsweek* made the error of reporting that a Koran was flushed down a toilet at Guantanamo, relying only on one anonymous source. The magazine presented the article to the Pentagon before publication and received no complaint. It turned out not to be verifiable, even though there have been published complaints by former prisoners claiming the same abuse. The *Newsweek* story was used by opponents of General Musharraf's government in Pakistan who oppose his close connection to the United States, and riots were fomented in that country and Afghanistan. *Newsweek* apologized, not for the accuracy or inaccuracy of the story, but for running it with only one source, a journalistic short cut.

The Bush administration demanded that the editors of *Newsweek* as good Americans do public penance by telling the "real story" according to the Bush administration scripture. But the *New York Times* reported that even Republican sources admitted that it was media manipulation: "Republicans close to the White House said that although Mr. Bush and Vice President Dick Cheney were genuinely angered by the *Newsweek* article, West Wing officials were also exploiting it in an effort to put a check on the press." The

Times quoted one Bush advisor as saying, "There is no check on what you guys (the media) do."

Of course there is no check. A free press is there to carefully watch those who hold power. The day that the press does not look upon any administration, Republican or Democratic, as the adversary, is the day that our liberties begin to erode. The press is a part of that delicate balance of power that protects us all. When Bush denigrates the press or tries to muzzle it, he is destroying a major pillar of a democratic society. Concerning the *Newsweek* incident, Marvin Kalb, formerly of CBS and now of Harvard, said, "This is not the first time that the administration has sought to portray the American media as inadequately patriotic."

The other story that emerged this past month is that the Bush administration appointees who control the Corporation for Public Broadcasting which provides PBS and NPR with $400 million per year have decided to redirect money into classical music and away from news shows on National Public Radio (NPR). The administration has also instigated an investigation into whether there is a liberal bias in public television programming (PBS). I am a long-time listener of NPR (both WXEL and WLRN) and I tell you that I cannot discern a bias. They tell both sides of a story, and that's true concerning Middle East coverage as well, despite the protestations of Cheryl Halpern, a former chairwoman of the Republican Jewish Coalition and a major Bush fund-raiser, who now sits on the Corporation for Public Broadcasting board. The problem is that balance is not what these people want.

I can feel the heat rising and I'm beginning to believe that I'm being boiled alive. Slowly our freedoms are eroding and we don't perceive it. We continue to follow stories of young run-away brides and the eternal saga of Michael Jackson and other such trivia. All the while freedom of expression is restricted in the name of moral codes promulgated by the Christian Right, and political commentary is diminished by pressure from the fundamentalist who resides in the White House. My fellow Americans: Feel the heat rising.

Self-Censorship in the Media
7/5/05

Censorship and media manipulation fit together like a chicken and an egg – if the power establishment cannot manipulate then it censors you. Before moving on from last week's discussion let me make one more comment on the whole *Newsweek* incident, since it is such an outrage.

White House press secretary Scott McClellan blamed *Newsweek* for setting off anti-American violence: "Our image abroad has been damaged."

Another source commented, "People died because of this story." Gee, the world hates us because of *Newsweek*. Talk about manipulation and getting off the hook. All this time I thought that our image was tarnished because we lied about the existence of weapons of mass destruction, the false assertion of a partnership between Saddam and Osama bin Laden, the fake story of Iraq's nuclear capability and the tangential fact that we have killed almost 200,000 Iraqis, mostly civilians, "collateral damage" as part of a preemptive war. I thought we were hated because we cavalierly invaded a Muslim country. I am glad that the Bush administration has put me straight – it's all *Newsweek's* fault.

Forget this little bit of legerdemain; the ultimate act of manipulation is when you get the media to self-censor. This is precisely what the Federal Communications Commission (FCC) has done through fear. First, it has warned broadcasters that it does not intend to hold itself to a specific definition of indecency. Thus they will forever be self-censoring for fear that they may cross an undefined line. (And remember the consequences -- the FCC fined Clear Channel $495,000 for *one* "violation" of its standards by Howard Stern, thereby forcing Clear Channel to drop him from their stations.)

Second, the FCC will not consider "context." If a forbidden word is uttered they intend to hold the broadcaster liable. This means that if I uttered the F-word on the air in an academic setting as part of a broader discussion of censorship, this very critique could be used to punish the broadcaster. Finally, previously the FCC required a repeated use of an obscenity. Now only one word slipped out of a guest's mouth puts the broadcaster in jeopardy. FCC Chairman Michael Powell (son of Colin Powell) really put the heat on the media when he urged them, under threats of major fines, to self-censor (in his construct, adopt a voluntary code). He then ominously warned: "It would be in your interest to do so." In mafia fashion, this is obviously an offer they can't refuse

And self-censor they do. This past year the British producers of "Masterpiece Theater" sent us two versions, one deeply and one mildly censored, of the critically acclaimed series "Prime Suspect." Some day, when we grow up, maybe we will be able to see what our more sophisticated British cousins can. Even Rush Limbaugh's talk show was censored, bleeping, on a few seconds' time delay, such offending words as "urinate," "damn," and "orgy."

When ABC aired Steven Spielberg's classic movie "Saving Private Ryan" 66 affiliates refused to broadcast it, denying it to such sophisticated markets as Boston, Detroit, Cleveland and Baltimore. In the heat of battle the F-word was used 21 times, and furthermore, it showed "graphic violence." As to the violence, the first 23 minutes of that film are almost unbearable in its recreation of the invasion of Normandy on D-Day. That is precisely what makes the movie a classic -- it shows the cruelty of war. That may also be precisely why certain people do not want to see it shown, as we are bogged down in a useless war based on lies. As to its profanity -- gee, I guess a real soldier in battle would never stoop to such language, especially if he were a born-again. Frank Rich, in the *New York Times*, called this self-censoring, "McCarthyism,' moral values' style." Many of the owners of these television outlets that saved us from Private Ryan also own newspapers. Do they self-censor there? The question is whether there is a spillover from the FCC into other areas of our lives?

The most egregious act of self-censorship was when Disney refused to distribute Michael Moore's movie "Fahrenheit 911" before our last presidential election. Moore's agent confirmed that Disney CEO Michael Eisner expressed concern that the film might jeopardize tax breaks for Disney World and its other ventures in Florida, given the fact that George's brother Jeb is governor. This is not only an act of self-censorship, but opens up an equally important debate as to the wisdom of corporate conglomerates owning media companies (out of the purview of this column).

I understand why this administration wants to curtail political debate. With their record, I, too, would be tempted. What is more difficult for me is their caving in to the religious right on so-called obscenity. There are absolutely no reputable studies that show that language, mere words, damage children. Actions, not words, damage children. Violence, hatred, loose guns around the house, withholding affection, these damage children, not words. My wife and I reared three children and we never censored their television, movies or reading material. They turned out pretty well. I know that they heard the forbidden F-word and other "obscenity" in their youthful years, but I am pretty sure that it hasn't compromised their good morals.

As part of self-censorship, the Bush administration wants broadcasters to return to the 1950s when most shows carried the seal of the Code of Good Practices. Jeff Jarvis, in *The Nation*, commented: "The code decreed that 'illicit sex relations are not treated as commendable.' So much for prime time. It insisted that 'attacks on religion and religious faiths are not allowed' and that clergy 'under no circumstances are to be held up to ridicule.' So much for TV movies about Jim Bakker and kiddie-diddling priests. 'The presentation of cruelty, greed and selfishness as worthy motivations is to be avoided.' Farewell reality TV. 'Unfair exploitation of others for personal gain shall not be presented as praiseworthy.' Donald Trump: You're fired!"

It would be a little ludicrous and comical if it weren't so serious. Before Michael Powell adapted to the Bush regime (who said that conservatives don't believe in evolution and adaptation?) he said, "I don't know that

I want the government as my nanny." In 1999, in accepting the Media Institute's Freedom of Speech Award, he said: "We should think twice before allowing the government the discretion to filter information to us as they see fit...Benevolent or not, we did not sign away to a Philosopher-King the responsibility to determine for us, like a caring parent, what messages we should and should not hear."

If we're lucky we'll survive the Bush administration and free speech will prevail before all media outlets self-censor us into total silence.

The Supreme Court and the F-Word
12/9/08

This past month the Supreme Court heard arguments on an important case involving censorship which focused on the use of the F-Word on television. I'm not delicate enough to discuss this case without frequent use of that word, not quite spelled out in deference to community standards. However, beware that the use of the F-Word will follow. If that will offend you I suggest you skip this column and return next week when I will discuss such non-controversial topics as Guantanamo or the West Bank.

Background to the case in point: the Federal Communications Commission, under the sway of the moral cops of the Bush administration, has been fining television networks for slips of the tongue involving what the FCC considers obscenity. Janet Jackson's "wardrobe malfunction" during the 2004 Super Bowl revealing her bare breast for nine-sixteenths of one second cost CBS a $550,000 fine. The agency set aside its decades-old policy of not imposing fines for isolated or fleeting material. After much litigation, probably costing CBS much more than $550,000 in legal fees, the Court of Appeals for the Third Circuit ruled that the FCC's fine was arbitrary and capricious and therefore illegal.

The present case in front of the Supreme Court, FCC v. Fox Television, (I never thought I would be rooting for Fox Television) involves a fleeting use of the F-Word. When accepting his Golden Globe award in 2003 pop star Bono, (I had to ask my son who he was) the lead singer of the rock band U-2, exclaimed in joy that the victory "was really, really f---ing brilliant."

The question before the Court is whether every permutation of that word involves sex. The Second Circuit, ruling in Fox's favor, stated, "As the general public well knows" four-letter words "are often used in everyday conversation without any sexual or excretory meaning." F---ing A. That's an expression from my youth in the 1950's that meant "I'm with you all the way, you're absolutely correct." Why it meant that I'll never know. But I'm sure that it wasn't referring to sex.

For my part I don't believe that there is such a thing as obscenity and I once proved it before a sort-of court of law. Here's the story. The year was 1968. I was teaching economics on the faculty of Miami University of Ohio. There was a national anti-Vietnam War student organization entitled, Up Against the Wall Mother-F---er. The leader of the local group held a protest and was expelled from school for the use of the F-Word. However, they could not throw him out without allowing him a hearing in front of an academic appeals board.

Here's where I came in. The student could not use an outside lawyer and Miami University does not have a law school. He could only use a member of the faculty as his counsel. The students knew that I was also a lawyer, so I was the natural choice. I was lecturing to a class when a member of Up Against the Wall Mother-F---er stormed into the lecture hall and exclaimed, "They threw Joe Blow out of school. Will you defend him?" I immediately said yes, and 120 students broke into thunderous applause. I was living through a Frank Capra movie.

I put a member of the English faculty on the stand and he testified on the changing nature of words. During the Victorian period the word "leg" was considered licentious. Think 1939 when Clark Gable uttered those immortal words, "Frankly dear, I don't give a damn." Damn, which the FCC would not consider obscenity today, was a scandalous word. When the student said that he didn't like the f---ing war he was expressing his dissatisfaction in the lingo of his generation. It was his version of "I don't like your damn war." I won the case. The student remained in school.

Adam Liptak, in his *New York Times* report on the current Supreme Court case, indicated that the Oxford English Dictionary has an approximately six-thousand word entry discussing the use of the F-Word in non-sexual contexts. I ran to my beloved 2,662 paged 1968 edition of the Webster's Third International Dictionary to see what it said about the F-Word. I was shocked, shocked I tell you, to find that it did not include one reference. It went from fuchsite (a mineral consisting of a common mica containing chromium) to fucold (resembling or having the nature of seaweeds). No F---. The word did not exist.

That's the point. In a 40-year span we went from zero to a six-thousand-word entry. There is nothing intrinsically obscene in language. I'll tell you what is really obscene – actions. Denying children health insurance is obscene. Using the N-Word is often obscene because it is an act that expresses bigotry and hate. Allowing people to live in poverty is obscene. Stealing is obscene.

Not caring for your neighbor is obscene. Language is a matter of taste. It is not obscene, unless it is used to denigrate another human being.

I think that this is an important Supreme Court case because it delineates the boundaries of the moral cops. They are never satisfied with policing our tongues. They want to police our actions. In 1960 when I was newly married in graduate school in New Haven, Connecticut, that state dictated that one could only have sex in the missionary position. The keepers of our morals were busy at work.

Censorship is a very dangerous tool that has to be handled carefully. It could lead to the loss of our precious freedoms, in and out of the bedroom. I hope that our f---ing conservative Supreme Court understands this. (There was no sexual reference in my use of the F-Word in that sentence.)

Civil Rights

The Danger of the "War" on Terror
6/20/06

Let's get something straight right now, before we discuss our eroding civil rights, because this is the bedrock of the attack on our freedoms: We are not in a War on Terror. Yes we are in a war of sorts in Iraq (a war defined by daily battles and huge casualties, a war against insurgents, but not against another nation). But we're not in a War on Terror as the Bush administration would have us believe.

We have a terror problem as do other nations. The English subways were bombed by Muslim radicals and their pubs were blown up by the Catholic IRA, but they did not define it as a war. It was and is a serious problem, but it is not war. The Spanish railway was bombed, but they do not consider themselves at war and they have not instituted draconian war legislation. The Germans were plagued by the Red Brigade for decades, but they did not restrict civil liberties. A serious problem, yes. A war, no.

We are at "war" only in a rhetorical sense, in that we define a campaign against any problem as a war, witness our War on Poverty under the Johnson administration, our War on Drugs under Bush I and Clinton and even Fox commentator Bill O'Reilly's supposed campaign to counter what he perceives as the War Against Christmas because we say Happy Holidays rather than Merry Christmas.

Why is this distinction so important? Because with war come hysteria and a general disregard for the checks and balances that define our liberty. With war comes xenophobia, the fear of anything different and foreign. With war comes a loss of civil liberties for everyone, liberal and conservative, foreign born and American bred.

If you don't believe me, look at history. From the beginning, war and fear of war have warped our collective commitment to civil rights. Starting with President John Adams, under fear of war with France, we passed the Sedition Act of 1797 that made it a crime to make "false, scandalous and malicious" writings against the president or congress or to attempt "to excite against them the hatred of the good people of the United States, or to stir up sedition." Although not widely implemented, Congressman Matthew Lyon of Vermont went to jail for describing Adams as having an "unbounded thirst for ridiculous pomp, foolish adulation and selfish avarice." A journalist in the employ of Thomas Jefferson to politically attack Adams, James Thomas Callendar, was also jailed.

These were relatively isolated incidents, but during the First World War sedition became the basis for widespread abuses of civil liberties. Under President Woodrow Wilson, Attorney General Alexander Palmer waged extensive raids on supposed revolutionaries. Armed with the passage of the Espionage Act of 1917 and the Sedition Act of 1918, Palmer, with his 24-year-old assistant, J. Edgar Hoover, arrested over 10,000 people. Palmer used the war fever to stir up emotions against supposed communist infiltration of this country, as well as blaming socialists for the country's ills. Emotions were running so high that the House of Representatives refused to seat Victor Berger (incidentally a Jew) who was elected as a socialist from Milwaukee, Wisconsin. Berger was convicted of sedition and sentenced to 20 years in prison because he opposed the war. The Supreme Court later overturned that conviction and he did serve in Congress.

Under cover of being at war, Palmer's man, J. Edgar Hoover, compiled a data base of 150,000 names (shades of what is happening today, except on a smaller scale) and broke into offices without warrants (again shades of the present). Palmer actually rounded up 249 "well-known radical leaders" and forcibly shipped them off on a boat to the Soviet Union. (Most of them who stayed were eventually shot by Stalin as potential traitors in the purges of the 1930's.) Palmer was attempting to obtain the Democratic nomination for president in 1920, and war fears were fertile ground for his demagoguery. Many people loved him because, after all, he was protecting them during a time of war.

Just this last month the current governor of Montana posthumously pardoned 75 people convicted under its sedition law during the First World War. One man was sentenced to 7 to 20 years in prison for calling wartime food regulations a "big joke." It was declared illegal to speak German and books written in that language were banned. (Twenty-seven states had sedition laws as well as the federal government.) At the pardoning ceremony the 90-year-old daughter of one of those convicted related how she was put up for adoption after the family farm failed when her father was imprisoned.

Governor Schweitzer said that he was saying what the governor back in 1917 should have said; "I'm sorry, forgive me, and God bless America, because we can criticize our government."

Moving on to the Second World War, we find the same disregard for civil liberties. Two and one half months after Pearl Harbor President Roosevelt signed Executive Order 9066 that incarcerated 120,000 Japanese Americans in detention camps.(Canada did the same with 23,000 Japanese residents there. War hysteria is not limited to these United States.) What is even more disturbing is that the Supreme Court in the infamous *Korematsu* decision of 1944 upheld the legality of this action. It took us until 1988 to formally apologize and award $20,000 to each of the surviving 60,000 internees, a pittance of the value of property lost and lives destroyed.

The Cold "War" produced its own hysteria through the machinations of the House Un-American Activities Committee (HUAC) and the McCarthy investigations. The stupidity of the era was reflected in an obituary this last January in the *New York Times*. Frank Wilkinson, age 91, died. He was an employee of the City of Los Angeles working on public housing in Chavez Ravine. He was summoned in front of HUAC and refused to respond based on his First Amendment rights. He was fired and eventually served time. The housing project gave way to the present Dodger Stadium. In the 1980's under the Freedom of Information Act he discovered the enormity of government snooping in that the FBI collected 132,000 documents on him. In 2002 the same City of Los Angeles that fired him issued a citation praising him for his "lifetime commitment to civil liberties and for making this community a better place in which to live." In 1999 he received a lifetime achievement award from the American Civil Liberties Union. It took society fully 50 years to redress its transgression.

We are going through a perilous period defined as the "War" on terror. We run the risk of the same loss of civil liberties as in the past, as long as we buy into the rhetoric of the Bush administration.

The great Justice William O. Douglas wrote: "As nightfall does not come at once, neither does oppression. In both instances, there's a twilight where everything remains seemingly unchanged, and it is in such twilight that we all must be aware of change in the air, however slight, lest we become victims of the darkness."

First Steps on the Road to a Police State
8/28/07

Earlier this month Congress passed a law allowing the National Security Agency (NSA) to eavesdrop on international telephone calls and emails made by Americans to people overseas without obtaining court warrants.

Previous to this the government had to comply with the Foreign Intelligence Surveillance Act of 1978 (FISA) which was passed to control government action against American citizens. That law was passed as a reaction to excesses of the Nixon administration. In an emergency the government could wiretap without a warrant, but it had to be reported to the FISA Court after the fact. It was this FISA Court approval that the Bush administration sidestepped in its illegal wiretapping after 9/11. Bush originally denied the existence of such wiretapping, but later came clean.

Under pressure from the telecommunication companies who feared civil lawsuits from ordinary Americans for invading their privacy, the Bush administration agreed to abide by FISA this last January. But the quantity of their eavesdropping was so great that Bush decided to pressure Congress for this new legislation so that he would not have to report to the FISA Court. His need to avoid the court and warrants testifies to the great volume of wiretaps happening at this very moment.

Of course we need the ability to use wiretapping in our fight against terrorism. But the question is how to effectuate this without wholesale trampling of our civil liberties. FISA's answer to this problem was to put some outside control over our spy agencies. That outside control was the FISA Court. Under the new legislation the NSA does not have to go to the court. Instead it merely needs the approval of Attorney General Alberto Gonzales. I'm sure that makes all of us feel more secure.

Having nothing to do with the current Bush administration in particular (although it is more scary than most), the real question is, can you trust government leaders not to distort the law and to misuse spy agencies that were intended for foreign operations against our own people? Put more simply, can we avoid a police state without some outside control?

History seems to say no. John F. Kennedy used the CIA to spy on Hanson Baldwin, a Pulitzer Prize winning *New York Times* reporter, because he was disturbed at what he wrote in his paper. Recent admissions by the CIA also report that it spied on other reporters as well. This was in direct violation of the 1947 charter of the CIA that barred it from operating in the United States, spying on Americans and acting like secret police. What is disturbing is that presidential aide Clark Clifford, who helped write the CIA charter, was a member of the small group of advisors to Kennedy that approved of its domestic spying. Even good men lose control of themselves.

In 1967 Lyndon Johnson ordered CIA director Richard Helms to spy on anti-Vietnam War protestors. In his memoir Helms wrote that he informed LBJ that it was illegal, but the president still demanded it. That domestic surveillance, code-named Chaos, went on for almost seven years under Johnson and Nixon.

I need not recount the illegal uses of spy agencies under President Nixon. The CIA went so far as to locate a good lock-picker for E. Howard Hunt and his gang for the Watergate escapade. Obviously, the misuse of authority did not begin with George W. Bush. It is endemic to anyone in authority. But it is exacerbated by the fact that our current president, to paraphrase the title of John Dean's book, is "worse than Nixon." Having served Nixon, and having gone to jail for doing it, he should know.

The danger is real. Referring to the misuse of the CIA and other government spy agencies, Robert Amory, chief of the CIA's intelligence analysis directorate under both Eisenhower and Kennedy, warned that, "You can get into Gestapo-like tactics."

The propensity for spy bureaucrats to go wild is reflected in the recent expose by ABC News that now the FBI has over 500,000 names on its terrorist watch list. A spokesperson for the ACLU commented, "If we have 509,000 names on that list, the watch is virtually useless. You'll be capturing innocent individuals with no connection to crime or terror." It is ludicrous. U.S. lawmakers and their spouses have been detained because their names were on the list. So was Saddam Hussein's name there while he was in U.S. custody in Iraq.

We can laugh at the ineptitude of our spy agencies, but it is no laughing matter. These bunglers have the power to get into Gestapo-like tactics, as Robert Armory reminds us. That's why I'm shocked at the broad discretion that congress just gave George W. Bush, of all people.

A Bush Victory and a Blow to Civil Liberties
9/11/07

This past month a federal jury in Miami convicted Jose Padilla of conspiracy to murder, kidnap and maim people in a foreign country. It was the final chapter in a sorry saga that began when the government arrested him in 2002 at Chicago's O'Hare airport and charged him with planning to explode a dirty bomb in this country.

To great fanfare then Attorney General John Ashcroft announced that

Padilla's capture marked an "unfolding terrorist plot to attack the United States by exploding a radioactive dirty bomb" that could have caused "mass death and injury."

Instead of charging Padilla with this crime in a civil court, the Bush administration branded him an "enemy combatant" and sent him into solitary confinement in a military brig in South Carolina for three and one-half years. What set Padilla apart from other supposed enemy combatants (persons subject to life confinement without a trial or evidence against them) was that Padilla is an American citizen, born in the Bronx, reared in Chicago and a Broward County resident.

Guilt or innocence aside, Padilla represented the concept that this government could pick an American citizen off the street and throw him into a three year incarceration without a lawyer or even the ability to communicate to his family that he was snatched. This went even beyond the Bush contention that he could eavesdrop on all of us without a court warrant. This was not just loss of privacy; it was loss of freedom.

Finally Padilla's case was about to end up in the Supreme Court when the Bush administration transferred him from the military prison into a civil court of law, where every American citizen has a right to be. Then Attorney General Alberto Gonzalez made this switch knowing that even this conservative Supreme Court would have embarrassed the administration by ruling against it.

When push came to shove, the grandiose claims about a dirty bomb aimed at the United States turned out to be more smoke and mirrors in league with the missing weapons of mass destruction and the nuclear capacity of Saddam Hussein. In the Miami courtroom Padilla was not charged with committing a crime. He was charged with conspiracy to commit a crime – meaning he had plans but never got around to doing anything.

Conspiracy is one of those crimes that opens the legal system to gross injustices. On the one hand, if a group could be shown to have manufactured bombs and stored lethal weapons, a conspiracy charge would be valid even though the criminal act did not occur. But at the other end of the spectrum, if a group of people sat at a bar and talked of how they could attack America as they drank their Budweiser, this would not rise to the level of conspiracy.

In Padilla's case the government had an application form with his fingerprints on it to attend an Al Qaeda training camp in Afghanistan. Padilla is a convert to Islam and was studying in Cairo to be an Imam. The government never placed him in Pakistan or Afghanistan. They tried him with two other supposed conspirators. The prosecution played literally thousands of recorded telephone tapes of the other two defendants talking to one another. Padilla's voice was on only seven tapes and his comments were innocuous.

We may never know to what extent Padilla was involved, but the evidence was slim indeed. Peter Margulies, a law professor, was quoted in the *New York Times*: "It's a pretty big leap between a mere indication of desire to attend a camp and a crystallized desire to kill, maim and kidnap." He further stated that the conspiracy charge against Padilla "is highly amorphous and it basically allows someone to be found guilty for something that is one step away from a thought crime."

When Padilla is sentenced on December 5 he faces up to life in prison. But more is at stake in this case than one person's travail. If this government can do this to one American citizen, it can do it to all American citizens. One can never forget the testimony of Pastor Martin Neimoeller who was deported to a concentration camp by the Nazis: "In Germany they came first for the Communists, and I didn't speak up because I wasn't a Communist. Then they came for the Jews, and I didn't speak up because I wasn't a Jew. Then they came for the trade unionists, and I didn't speak up because I wasn't a trade unionist. Then they came for the Catholics, and I didn't speak up because I was a Protestant. Then they came for me, and by that time no one was left to speak up."

Padilla's conviction comes amidst the fears of post 9/11 and almost 80 years to the day since the executions of Sacco and Vanzetti, two minority immigrants who were caught up in the anti-terrorist show trials after the First World War. History will tell whether Padilla will join them on the acknowledged list of victims of hysteria and government duplicity.

The Bush Administration Attacks Our Civil Rights
1/31/06

I plead guilty. I approach the extension of the Patriot Act and the Bush administration's massive eavesdropping on American citizens from the perspective of my own life experiences. I know what it is to be the target of government surveillance. It was the early sixties and my wife, Lynne, and I were active in the Cleveland, Ohio chapter of the Congress of Racial Equality (CORE), a civil rights organization. We did "radical" things such as check the local hotels and motels as to whether they conformed to the newly passed Civil Rights Act of 1964. We organized a busload of activists to travel to Washington, D.C. where we heard Martin Luther King give his "I Have a Dream" speech and we picketed a local hospital that discriminated against blacks. We also protested the building of a new grade school that would not be integrated due to its location. Really "radical" stuff. Yet we were under constant government surveillance.

Sgt. John Ungvary of the Cleveland Police Subversive Squad, in cooperation with the FBI, would carefully record the license plates of every car that attended a CORE meeting. Our home telephone was tapped. This was the early sixties and electronics were not too sophisticated. Our phone was the only line in the apartment building that clicked when the receiver was lifted. One of these years I will ask for my file under the Freedom of Information Act to see what the government thought of me. I know what I thought of them. What fools they were to think that Martin Luther King was a subversive and that the civil rights movement was akin to communism.

Arianna Huffington summarized those times on her blog: "Our government lied, cheated, harassed, intimidated, burglarized, vandalized, framed and spread false rumors – to say nothing of keeping voluminous files on everyone from John Lennon to Lucille Ball – in an effort to quash legitimate dissent against the Vietnam War and the racist practices of the South." But it's happening once again. It was recently reported that the FBI has been monitoring antiwar protestors, anti-logging advocates and the Catholic Workers Group, which promotes antipoverty efforts and social causes. An ACLU spokesperson commented, "You look at these documents and you think wow, we have really returned to the days of J. Edgar Hoover, when you see in FBI files that they're talking about a group like the Catholic Workers league as having a communist ideology."

It's not only the FBI. It's the undercover New York City Police surveillance of people protesting the Iraq War. It's the National Security Agency (NSA) eavesdropping on thousands of citizens. One wonders whether there are any intelligence agents left to search for Al Qaeda operatives, when they are all checking on antiwar and anti-logging advocates. But most important, our president maintains that he has the authority under the executive powers of Article II of the Constitution to contravene laws and to continue to invade our privacy. He also maintains that he has the right to arrest an American citizen and brand him an "enemy combatant" and deny him a trial in an American court. (Ask Jose Padilla about the protection that he has received under the Constitution, as he continues to sit in a military brig in North Carolina.)

All of this domestic spying violates the Foreign Intelligence Surveillance Act of 1978 which was passed in response to the excesses that Arianna Huffington described. Under that act the government must first obtain a warrant from a special court to spy upon an American citizen, something which the Bush administration, under the guidance of our vice president, refuses to do. Under the heading, "Mr. Cheney's Imperial Presidency," the

New York Times editorialized: "George W. Bush has quipped several times during his political career that it would be so much easier to govern in a dictatorship. Apparently he never told his vice president that this was a joke."

Rather than deny that the NSA violated the law by eavesdropping without warrants, Cheney vigorously defended the practice based on executive powers. He has been the prime mover in this administration to assert the power of the presidency: "I believe in a strong, robust executive authority and I think that the world we live in demands it." It was this same kind of thinking that produced the excesses of the FBI snooping during the civil rights era and the executive order that displaced 120,000 innocent Japanese-Americans into detention camps during the Second World War.

This is not a partisan issue. The ramifications affect Republicans as well as Democrats. It is an attack on the balance of powers within the Constitution that protect us from autocratic rule or impulsive legislation. The Constitution carefully split power between three branches: executive (the president), legislative (the Congress) and judiciary (the courts). Within the legislative branch it purposely created two bodies (the Senate and the House) which act as a check and balance against each other. Within the Senate, by its rule, not by constitutional law, the filibuster acts as another check against majority rule requiring a super-majority of 60 percent to pass legislation when a group of senators feels strongly enough to oppose something. The president can veto legislation that finally makes it through the two legislative chambers. That's his check on the legislative branch. But, in turn, he can be overruled by a two-thirds vote of Congress. Our founding fathers argued whether this should be a two-thirds or a three-fourths vote. They opted for the former because they thought that a three-fourths vote would put too much power in the executive branch. They were constantly and consciously balancing power.

The framers of the Constitution were balancing power because they distrusted human nature. They realized that power corrupts. They lived under King George and they knew the history of imperial power typified by the French King Louis XIV who declared "L'etat, c'est moi, I am the State," when questioned by the Parliament of Paris. They were determined to create checks and balances to avoid that on American soil. It is this understanding of the Constitution that President Bush challenges when he blatantly negates the legislative process by contravening the Foreign Intelligence Security Act of 1978 which prohibits domestic snooping without a warrant. It is an act of import that may very well constitute a "high crime" under the impeachment clause of the Constitution.

The importance of this constitutional question was best summed up by Robert A. Levy of the Cato Institute, probably the most conservative (libertarian) think tank in Washington. He was referring to the Patriot Act, but his comments apply just as well to the Foreign Intelligence Security Act of 1978: "If you think the Bill of Rights is just so much a scrap of paper and the separation of powers doctrine has outlived its usefulness, then the USA Patriot Act…is the right recipe to deal with terrorists."

Someone should tell both the president and his vice president that this is still a democracy with a rule of law under a Constitution before it's too late for all of us. How many more Jose Padillas will there be before we wake up and protest?

Immigration

On Illegal Immigrants
4/10/07

Here's the bottom line: There are approximately 12 million illegal immigrant workers in this country. (Lou Dobbs of CNN speaks of up to 20 million, but I'll use the generally accepted 12 million.) We have 146 million legal workers in our work force with a 4.5 percent unemployment rate. This means that there are a little over eight million unemployed. Not all of them are poor unskilled workers. We have a good share of middle class accountants, computer specialists, salespeople, dentists and other who are not ready to do the jobs these immigrants do. In fact, how many unskilled native-born Americans are ready to do the back-breaking work of picking fruit and vegetables?

Let's say for the sake of argument that three million of our legally unemployed workers would replace these illegals. That leaves nine million jobs unfilled in this country if we were to deport all illegal immigrants. This means that fresh fruit will rot on the vine. White collar workers will have to learn to work in filth since the night crew will not be there to clean. You may not be able to get meat at the supermarket since most of the packing houses will not have workers to cut and process the animals. At a recent INS (the Immigration and Naturalization Service of the Justice Department) raid on a Swift Company meat processing plant in Marshalltown, Iowa, fully 58 percent of the workers were illegal.

I know that without illegal workers my son's family would be in chaos. Let me explain. Both he and his wife are upwardly mobile professionals and they require a full time nanny for their three children. Although their nanny is legal, if all of the illegal nannies were expelled from this country, either the price of nannies would skyrocket or, worse yet, they would not be able to find one. My daughter-in-law would not be able to work outside the home. There goes the fancy house, etc.

The fact is that this country has needed cheap labor as we have grown over the past 25 years, and this cheap labor has come from illegal immigration. When my grandparents came to this country in the 1890's America also needed cheap labor, but we were smart enough to welcome immigrants. My *bubbe* and *zayde* worked in the sweatshops and began life in this country the same way that the illegals are starting out today. The only difference is that our politicians have not been smart enough to make the immigration legal, so the capitalistic marketplace took over. These immigrants have been drawn to this country by the availability of work. And big business has welcomed them because they are essential to our prosperity.

There have always been xenophobic Americans who are against immigration. We Jews scared the daylights out of mid-America and a Republican congress closed the gates to the American dream in 1924, except for a select few under a restrictive quota system. There was such a backlash against the Irish immigration in the 1840's that a new political party was formed based on the fear of Catholicism and immigrants. The Know Nothing Party even ran ex-president Millard Fillmore for president in 1856, and he received fully 22 percent of the votes cast. Yet we have lived to see an Irish Catholic become president.

Unfortunately we are in an anti-immigration frenzy today comparable to that period.

The pious establishment asks, how can we give these people amnesty, for they have broken our laws by illegally entering this country? Amnesty is the same as a pardon. We pardoned Nixon, the Iran-Contra convicts under Reagan, and Bush will probably pardon Scooter Libby before he leaves office. Why can we not pardon hard-working poor people whose only crime is that they sneaked across a border to work at low paying jobs to support families here and back home?

Let us Welcome the Illegal Immigrants
4/17/07

In last week's column I pointed out that if we deported the 12 million illegal workers in this country a minimum of nine million jobs would go unfilled, bringing vast parts of our economy to a literal standstill. As much as we need this immigration, whether it is legal or illegal, there is a nativist reaction spreading across America that no longer welcomes the stranger. If this were the case in the late nineteenth century, very few of us Jews would be here today. The late Molly Ivins wrote: "Old-fashioned anti-immigration prejudice always brings out some old-fashioned racists. This time around, they have started claiming that Mexicans can't assimilate... Racists seem obsessed by the idea that illegal workers – the hardest working, poorest people in America – are somehow getting away with something, sneaking goodies that should be for Americans."

This feeling is affecting the chances for immigration reform in congress. It was originally thought that a new version of the Kennedy-McCain Senate bill could come to vote in April. Now they are talking about May or June, if ever. McCain has distanced himself from his own legislation in his continual movement to the right in his presidential bid. Mitt Romney, who in November of 2005 praised the Kennedy-McCain bill as a "reasonable proposal," is now attacking it, as he positions himself as the candidate of the right-wing of his party. An earlier House bill called for branding all illegal immigrants as felons. It appears that during this ridiculously extended political period (after all, the next election is 19 months in the future) we may lose the chance to bring rationality to this pressing issue.

Meanwhile the conservative talk-radio hosts are fanning the fires, playing upon irrational fears. Reflecting this, an Iowa housewife approached one of the candidates and asked, "What are we going to do with illegal immigrants who come here and become criminals?" They come here to work, not steal. Studies have shown that crime among illegal immigrants is lower than the national average for legal Americans. Yet Congressman J.D. Hayworth, Republican from Arizona, wants to track all illegal workers using electronic bracelets as well as denying citizenship to their children born in the U.S..

A more common fear is that we will lose English as the national language. This is not a new fear. It was there as a reaction to the German immigration in the mid nineteenth century. It was there in New York City when we Jews swamped these shores with Yiddish-speaking immigrants. It is now the reaction to Spanish-speaking immigrants, both legal and illegal. Yet the Pew Center research reports that nearly all second-generation Latinos are either bilingual or English-dominant and by the next generation 80 percent are English-dominant and virtually none speak only Spanish. It is the Jewish experience played out in Spanish – how many Jews today can speak Yiddish?

There is the fear that illegal workers are a drag on our health system, sucking up millions of dollars of Medicaid money. It is true that they get sick just like Americans and that they end up using public health services just like many of the 48 million Americans without health coverage. But this is an American problem, not an illegal immigration problem. We must figure a way to provide health coverage for all poor workers, legal and illegal.

There is an irony in singling out illegal workers. Since a vast majority of them work with fake documents, they pay social security and payroll taxes that they never draw upon, forfeiting the money to the federal government. The IRS does not release this information, but it would be interesting to see how much money illegal workers forfeit in taxes that would be refunded to them if they filed tax returns and how much money goes to Social Security which they cannot use. It could well be more than their cost of health care.

Certainly the INS (the Immigration and Naturalization Service of the Justice Department) knows where a good majority of these illegal immigrants work. The government also knows that we need these workers for the health of our own economy, so it produces the American version of the old Soviet show trials. We are feted to theater. Every month or so the INS raids a factory and deports some unfortunate illegals to great fanfare. The *New York Times* editorialized: "A screaming baby girl has been forcibly weaned from breast milk and taken, dehydrated, to an emergency room, so that the nation's borders will be secure. Her mother and more than 300 other workers in a leather-goods factory in New Bedford, Mass., have been terrorized – subdued by guns and dogs, their children stranded at school – so that the country will notice that the Bush administration is serious about enforcing immigration laws."

Even worse and crueler and more un-American is the practice of arresting some of these illegal workers as felons. They will then face years in jail. This is how it plays out. At a recent raid upon a Swift Company meat-packing plant in Iowa, out of 1,282 illegals rounded up it was found that 148 of them were using Social Security numbers of living Americans. This technically is identity fraud, for which they have been charged as felons. They did not use this information to buy television sets or to defraud anyone. The used the other person's identity to be able to work.

The *Times* interviewed one woman detained. Hunched in a gray-and-white striped jail uniform, she began to cry. Referring to her children, she said, "I risked everything so they could grow up in the United States. I'm only asking for permission to do honest work. I'm not a bad person. My record is clean. My only mistake was to do hard work in someone else's name." Her attorney commented: "She's a mother who cut my pork chops and gave Social Security a lot of money. She deserves a medal, not an indictment."

I want to end this column on a Jewish note, so let me relate a situation that sounds like a digression, but really is not (stay with me on this). At a recent gathering in Jerusalem to discuss the situation in the West Bank and the checkpoints, a participant said of the Palestinians, "These people are not like us. They come to our faces and they lie to us." At that point Uriel Simon, an Orthodox Jew and professor emeritus at Bar-Ilan University (an Orthodox institution) said, "As for liars, my father was a liar. My grandfather was a liar.

How else did we cross lines to get to this country? We stayed alive by lying. We lied to the Russians, we lied to the Germans, we lied to the British! We lie for survival! Jacob the Liar was my father. Of course they lie! Everyone lies at a checkpoint! We lied at checkpoints, too."

As Jews we should know a little about survival and have empathy for those just trying to survive. So they sneaked into this country. Big deal. They are just trying to survive by doing honest work. In many respects, they are modern-day Jews. Rather than oppressing them, we should legalize them so they may share in the American dream.

A Seriously Flawed Immigration Bill
6/12/07

As I write this on May 26th the Senate is debating the bi-partisan compromise immigration bill. But before I discuss that, I want to bring to your attention a little noticed Bush administration policy that was implemented last October.

Children born in the United States to illegal immigrants are no longer automatically entitled to health insurance through Medicaid. Our government now requires that the parents provide documents to prove their citizenship. Many illegal immigrants fear contact with the government for obvious reasons and are hesitant to obtain the legal documents needed to provide health care for their children. As head of the California Health and Human Service Agency said, "By virtue of being born in the United States, a child is a U.S. citizen. What more proof does the federal government need?"

These infants go without immunization and other crucial health care in the first years of their lives, thanks to a Bush administrative policy having nothing to do with new legislation. This pernicious ruling is indicative of the mood of conservatives in this country and provides a backdrop for the discussion on the current proposed immigration bill. Are not these children and are not their parents, children of God? To paraphrase Shylock's famous defense of Jews, if you prick them, do they not bleed?

Senator David Vitter, Republican from Louisiana, says the current bill offers "pure unadulterated amnesty" and would "reward lawbreakers "with "a large-scale get-out-of-jail-free pass." Let's look at this so-called free pass. The legalization process would not begin until after certain "triggers" were reached, including the construction of at least 370 miles of border fence and 200 miles of vehicle barriers. Homeland Security must also create a new fraud-proof system to verify the legal status of all American workers.

These triggers would not be in place for at least 18 months after the legislation is passed, possibly years later. Then an illegal immigrant family of four would have to pay fines of $4,500, after which they will have to pay $1,500 to renew their temporary visas every four years. They must then learn English and once again pay an additional fine of $4,000. Finally, they must return to their home country to file for U.S. citizenship before returning here for permanent residency.

Experts estimate that it will take a minimum of 13 years to complete the process. Where poorly paid immigrant subsistence workers will get the money to pay the fines, the visa renewal fees and the return trip to their former countries is a question up in the air. And when is the last time you paid $1,500 for a visa renewal? This is not humane behavior.   Yet Senator Vitter and his ilk call this a free pass. Truth be told, the bill stinks and there is good reason for liberals to oppose it (contrasted to conservative bogus reasons).

The most odious section provided in its first draft for 600,000 temporary workers a year who would not be allowed a path toward citizenship. That number could be increased to 800,000 in response to demand from employers. Senator Jeff Bingaman, Democrat from New Mexico, said that the bill as written "puts us on a par with Kuwait or other countries who just depend on foreign workers and have a second class group of workers doing inferior jobs but not having any real rights or privileges." By an amendment introduced by Bingaman the amount of temporary workers has been reduced to 200,000 a year, but it is unclear at this point whether it can balloon to 800,000 on demand of employers.

It is little known that such a program currently exists for unskilled workers. It is the H-2 guestworker program. In 2005 about 120,000 worked in this country, approximately 32,000 in agriculture and another 89,000 in forestry, seafood processing, landscaping, construction and other non-agricultural jobs.

One of the perks of contributing to the Southern Poverty Law Center is receiving their in-depth studies on social topics. They have recently released a critique of the H-2 program entitled "Close to Slavery." Although American law explicitly protects agricultural workers (and excludes protection to non-agricultural temporary workers – I wonder what lobbyist got to whom?) the law is not enforced. The same protections existed under the bracaro program that brought temporary workers to this country before it was abolished in 1964, yet the U.S. Department of Labor officer in charge of that program, Lee G. Williams, described it as a system of "legalized slavery."

The Southern Poverty Law Center report describes the abuses under the current H-2 program which will be magnified under an expanded version under consideration in the immigration bill before the Senate. The key to the abuse is that the temporary worker is tied to the employer and cannot leave him no matter how much abuse, legal and illegal, he sustains. In essence, if a worker cannot leave his employer, he is an indentured servant at best, and a slave at worst.

The Southern Poverty Law Center report documents cases where the employers confiscate the workers' passports when they arrive as a tool to keep them in tow, pay them illegal subsistence wages as low as $2 per hour, provide squalid housing which is often in rural and isolated areas, and then charge them exorbitant fees to transport them to a grocery store or other civilized amenity.

Worse, the Department of Labor makes no effort to enforce what little protection these temporary workers have under our laws. In 2004 there were 6,700 businesses certified to employ temporary agricultural workers under the H-2 program, yet the Department of Labor made only 89 investigations. There were 8,900 businesses certified to employ non-agricultural temporary workers and there is not one investigation on record.

Even more atrocious, the Southern Poverty Law Center report states: "When employers do violate the legal rights of workers, the DOL takes no action to stop them from importing more workers. The Government Accountability Office reported in 1997 that the DOL had never failed to approve an application to import H-2A (agricultural) workers because an employer had violated the legal rights of workers."

Concerning our current temporary worker program, House Ways and Means Committee Chairman Charles Rangel has said, "This guestworker program's the closest thing I've ever seen to slavery." What makes anyone think that the proposal in the new immigration bill would be any different, except that it would increase the number of indentured servants in this country?

Yes, we need these workers if our economy is to continue to prosper. The simple answer would be to allow them to come legally and not to be tied to a single employer. Let them have the same privilege of movement as any other person in the workforce. Give them a chance to become Americans in a reasonable time without onerous fines and fees and let them and their children contribute to the American dream. This is not what this immigration bill does. This bill is seriously flawed. Let us treat them humanely. If you prick them, do they not bleed?

Reflections on George W. Bush

Is George W. the Worst President?
5/23/06

Historians are constantly rating American presidents. Like the stock market their value goes up or down over the years. There are consistent winners over time. The general historical consensus is that Washington, Lincoln and Franklin Roosevelt were the three greatest men who served. In the CSPAN poll of 1999 the historians rated Harry Truman fifth, immediately behind the big three and Teddy Roosevelt.

What is just as interesting is the speculation as to who were the worst presidents. Although the various polls of historians differ somewhat, all of them focus on Franklin Pierce, James Buchanan, Warren Harding and Andrew Johnson. Now we have a new contender for the infamous honor of being the worst president of these United States: George W. Bush. This is precisely the question asked by the Princeton historian Sean Wilentz in a recent front cover story in *Rolling Stone*.

Wilentz doesn't like Bush, but as an ever-cautious historian he never comes to a definitive conclusion. Trying to be intellectually honest, I struggle with this same question; therefore let me share with you my thought processes.

Pierce served from 1853 to 1858. His major blunder was the approval of the Kansas-Nebraska Act that exacerbated the slavery question. Likewise Buchanan, who followed Pierce, was destroyed by the issue of slavery. Buchanan was the Nero of America. He fiddled while the flames of insurrection were around him. While he was in office the Confederacy was being formed under his nose. He left the mess to Lincoln. Warren Harding, who served from 1921 to 1923 when he died in office, is remembered as presiding over one of the most corrupt administrations in our history. Most people remember the Teapot Dome scandal as synonymous with Harding.

Of all the contenders my choice for the worst, or possibly the second worst after George W. Bush, is Andrew Johnson who became president after the assassination of Lincoln and served from 1865 to 1869. He was a rabid racist who stumped against the Fourteenth Amendment to the Constitution that prohibits states from depriving any person of life, liberty or property without due process of law. A slave holder himself, he declared that, "This country is for white men and by God, as long as I am president, it shall be governed by white men." His role was crucial in denying civil rights to the newly freed slaves. One hundred years of Jim Crow was his legacy.

You have to go a long way to deny Andrew Johnson the title of worst president. Now let's look at George W. Bush's record to see if he has accomplished this task.

War has always been last resort, an acknowledgement of the failure of diplomacy. Bush has made war a tool of diplomacy by proclaiming the right of preventive action. Most presidents listen to their generals or other learned counselors before sending our youth into a battle zone. When asked if he consulted his father (someone who knew a little bit about war), George responded, "There is a higher Father that I appeal to." As a corollary to this war Bush has established an American gulag where we reserve the right to torture prisoners and to hold them indefinitely without the right to trial. This blemish on the soul of America is not inconsequential.

Credibility is the hallmark of greatness; the lack thereof damns one to the category of worst or near-worst. Bush's honesty is seriously doubted by the American public and is a major reason why his approval rate is currently at 31 percent. Only the die-hard loyalists refuse to believe that he lied to us concerning the weapons of mass destruction, the nuclear capacity of Saddam and the Iraqi-Al Qaeda connection. Credibility and corruption go hand in hand. We have only seen the tip of the iceberg in the Jack Abramoff lobbying scandals. The Democrats are correct when they talk of a "culture of corruption." And Bush is doing nothing to change this culture. Under his aegis the House has just passed a "reform" bill for lobbying that even a Republican, Representative Christopher Shays of Connecticut, calls "pathetic."

It's also pathetic when an administration leaks the name of a covert CIA agent in an attempt to silence criticism of his administration by her husband. It may not be illegal, but then again it may, to award no-bid contracts worth billions to your cronies at Halliburton, the very people who put you in the White House. Only a Democratic Congress could ferret out the particulars. Of course, this highlights the importance of the upcoming off-year elections.

War, credibility and corruption aside, Bush will be judged on his domestic policies.

We have just passed another $70 billion of tax cuts that favor the rich in the face of a rising deficit. This deficit will be paid by our children and grandchildren in the form of higher taxes to pay the interest to foreign powers who buy our debt. In the pursuit of science: Bush has stymied stem-cell research and allowed other countries to become the leaders in this new scientific frontier. He has denied evolution and pushed "intelligent design" in school curriculums. He has denied the scientific proofs of global warming, pulling us out of the Kyoto Protocol. Along with his brother Jeb, he has redefined the meaning of life in the Terri Schiavo case.

Bush has belatedly declared that we are addicted to oil, but has done nothing to fight this addiction. Our tax laws actually subsidized the purchase by corporations of gas-guzzling Hummers until the loophole was partially plugged in 2004. During Bush's tenure the congress has not seriously implemented federal fuel efficiency guidelines. It is a disgrace that SUVs, which have accounted for over 50 percent of vehicular sales, were classified as trucks, thereby avoiding gas efficiency requirements.

Cronyism, which leads to incompetence, has been rampant in this administration. "You've done a heck of a job, Brownie," sums up the whole Hurricane Katrina disaster. Most important, Bush's push for an Imperial Presidency that negates checks and balances built into our Constitution may be his most lasting legacy. He doesn't veto legislation; he merely ignores it. He claims the right to be above the law based on war powers. Even President Lincoln never claimed this right and the Confederate Army was merely 60 miles from the White House. Finally, his judicial appointments may cripple this country for the next 30 years. I am referring to right-wing judges placed on the Supreme Court as well as atrocious nominations to the Circuit Courts of Appeal.

Robert Scheer, the respected columnist for the *L.A. Times*, until he was recently canned, spent over 30 years interviewing presidents. His new book is entitled, "Playing President: My Close Encounters with Nixon, Carter, Bush I, Reagan and Clinton – and How They Did Not Prepare Me for George W Bush." In a recent interview he commented, "This administration doesn't feel they need a mindful audience. They don't care about facts, logic or consequences. They are the most cynical people that I've ever encountered in politics...I don't think I've ever seen that kind of cynicism before, and I'm the guy who interviewed Richard Nixon."

Andrew Johnson or George W. Bush? It's still a toss-up. But I'm leaning toward George.

The Dangers of the Imperial Presidency
5/8/07

There are many reasons to believe that George W. Bush may be the worst president in American history (acknowledging that Andrew Johnson gives Bush a run for his money). Listing just a few: reducing taxes for the rich while services for the poor are diminished; packing the federal court system with right-wing ideologues; filling important government positions with incompetent cronies and political operatives ("Brownie, you're doing a heck of a job"); stifling stem cell research, so that the rest of the world will outstrip us in the new technological frontier; denying global warming because it may cost his big business friends a few shekels to retool; emasculating the EPA and other regulatory agencies so that basic health laws like the Clean Air Act are ignored; lying to us about weapons of mass destruction and nuclear material in Niger to entice us into a useless war; total incompetence as commander in chief, resulting in the deaths of over 3,000 young American kids, reaching for a "victory" that is impossible to achieve; and generally handing over the reigns of the government to lobbyists for Halliburton and other big business interests. OK, it sounds like he's even worse that Andrew Johnson.

But in the long run, more important than all of the above, Bush's greatest assault on American values is his quest to create an imperial presidency. The framers of the Constitution created a delicate balance of power between the president, the congress and the courts. Of the three branches they feared most the unbridled power of the presidency. Many delegates to the Constitutional Convention proposed an executive committee rather than one president. Governor Edmund Randolph of Virginia proclaimed, "A unity in the Executive is the fetus of monarchy."

This fear was so prevalent that when a single presidency was first put to a vote on May 29, 1787, it was postponed for a week for lack of support. Finally on June 5th the Convention approved the concept of a one-person presidency, but not without New York, Delaware and Maryland dissenting. When you hear talking heads on television telling us that the framers of the Constitution intended us to have a strong president and nearly unlimited powers during times of national crises, think back to those original debates and the anguish with which they formed the executive branch.

This is not to say that we should have a weak executive. It is to say that the president cannot run roughshod over the dictates of congress or the courts. In fact, that is precisely what the founding fathers feared. The framers of the Constitution were aiming for a delicate balance amongst the three branches of government. It is important to understand this history to evaluate the claims of George W. Bush. In light of this history a statement by John Yoo (professor at the University of California Law School and ex-Justice Department official – one of the framers of the famous torture memo) is most egregious: "The founders intended that wrongheaded or obsolete legislation and judicial decisions would be checked by presidential action." Just the opposite! Although all three branches check on one another (that's the meaning of checks and balances) the founders anguished over how to check presidential actions. In view of this history it's hard to accept Bush's ignoring legislation and court decisions in the name of presidential power.

Here are a few examples of the manifestation of the imperial presidency. In six years Bush has vetoed only one bill. In May of 2006 the investigative reporter Charlie Savage of the *Boston Globe* unearthed the hidden fact that, instead of using his veto power, Bush signed 750 "presidential signing statements" that declared that he would ignore the law as passed by congress. I'll be honest. I never heard of a signing statement until this expose. It was invented by Edwin Meese when he was attorney general for Ronald Reagan in an effort to expand presidential power. He was aided by a young lawyer named Samuel Alito, Jr., now on the Supreme Court, thanks to George Bush.

The original concept was that a signing statement was to reflect the president's interpretation of the law for the purpose of enforcing it, not for the purpose of ignoring it. If a president disagrees with congress he has the power of the veto, and, in turn, the congress has the power to override that veto with a two-thirds majority. This is called checks and balances. (The Constitutional Convention pondered requiring a three-fourths majority to override a veto, but decided that would put too much power in the presidency.) As of now these signing statements have not been legally challenged. Given the makeup of this Court (with Alito and his cohorts) overruling this power grab by Bush would be in doubt.

Another example of the imperial presidency is Bush's ignoring the Foreign Intelligence Surveillance Act of 1978. It was passed as a reaction to the abuse of power by the Nixon administration. The Act declares that a president cannot be involved in electronic surveillance without first acquiring a warrant from a special eleven-person court, commonly referred to as the FISA court. If there is an emergency, the president has the authority to tap the phone but report it to the court immediately thereafter. There is no danger to national security because of the existence of the FISA court.

But Bush decided that he did not want judicial oversight (part of the normal checks and balances of a democratic government) and without court warrants he has proceeded to tap the phones of thousands of Americans since 9/11 and to data mine every call made in the country. This data mining means that the NSA has tracked the number of everyone whom you have called these past four years. The potential for abuse is enormous. Can you image Nixon sitting there tracking the calls of the people on his "enemies list?" Can you imagine Cheney (the Darth Vader of the administration) doing the same? Despite congressional outcry, this practice continues.

A final example of the imperial presidency is the passage by a Republican controlled congress of the Military Commission Act of 2006. It denies the right of habeas corpus (the right to a speedy trial by a competent court). Under the Act, Bush can imprison a suspected terrorist, never bring him to trial, deny him an attorney and never let him confront his accuser. If brought to trial, he will go before a special military commission where hearsay evidence is allowed and classified evidence can be used against him without giving him the right to see it. It is a travesty of American justice.

Jonathan Turley, George Washington University Constitutional Law Professor, summed it up well: "What the Congress did and what the president signed essentially revokes over 200 years of American principles and values... Congress just gave the president despotic powers... I think people are fooling themselves if they believe that the courts will once again stop this president from taking –overtaking- almost absolute power." As of now the conservative Supreme Court has refused to review the Military Commission Act.

Wars come and go (unfortunately the dead cannot be resurrected), but the imperial presidency is by far the greatest danger that George W. Bush foisted upon our nation. It will be the most difficult to redress of his legacy of atrocities and incompetence.

Bush through the Reflection of Eisenhower
9/19/06

What follows has everything to do with George W. Bush, but first I must tell the story.

Two weeks ago Lisa Myers, a senior investigative reporter for NBC Nightly News, reported a most disturbing tale of government conduct that borders on criminality.

We have lost more than 130 soldiers in Iraq and nearly 40 soldiers in Afghanistan to rocket-propelled grenades, or RPGs. They are the favorite weapons of insurgents. They are cheap, easy to use and deadly.

Last year a special Pentagon unit (ironically established by Donald Rumsfeld) found the ideal answer to the RPG problem. It is a system created in Israel called the Trophy Active Defense System. Trophy is a miniaturized version of the anti-ballistic missile system that automatically detects an incoming threat and launches an interceptor rocket that homes in on the missile (the RPG) and destroys it at a safe distance. It does this by having a 360 degree scanning device on the tank or other military vehicle that automatically detects the RPG when it is launched.

This system is so good that General Dynamics entered into an agreement with the Israeli company to market Trophy throughout the world. In cooperation with the Pentagon, Trophy was subjected to 30 tests. It knocked the RPG out in 29 of those instances. An official with those tests told NBC that Trophy "worked in every case. The only anomaly was that in one test, the Trophy round hit the RPG's tail instead of its head. But according to our test criteria, the system was 30 for 30."

So why are we not purchasing Trophy to protect our soldiers? Because the Army put a stop to it since they have an existing contract with Raytheon to develop the same product, except that, by its own admission, the Raytheon version will not be ready until 2011. That's not a misprint – it won't be ready for another five years, but this administration will not purchase the Israeli system to protect our own soldiers now.

Where is Secretary of Defense Rumsfeld? Where is Commander in Chief Bush? Harry Truman had that famous plaque on his desk: "The buck stops here." Why have they not intervened for the past year in what is obviously an internecine struggle in the military establishment. Obviously, the Pentagon feels frustrated that it cannot get around the Army veto of a needed weapons system; so frustrated that it leaked the whole issue to NBC. To be fair to Bush, he reads only what his managers put in front of him. His White House is notorious for not being accessible to other departments of government. The poor soul probably didn't know what was happening. The same cannot be said for Rumsfeld.

But the question still remains: why would the Army nix the Trophy? The NBC report quoted a Pentagon senior official: "This debate has nothing, zero, to do with capability and timeliness. It's about money and politics. You've got a gigantic (Army procurement) program and contractors with intertwined interests." When a Pentagon official tells you that military contracts and politics are more important than the lives of our kids fighting in Afghanistan and Iraq, you better believe it. This validates Mark Hanna's famous statement over a century ago (He was President William McKinley's Karl Rove): We are ruled by "a business state" and that "all questions of government in a democracy were questions of money."

This whole story sent me scurrying to read President Dwight Eisenhower's famous farewell speech in 1961. Eisenhower was not the perfect president. He was weak on civil rights. He did not stand up to McCathyism and he engineered coups in Iran and Guatemala. But he was cool-headed and thoughtful in his response to the pressures of the Cold War. In his farewell speech he warned against the ascendancy of the "military-industrial complex."

He said, "The potential for the disastrous rise of misplaced power exists and will persist." I am sure that Eisenhower never heard of Halliburton (he probably knew of Raytheon), but he understood the danger of an administration 50 years hence succumbing to management by lobbyists.

President Eisenhower had four other points that he made in that speech that are largely forgotten today but should be noted for their relevance to the Bush administration. He said that we "must avoid the impulse to live only for today, plundering, for our own ease and convenience, the precious resources of tomorrow. We cannot mortgage the material assets of our grandchildren without risking the loss also of their political and spiritual heritage." As we reduce the taxes on the rich and deficit-spend billions on Iraq, creating debt that our children and grandchildren will have to pay, we can ponder Eisenhower's words.

In the context of the Cold War that he faced during his eight years in the White House, he cautioned that "we must avoid becoming a community of dreadful fear and hate." But that is precisely what this administration fosters -- from bogus orange and red alerts to campaign rhetoric that plays upon our fears and stereotypes 1.3 billion Muslims worldwide.

Writing "as one who has witnessed the horror and the lingering sadness of war," Eisenhower warned, "that (the conference) table, though scarred by many past frustrations, cannot be abandoned for the certain agony of the battlefield." We can imagine what Eisenhower would have said about preemptive war and the neo-conservative master plan of fostering American dominance through the use of military might. Bush never witnessed the horrors of war, and, unfortunately, he is not reflective enough to imagine them. And none of his friends have children in Iraq that need the protection of the Trophy Active Defense System, or who have to worry about receiving notification of the death of a child.

Finally, President Eisenhower understood the need for self-control when leading a superpower. He talked of balance and he said, "May we be ever unswerving in devotion to principle, confident but humble with power." Could we ever envision General or President Eisenhower saying, "Bring Em On?" He managed existential dangers to our country that far outweigh our problem with terrorism, no matter how frightful it may be, and Eisenhower did it without a preemptive war, without ever reverting to wearing a flight jacket as president and without taunting an enemy to "Bring Em On."

The comparison between President Eisenhower and President Bush should embarrass the Republican Party and should severely depress the rest of us. Meanwhile, our soldiers will continue to die at the hands of RPGs, and Raytheon will continue to work on its contract until 2011. It is not hard to imagine what President Eisenhower would have done.

Roosevelt and Truman

Franklin Delano Roosevelt and the Jews
5/25/04

Last month in the *Journal* a guest columnist wrote: "Democratic President Franklin Delano Roosevelt whom I, like most Jews, used to worship, first took office in 1933, the same year Adolf Hitler hijacked Germany. Yet, he was unmoved by what the Nazis did to the Jews. In 1939, he forbade Jews on the German ship Saint Louis from entering the United States. And in 1944, aware that the gas chambers were working overtime, he rejected pleas by his wife, Eleanor, and British Prime Minister Winston Churchill to bomb the railroad tracks leading to and from the death camps." The writer made reference to Arthur Morse's book "While Six Million Died" which put forth the above facts, and he concluded: "Morse's book so disturbed me that it began the process, which took 36 years, of turning an old Jewish Democrat into a new Jewish Republican."

The fact is that Morse's book was flawed history. But it has been popular among Jews because it reinforces our sense of victimization. It tells us that we can't trust anyone who isn't Jewish, even a great friend such as FDR. For a concise history of the real story I recommend a seminal article that appeared in *American Heritage*, July/August 1999 by William J. vanden Heuvel (worth a trip to the library) and a compendium of monographs by 15 scholars in a book entitled "The Bombing of Auschwitz, Should the Allies Have Attempted It?" published in 2000 by St. Martin's Press in association with the United States Holocaust Memorial Museum (Michael Neufeld and Michael Berenbaum, Editors).

Here are the real facts. FDR was very moved by the plight of Jews in Germany during the rise of Hitler, but he was confronted with an isolationist Congress and public that opposed immigration to the United States at a time when 25 percent of Americans were unemployed. Still he succeeded in bending the law to the extent that from 1933 to 1941 fully 35 percent of all immigrants to America under the quota guidelines were Jewish and after *Kristallnacht* over 50 percent were Jews. In reaction to *Kristallnacht* FDR extended the visitors' visas of 20,000 Austrian and German Jewish visitors in the United States so that they would not have to return.

Many contemporary Jews don't understand why FDR did not try to liberalize the immigration quotas. They forget the times in which he lived. The pro Nazi German American Bund was holding rallies in Madison Square Garden. Father Coughlin was espousing his venom over the airwaves. Anti-Semitism was more prevalent than in any other time in the history of this nation. Even Representative Emanuel Celler of Brooklyn, truly a champion of Jewish interests, warned FDR against attempting to change the immigration formula. His colleagues in Congress had warned Celler that if the administration attempted to give asylum to refugees or to liberalize the immigration quotas, other bills "to cut the quotas in half or to stop all immigration would be introduced and probably passed."

As for the *Saint Louis*: It was May of 1939. Roosevelt was one year away from one of the most momentous political acts in American history, the decision to run for a third term. Even George Washington did not attempt that. He was not about to muddy the waters with an unpopular immigration issue. Joseph Goebbels, the German Minister of Propaganda, was calling Roosevelt "that Jew Rosenfeld." Given the political climate FDR's hands were tied. But he did not forsake the 936 Jewish passengers on the *Saint Louis*. Working through our State Department he made sure that not one was returned to Germany. They all went to democratic countries – 288 to the United Kingdom, the rest to France, the Netherlands, Belgium and Denmark. They were not forsaken. We cannot fault FDR for not foreseeing in May of 1939 the Final Solution. Little did anyone know that the Nazi killing machine would follow the *Saint* Louis refugees into these other countries.

And now the Auschwitz charges. There are actually two. First, FDR should have bombed the camps, killing Jewish prisoners to save potential future detainees. Second, the least he could have done was bomb the railroad tracks leading to the camps.

As to bombing the camps, even the Rescue Committee of the Jewish Agency in Jerusalem, headed by David Ben-Gurion, voted against making the bombing request. The dilemma was succinctly put by James Kitchens, "Would it be moral to kill a minimum of several hundred internees in trying to save others – with no assurance of success – and if so, what tragic ratio would have been acceptable?"

As for the railroad lines, the respected Jewish historian Gerhard Weinberg derides the notion that a few line-cuts on the railways would have deterred the "men who were dedicated to the killing program." The fact is that there were many camps besides Auschwitz and even there the Nazis were experienced in rail repair and would have had the railroad running within days. The Holocaust expert Deborah Lipstadt derides this whole campaign to fault FDR as an ex-post facto writing of history by neo-conservatives.

It is true that the American war machine was geared for "victory in the shortest time." This meant that our limited air capacity would not be diverted to save anyone, Jews included. But this was not anti-Semitic. In northern Holland during the last seven months of the war more than 80,000 citizens starved to death because the Germans wanted to punish the Dutch for insurrection and strikes following the failed assault on Arnhem. The Allies knew what was happening, but they refused to divert air power for food drops because it would have deflected their attention from the objective of victory in the shortest possible time.

One can argue the morality of this position, but no one has ever suggested that anti-Dutch animus was involved in the decision. Thus it was with Auschwitz. We may disagree with the policy, but one should not easily jump to a conclusion of anti-Semitism (unless it really makes you feel perversely good through a sense of victimization). Weinberg argues that the American policy of victory in the shortest time actually saved Jewish lives, for every day the war continued more Jews were led to the ovens.

If you are or were a liberal Jewish Democrat and want to become a conservative Republican, that is your prerogative, but your decision should not be based on FDR bashing. I was an 8-year old child when Franklin Delano Roosevelt died. I remember that adults cried for the loss of their hero. Today he is still my hero and I vigorously fight the tarnishing of his memory. May he rest in peace.

Franklin D. Roosevelt and the Jews
2/20/07

The trashing of Franklin Delano Roosevelt started in 1967 with the publication of Arthur Morse's book "While Six Million Died." In it he maintained that FDR was oblivious to the fate of Jews in Europe and that he was particularly culpable in his turning away of the refugee ship the *St Louis* and in not stopping the Nazi murder machine by bombing Auschwitz, either the railroad tracks or the camp itself. Other books followed in this same vein. The mantra was then picked up by neo-conservatives in their campaign to turn Jewish Democrats into Republicans.

In an earlier column in May of 2004 I referred the reader to a seminal article in defense of Roosevelt by Ambassador William J. vanden Heuvel in the July/August 1999 issue of *American Heritage* (truly worth a trip to the library) and to a compendium of monographs by 15 scholars in a book entitled "The Bombing of Auschwitz, Should the Allies Have Attempted It?" published in 2000 by St. Martin's Press in association with the United States Holocaust Memorial Museum (Michael Neufeld and Michael Berenbaum, Editors).

If the above references do not convince you that Morse and his followers are spouting faulty history, then a new book entitled "Saving the Jews, Franklin D. Roosevelt and the Holocaust" by Robert N. Rosen will. Rosen's finely researched 654-page book proves without a doubt that President Roosevelt was not derelict in his concern for our Jewish plight, but was a passionate advocate who did as much as he could, given the military and political environment during those years. The environment is the nub of the issue: From hindsight (knowing how it all unfolded) we scream with anguish: why did he (or for that matter, the Jewish community) not do more? The answer is that we must understand history in the context of the time.

Getting to the particulars, Rosen reviews the whole *St. Louis* saga. The ship, carrying 936 German Jewish refugees, was turned away from Cuba in May of 1939. Roosevelt immediately directed the American Consul-General in Havana, Coert DuBois, and Ambassador J. Butler Wright to work closely with Jewish aid groups. Both DuBois and Wright were in intimate contact with Lawrence Berenson, the Cuban representative of the Joint Distribution Committee (JDC, commonly referred to as the Joint).

The Joint offered a $500 cash bribe per passenger to allow the Jews asylum. This amounted to nearly $500,000. The Cuban president countered with a $650 offer. Rosen comments that, at this point, Berenson "made a major blunder." He told the Joint leadership back in New York that he could save them "a considerable amount of money." He began to bargain with the Cubans, upon which they immediately declared to the world that the *St. Louis* was barred from their country. Thus began the ship's journey up the American coastline.

Given the political climate Roosevelt could not contravene our immigration laws and allow the *St Louis* entry to American ports. Mid America and the Republican Party were paranoid about being invaded with radical immigrant refugees, especially Jews. It is hard for us to understand from the vantage point of 2007, but as late as June, 1943, the Senate overwhelmingly defeated a bill that would simplify the naturalization process for resident aliens *with children in the American armed forces.* What FDR did was to assure that every one of the *St Louis* refugees was placed in a free democratic country. He enlisted the help of our Ambassador in London, Joe Kennedy, to pressure the British to cooperate.

In the end, 29 disembarked in Havana, and 907 sailed back to Europe, of which 288 disembarked in England, 181 in Holland, 224 in France and 214 in Belgium. Because of Roosevelt, not one returned to Germany. Little did he or anyone else anticipate that four months later Hitler would invade Poland and put most of these refugees in danger once again. But, according to the U.S. Holocaust Memorial Museum more than two-thirds of the passengers of the *St. Louis* did survive the Holocaust, a percentage higher than the overall Jewish population in Europe. No one gives Roosevelt credit for this.

As to the bombing of the death camps, why criticize Roosevelt when most Jewish organizations opposed it at that time? In June of 1944 David Ben Gurion responded, "We do not know the truth concerning the entire situation in Poland, and it seems that we will be unable to propose anything concerning this matter." Ben Gurion wrote: "The opinion of the Jewish Agency's Executive Committee is not to propose to the Allies the bombing of sites in which Jews are located."

Some Jews did advocate precisely that, and the World Jewish Congress objected: "The destruction of the death installations cannot be done from bombing from the air, as the first victims would be the Jews who are gathered in these camps, and such a bombing would be a welcome pretext for the Germans to assert that their Jewish victims have been massacred not by their killers, but by the Allied bombing." The WJC's preference was for Auschwitz to be dismantled by Soviet paratroopers and the Polish Home Army. Of course, they didn't give a damn.

On August 16, 1944 representatives of all the major Jewish organizations met with John Pehle, the Executive Director of the War Refugee Board (which Roosevelt personally established) and with other State Department officers. Afterwards these groups sent a memorandum outlining the Jewish request for rescue. No request to bomb Auschwitz or the railroad lines was included on the list of Jewish priorities.

There is no historical doubt that Assistant Secretary of State Breckinridge Long, who was in charge of the Visa Division, was anti-Semitic and did what he could to undercut Roosevelt's concern for Jewish refugees. In one instance Rabbi Stephen Wise informed Under Secretary of State Sumner Welles that the WJC felt that a group of Jewish children in hiding in Romania and France could be bribed out. Welles sent him to Treasury Secretary Henry Morgenthau. Before going there Wise spoke with the president. In his memoirs Wise reports that FDR responded, "Stephen, why don't you go ahead and do it?" But Wise was unsure that Morgenthau would cooperate. At that moment the president called the Treasury Secretary and said, "Henry, this is a very fair proposal which Stephen makes about ransoming Jews." Morganthau recalled in 1947 that, "The president was deeply moved by the situation" and "could not have been more receptive." Long and his clique at State dragged their feet and nothing was ultimately accomplished.

After Roosevelt finished the Yalta Conference, in February, 1945, an ill and tired FDR, only two months before his death, did not proceed directly home. Instead he stopped at Great Bitter Lake in the Suez Canal to meet King Ibn Saud, the leader of Saudi Arabia to attempt to facilitate Arab acceptance of a Jewish homeland in Palestine. Earlier FDR had boasted to Secretary of State Edward Stettinius that "he could do anything that needed to be done with Ibn Saud with a few million dollars." Roosevelt was wrong. Ibn Saud vowed unswerving opposition to a Jewish state.

Rosen asks this question: "How was it that the same man, who, according to his critics, did not care one whit about Jewish people, tried his best in the final weeks of his life to establish a Jewish homeland for the victims of the holocaust? Roosevelt faced no election. He had no obligation to see Saud. Yet he did. Why?"

The answer is simple: Franklin Delano Roosevelt was a true friend of the Jews.

Harry Truman and the Jews
5/29/07

The noted historian Michael Beschloss' new book "Presidential Courage" was recently excerpted in *Newsweek*. There he wrote of Harry Truman's *de facto* recognition of Israel only 11 hours after David Ben Gurion declared its independence. But Beschloss also left the impression that Truman had an anti-Semitic streak within him. It is this on which I want to focus.

In 2003 the Truman Library made public a hitherto unknown small diary written by President Truman in 1947. Beschloss quotes Truman from that diary: "The Jews have no sense of proportion, nor do they have any judgment on world affairs...The Jews, I find, are very selfish." This is somewhat out of context. Truman was being pressured incessantly by us Jews to recognize Israel while his state department counseled that recognition would jeopardize our oil supply and alienate the entire Arab world. Truman wrote to his sister Mary Jane, "I'm so tired and bedeviled I can't be decent to people. Truman presidential aide George Elsey commented, "So here was a guy under pressure, and occasionally he blew his stack...Who wouldn't under the circumstances?"

Getting back to the diary entry, Bleschloss does Truman a disservice by not quoting the whole entry. Truman lamented that we Jews were not interested in the millions of others who died or were displaced because of World War II, "as long as the Jews get special treatment. Yet when they have power, physical, financial or political neither Hitler nor Stalin has anything on them for cruelty or mistreatment to the underdog. Put an underdog on top and it makes no difference whether his name is Russian, Jewish, Negro, Management, Labor, Mormon, Baptist he goes haywire. I've found very few who remember their past condition when prosperity comes."

If we analyze what he wrote about us, the comparison to Hitler and Stalin aside, he was not too far off the mark. He accused us of being "selfish" for not caring for others who were killed or displaced in the war. We must remember that the world had just finished a war that cost over 50 million lives. Not only were we Jews suffering. Our strength is caring for the Jewish people, but for the outside world, even including friends, it is quite possible to see this as selfishness. Truman had many problems on his plate. We Jews correctly acted as if the Jewish problem was the only one around. That was our job, but it didn't make Harry Truman's life any easier.

We must also remember that he included his Baptist brethren as well as management and labor in the group, including Jews, who once they gain power, will abuse it. He was ranting against the Jews in the diary, but it was not from a particular animus against us. He was commenting on human nature. I am sorry to report that he was probably correct. When dissected line by line the diary becomes less venomous. If only he had left out the Hitler and Stalin reference. But Ole Harry was an emotional guy and could go over the top occasionally. Remember when he defended his daughter excoriating the *Washington Post* music reviewer, threatening to kick him in his testicles? Actually he wrote, "Some day I hope to meet you. When that happens you'll need a new nose, a lot of beefsteak for black eyes, and perhaps a supporter below!"

Bleschloss made a point of the fact that Truman never had a Jew or a black as a guest in his house in Independence, Missouri, including his pal and ex-partner Eddie Jacobson. This is true. The home was owned by his mother-in-law who was a bigot. We must remember that Truman was raised in a racist home in a racist border state. Both his grandparents owned slaves. The liberality of his wife Bess is very much in question. Given this environment his accomplishments for Jews and African-Americans are amazing.

Not only did he recognize Israel but he desegregated the Armed Forces by executive order because he knew that the legislature would not do it, at a time when over 80 percent of the people opposed it. And out of that home, which he did not control, he surrounded himself with Jews. When Eddie Jacobson died, as Bleschloss does recount, Truman made a shiva call to the

Jacobson home and "put his head in his hands and started to sob, 'I've lost my brother!'" This is not the conduct of an anti-Semite.

David Ben Gurion noted in his memoirs that in a New York hotel suite, when he thanked Truman for his steadfast support of Israel tears suddenly sprang from Truman's eyes, and "his eyes were still wet when he bade me good-by." Abba Eban also wrote that in 1952 when he praised Truman in public, "As I glanced at him he was wiping away a tear." This is the conduct of a person who felt close to our community, not an anti-Semite.

Bleschloss writes that among other factors Truman recognized Israel because he "was also motivated by sheer politics. With a tough campaign ahead, he felt that if he did not recognize Israel, the backers of a Jewish state would make his life a living hell." Rabbi Abba Hillel Silver and the Jewish lobby had already accomplished the hell factor. Silver had the chutzpah to pound on Truman's desk and verbally attack him. Abba Eban wrote: "Truman regarded Silver with severe aversion regarding him not inaccurately as a supporter of the Republican Party which came second only to the Soviet Union as a primary target of Truman's distrust." We Jews had already bombarded the president with 48,600 telegrams, 790,575 postcards and 81,200 pieces of other mail. In one three-month period alone in 1948 he received 301,900 postcards. Michael Benson in his book "Harry Truman and the Founding of Israel," comments, "Such a steady stream clearly annoyed the president."

As for politics, Truman had already written off New York due to the Henry Wallace factor. If Truman's motivation were political, he would not have continued the American arms embargo against Israel throughout the election period of May to November 1948 (Israel bought its armament from Europe), and he would not have withheld *de jure* recognition until January of 1949, after the first elections in Israel.

Truman was not pandering to the Jews. I agree with David McCullough, the respected Truman biographer, when he said that the assumption that Truman was motivated by politics in his support of a Jewish state "is a cynical, unrealistic misunderstanding of the people involved."

Harry Truman was a white male born in the nineteenth century. He was also a very emotional person, which made him a real human being unlike most politicians. He was definitely not PC (politically correct). Things came out of his mouth that today may sound bigoted, but, put in context, are merely the jargon of the day. If we look at his accomplishments and at his friendships, we realize that Harry Truman was a real friend of the Jews. I believe that Michael Bleschloss is a great historian, but in this case he has done Harry Truman a great disservice. He's still my hero.

Harry Truman and Civil Rights
6/1/04

This past month we celebrated the 50th anniversary of the *Brown v. Board of Education* decision, widely acclaimed as the impetus for the modern civil rights movement. Yet there is another historical perspective that gives this honor to the actions of President Harry S. Truman, beginning nine years before *Brown*.

I write this column immediately after attending a symposium on Truman and Civil Rights held at the Little White House in Key West. It is an annual event organized by Bob Watson, an energetic political science professor from Florida Atlantic University.

Of all the scholars in attendance, I was most impressed by Michael Gardner. I recommend his book, "Harry Truman and Civil Rights, Moral Courage and Political Risks" published by Southern Illinois University Press. There he fully documents Truman's personal commitment to civil rights.

The problem is that Truman's presidency was so full of momentous events such as the establishment of the Truman Doctrine, the Marshall Plan, the founding of NATO and the U.N. and the dropping of the atomic bomb, that his commitment to civil rights and the plight of black Americans gets secondary treatment by historians. But it shouldn't.

Truman was an unlikely candidate to be a civil rights activist. He was reared in a racist home in a racist border state. Both his grandparents owned slaves. Union soldiers evacuated his mother at age 11 from her home. She never forgot the trauma and hated Lincoln to her dying day at age 94. When she visited her son in the White House he told her that she would have the honor of sleeping in the Lincoln bedroom. Truman's aide, Clark Clifford, reported that there was a moment of silence and then the senior Mrs. Truman turned to her daughter-in-law and said, "Bess, if you'll get my bags packed, I'll be going home this evening."

But ole Give-em-Hell Harry surprised everyone. In September of 1946 the president of the NAACP Walter White visited Truman in the White House. He told the president of incidents of returning black veterans who were maimed and murdered by Southern bigots, soldiers who fought the Nazis so that this country could be free. Truman was so moved that the next day he wrote a memo to his attorney general (later supreme court justice) Tom Clark suggesting federal action.

The mid-term elections in November of 1946 clearly showed Truman's unpopularity. The Republicans took both houses of Congress. A less courageous man would have reacted by bending toward popular sentiment. Harry Truman took the harder road. He ignored the polls and continued his commitment to an unpopular cause. In December of that year he appointed a Presidential Civil Rights Committee by Executive Order (since he knew that it would never pass Congress). The president of General Electric Charles Wilson headed the Committee and the great Rabbi Roland Gittelsohn served on the 15-person commission. The next year it issued a final report with 35 recommendations that served as the roadmap for the civil rights acts of 1964 and 1965.

In June of 1947 Truman ascended the steps of the Lincoln Memorial and addressed the closing session of the NAACP convention. He did this at a time when Washington, D.C. was a totally segregated city and the polls indicated that 82 percent of Americans were against his civil rights program. (It is a blot on John Kennedy's legacy that he could not move himself to ascend those same steps at the 1963 rally where Martin Luther King delivered his famous "I Have A Dream" speech.) Immediately before this speech in a letter to his sister Mary Jane, Truman wrote, "Mamma won't like what I say because I wind up by quoting old Abe. But I believe what I say and I'm hopeful we may implement it." Truman called for the equality of the races. Immediately after the speech Truman sat next to White and said to him personally, "I said what I did because I mean every word of it – and I am going to prove that I do mean it." In his autobiography Walter White concluded that it was this speech, which was broadcast to over 100 million Americans, that launched the federal civil rights program.

Truman went on to espouse equality for blacks in his State of the Union speech in January of 1948 and his Special Message to Congress on Civil Rights the following month, only 5 months before the Democratic Convention and 9 months before the general election in November. He knew that pushing civil rights was not politically wise. He also knew that he had to do the right thing. In July of 1948 Truman issued his famous Executive Orders that integrated both the military and the entire federal government. At the Democratic convention Truman pushed for a strong civil rights platform with the help of the young Minneapolis Mayor Hubert Humphrey.

The ultimate outcome of all of this was the famous Dixiecrat break-off that was supposed to throw the election into the House of Representatives. The conventional wisdom was that Truman needed the votes of the progressive western states, the unions and the conservative south to win. The irony is that black voters in the industrial northern states won the election for him. But that was the historical outcome, not the political strategy of the time.

Truman never worried about his popularity. He wrote: "I wonder how far Moses would have gone if he'd taken a poll in Egypt ... It is right and wrong and leadership – men with fortitude, honesty and a belief in the right that makes epochs in the history of the world." His White House aide

General Donald Dawson wrote, "When people on the staff would caution the president about this or that issue – claiming that public opinion was against some action that the president was planning to take, Harry Truman would interrupt by asking his advisors to tell him what they thought was the best thing – the right thing for the country. It was just that simple – polls didn't matter; the good of the country did."

People remember that Harry Truman had the message "The Buck Stops Here" on his desk. But he also had a neatly lettered card in the Oval Office quoting Mark Twain: "Always do right. This will gratify some people, and astonish the rest."

When Truman left office his approval rating was at 31 percent. This didn't bother him. History has since rated him among the top five presidents to have served our country. Maybe more leaders should follow his example. Maybe we should ban the Karl Roves of this world from stepping inside the Beltway. I have very few personal political heroes, but Harry is definitely one of them.

Foreign Policy and War

Spreading Freedom Throughout the World
2/8/05

We have witnessed the inauguration of President Bush for another agonizing four years. If his inauguration speech has any validity, the next four may be worse than the last four. In his speech he mentioned the word "freedom" 27 times in approximately 20 minutes, capsulized in the following quote: "It is the policy of the United States to seek and support the growth of democratic movements and institutions in every nation and culture, with the ultimate goal of ending tyranny in our world."

Peggy Noonan, the former Reagan speechwriter, called it "mission inebriation." This is not the first time that our president has been inebriated. In his earlier years his drug of choice was alcohol, now it is power. Then he could only do damage to himself and his family. Now he is responsible for the deaths of over 1400 American kids, whom we dress up in uniform and send to combat in Iraq, and the count continues. How far has this new inebriation gone? The *New York Times* reported that at the White House dinner following the swearing-in, they served a menu inspired by the food served during the presidency of Teddy Roosevelt. Inebriation and delusion are an even greater danger than drinking and driving. To paraphrase Lloyd Bentsen, I have studied Teddy Roosevelt, and Bush is no Teddy Roosevelt. The problem is that with America as the only standing super power, his stick is actually bigger than TR's. It takes a Teddy Roosevelt to understand how to use such power.

The *Times* also reported that in delivering the speech, "his tone was proud, unapologetic, even defiant." Also his speech had "missionary zeal." Mix intoxication with religious zeal and we get a heck of a lot more than a good revival meeting. In this case we get a leader who could duplicate Iraq over the globe.

Is this alarmist? I really don't know. I have hopes that this whole freedom gig is a cover-up for past ineptitude. Bush asked us to go to war because Iraq had weapons of mass destruction. Turned out to be a lie. They were working on a nuclear capability. Turned out to be a lie. Iraq was implicated in the tragedy of 9/11. Turned out to be a lie. And that Saddam Hussein was in serious contact with Osama bin Laden. Turned out to be a lie. Obviously he had to present a new rationale for our involvement. Why not freedom? I can see Karl Rove licking his chops as they formulated this new raison d'etre for the administration.

Given what the Congress knows today, would it have voted for an invasion of Iraq merely to topple Saddam, a sadistic tyrant? I think not. For the record, I do not like dictators, sadistic or otherwise. But we have to be realistic. Out of the 150-plus nations on this planet, I would guess that 30 to 50 are ruled by dictators of varying villainy. Where should we start? I expect that if we really mean this, my grandchildren and possibly great-grandchildren will be fighting these wars.

But what the heck, for a good cause we can sacrifice our children and grandchildren. Let's figure where we can start. Condi Rice, at her confirmation hearing, suggested six countries: Iran, North Korea, Cuba, Myanmar (Burma), Zimbabwe and Belarus. An odd mixture. To make this campaign efficient I believe that we should go after the biggest and the worst dictatorships to begin.

The biggest – China and Russia. We know that China is an oppressive dictatorship. True, they are becoming more capitalistic every day and they buy large quantities of our debt so that we can finance our crusade (that's the word, religious connotations and all) in Iraq. It's also true that this week China signed a deal with Boeing to buy 60 new 787s. But if we're serious about this freedom thing, we will just have to give up this playing footsies with dictators. If times get tough in Seattle, let them move to Florida. And there's a little problem that China may retaliate with an atomic bomb. But for freedom we should take chances, and Florida probably won't be a prime target.

Now Russia. We know that Putin has restricted freedom to the point where it is an embarrassment to call that country a democracy. We never trusted those commies in the first place. Let's show the world that we mean it when we say we will spread freedom.

The hypocrisy of Bush and his speech writers cries out when one looks at the oil producing dictatorships that we befriend and coddle. Saudi Arabia is the best example. You want freedom; take a look at freedom Saudi style.

I have a friend who spends six weeks there periodically as a consultant. He describes life among the freedom-loving Saudis. No movies allowed (they may impart strange beliefs), no liquor allowed (except when the princes secretly imbibe at home), all women must cover themselves in public and cannot leave their homes without their husbands or guardians accompanying them. Of course, no women are allowed to drive an automobile (it may give them idea that they are semi autonomous human beings). Why don't we invade Saudi Arabia? Because the oil interests (starting with ex-oil men Bush and Cheney) have too much at stake. It would be bad for business.

Amitabh Pal, writing in this month's *Progressive* (a venerable magazine since 1909), describes the Bush administration's embrace of four Central Asian dictatorships. In Azerbaijan, where western oil companies have invested $4 billion, the dictator Ilham Aliyev recently was "elected" in a rigged election that involved severe brutality according to Amnesty International and European observers. Ilham's recently deceased father was a guest of Bush in 1996 when he made him an honorary Texan. They are our allies. They sent 159 troops to Iraq to fight for freedom.

In Kazakhstan, where Chevron Texaco has an investment of billions of dollars, Human Rights Watch has documented the jailing of opposition figures, the death of a journalist and constant harassment of non-governmental agencies. The European Union has condemned a recent "election" as a fraud. Secretary Rumsfeld has praised their leadership as "wonderfully helpful in Iraq." They sent 28 soldiers there to fight for freedom.

In Uzbekistan, the dictator Islam Karimov has jailed 6,500 political prisoners, according to *The Guardian*. The British Embassy reported that at least two prisoners have been boiled to death. Currently there are 1,000 U.S. troops stationed there, and Rumsfeld has lauded "the wonderful cooperation we've received from the government of Uzbekistan."

Finally, Turkmenistan, which Human Rights Watch calls "one of the most repressive countries in the world', works closely with Bush and company. We train their officers and recently donated a Coast Guard cutter to them. They have been praised by General Tommy Franks and Rumsfeld, who expressed gratitude for their "very fine contribution with respect to humanitarian assistance for Afghanistan."

So what do we make of all this? Is Bush really serious about spreading freedom throughout the world, or is it business as usual? For the safety of this world, for better or for worse, we hope it is business as usual. But this still leaves us with a president that lies to American people in the name of freedom and religion. I hope our born-again president can live with himself. Does he ever look in the mirror?

A History of Avoiding War
2/21/06

I am in the process of lecturing on American history and it has dawned on me that we Americans are a bellicose people, either always ready to go to war or quick to support a war that our leaders dragged us into. I am also struck by the sagacity of many of our presidents who were smart enough to temper the emotions of the masses. I must say that this interests me because of the sorry state of affairs brought upon us by the current resident in the White House.

Let me review this propensity for belligerency in a chronological order. In the late 1790's American ships were caught in a continuing war between France and England. Perceiving that we were pro-British, France harassed our vessels, thereby causing a great wave of anti-French sentiment here. Congress was ready to declare war; however, President John Adams kept a cool head and finally arrived at a peace treaty with France. New York State was pro-war and voted against Adams, thus denying him a second term in the very close race against Jefferson in 1800. Nevertheless, Adams wrote his own epitaph, "Here lies John Adams, who took upon himself the responsibility of peace with France in the year 1800."

Not much later Jefferson faced an outcry of public opinion favoring war with England. In 1807 the British intercepted the U.S. frigate Chesapeake. England claimed the right to control the seas under a British law called the Orders of Council. It was British colonial hubris at its worst. Most Americans wanted to react militarily. To his credit, Jefferson kept his composure and answered this provocation with an embargo against all foreign trade with the United States, which hurt this country more than any other. He definitely "wimped out" by current standards. But he did avoid war.

His successor, James Madison, was not so wise. Historians argue whether the War of 1812 was fought over this issue or whether the western war hawks, led by Henry Clay, forced us into war in order to annex Canada. Whatever the case, by the time we declared war, the British had already repealed the Orders of Council, thereby making war unnecessary. Unfortunately, since there was no Internet at the time, we were not aware of their repeal. We paid a heavy price for our war fever. If we didn't lose the war, we certainly didn't win it. The British burned Washington, D.C. and we saw the spectacle of Dolly Madison frantically carting away Gilbert Stuart's portrait of George Washington as she fled the president's mansion. (When it was rebuilt the charred walls were painted white, thereby creating the "White House." Teddy Roosevelt finally formalized the name by printing it on his stationery)

Temperance and an avoidance of war have been the norm for responsible presidents. Martin Van Buren in 1837 quietly calmed jingoistic sentiment to go to war over the seizure of an American ship that was illegally carrying weapons to Canadian rebels, and again in 1840 he diplomatically solved a border dispute with Canada that could have precipitated another military clash.

Even James Polk, who started the Mexican-American War because he wanted to annex California, avoided war over what he thought were less important issues. In 1846, though he ran for president on the slogan "54*40' or Fight," he compromised with the British and accepted the 49th parallel as our northwest boundary. (Had it been 54* 40', Vancouver would be a part of the United States.)

Ulysses Grant knew the price of war. He was cognizant of the 620,000 soldiers who died in the Civil War, many of whom served under him. Although he was Lincoln's best general, he abhorred violence. He wrote, "I never went into battle willingly or with enthusiasm." As president, Grant avoided a war with Spain. The public clamored for us to recognize Cuban rebels which would have meant certain war. Since the Constitution clearly gives the president the right to recognize foreign powers, congress tried to force recognition, but to no avail.

Of course, we eventually did go to war with Spain over Cuba in 1898 under President William McKinley. In his inaugural address McKinley vowed, "No wars of conquest; we must avoid temptation of territorial aggression… no jingo nonsense under my administration." But he succumbed to the public clamor for war, fueled by the newspapers of William Randolph Hearst. When Hearst sent the noted sculptor and painter Frederick Remington to Cuba to cover the "war," Remington told Hearst that there was no war to cover. Hearst famously replied, "You furnish the pictures and I'll furnish the war."

With our victory in the Spanish-American War we colonized the Philippines, only to give them independence in 1946. McKinley wrote, "I walked the floor of the White House night after night until midnight and…I went down on my knees and prayed to Almighty God for light and guidance more than one night. And one night late it came to me… that there was nothing left for us to do but to take them all, and to educate the Philippinos, and to uplift them and civilize and Christianize them."

This was McKinley's version of the current white man's burden to spread democracy across this planet by the sword or, more precisely, by the lives of 2300 young Americans, many of whom joined the Reserves to get a little extra money to survive in an American economy that is producing great wealth for the rich and diminishing returns for the poor.

Yes, all of this history is relevant to what is happening today. Good presidents, presidents who have served in the military (not played around in the

National Guard in Alabama), presidents who actually felt the responsibility of sending young kids into battle, did everything they could to avoid war. They did not lie about military intelligence. They did not take that intelligence and stretch it into a preconceived decision to go to war.

This is not a column against war. I am not a pacifist. Franklin Delano Roosevelt led us into war against Hitler over the objections of an isolationist congress and he was morally correct. But the "Greatest Generation" knew for a surety that they were fighting for the future of humanity. It was not a war of choice. It was not a war that could have been avoided by negotiations. Munich taught us that.

The neocons of this administration, most of whom never served in the military (thus earning the moniker "chicken hawks"), came into power with a master plan to spread American dominance over this planet, and they anticipated using war as a strategic tool. This is where they differed from Adams, Jefferson, Grant and other presidents in our history who understood that war should never be a tool, only a last resort.

I will respect President Bush when he sends his two daughters who are of military age to Iraq in defense of his "crusade." Then let us see what he thinks about a war of choice rather than of necessity.

Fear of Muslims

Anti Muslim Hysteria Rising
1/18/05

As a by-product of Iraq and Al Qaeda there is an increasing animus in this country against the ancient and honorable religion of Islam. With Muslim-bashing an everyday occurrence on talk radio and the fears elicited by the ever-changing colors of terrorist awareness by Attorney General Ashcroft, it is no wonder that reported hate crimes against Muslims were up 70 percent in 2003, the last year of statistics.

Now this past month Cornell University reported that almost every other American (44 percent) is in favor of restricting the civil liberties of Muslim Americans. Fully 27 percent of respondents supported requiring all Muslim Americans to register where they live with the federal government. The survey also found that people who describe themselves as Republicans and "highly religious" were more apt to support the curtailing of civil liberties for Muslims than Democrats or the less religious.

It is obvious that for a large percentage of Americans the war on terrorism is equated with a war on Islam. This misperception is fueled by academics like Bernard Lewis of Princeton who preach the concept that terrorism is only a part of the greater problem of the "clash of civilizations" between the West and Islam. This ignores the fact that less than 20 percent of the 1.3 billion Muslims in this world are Arabs and only an infinitesimal portion of them are terrorists (however you define that term).

I am not surprised at these findings. I believe that the psychological makeup of mankind is essentially xenophobic. I remember the slogan that the NCCJ (the National Conference for Community and Justice, formerly the National Conference of Christians and Jews) used to promulgate: "You have to teach a child to hate." It sounds nice, but I think that the reverse is true. Our natural state is to fear the other, or at least to fear anything that is different than we are (the definition of xenophobia). Respecting the stranger is a result of a civilizing process that goes against human nature. That is the reason that Torah and the holy writings of other religions are so important – they change our natural instincts to distrust the other if that other is different.

This is not just an American or Western problem. After 12 Nepalese workers were murdered by terrorists in Iraq, Hindu mobs turned their wrath upon the 3 percent Muslim minority in Nepal, storming the mosques and ransacking Muslim-owned businesses. Hysteria knows no national or religious boundaries. In America we have not yet stormed the mosques (but remember, we put the Japanese Americans in concentration camps during WWII, so anything can happen), but our prejudice has manifested itself in more sophisticated realms. This past October the State Department refused entry into this country to Tariq Ramadan, a European Muslim academic who had a job waiting for him at a peace institute at Notre Dame. Ramadan has written 20 books and numerous articles that reflect his moderate social views. He has traveled in America more than 30 times in the last five years. Nevertheless the rising anti Muslim hysteria in this country moved the State Department to deny him entrance. This is so counter productive, since this is precisely the time that we need more articulate moderate voices of Islam in this country.

Americans, including Jews, do not realize that Islam is a sophisticated religion. Both the Christian and Jewish philosophers owe a debt to their Muslim predecessors. Yes, there is a fundamentalist movement within Islam that distorts Muhammad's teachings, but both Judaism and Christianity have this same problem.

The *New York Times* columnist Nicholas Kristof points out that the "Left Behind" series are the best selling novels for adults in the United States. As a Christian he is appalled by their description of the Second Coming. In these American best-sellers when Jesus returns he will slaughter everyone who is not a born-again Christian. Jews, Hindus, Moslems, agnostics, Catholics, all of us are heaved into an everlasting fire: "Jesus merely raised one hand a few inches and…they tumbled in howling and screeching." Kristof comments, "If a Muslim were to write an Islamic version of "Glorious Appearing" (the latest book in the "Left Behind" series) and publish it in Saudi Arabia, jubilantly describing a massacre of millions of non-Muslims by God, we would have a fit." Kristof understates our reaction. We would be well along the road to storming those mosques.

Let's not let the Jews off the hook either. Jewish fundamentalism has practically made the term modern-Orthodoxy an oxymoron. Its narrow focus on messianism has distorted the universal message of Judaism as reflected in the prophetic books of the bible and elsewhere in our literature and tradition. It has dragged American Jewry to the right in defending fanatical settlements on the West Bank and it has helped seduce us into actually believing that somehow Islam is our enemy.

I was recently saddened when a good friend, a prominent Jewish community leader, forwarded an email to me protesting an American stamp commemorating the Muslim holiday season. In a tirade reminiscent of the anti-Semitic tracts of the 1930s, the email asked me to remember the MUSLIM bombing of the Panama Flight 103, the MUSLIM bombing of the World Trade Center, the MUSLIM bombing of American embassies, etc., etc. It then asked me to BOYCOTT this stamp, and "Remember to pass this along to every patriotic AMERICAN you know." It ended with, "God Bless the USA". Remember that this junk is floating around in the Jewish community, among our leadership.

Yes, there are Muslim fundamentalists who are a threat to America. But it should humble every Jew and Christian to remember that we are not without our own fundamentalist problems. Yes, we should be vigilant. But the sins of the few should not be visited upon the vast majority of law abiding patriotic Muslim Americans. If we were to hold all Muslims responsible for Al Qaeda, then it would justify the anti-Semites who held the Jewish community responsible for Ethel and Julius Rosenberg.

Fortunately, despite the anti Communist hysteria of the period, the American public remained cool and did not turn against its Jewish minority. We can hope for the same outcome today on behalf of our Muslim neighbors. As Jews, we should have some *rachmunis*. There but for the grace of God, go us.

Irrational Fear of Islam
8/23/05

In the aftermath of the London subway bombings, Representative Tom Tancredo, Republican from Colorado, suggested that if this were to happen in our country we should "take out" Islamic holy sites. The talk-show host asked, "You're talking about bombing Mecca?" Tancredo responded, "Yeah." (Moderate Muslim Turkish officials   protested and our State Department called the statement, 'insulting and offensive.") But Tancredo's remarks were just the tip of the iceberg of anti-Muslim sentiments in the United States. Republican polemicist Ann Coulter wrote, "We should invade their countries, kill their leaders and convert them to Christianity." This is pretty simplistic, but unfortunately pretty representative of the unthinking masses in our country.

In contrast to these Neanderthals, I would like to share with you a lecture on Islam that I attended by a Muslim political scientist. I was privileged to share the podium with Dr. Ahrar Ahmad at the Truman Symposium in Key West this past May. I presented a paper on Truman and the Jews and Dr. Ahmud spoke on peace in the Middle East as it relates to Islamic thought. He was most impressive.

He began, "One of the most delicious and dangerous ironies in human history is that while the three great monotheistic faiths have talked peace, and taught peace, feted peace and greeted peace, unfortunately the faithful have not. Indeed they are more apt to say, my religion is the religion of justice, compassion, mercy and love, therefore I hate you."

I plead guilty with most Americans in having an imperfect understanding of Islam and the Quran. I was an adult, probably in my thirties, before I even met a Muslim. (And we Jews are always amazed when we hear of someone who hasn't met a Jew – and when they do meet us, they find that we don't have horns.) It is this ignorance that makes Dr. Ahmad's remarks so important.

He continued: "In directly addressing Jews and Christians, the Quran states: 'O People of the Book, Ye have no ground to stand upon unless Ye stand fast by the law, the Gospel, and the revelation that has come down to you from your Lord' (5:71). In other words it is not only accepted, it is expected, that Jews and Christians remain loyal to the teachings and commitments contained in their sacred texts…There is a pluralism evident in Chapter 109 where we find the entire chapter of eight lines dedicated to only one message, 'you will not worship what I worship, nor will I worship what you worship, to you your way, to me mine.'…It is that spirit which hints at Islam's commitment to democracy"

Is Ahmad cherry picking quotes from the Quran to put on a good face? He comments: "Is it possible that I am using the Quran selectively to make my argument? Perhaps. But I am convinced that I am capturing the ethos of Islam accurately and honestly. However, one can read into Scripture whatever one wants. Every act of reading is a textual deconstruction, every act of understanding an interpretation. What you read into a text is what you bring to it and want from it. If you want to find peace, justice and tolerance in the Quran you can. If you want to read anger hate and violence you can do that too, as you can in every other sacred text." Ahmad admits, as should any honest Jew, Christian or Muslim, that our scriptures are ancient texts that contain both sublime teachings and horrid hatred. It is up to us to reach into them and extract the Godly passages. Back in July of 2003 I wrote about this and discussed how there is a prescription for genocide in our Jewish bible.

(You can find that column in this book in the Israel Section, Peace Process subsection, entitled "Koran and Bible – Irrelevant to Peace Process.")

If you want to fear another religion I would suggest that Christians who pervert Christianity are far more dangerous to us than their Muslim counterparts. Try these chilling quotes. Gary Bauer (who ran for president in the Republican primary): "We are engaged in a social, political and cultural war. There's a lot of talk in America about pluralism. But the bottom line is somebody's values will prevail. And the winner gets the right to teach our children what to believe." Gary North (Institute for Christian Economics): "The long-term goal of Christians in politics should be to gain exclusive control over the franchise. Those who refuse to submit…must be denied citizenship…Christians are the lawful heirs, not non-Christians." And finally, Randall Terry of Operation Rescue, the man behind the Terri Schiavo fiasco, who is now running for the Florida State Senate: "I want you to just let a wave of intolerance wash over you. I want to let a wave of hatred wash over you. Yes, hate is good. Our goal is a Christian nation. We have a biblical duty. We are called by God to conquer this country. We don't want equal time. We don't want pluralism. Our goal must be simple. We must have a Christian nation built on God's law, on the Ten Commandments. No apologies."

These people are an embarrassment to "normative Christianity," but they exist and are a potent force in this country, more dangerous to America than either internal or external Muslims.

Of special Jewish interest is this comment from Dr. Ahmad: "In the Muslim world we do not see the kind of vicious anti-Semitism that we see elsewhere. The Muslims did not destroy any Jewish or Christian places of worship when they captured Jerusalem in 638, in fact the Muslim Caliph ordered the Wailing Wall area to be cleaned up. It was not the Muslims that drove out the Jews from Jerusalem in 1099 when the city went under Crusader control; in fact Salah al din invited them back after he recaptured it in 1187. The Muslims did not expel the Jews from Spain in 1492 (indeed in Spain they lived in particularly harmonious amity), it was the Muslims who welcomed the expelled Jews into the Ottoman Empire (where they were allowed legal autonomy and spiritual jurisdiction over themselves). In fact by the 17th century almost 30% of the population of Istanbul was Jewish, who were there by choice not conquest or coercion."

Ahmad is totally honest when he continues, "This does not mean that Jews and Christians in Islamic rule lived in absolute peace and justice, and that they sat around in campfires roasting marshmallows and singing Kumbaya. Surely there were bitter misunderstandings and savage encounters between Muslims and others. But, and this is my point, these incidents were episodic and determined by circumstance, neither systematic nor governed by doctrine."

There is no doubt that those who pervert Islam by committing atrocious terrorism in its name are a threat to humanity. Also, there is no doubt that Islamic leaders have to condemn these outrages from an Islamic perspective. We need more Dr. Ahrar Ahmads to speak out. This is beginning to happen, and I believe that it will gain momentum.

But the core points that I am trying to make are: (1) From a Jewish standpoint, anti-Muslim animus is irrational. Of our two daughter religions, Judaism is philosophically closer to Islam than to Christianity. (2) From an American standpoint, we should fight the terrorists who use a distorted version of Islam without branding the 1.3 billion Muslims in this world, and especially without scapegoating the six million Muslims who live in this country. We are not in a war of civilizations, the Judeo-Christian West against Islam. We are fighting terrorists, who happen to be Muslims. Let's be a little sophisticated.

End of Life Issues

Checking Out is Not Easy to Do
4/25/06

This column is occasioned by the fact that earlier this month I attended a symposium on end-of-life issues that featured Rabbi Elliot Dorff, one of the Conservative Movement's brightest scholars and the Rector at the University of Judaism, and Rabbi Edward Reichman, an Orthodox physician who teaches medical ethics at Albert Einstein College of Medicine.

This is not new territory for me. The very first piece that I wrote in May of 2003, when I started these weekly columns, was on this topic. Then, as now, I am acutely aware of the pain of these issues. I am a senior citizen and not immune to the fears and anxieties of growing older. But we cannot ignore our own finitude and we cannot avoid making these decisions for ourselves, otherwise others will do it for us, and not necessarily in the way we would want.

Before any discussion one point of departure must be emphasized: There is not one Judaism, but many. We cannot ask the question, what does Judaism say? In fact, there was never one Judaism. The Sadducees fought with the Pharisees. The Karaites denied rabbinic authority. The Sephardim created different rules than the Ashkenazim. Chabad believes differently than the misnagdim Orthodox on many crucial philosophical points and the Orthodox differ from the Conservative, Reform, Humanistic, Reconstructionist movements, and they all, in turn, differ from one another.

Understanding this gives us the ability to analyze the arguments and reach our own conclusions. It fascinates me that Jews who do not keep kosher, are not *shomer shabbos* and generally do not lead their lives according to *halacha* (Jewish Talmudic law), ask the question, what does Judaism say about end of life issues. If we have autonomy in all other aspects of Jewish practice, we surely have it when it comes to the right to die.

At the symposium, needless to say, there was disagreement between Rabbis Reichman and Dorff. The former made it clear that Orthodox law would have supported the parents of Terri Schiavo, insisting that the feeding tubes keep her alive indefinitely, since you cannot deny a patient food. Rabbi Dorff came to the opposite conclusion, arguing that artificial nutrition and hydration are medicine, not food, since they have no taste, no texture, not different temperatures, and they do not come into the body the way food does. He points to *halacha* which says that you have a duty to remove medication if it is not working. Thus he would have removed the feeding tubes three months after the onset of a persistent vegetative state.

As liberal as Rabbi Dorff is on passive euthanasia, he is adamantly against active euthanasia – the choice to voluntarily check out. He worries about children who are more interested in their inheritance than in keeping their parents alive. I share these same fears with him and therefore I believe that active euthanasia should be limited only to a person over his or her own life. No relative should be able to make an active decision on behalf of another. But in the Q and A session I challenged him with this case: I am informed that I have Alzheimer's disease and that in a short time I will not know the difference between by *pupik* and my elbow. I do not want to burden my spouse with personally caring for me for an extended period of time and if I were to be put in an institution it would deplete my resources which I want to leave for my wife and children. Putting aside the slippery slope (or domino theory) argument, which I will discuss in a moment, why should I not be able to take a pill and meet my Maker with dignity?

Rabbi Dorff's answer relied on the traditional *halachic* text that says that a person does not own his or her own body: "The soul is Yours (i.e. God's) and the body Your handiwork." He analogized it to a person renting an apartment. As a mere renter, not the owner, he cannot destroy the apartment without the permission of the owner. Thus each of us has a fiduciary responsibility to God during our lifetime to keep the body alive and not to destroy it.

This analogy does not speak to me. If God is my landlord, I expect him to be a good owner and to direct me how to keep his property. If he is an absentee landlord who is mysteriously absent then he forfeits his right to make decisions. I'm here, living in this building. If a hurricane extensively damages it, and my landlord has been absent since he visited the neighborhood circa 1250 BCE when he supposedly spoke to a relative of mine named Moses, then he forfeits his right of approval. I am left to decide whether the building should stand or be destroyed. When it becomes too painful or degrading to live in the structure that God gave to me, then I should have the right to check out.

Now to the domino or slippery slope argument against active euthanasia, which is a practical, *non-halachic* consideration, and which I acknowledged in my first column three years ago as an important caveat. First, the thinking goes something like this: If we allow anyone to terminate life, it is a short step toward government deciding that it would be more humane and cost effective to end the lives of old and sick patients and other "drags on society." As I have pointed out, this certainly has resonance within the Jewish community, thinking of the Nazi atrocities on "defectives" as well as Jews. It evokes the fear of a slippery slope into a moral abyss. It starts with pulling the plug of a respirator; it continues with allowing a person to end his or her own life; it ends with our killing "defective" babies when they are born. It is a powerful argument of fear, but not necessarily logic.

After Auschwitz we know that anything is possible. Yet fear of ultimate consequences down a long, long road can totally immobilize a person or society. No humane social laws or curbs on unbridled capitalism would ever be passed because they would be the first steps on the inexorable road to socialism or communism. It was precisely this kind of reasoning that kept America 50 years behind Europe in the evolving of social legislation such as social security and Medicare. The bottom line is whether we feel comfortable in the stability of our own social system or whether we see a rising Nazi-ism in the future. I feel comfortable enough not to worry about the domino effect.

The modern Jew walks a tightrope between the personal autonomy that we receive from the Greek philosophical tradition and our American ethos and the communal responsibilities that are part of belonging to the Jewish peoplehood. The wisdom of our Talmudic forefathers should never be ignored nor underestimated, but ultimately we do have personal freedom, and in this case I choose the path of exercising my right to decide my own end of life solutions.

Death With Dignity – Painless and Calm
11/2/04

I am writing this one week before the election, so I have no idea whether we will have to live with Attorney General John Ashcroft for another four years. It is an important question because he has attempted to overturn Oregon's Death With Dignity Act that allows a terminally ill person to end his or her life without pain and degradation. Ashcroft and Bush aside, this is an important issue that must be more widely discussed.

The Oregon law allows adults who are likely to die in six months from incurable diseases to obtain lethal drugs from their doctors. In plain language, this is legal suicide. And, as a rabbi I support it. I believe that this would be a minority position in the rabbinate. The traditional hallachic Jewish stance states that a person does not own his or her body: "The soul is Yours (i.e. God's) and the body Your handiwork." This biblical statement is taken literally, and the conclusion is that we have no right to determine the length of our days without God's permission.

As a liberal Jew, I respectfully disagree. I cannot conceive that God wants us to suffer pain and indignities. I cannot conceive that God wants us to continue existing while not recognizing our spouses or children. There has to be a better way to exit this world. The bible also tells us that we are made in the image of God. To me that image connotes dignity and a clear cognitive process, not helplessness, pain and despair. It also connotes control, probably the most important ingredient of the human condition.

Leaving theology, the one argument against a Death With Dignity law that has some appeal is the fear of the slippery slope (the domino argument). It goes something like this: If we allow anyone to terminate life, it is a short step toward government deciding that it would be more humane and cost efficient to end the lives of old and sick patients and other "drags on society." Anything in life is theoretically possible, but exaggerated fears for the future should not stand in the way of practical humanitarian relief in the present

The above arguments become somewhat academic because we now have a five year report from Oregon on what has actually happened in that state. In that five year period 198 prescriptions were written, of which only 129 were used. This represents less than one-eighth of one percent of the deaths during that same period. People are not rushing to end their lives in Oregon. There were fears that legalized physician aid would put pressure on the most vulnerable, i.e. the poor. But statistics show that almost all of the patients who died after ingesting the lethal medication were middle class with health insurance. Eighty-three percent were in hospice care, and none were African American.

Also there is almost a ten year history under a comparable law in the Netherlands. The reports show that there is no "slippery slope" effect there either. A little less than three percent of deaths there are attributable to their Death With Dignity law, and this figure has been consistent throughout the years. Nor is there any evidence that the poor and vulnerable were victimized. Opponents of aid in dying make much of the fact that there have been 900 cases of termination of life without the specific request of the patient in the Netherlands. In reality this reflects "terminal sedation", a practice that is humanely practiced in this country as well. The only difference is that the occurrences are openly recorded in the Netherlands, while they are quietly suppressed in our country.

Death with dignity is a concept whose time is about to arrive. In 1991 fully 46 percent in the state of Washington voted for such a law. In 1992 it was also 46 percent in California. In Maine in 2000 fully 49 percent voted for a Death With Dignity law. Vermont is on the verge of being the second state to actually pass such a law. It's only a matter of time. Many states would already have passed a law were it not for the immense amount of money spent by the Catholic Church and right-wing Protestants against these efforts. In Michigan in 1998 the Catholic Church spent $6 million to defeat the proposal, while proponents spent less than a quarter of a million dollars.

But times are changing. In a recent poll, 60 percent of physicians in the East are in favor of an Oregon type law. This figure drops to 43 percent in the Midwest and 46 percent in the South, but climbs above a majority in the West where 53 percent of the physicians support such a law.

Meanwhile, we who live outside of Oregon are not entirely at a loss if we want to contemplate our options. And contemplate is the key word. Most of us want control. We want to know that if we want to exit this existence before we are a burden to ourselves and others we can. Whether we take the pill or not is not important. Our sense of control is what counts.

If we want control we can turn to a Zurich, Switzerland based not-for-profit association called Dignitas. They do everything that the Oregon law does, but you have to fly to Zurich. Yet 75 percent of their 2500 members are foreigners. Most of the members are German, but some people come from as far away as Israel and the United States. To join it costs 76 euros (a little under $100) and yearly dues of 38 euros (a little over $50). Their web site is www.dignitas.ch. It is written in translated German and is almost impossible to decipher, but it is worth the effort.

There is one crucial difference between Dignitas and the Oregon law. Under Swiss law it is permissible to have an assisted death not only when death is imminent within six months but when there are "unreasonable handicaps." This would cover a person who has Alzheimer's disease and wants to check out in time. He or she would not be covered in Oregon. Relief may be only a short six-hour plane trip away.

This is not a pleasant topic. Since I am a senior citizen, I am painfully aware of that. I am also a realist. Death is part of living, and how we do it should be discussed. The Dignitas web site describes the process: "A completely painless barbiturate dissolves in tap water. After ingestion the patient falls asleep within a few minutes. The sleeping state leads to a painless and calm death." We all hope that we never have to make such a decision. But a painless and calm death is not to be dreaded.

Postscript: In 2008 the State of Washington passed a Death With Dignity law identical to the one that exists in Oregon.

Social Security

Privatizing Social Security, Part I
2/15/05

The revamping of Social Security will be President Bush's keystone domestic issue in his second term. Since it is a very big topic, this will be only part one of a three week series. It is expected that his push to get congressional approval will equal in intensity his drive three years ago to get approval for the war in Iraq.

But there is a difference. Then he could lie to us concerning weapons of mass destruction, Iraq's nuclear intentions and Saddam's tie to Al Qaeda and we had no way of checking his facts. We knew from United Nations' reports that he was lying (if you want to be charitable, you can say that he was relying on faulty intelligence – but I honestly believe that he outright lied), but it was hard to refute him since we did not have the same access to his intelligence reports.

With the Social Security issue we are on equal footing. He cannot rely on secret information from the FBI or CIA. All of the economic facts are out there for any ambitious reader. Hillary Clinton recently spoke in West Palm Beach on this topic. She quoted Daniel Patrick Moynihan to the effect that every person has the right to his own opinions, but he does not have a right to his own facts.

These plain incontrovertible facts are what I will present in these columns. I do not claim to be an economist, although I did earn a masters degree in economics from Yale. You don't have to be an expert to understand the arguments. The problem is that when technical information is presented many people's eyes seem to glaze over and they lose concentration. They much prefer a 30-second sound byte to explain the issues. Unfortunately, Social Security can't be explained in 30 seconds.

In these columns I rely on many sources, but I am primarily indebted to Paul Krugman, an economist on the faculty at Princeton and a *New York Times* columnist. Krugman, who previously taught at MIT, has the ability to discuss complex issues in laymen's terms. I strive to be as concise and clear. I also recommend a seminal article by Roger Lowenstein in the *New York Times Magazine* on January 16th. It is one of the best explanations of the history of Social Security as well as the current "crisis." (It's interesting that Krugman recommends this article, which is written by a non-economist.)

One small but important point must be made before we begin. The president, leading up to his State of the Union address, had the unfortunate habit of referring to a crisis in Social Security and Medicare, as if they were one program. Obviously, they are not. We may have a looming crisis in Medicare, but that is an entirely different issue that involves many complex issues in medical care. It has nothing to do with Social Security, which is a relatively simple insurance program.

Now to the issues. In his State of the Union address Bush proposed to privatize Social Security to the extent that an individual could direct 4 percent of his contributions into a private account to be invested in the stock market. This would represent nearly two-thirds of his 6.2 percent tax on wages. The president insisted that the present system will be "exhausted and bankrupt" by the year 2042.

First and foremost one must ask, is the president telling us the truth? Given his record on Iraq, this is a legitimate question. Can he be correct, or is this just a give-away to the financial institutions that will reap billions in commissions on these private accounts? I admit that I don't trust this man, but even a moderate Republican should ask this question.

The clear economic facts show that there is not a crisis in Social Security; in truth, the president is crisis-mongering. The Social Security Administration has about 40 actuaries on staff who try to project 75 years into the future. They present an "intermediate" case and an "optimistic" scenario. Using the more conservative intermediate figures they predict that by the year 2018 Social Security will begin to pay out more than it receives. The president in his State of the Union address proclaimed that after this date "the government will somehow have to come up with an extra $200 billion to keep the system afloat." That's just a lie. He ignores the fact that presently there is $3 trillion (that's trillion with a "T") in the Social Security trust fund and that fund will continue to grow until 2018. At that time the trust fund will be drawn upon to make up the shortfall in income. That's exactly why the trust find was founded. The system is working the way it is supposed to. In 2042 (or possibly 2052) the trust fund will be exhausted, and thereafter Social Security will be able to pay only 75 percent of benefits unless the government raises new taxes.

That's the scenario under the intermediate forecast. If we accept the optimistic posture, and it has been pointed out that previous forecasts have proved the optimistic outlook more accurate than the intermediate, then Social Security will remain solvent for another 75 years, until 2080. There is a desire to push solvency out to the year 2080 under an intermediate assumption, which means that some slight tinkering on the system is in order. We will discuss what this means in the third installment. But one thing is for sure – we do not have a Social Security crisis. It is crisis-mongering by a president who has difficulty delineating truth from fiction.

The president has told the American people that they could get better returns with "your money" than what the Social Security trust fund receives from the government. That is a subject that we will also discuss in the third column, but the argument totally distorts what the payroll tax is. It is not a pension system. It is an insurance policy. If you die young, you paid more money into the system than you collected. If you live to an old age, you collect more than you put in. Under a privatized system you could outlive your money, thereby enduring old age without any Social Security income. Social Security was designed to provide only 40 percent of needed retirement funds. It is expected that people will also have private 401Ks and other retirement vehicles. But Social Security was not meant to maximize income. It was meant to be a safety net for those who invest their own money poorly (remember the recent technology bust) or for poorer people who could not scrape together enough money to provide for their old age. This point totally eludes David Brooks, the resident conservative *New York Times* columnist (now that Bill Safire is gone). He frames the argument in terms of people who instinctively trust the markets and support Bush's reforms and those who are suspicious of capitalism. I trust the markets and am invested in the markets, but not with my Social Security taxes. I know when to buy insurance and when to play the market. In sum, Social Security is a system that has worked and will continue to work, if we can keep those who want to shrink government and the greedy hands of the financial institutions off the money.

Next week we will continue to discuss this complex issue.

Privatizing Social Security, Part II
2/222/05

This is the second in a three-part series. Last week I discussed whether there is really a crisis in Social Security, and I came to the conclusion that there is not, and that President Bush is crisis-mongering to sell an Edsel to the American public.

To accept the president's privatization plan is to add anywhere from $1 trillion to $5 trillion dollars of debt (most people settling on a $2 trillion figure) over the next two decades. This debt is the result of the "gap." Let me explain. The way Social Security works is that current retirees are paid from contributions from current workers. When they age and retire their benefits will be paid by future workers. Now if we take two-thirds of a current worker's payroll tax and divert it into private accounts that the workers own, then that money will not be available to pay the retirement benefits to current retirees. The government will have to step in and pay what was promised to them. This figure is referred to as the gap and will probably total $2 trillion or more.

There would not be a gap problem if Bush were to raise taxes to cover this expense. But not only is he not willing to do this, he is continuing to lower taxes, excluding the Social Security issue. (This is the first time in American history when we are fighting a war and reducing taxes at the same time. We are essentially funding Iraq on a credit card on which our grandchildren will pay the interest.) Bush should have had the decency in his State of the Union address to at least make some reference to the gap problem. He totally ignored it, as if he expected the American people not to realize his sleight of hand. Does he not have any respect for our intelligence?

What is even more disturbing is that he expects to pay this debt off the books, not even acknowledging it as debt. Senator Judd Gregg (Republican, New Hampshire), who is the Chairman of the Senate Budget Committee, explains it this way: "You've got to look at this as a very significant long-term fiscal policy decision where you're going to have a loss in the first 10 to 20 years and a significant move toward solvency in the last 20 to 30 years. That mitigates against doing it in the context of a typical budget resolution."

The *New York Times* in a lead editorial calls this what it is – a ruse. "To convince the public that those costs won't matter, privatization advocates are concocting a ruse something like this: Borrow, say $2 trillion today to establish private accounts, with the expectation that they'll generate such tremendous personal savings that the government will be able to cut future Social Security benefits by an even larger amount and use the savings to erase the debt, plus interest, some 40 years down the line. By this sleight of hand, the money borrowed is not new debt, and there's no need to count it toward the deficit. Remember how Enron used off-the-books maneuvers to pretend it had no debt? Remember how well that worked out?"

The problem is that we are already piling up debt at an alarming rate. Our total national debt is $7.5 trillion and we are adding to it at almost half a trillion per year. Debt ultimately impoverishes a country. As the government has to sell more and more government bonds (as it increases its debt) it will have to raise interest rates to lure increasingly scarce money. The higher interest rates slow the economy and weaken the dollar, thereby decreasing our standard of living.

This would not be a major problem if our debt were owed to our own people. In that case, the interest money would be paid to Americans, and they, in turn, would spend the money back in our own economy, thereby stimulating the economy and offsetting the drag of the higher interest rates. But approximately half our debt is owned by foreigners, primarily the central banks of China, Korea, Saudi Arabia and other countries. When we pay interest on an external debt, the money does not necessarily return back to our system. The interest payments to foreigners shrink the money circulating in our system and thereby impoverish the economy for a future generation.

And there is one other specter of disaster that hangs over our debt. As our dollar drops in value, will these other countries want to buy our debt? If they switch in great numbers it could trigger a collapse of our economy some time down the road. The argument against this is that they will not do this, since if we collapse they are holding trillions in bad debt. But we can't be sure about this. They are already beginning to switch. The International Monetary Fund reports that dollars account for 63.8 percent of all assets in the vaults of foreign central banks and national treasuries at the end of 2003, down from 66.6 percent in 2000. Bloomberg reported that last November Alan Greenspan said that foreign investors may tire of financing the U.S. current deficit.   We have to live with the fact that a miscalculation in the future could trigger an economic disaster for our economy. But that's down the road, and our president and his political party do not seem to think too far down the road. They act like teenagers with a free credit card. Certainly the Social Security gap of a mere $2 trillion does not seem to deter them.

I am well aware that most Americans don't want to get as deep into these arguments as I have, but without knowledge we cannot intelligently refute the juggernaut that will descend upon us by Karl Rove and company in support of a give-away to the financial industry.

Next week we will review whether private accounts would really yield higher returns than the current Social Security trust fund, how privatization would affect the 55-year and older population and a few other aspects of Bush's proposals.

Social Security, Part III
3/1/05

This is the last in a series of three columns on Social Security. .

President Bush has claimed that it is a certainty that if a person put his money in a private account that it would out-earn the current 3 percent that the Social Security trust receives from its purchase of government bonds. This sounds reasonable, but it may not be. This may have been true in the past 50 years, but it is far from a certainty in the next half century. For one, securities sell on an average of double the PE ratios (price as relates to earnings) a generation ago. This means that stocks are more expensive today than in the past. There is no guarantee that they will appreciate over a 50 year period in the future fast enough to outstrip the slow but steady returns on government bonds.

In any case, if it were a surety that the market will out-perform government bonds over the next 50 to 75 years, all Bush has to do is push for a change in the law to allow the Social Security fund to invest in the market, as do private and state retirement funds. It would avoid the immense costs of brokerage fees and also spread the risk.

Even assuming that private accounts could earn more than the present Social Security trust, there is the ever present problem of timing. What would have happened to a worker who was ready to retire immediately after the stock market meltdown in 1987 or the more recent bust in technology stocks? Finally, private funds undermine the concept of a safety net for everyone. It undermines the concept, discussed in a previous column, that Social Security is an insurance policy, not a pension policy. It's there to protect us, not necessarily to maximize income

It was precisely Bush's concept that the market would out-perform the Social Security fund that was peddled in Chile 24 years ago when they privatized their system. Yet the *New York Times* reported that the outcome has been a disaster. The *Times* described the plight of one worker: "Dagoberto Saez, for example, is a 66-year old laboratory technician here who plans, because of a recent heart attack, to retire in March. He earns just under $950 a month; his pension fund has told him that his nearly 24 years of contributions will finance a 20-year annuity paying only $315 a month. 'Colleagues and friends with the same pay grade who stayed in the old system, people who work right along side me,' he said, 'are retiring with pensions of almost $700 a month –

good until they die. I have a salary that allows me to live with dignity, and all of a sudden I am going to be plunged into poverty, all because I made the mistake of believing the promises they made to us back in 1981.'"

A government official who remained anonymous because he feared retaliation from corporate interests told the *Times*: "If people really had freedom of choice, 90 percent of them would opt to go back to the old system." The *Times* also reported that Jose Pinera who devised the Chilean privatization system from 1978 to 1980 under the Pinochet dictatorship is now an employee of the Cato Institute, the chief conservative Washington think tank that is pushing for privatization in our country. Pinera still writes columns praising the success of the Chile experiment.

President Bush has also promised that anyone 55 or older would continue to receive full Social Security benefits. But if the gap of $2 to $5 trillion is added to the debt (discussed last week) and 30 years from now the pigeons come home to roost and the economy begins to collapse under the debt burden, who among us believes that Social Security will not have to be cut along with all other government programs? The 55 year old of today will be 85 and wondering how he could have added to the debt 30 years earlier. Yes, Bush did sound so certain of his facts. But then again, he was certain of WMDs as well.

Many conservatives are resurrecting the ghost of Alfred Landon, who was the Republican candidate against FDR in 1936. He called Social Security "a cruel hoax" on the American people and attacked the validity and solvency of the Social Security trust fund: "The so-called reserve fund…is no reserve at all, because the fund will contain nothing but the government's promise to pay." Since the trust fund money is loaned to the treasury (by buying government bonds), it is true that it relies only on the government's promise to pay. But wait a minute, the Social Security trust fund is in the same boat with the other governments and individuals that hold bonds on our $7.5 trillion debt. The day that the U.S. government defaults on payment, we can worry about a lot of things even more important than just Social Security.

Having said that Social Security is not in trouble, most liberal economists will agree that it is now time for minor tinkering to stretch our forecasts out another 50 or 75 years. The Social Security law has never been sacrosanct. It has been amended a few times over the years. But the tinkering does not have to be great. Just upping the $90,000 income cap on which we levy the Social Security tax would go a long way to solving any problems that we might have. Presently increases in Social Security payments are pegged to the wage index, not the CPI (Consumer Price Index). The wage index increases the payout at a three times higher level than would the CPI index. This could also assure solvency well into the 22nd century. But we must be careful about this. I would want to see the calculations, because according to Roger Lowenstein this could reduce a person's Social Security income over a lifetime well over 50 percent. Let's see the actual calculations before we jump on any bandwagons.

Finally a Jewish note to this argument. UJC (the United Jewish Communities, representing the merger of the UJA and the Council of Jewish Federations) is "remaining uncharacteristically quiet" on this issue, JTA (Jewish Telegraphic Agency, the AP of the Jewish world) reports. The reason? JTA explains: "Insiders say the pressure to stay out of the debate is coming in part from UJA-Federation of New York, which has many donors and activists tied to the financial sector." Money speaks louder than Jewish ethics.

Three columns ago I began this discussion with the comment that Bush can't lie to us about the Social Security facts which are out in the open the way that he did about WMDs and other Iraq intelligence. That's our salvation. I write this only three days after the State of the Union address and the press reports that opposition is building to his scheme. Both Hadassah and the National Council of Jewish Women are working against privatizing the system.

NPR reports that over $100 million will be spent on television ads both for and against Bush's proposal. This presents us with the depressing fact that most Americans will formulate their opinions based on 30-second sound bytes. In spite of this, we know that the true facts are out in the open. All we have to do is spread the word. This time Bush and company may come up short. It could actually wipe that smirk off his face.

Postscript: Thank God that Bush's drive to privatize Social Security failed. The 2009 collapse of the stock market shows what could happen when your safety net is linked to private accounts.

Additional Topics

Creationism, Evolution and Torah
12/6/05

Fifty one percent of Americans reject the theory of evolution, according to a recent poll by CBS News. More alarming, The Pew Research Center in Washington reports that 38 percent of Americans believe that creationism should be taught in schools *instead of* evolution. Kansas has once again mandated "intelligent design" be taught in the classroom to challenge the theory of evolution. One prominent conservative, John West of the Discovery Institute, gushed that Kansas now has "the best science standards in the nation." And let us not forget that our illustrious president does not believe in evolution, along with other scientific phenomena such as global warming.

As a rabbi, these headlines force me to go back to Torah and review the passages on which creationism stands. The born-agains believe in the literal truth of the first eleven chapters of Genesis. Let's look at some of these biblical verses. Chapter 1: God created the world in six days and rested on the seventh. The problem is that the text says that the moon and sun were not created until the fourth day. Without the moon and sun, how did we reckon the first three days? This is not a new insight. Thomas Paine (the great American author of "Common Sense" that spurred us on to independence) discussed all of this in his "Age of Reason," for which he was marginalized. He died forgotten and impoverished. Such is the fate of people who oppose religious fundamentalists (hopefully with the exception of this writer). Our ancient rabbis also understood that there were problems with the text and went to great lengths to try to reconcile them.

But let us go on to other textual problems. In chapter 1, verse 27, we are told that God created man in His image, *male and female*. Yet in Chapter 2, verses 18-22 we find the well known story of Eve coming out of Adam's rib.

But wasn't she already in existence back in Chapter 1? Obviously we have two separate creation stories in Torah. Which one should we teach in our public schools?

God created Adam and Eve. They had two kids, Cain and Abel. Tragically they lost one to fratricide. They then had a third son, Seth, when Adam and Eve were 130 years old (Chapter 4). The vitality and length of years of these biblical characters are amazing. Methuselah lived the longest at 969 years. Think of this: they prospered and propagated without the aid of modern drugs such as penicillin or Viagra.

But back to the origins of life: With whom did Seth and Abel consort? No women are in the picture. Chapter 5, verse 5, tells us that Adam lived 800 years "and begot sons and daughters." Maybe Seth and Abel slept with one of their sisters or possibly with their mother. Who else was there? Heavens to Betsy (whoever she may be), what are our born-agains going to believe? This text may force the religious right to endorse incest!

I do not mean to ridicule the Torah, only those who misconstrue its value and meaning by taking it literally. The Torah contains wonderful legends and stories. They represent the history of my people trying to make sense of existence during a pre-scientific period. And there is much beauty and morality in these myths. Example: If we trace our ancestry to one pair of progenitors, racism is eliminated. If Adam and Eve were the parents of all mankind, how could a bigot say that one race is superior to another, since we are all cousins? Example: The outcome of that peculiar story of eating the apple from the tree of knowledge, for which Eve is punished by the declaration that her husband "shall rule over you" (Chapter 3, verse 6) is that mankind now knows the difference between good and evil, which is the foundation of free will. (Talking about fundamentalism, if you want to believe in the literal truth of these passages, you have to believe that God dictates that a husband rules over his wife – so much for women's lib.)

Chapters 6 through 11 tell us the story of Noah and his ark. We know that this is just a retelling of old Mesopotamian flood stories, many of which predate the bible by a thousand years. But what is important is that in the biblical version the flood is the result of God punishing mankind for immoral behavior. The Jewish contribution to flood story myths is that we breathed morality into the tales. Yet we still read that fundamentalist "scholars" hope to find remnants of the ark on Mount Ararat proving the "truth" of the bible. The truth is that Jewish geniuses took old stories and used them to create moral guidelines. Morality should be taught in classrooms, but not in science classes, and certainly not in lieu of scientific knowledge.

My belief in God does not require me to take these opening chapters of Torah literally. It does require me to take their search for moral conduct seriously. Science is inherently amoral (not immoral) and it needs to be tempered by morality. Kenneth Miller is a believing Catholic and professor of biology at Brown University. He puts it this way: "Evolution may explain the existence of our most basic biological drives and desires, but that does not tell us that it is always proper to act on them. Evolution has provided me with a sense of hunger when my nutritional resources are running low, but evolution does not justify my clubbing you over the head to swipe your lunch. Evolution explains our biology, but it does not tell us what is good, or right, or moral."

Finally, Miller eloquently writes: "Each and every increase in our understanding of the natural world is a step toward God and not, as many people assume, a step away. If faith and reason are both gifts from God, then they should play complementary, not conflicting, roles in our struggle to understand the world around us. As a scientist and as a Christian, that is exactly what I believe. True knowledge comes only from a combination of faith and reason."

Tell this to the Christian right. Tell this to Chabad (The Lubavitcher Rebbe, Menachem Schneerson, wrote a paper against evolution). Tell this to every fundamentalist who would destroy scientific education in this country at a time when only our expertise in science will keep us leaders in this world. We cannot export cheap clothing. We must rely on knowledge-based industries. One can envision our exporting advanced biological breakthroughs if the scientific curriculum in our schools is not replaced by creationism. Not only does our moral future depend on this issue, but our economic future as well.

Gun Control and the Supreme Court
7/8/08

This month the Supreme Court ruled on the meaning of the Second Amendment and its effect on gun control. It was another 5to4 decision written by Justice Antonin Scalia for the majority.

The *New York Times* described Scalia's decision as his "most important in his 22 years on the court." This may be a gross exaggeration. Someone should tell Chicken Little that the sky is not falling. Although extremely important, the Court's decision, by its conservative majority (thanks to Bush's appointments of Roberts and Alito) does not affect most state and local gun control laws, at least not for the moment. Everything is contingent upon what the Court will rule in the future, and that's dependent on who the next president will be and whom he will appoint to the Court.

The present case came for the District of Columbia which has had an absolute ban on handgun ownership for the last 32 years. The rationale is obvious – Washington is a dangerous city. In fact, the United States is a dangerous country. Thirty thousand Americans are killed by guns every year. Washington, Chicago, Detroit, San Francisco and other major cities have stringent laws concerning handgun ownership to protect its citizens but none has an absolute ban. Washington is the only city that has such an absolute ban on ownership rather than restrictive licensing and other controls. It is this ban that the Court ruled illegal.

The case centered on the meaning of the Second Amendment to the Constitution. It reads: "A well regulated militia being necessary to the security of a free State, the right of the people to keep and bear arms shall not be infringed." The question before the Court was whether this amendment conferred the right to an individual to own a handgun or whether it applied only to the States to maintain their own militias (now called the National Guard). Most historians believe that it applied to the states, not to individuals, although it is poorly written and is admittedly vague.

The Supreme Court in 1939 clearly ruled that the right to bear arms did not apply to individuals and that has been our law for 70 years. Now this 5-4 Supreme Court decision changes that. But the decision clearly stated that it does not apply to assault weapons and other reasonable restrictions such as permitting laws. Without analyzing the 154 page decision it is fair to say that most existing local regulations will meet constitutional muster.

The Court decision involved Washington, D.C. and thus only a federal jurisdiction was covered. There is a strong argument that the decision will have absolutely no effect if a future Supreme Court rules that the Second Amendment does not apply to the state and local governments. The civil rights that protect us in the first ten amendments originally applied only to the federal government and the territories that had not yet become states. After the Civil War the Fourteenth Amendment extended most of the ten original amendments over the states. But three Supreme Court decisions dating to 1875, 1886 and 1894 ruled that the Second Amendment does not affect the states. Thus, if a state or municipality were to totally ban the possession of handguns, this month's ruling would not apply.

This leaves us in the odd position that in the future conservatives, who usually protect state rights, will argue that the Second Amendment applies to the states and liberals, who usually argue for increased federal authority, will argue the Second Amendment was not extended to the states. This will be the next question that the Court will have to decide.

Before we Floridians become too agitated over this ruling we must realize that it in no way affects us. We are in the shameful position of having basically no regulation of handguns. Florida has no law banning assault weapons; does not require background checks at gun shows; does not require gun dealers to keep record of sales; and forbids property owners and employers to ban guns from their property. (Yes, Florida counties can require background checks at gun shows, but this will only drive the shows to Dixie and Citrus counties and the like.) We should not be as upset over a bad decision by five conservative judges as over the state of anarchy in our own backyard.

There are over 200 million guns floating around our country. The very same day that the Supreme Court issued its opinion a worker in a Kentucky plastics plant shot his supervisor, four co-workers and himself to death. Scalia's opinion specifically stated that the government has the right to ban handguns in "sensitive places" like schools and government buildings. It's good that in spite of their own opinion the members of the Court will work in a secure environment. The rest of us will just have to keep an eye open for pistol handles protruding from the pockets of our fellow workers.

Bring On the Draft
1/11/05

The bills have already been filed in the House and the Senate (HR163 and S89). The Pentagon has already quietly begun to fill the 10,350 draft board positions and 11,070 appeals board seats nationwide. The question is when this administration will implement the inevitable.

I am not a military expert, but I know that we cannot fight a ten year war, reminiscent of Vietnam, without the draft. Not since the 19th century has America fought a protracted war with an all-voluntary army. Even at this relatively early date in the Iraq debacle we have used virtually every active-duty Army combat brigade and most of the Marine units in that conflict. I also know that it will become increasingly harder to recruit new enlistees. "Join the Army and have the privilege of house-to-house combat in Falluja" is not exactly a recruiter's ideal sales pitch. Only the truly desperate will respond, which, of course, will reflect on the quality of our armed forces. There is also the specter of the Bush Doctrine (the right to pre-emptive war) that hangs over our future. If Cheney-Rumsfeld-Wolfowitz decide to expand this doctrine to include Iran, Syria or any other axis of evil nominee, the need for more soldiers will increase immensely, well beyond the capabilities of an all-volunteer system.

Truth be told, we already have a draft in place. It's a backdoor draft. Thousands of soldiers who have completed their tours of duty in Iraq are being forced to remain there – even if their voluntary enlistments are up. In the third presidential debate President Bush had the chutzpah to say that these soldiers "didn't view their service as a backdoor draft. They viewed their service as an opportunity to serve their country." I guess that they just couldn't wait to get to the streets of Falluja.

The administration is also calling up reservists who completed their duties years ago. The *New York Times* (reprinted in the *Sun Sentinel*) reported the case of Rick Howell, a major who left the Army in 1997, who responded: "I consider myself a civilian. I've done my time. I've got a brand-new baby and a wife, and I haven't touched the controls of an aircraft in seven years. How could they be calling me? How could they even want me?" Of 2500 call-ups in his same situation almost one third never even showed up on military bases for refresher training. Law suits are now being filed in federal courts to negate these conscriptions.

Yes, we do have a quiet draft now, but it does not affect enough people. I believe that we need a full blown draft with no exceptions, as stipulated in the proposals before Congress. I believe this because I oppose the war, not because I am some kind of jingoistic nut. (For the record, I vehemently opposed the Vietnam War, but at the request of my seminary I volunteered to serve. I was rejected because I was over-age. I was 33; they took a 26-year old.)

We know who joins the military. With the exception of military brats, it is the economically needy, often fighting to get out of the ghetto. A job, any kind of a job, and the ability to get training that could some day earn them a decent living are powerful motivators. The middle and upper classes declare our wars while the lower classes fight them. There is no shared sacrifice in this country. The middle and upper classes are not even paying for this war. We are putting it on our credit cards through increasing the federal debt, thereby passing the bills on to future generations.

Shared sacrifice is what we need. Certainly the politicians are not sharing the sacrifice. Only one of 535 members of Congress has a child in the war. Compare this to Franklin D. Roosevelt who had sons in World War II and Lyndon B. Johnson whose sons-in-law served in Vietnam. It has been pointed out that in three generations the Bushes have gone from war hero in World War II, to war evader in Vietnam, to none of the extended family showing up in Iraq.

Here's my thesis: I learn just a little bit from history. This country understood the folly of Vietnam only after the children of the middle and upper classes either had to die there or spend great energy to avoid being drafted. As long as poor rural white and urban black kids were dying, it was a convenient war. When we had to share the sacrifice equally, we came to our senses. I believe that as long as we have an all-voluntary Army this country will follow our president and his hawkish advisors to ludicrous ends. When the great middle class has to pay with the lives of our children we will come to our senses.

Katha Pollitt in *The Nation* argues against this thesis. She believes that under any draft the rich will find ways to evade service. This ignores the stringent requirements of the two bills currently before Congress. And even if there is a certain amount of evasion, that very effort and fear of service mobilize the middle class. There was a lot of evasion, but the draft still played an important role in marshalling opposition to the Vietnam War.

She argues that we should not use the draft to promote indirectly politics we should champion openly. There is a purity and naiveté to this argument that is refreshing, except that it does not work in the real world. The death of loved ones – that focuses attention on a real problem, attention that is lacking from most of the populous, those 50% of our people who watched sitcom re-runs during the presidential debates.

Finally, she argues that a draft would further militarize the nation, making our country more authoritarian and "probably more violent, too, if that's possible." One could counter this with the reality that many who are truly exposed to the brutality of war return home with a healthy distrust of militarism. In any event, in a country where every other person owns a handgun and you can openly purchase an AK47 submachine gun if you choose (now that Bush let the ban on their sale lapse) it is hard to argue that a draft would make us more militaristic.

The bottom line is that we have a war that is being fought by Other People's Children, to use a phrase borrowed from William Broyles (the editor of *Texas Monthly*). He comments that, "If you support this war, but assume that… Other People's Children should fight it, then you are worse than a hypocrite. If it's not worth your family fighting it, then it's not worth it, period." I do not, and never did, support the war, but I believe that it is immoral for us not to share the sacrifice equally. It's time that we stop taking advantage of economically disadvantaged kids. I also believe that the only way to stop the madness is to institute the draft. Bring it on.

Wealth And The Downfall Of America
7/22/03

In contrast to early and medieval Christianity, rabbinic Judaism had nothing against amassing wealth. Maybe this is because the rabbis who wrote the Talmud actually worked at regular jobs for a living and did their "rabbi-ing" after hours. They understood the need to accumulate wealth, if for no other reason that it provided the leisure time in which to pursue their religious studies. The prophets of the Bible were generally less understanding. On the whole they didn't like rich people, primarily because the wealthy that they saw got there by trampling on the poor, the widows and the orphans. Such was the world of the eighth to the fifth centuries before the Common Era (BCE). Perish the thought that the wealthy today would do the same.

Which brings me to an intemperately written attack by Jeff Gates upon the modern amassing of wealth in this country in the July/August issue of *Tikkun* magazine. At least this moderate liberal has some *rachmonis* for the rich. After all, they, too, have problems in life, many of which are caused by their wealth. Of course, *Ahf mir gezogt*, it should happen to me. Putting aside Gates' rhetoric, he presents statistics that can't be refuted and must be faced.

In 1982 the average wealth of the people on *Forbes* magazines' list of the wealthiest 400 was $200 million. By 2000 their average wealth was $1.4 billion. From 1998 to 2000 the wealth of these people grew an average of $1.9 million per day, which translates into $240,000 dollars per hour, which is only 46, 602 times the minimum wage. The number of billionaires in America increased from 13 in 1982 to 274 by 2000.

Over the past 30 years, *Fortune* magazine reports that the average pay of the top-paid 100 executives skyrocketed from $1.3 million to $37.5 million, or from 39 times the average employee's pay to 1,000 times. Just looking at the top ten CEOs in this country, their average annual pay soared from $3.45 million in 1981 to $154 million in 2000.

All of this amassing of wealth has an effect on poor people. It wouldn't be so bad if everyone were getting richer at the same time. But this isn't the fact. Income distribution is becoming increasingly skewed. By 1998 the richest one percent had as much income as the poorest 100 million Americans, that's over one-third of our population. For the poorest 20 percent of our population, their average after-tax income fell nine percent from 1977 to 1999. The rich are getting richer and the poor are getting poorer.

These startling statistics are linked directly to the tax-cutting, trickle-down economics started by Reagan's supply side economists (what Bush The Father once called "voodoo economics"), and continued by Bush The Son. Princeton economist Paul Krugman has pointed out that over the next 75 years the Social Security system, including Medicare and Medicaid, should come up about $10 trillion short of money – but the current round of Bush The Son's tax cuts will deny the federal government $14 trillion income for the same 75 year period. Of course, the 400 richest and their friends in the top 20 percent of income brackets won't need social security anyway.

When the crunch comes, taxes won't go up. Services will be cut, and our safety net will evaporate. Putting aside the very Jewish concern of the effects of poverty on the poorest among us, the loss of the safety net will mean a loss of safety for the middle class, or what's left of it. Poverty breeds crime and violence. I can envision seventy-five to a hundred years from now that Americans will live behind large electronic walls and ride in specially armored cars to protect against kidnapping, as is common in third world countries today, those very same countries that have no safety net.

We Americans were never very good at communal responsibility. It went against our sense of rugged individualism, which was a part of our frontier mentality. We came late to this sense of communal responsibility, under FDR, while Europe faced up to it in the late eighteen hundreds. History will show that not only were we latecomers, but that we also made an early exit. History will also show that it was during the reign of Bush The Son that this country made that irresponsible turn toward disaster.

Maybe the prophet Isaiah was correct when he wrote in the eighth century BCE: "Woe to those who annex house after house, and make field after field adjacent."

Jonathan Pollard and Washington Secrets
11/11/03

In early September Jonathan Pollard made his first public appearance in 15 years before a United States district judge in Washington, D.C. It may auger well for him in his bid for freedom. What it did for a surety is reignite passions in the Jewish community over the Pollard affair.

The conservative ideologue Mitchell Bard wrote a column entitled, "Let Pollard Rot." In it he labeled Pollard a traitor, even though he was never charged as such, only as a conspirator to commit espionage for a friendly country. The usual sentence for this latter crime is 5 years in jail, not a life sentence, as Pollard was dealt. The more common reaction of late in the Jewish community is the recognition that Pollard has served enough time for his crime. After 18 years in prison, Jewish organizations ranging from the Orthodox Union to the UAHC (Reform Judaism's central body) are asking for clemency.

I had always assumed that the government reneged on its plea bargain with Pollard based on at least a tinge of anti-Semitism. Why else would then Secretary of Defense Caspar Weinberger write his famous secret brief to the judge practically demanding a life sentence? But I have changed my mind, based on a recent article written by my friend John Loftus, a former Justice

Department attorney and spy maven, and the author of "The Secret War Against the Jews." (St. Martin's Press)

Loftus points out that immediately after the Pollard incident more than 40 American agents in the Soviet Union were either captured or killed. It was assumed by the Defense Department that Pollard gave their identities to Israel where a Soviet spy in the Mossad picked them up and transferred them to Russia. This would make Pollard complicit in mass murder. This not only explains Weinberger's plea to the judge, but the harsh treatment Pollard received after incarceration. He spent over a year in solitary confinement, incommunicado, in a ward reserved for the criminally insane. This was followed by 5 years in solitary confinement in Marion, IL, one of the toughest prisons in the federal system.

But the assumption was wrong. Pollard did not provide these names to Israel. As Loftus points out, it has come to light that the Navy Department, where Pollard worked, kept these names in a locked safe with a "blue stripe" security clearance, a level that Pollard never reached. Subsequently, the CIA agent Aldrich Ames and the FBI Special Agent Robert Hanssen have been convicted of passing these names to the Russians. Both had "blue stripe" clearance.

So why, at this point, do not the Washington spooks admit their errors and agree to clemency for Pollard? It could be out of bureaucratic hubris, which demands that you never admit that you made a mistake, or it could be something more embarrassing. Loftus claims that Pollard sent Israel the names of Arab terrorists in the employ of Saudi Arabia, secretly financed by the American Defense Department. Loftus met Pollard in jail and Pollard verified this.

Why would America want to finance Arab terrorists, including one young man by the name of Osama Bin Laden? Simply because we were using them to attack the then Soviet regime in Afghanistan. In essence, we created a monster that eventually turned on us. (This is analogous to the Mossad creating Hamas as a counterbalance to the PLO in the late 1980s. They are living with the horror of their own creation today.) Loftus maintains that it is this fact that keeps the Washington establishment insisting on Pollard's continual incarceration. As a free man he could embarrass the Defense Department, the spy agencies and many influential current leaders in the Administration who were involved in this case.

There are no winners in this saga. The U.S. government violated its plea agreement, and has not confronted its own mistake of blaming Pollard for the actions of Ames and Hanssen. But Pollard and Israel are not blameless. Starting with Pollard. He is no hero. He is an embarrassment to the Jewish community. As a naval intelligence analyst, he owed an allegiance to this country. He violated that commitment in passing along classified information to Israel, albeit a friendly ally of the U.S. He deserved to be incarcerated, but not for life.

Israel committed a much graver error than Pollard. We know that it is common for nations to spy on its own allies (the U.S. was caught spying on France about 5 years ago), but for Israel to use an American Jew endangered the American Jewish community. It exposed us to the anti-Semites who have falsely charged us with dual loyalty. It was a stupid act with no consideration for its consequences. It is a testimony to the liberality and openness of American society that there was no anti-Semitic backlash from the Pollard affair.

Meanwhile, Pollard has shown genuine repentance. In his appeal to President Clinton asking for a pardon he wrote: "I fully appreciate that what I did was wrong. Grievously wrong. My intent was to help Israel, but I had no right to violate the laws of this country or the trust it had placed in me. I had no right to place myself above the law." In that plea to the President, Pollard spoke of his "unmitigated remorse." Instead of aiding Pollard, then Israeli Prime Minister Ehud Barak pressured Clinton for a pardon for Marc Rich. So much for Israeli integrity. Rich continues to live in freedom in Switzerland, while Pollard is slowly dying in jail in North Carolina.

This whole affair was best summarized by Representative Anthony Weiner, who attended the recent Pollard hearing: "Jonathan Pollard committed a very serious crime, but he has now served 18 years for a single plea of conspiracy to commit espionage on behalf of an ally. There is no case in American history that has been judged so harshly."

Never Again, But What About Darfur?
7/12/05

On August 22, 1939, days before the Nazis invaded Poland, Hitler addressed his military chiefs in Obersalzburg. There he asked a rhetorical question: "Who today still speaks of the massacre of the Armenians?" (The Turkish genocide of the Armenians from 1914 to 1922 cost two million lives) It is such cynicism that allows evil people to continue to perpetrate genocide anew in succeeding generations. As a reaction to the Holocaust we Jews say "Never Again," but it is happening as you read this column in West Darfur, a province of the Sudan – and no one is paying attention.

Here are the bare facts: The current genocide has its roots in a political and religious conflict between the Christian south and the Muslim north of Sudan. The civil war that began in 1983 has recently concluded with a shaky truce. However, a hard line Muslim opponent of Omar Hassan Ahmud al-Bashir, the Muslim president of Sudan, solicited the support of black Muslims in the province of West Darfur in an armed struggle against Bashir. In retaliation, Bashir has decided to annihilate the entire black population of Darfur, who are also Muslim. The Sudanese Army has been utilized, but the mass killings have been perpetrated by a government financed militia called the Janjaweed. They have done their job well. According to the Coalition for International Justice 400,000 people have been slaughtered, and rising by 500 per day, and over two million people have been driven from their homes and fled over the border to Chad.

No one cared or knew about this emerging genocide until the *New York Times* columnist Nicholas Kristof visited Darfur in March, 2003 and began graphically to record the horror. Denied entrance into Darfur by the Sudanese government, Kristof snuck across the border from Chad to continue to alert the world. It was only after his opinion columns were published that the *Times* began to cover the Darfur story from its newsroom. If life were fair, Kristof would receive a Pulitzer Prize for this service to humanity. (Postscript: the next year he did receive the prize.)

The problem with alerting the world about an emerging genocide is that statistics do not tell the whole story. To say that six million died in the Holocaust is not to communicate the horror and inhumanity. Only individual stories can touch us to the core. Kristof has written about the people he personally met in Darfur. Here are some of their stories: Zahra Abdel Karim, a 30-year old woman, recounted how the Janjaweed shot to death her husband, her 7-year old son as well as three of her brothers. They then grabbed her 4-year old son from her arms and cut his throat. They proceeded to gang-rape her and her two sisters. Later, the troops shot one sister and cut the throat of the other. One Janjaweed said, "You belong to me. You are a slave to the Arabs, and this is the sign of a slave." He then slashed her leg with a sword, and let her hobble away.

Magboula Muhammad Khattar, a 24-year old woman, hid in a hollow, peeking out, when the Janjaweed attacked her village. They rounded up all the males including her husband and his three young brothers, ages four to eight. They tied their hands and forced them to the ground and executed them. The women were taken away to be raped and most eventually killed. Roaming the Sudan-Chad border, Kristof wrote: "There is no childhood here. I saw a 4-year old orphan girl, Nijah Ahmed, carrying her 13-month-old brother, Nibriz, on her back. Their parents and 15-year-old brother are missing in Sudan and presumed dead."

Kristof reports: "The stories of those hiding in Darfur are heartbreaking. Zahra Mochtar Muhammad, from the village of Darma, saw the Janjaweed kill her husband. In the chaos of the gunfire and burning huts, she and her children ran in different directions, and she lost her 4-year-old daughter and 2-year-old son. Later, she found her children's bodies where they had died of thirst. They were together – the older one had apparently tried to protect her brother." And then there is Hatum Bahir, a 35-year old woman who is pregnant with the baby of one of the 20 Janjaweed raiders who murdered her husband and then gang-raped her. The twist to this atrocity is that now the Sudanese government is arresting women like Hatum who are not yet married and they are imprisoned for adultery.

Where is the world? France has oil interests in Sudan and the Russians sell lucrative arms to the Khartoum government. The rest of Europe turns its head. In September of 2004 Bush did acknowledge that genocide was in progress, although the United Nations has hesitated to use that word. But Kofi Annan, in an opinion piece in the *Times* pleaded, "We know what is happening in Darfur. The question is, why are we not doing more to put an end to it?...We saw this all too well in Bosnia a decade ago...Are we now going to stand by and watch a replay in Darfur?"

The apparent answer to that question is: Yes. Certainly the United States does not have the capability to send forces there, given the fact that we are bogged down in a useless war in Iraq. But we could enforce a no-fly zone over Darfur, thereby stopping the Sudanese Army from strafing villages. We could freeze Sudanese assets in this country. This is precisely what the Darfur Accountability Act calls for. It passed the Senate, but in mid-May the Bush administration stripped it from the supplemental military appropriations bill in the House, thereby killing this bipartisan effort

"Never Again" should resonate in the Jewish community with greater emotion and commitment than in general society. If the lessons of the Holocaust are not universalized, then we cease to be witnesses to the world and we betray our own history. Politicians aside, where is the Jewish community? I do not hear any dialogue in the Jewish press, in the corridors of our synagogues or in the board rooms of our Federations. The entire Jewish community did sign on to an inter-denominational appeal by the Save Darfur Coalition in August of 2004, but there has been an eerie silence since then, with the possible exception of the Religious Action Center of Reform Judaism.

As we enjoy the beautiful sunshine of South Florida in early June, let us take a few seconds, nay, a few minutes and contemplate the cruel fact that someone in Darfur is being exterminated as we continue our privileged lives. It's time for us to take seriously our own slogans. Never Again.